CONDUITS OF GRACE

KIM KRULL

Cathy,
Oh that you
might know
how fiercely
loved you are
by God! - You
my friend are
a light in
the dark!
fondly,
Kim Krull

ISBN 978-1-64471-517-8 (Paperback)
ISBN 978-1-64471-518-5 (Digital)

Covenant Books, Inc.
11661 Hwy 707
Murrells Inlet, SC 29576
www.covenantbooks.com

PREFACE

Friends, in the following pages, you will find daily writings that started out with just a few friends. We all had the desire to grow in our faith and not only personally change but also begin to affect the lives around us. We desired to become conduits of God's grace. We wanted to become so filled by the Holy Spirit that we could not help but "leak Jesus" on those we came in contact with! Over the years, our spiritual journey together continued on through many seasons. Some very painful, others filled with joy. During the painful times, we encouraged one another with the phrase, "You know, it's gonna be good!" We prayed for each other, for each other's families, and we questioned each other and challenged each other to be authentic and honest! We met a few times a year for conversation, but mostly we exchanged thoughts and prayer requests through e-mail.

We didn't all live in the same town or even the same state, so getting together was a challenge. It didn't matter. We grew to love each other and referred to each other as "soul sister."

It is with great pleasure that I welcome you to "our group!" Never, ever forget WHOSE YOU ARE! Because, soul sisters, your light matters! Your life can have a powerful impact on the lives around you! You can be a living, breathing, conduit of grace! SHINE BRIGHT, SISTERS! The world is watching, and it needs your light!

All scriptures are NIV or ESV unless otherwise noted.

Also, I have changed the pronoun in the scripture texts to reflect the gender of the readers.

JANUARY 1

But seek first the kingdom of God and His Righteousness, and all these things will be added to you. (Matthew 6:33)

He must increase, but I must decrease. (John 3:30)

The law always ended up being used as a Band-Aid on sin instead of a deep healing of it. And now what the law code asked for but we couldn't deliver is accomplished as we, instead of redoubling our own efforts, simply embrace what the Spirit is doing in us. Those who think they can do it on their own end up obsessed with measuring their own moral muscle but never get around to exercising it in real life. Those who trust God's action in them find that God's Spirit is in them—living and breathing God! Obsession with self in these matters is a dead end; attention to God leads us out into the open, into a spacious free life. Focusing on self is the opposite of focusing on God. Anyone completely absorbed in self ignores God, ends up thinking more about self than God. That person ignores who God is and what He is doing. And God isn't pleased at being ignored. (Romans 8:5–8, Message)

And He said to him, "You shall love the Lord your God with all your heart and with all your soul and with all your mind" (Matthew 22:37, NIV). Jesus said, "Love the Lord your God with all your passion and prayer and intelligence." (Matthew 22:37, Message)

Lord, I pray that the new year will bring excitement, adventure, growth…that at the end of the year, should You choose to give us breath that long…we will be wiser and totally surrendered, everywhere and always to You.

Personally, the last year has taught me some things. You, God, can be trusted...all the time. What You choose to do in my life and in the lives of my loved ones is totally Your decision. When I surrender to You, I give up my choice. I give it to You! YOUR WILL be done! Heck, most of the time, I don't even understand why I want what I do!

Along with wisdom, Lord, I ask for patience and supreme and unwavering trust. Give me eyes to see and a mind to understand that absolutely nothing takes place in my life, or in any surrendered life, without Your direction. Help me to stop fighting You, consciously and unconsciously, and help me let go, back off, and let God—let YOU—orchestrate and direct my life. Your will be done. Amen

Prayers for all of you, my friends, in the new year. I cannot wait to see what God has in store for us! The thought that is foremost in my thinking this morning is, "God doesn't waste a surrendered life." I'm bouncing on tiptoes to see where we are going!

Love you, ladies!

JANUARY 2

My soul thirsts for God, for the living God. When shall I come and appear before God? (Psalm 42:2)

O God, You are my God. I shall seek You earnestly. My soul thirsts for You, my flesh yearns for You, in a dry and weary land where there is no water. (Psalm 63:1)

So whether you eat or drink or whatever you do, do it all for the glory of God. (1 Corinthians 10:31)

Love the Lord your God with all your heart and with all your soul and with all your mind and with all your strength. (Mark 12:30)

I am the vine, you are the branches; she who abides in Me and I in her, she bears much fruit, for apart from Me you can do nothing. (John 15:5)

But seek first the kingdom of God and His righteousness, and all these things will be provided for you. (Matthew 6:33)

Why do we waste our lives pursuing our "lesser loves"?

What are my "lesser loves" that push God out of my thinking? Lesser loves are things that occupy my thoughts and motivate me to do one thing or another. Sometimes it's public opinion, wanting others to think highly of me. Sometimes it's greed. Sometimes it's laziness, and sometimes it's just plain selfishness! Wanting my way, my plans, my priorities, my ideas for my glory! All those "lesser loves" get in the way of our love and devotion for God.

My dear sisters, God is indeed pursuing us, drawing us to Himself, and stripping us of lesser loves that stand in the way of our intimate relationship with Him. We are a work in progress. Being molded by the hands of the Master Potter! But that being said, we have a choice to make. Will we let go of the things and lesser loves that are holding us back from desiring the "One Thing" that will truly fulfill us and challenge us and delight us? Or will we stubbornly hold on to our will? The choice is ours. And speaking from experience, it is a choice we make daily—hourly, in fact. When my mind is on my Lord, my heart's desire is to hear the words, "Well done, good and faithful servant." To finally see Him face-to-face, to understand all the times He has intervened in my life and drawn me to Himself. I know that when my life here is over, I will finally "get it." I will no longer wonder if God is in the details and events of our lives, but I will know with a certainty that God is worthy of praise, worship, and adoration! That He is always present, active, and powerful in the lives of His children! We don't have to run to "lesser loves" to be content. Our true contentment comes only from the One Who loves us with a love that our little minds cannot begin to comprehend! The One Who directs our steps, protects, and provides. The Lover of our souls! He alone is the ONE THING that matters!

Have a great day, friends! You are greatly and eternally loved by the Master of the universe! Everything else pales in comparison!

JANUARY 3

Let the favor of the Lord our God be upon us, and establish the work of our hands. (Psalm 90:17)

But His favor lasts a lifetime! Weeping may last through the night, but joy comes with the morning. (Psalm 30:5)

My times are in Your hands. (Psalm 31:15)

And we know that in all things God works for the good of those who love Him who have been called according to His purpose. (Romans 8:28)

As for you, you meant evil against me, but God meant it for good, to bring it about that many people should be kept alive, as they are today. (Genesis 50:20)

For you bless the righteous, O Lord; You cover her with favor as with a shield. (Psalm 5:2–12)

For the Lord God is a sun and shield; the Lord bestows favor and honor; no good thing does He withhold from those who walk uprightly. (Psalm 84:11)

My dear friends, God's favor does indeed rest upon us. How I wish that meant trouble-free lives and immediate answers. But we all know that it does not. Very often, we cannot begin to understand just what God is up to...and we begin to doubt that He is listening at all. But you can rest assured that the very God who hung the stars and created us for His purposes in this very time and in the very place has not forgotten you! The testing will not last forever, the trial will eventually pass, and mourning will subside; and then God will reveal His awesome, perfect plan and purpose. We, oftentimes, just have to hang on and trust that what He says is true. That He will indeed work all things out for good for those who love Him. That He will open doors and transform lives that without Him would remain hopeless. Sometimes, the prayer of our heart may simply be, "Help me hang on to You." "Help me trust You in this…" "Help me get through so that I can see Your goodness and faithfulness on the other side." I found comfort in Job's words in our times of trial and pain: "Though He slay me, yet, I will trust in Him."

God is proud of our efforts to remain faithful. He WILL answer in His timing, and He can be trusted. This I know.

JANUARY 4

O h, the depth of the riches both of the wisdom and knowledge of God! How unsearchable are His judgments and unfathomable His ways! For who has known the mind of the Lord, or who has become His counselor? Or who has first given to Him that it might be paid back to him again? For from Him and through Him and to Him are all things. To Him be the glory forever. Amen. (Romans 11:33–36, ESV)

Have you ever come on anything quite like this extravagant generosity of God, this deep, deep wisdom? It's way over our heads. We'll never figure it out. Is there anyone around who can explain God? Anyone smart enough to tell Him what to do? Anyone who has done Him such a huge favor that God has to ask his advice? Everything comes from Him; Everything happens through Him; Everything ends up in Him. Always glory. Always praise. Yes. Yes. Yes. (Romans 11:33–36, MSG)

It wasn't so long ago that you were mired in that old stagnant life of sin. You let the world, which doesn't know the first thing about living, tell you how to live. You filled your lungs with polluted unbelief, and then exhaled disobedience. We all did it, all of us doing what we felt like doing, when we felt like doing it, all of us in the same boat, it's a wonder God didn't lose His temper and do away with the whole lot of us. Instead, immense in mercy and with an incredible love, He embraced us. He took our sin-dead lives, and made us alive in Christ. He did all this on His own, with no help from us! Then He picked us up and set us down in highest heaven in company with Jesus, our Messiah. (Ephesians 2:1–6, MSG)

Or do you think lightly of the riches of His kindness and tolerance and patience, not knowing that the kindness of God leads you to repentance? (Romans 2:4)

So that in the ages to come He might show the surpassing riches of His grace in kindness toward us in Christ Jesus. (Ephesians 2:7)

And my God will supply all your needs according to His riches in glory in Christ Jesus. (Philippians 4:19)

My dear much-loved sisters, it is high time we take God out of this box we have placed Him in by our own design. This "box" that confines, limits, and expects little from Him. It is high time we blow that box apart, or rather stop confining, limiting, and underestimating God! Our Lord is limitless in knowledge, wisdom, and riches! Spiritual riches as well as material riches! He can heal, He can restore relationships and lives, He can frankly do absolutely anything He sees fit to do! We are the weak, timid, grave tending ones, cowering and crying, sniffling and whining, afraid and unsure. GOD IS NONE OF THOSE THINGS! He is never at a loss for what to do. He always completely understands any relationship or situation. He can supply ALL our needs through His glorious riches! Let's stop believing for even a millisecond that God is not able, not available, or not interested! We are MORE THAN CONQUERORS through Jesus Christ! If God is for us—which He is—who or what can dare stand against Him and, in turn, us?

May we stop living small, frightened, timid lives and embrace this big, bold, beautiful, exciting, adventurous life that God is offering every one of us! Sisters, we serve a MIGHTY GOD, let's live like we believe it!

Have a wonderful week, dragon slayers! Get out there! Be bold, shine bright, trust mightily! Our great God is FOR us!

JANUARY 5

All this is for your benefit, so that the grace that is reaching more and more people may cause thanksgiving to overflow to the glory of God. (2 Corinthians 4:15)

I will give thanks to You, LORD, with all my heart; I will tell of all Your wonderful deeds. (Psalm 91:1)

Do not be anxious about anything, but in every situation, by prayer and petition, with thanksgiving, present your requests to God. And the peace of God, which transcends all understanding, will guard your hearts and your minds in Christ Jesus. (Philippians 4:6–7)

Let the message of Christ dwell among you richly as you teach and admonish one another with all wisdom through psalms, hymns, and songs from the Spirit, singing to God with gratitude in your hearts. And whatever you do, whether in word or deed, do it all in the name of the Lord Jesus, giving thanks to God the Father through Him. (Colossians 3:16–17)

The LORD is my shield; my heart trusts in Him, and He helps me. My heart leaps for joy, and with my song I praise Him. (Psalm 28:7)

Where does gratitude rank on your priority list?

There are so many things to be thankful for, let me list but a few. Art—beauty, birds, books—because they grow your mind. Challenges—without them there's no achievement. Change, because it causes growth. Clothes—enough said. Conversation, creativity, candy, dancing, daydreaming, doctors, dogs, education, electricity, expectation, experience, family, food, forgiveness, friends, games, gardens, gifts, health, help, humor, hobbies, home, honesty, hope, hugs, inspiration, kindness, laughter, life, love, marriage, memories, money, music, nature, oceans, opportunities, parents, perspective, possibilities, purpose, relationships, romance, science, sex, sharing, sleep, smiles, soap, stars, sunsets, technology, travel, veterans, vision, wisdom, work—and YOU!

I have to admit, I am slow to be grateful! Quick to approach the throne with a prayer request list, quick to call out for help, quick to get upset with God when I am frustrated, tired or weary—but not so quick with gratitude. My prayer over the last few years was "for God to give me a grateful spirit." I am admittedly a work in progress. My dear sisters, we have indeed been blessed in so very many ways. I think that today's reminder to give thanks with a grateful heart is a much-needed reminder. And with that thought in mind, I am going to challenge every one of you to grab a notebook, journal, or random piece of paper and start your own gratitude journal. Every single day, take a second and write down one thing (minimum) that you are thankful for. Then if you feel so inclined, share it with someone. Perhaps if we tune our thinking in to the mind-set of thankfulness, God will daily open our hearts and our minds to see His provision, protection, and proddings!

Today, this morning, this minute, I am thankful for sustaining faith, for spell-check, and for this group of women to share this journey with!

Have an eye-opening day…open to God's gifts, generosity, and grace!

JANUARY 6

For from days of old they have not heard or perceived by ear, Nor has the eye seen a God besides You, Who acts on behalf of the one who waits for Him. (Isaiah 64:4)

Since before time began no one has ever imagined, no ear heard, no eye seen, a God like You Who works for those who wait for Him. (Isaiah 64:4, MSG)

For it is God Who is at work in you, both to will and to work for His good purpose. (Philippians 2:13, ESV)

Be energetic in your life of salvation, reverent and sensitive before God. That energy is God's energy, an energy deep within you, God Himself willing and working at what will give Him the most pleasure. (Philippians 2:13, MSG)

For we are His workmanship, created in Christ Jesus for good works, which GOD prepared beforehand so that we would walk in them. (Ephesians 2:10)

For I know the plans I have for you, declares the Lord, plans to prosper you and not to harm you, plans to give you hope and a future. (Jeremiah 29:11)

Friends, God is intimately involved in the details of our lives. We cannot possibly see the end or the outcome of what He is doing. He is God, and He is working—purposefully, skillfully, and lovingly. And one day when we look back on our journey from heaven's perspective, we will see His Hand in those inexplicable circumstances, and we will say with wonder and worship, "You have done all things well!"

Sisters, how today's scriptures should encourage and delight us! How does it change or adjust your thinking to realize that everywhere and always, God is at work? In every situation and circumstance of our lives, God is at work! Now, stop for just a moment and think about this statement by John Piper, "God is ALWAYS doing a thousand different things that you [we] cannot see and do not know." God is GOD! He is capable to deliver us from any trial or circumstance. He is wise enough to see all the truth about any situation and He is loving enough to "work all things out for good…for those who love Him."

I realize how easy it is for me to type that word *trust* and just how difficult it is for all of us to live in that deep and abiding trust. But, sisters, that is the work of our lives this side of eternity: learning to TRUST. Trusting Him daily, moment by moment, in the confusion, trials, frustrations, disappointments of life as well as in the times of laughter, joy, and celebration. Remembering that God is involved in both! God is FOR you, He is working behind the scenes in ways that we cannot fathom! He ALWAYS knows what is best and will benefit His children, and He can be trusted! Friends, our God, our Father, the Lover of our souls does ALL things well! We can relax in His loving arms and trust that He knows what He is doing! May we embrace the day before us, always looking for God's hand in the people and events happening around us, because He's there! He is moving and working and arranging and orchestrating and creating, and He calls us as His daughters to join Him! Let's not miss another moment by living in fear and distrust! WE ARE LOVED, CALLED, and CLAIMED!

Have a great week! Hang on tight to the Hand holding yours… it's gonna be good!

JANUARY 7

The one who has knowledge uses words with restraint, and whoever has understanding is even-tempered. (Proverbs 17:27)

My dear brothers and sisters, take note of this; Everyone should be quick to listen, slow to speak and slow to become angry, because human anger does not produce the righteousness that God desires. Therefore, get rid of all moral filth and the evil that is so prevalent and humbly accept the Word planted in you, which can save you. (James 1:19–21)

Love is patient, love is kind. It does not envy, it does not boast, it is not proud. It does not dishonor others, it is not self-seeking, it is not easily angered, it keeps no record of wrongs. (1 Corinthians 13:4–5)

I can do all things through Him Who gives me strength. (Philippians 4:13)

Trust in the LORD with all your heart and lean not on your own understanding; in all your ways submit to Him, and He will make your paths straight. (Proverbs 3:5–6)

Moodiness, complaining, ingratitude, toxic attitudes—all these things are destructive to living our best life.

Eternal Father, we admit to You now that we all have areas of our lives that are not glorifying to You. We put social media, TV, activities, and many, many other things before our time and devotion to You. We are so busy running, doing things for so many reasons without even pausing long enough to thank You, to examine our hearts, and to come to You for guidance. What fools we are!

How can we expect You to order our steps and make our paths straight if we don't come to You with a sincere heart? If we don't approach Your throne ready to listen, to respond to what YOU are telling us? As we begin this new year, embracing a time of new beginnings, may our sincere prayer be more of You, Lord Jesus, more of You and less of me!

We love You, we praise You, and we thank YOU for WHO You are, for what You have done, and for what You are going to do! We trust You with our lives, our schedules, and our hearts. Please, Father, as You have begun a "good work" in us, bring it to completion so that our lives may glorify You! Amen.

JANUARY 8

Therefore encourage one another and build each other up, just as in fact you are doing. (1 Thessalonians 5:11)

The LORD Himself goes before you and will be with you, He will never leave nor forsake you. Do not be afraid, do not be discouraged. (Deuteronomy 31:8)

Praise be to the God and Father of our Lord Jesus Christ, the Father of compassion and the God of all comfort, Who comforts us in all our troubles, so that we can comfort those in any trouble with the comfort we ourselves receive from God. (2 Corinthians 1:3–4, ESV)

All praise to the God and Father of our Master, Jesus the Messiah! Father of all mercy! God of all healing counsel! He comes alongside us when we go through hard times, and before you know it, He brings us alongside someone else who is going through hard times so that we can be there for that person just as God was there for us. (2 Corinthians 1:3–4, MSG)

Therefore my dear brothers and sisters, stand firm, Let nothing move you. Always give yourselves fully to the work of the Lord, because you know that your labor in the Lord is not in vain. (1 Corinthians 15:58)

And let us consider how we may spur one another on toward love and good deeds, not giving up meeting together, as some are in the habit of doing, but encouraging one another—and all the more as you see the Day approaching. (Hebrews 10:24–25)

May the God Who gives endurance and encouragement give you the same attitude of mind toward each other that Christ Jesus had. (Romans 15:5)

In the movie *Gladiator*, Russell Crowe speaks the line, "Brothers [sisters] what we do in life echoes in eternity!" I love that line! It affirms my belief that "our lives matter!" How we treat others…matters! How we love ourselves…matters! The wake we leave behind when we leave a room or conversation…matters! When we build up and affirm other people, it matters! Now, I am not talking about empty flattery. But about speaking honest, true affirmation of another person's worth or contribution.

When I remember the people that have encouraged me in my life, it makes me smile! I strive to be one of "those people" to bring comfort, encouragement, hope, and confidence through speaking honest words of affirmation.

We all know plenty of "Debbie Downers." Heck, we've probably played that role from time to time. May we make it our aim and goal to fight the negativity around us; look for the positive, the good, and the beautiful; and encourage with sincere hearts and motives those God has placed in our paths. Because, my dear friends, people may not remember our names or our attire, but they will remember how we made them feel!

Have a great day, soul sisters!

JANUARY 9

Surely goodness and love will follow me all the days of my life, and I will dwell in the house of the Lord forever. (Psalm 23:6)

For thus says the Lord God, "Behold, I Myself will search for My sheep and seek them out." (Ezekiel 34:11)

I will seek the lost, bring back the scattered, bind up the broken and strengthen the sick, but the fat and the strong I will destroy I will feed them with judgment. (Ezekiel 34:16)

For the Son of Man has come to seek and to save that which was lost. (Luke 19:10)

But an hour is coming and now is, when the true worshipers will worship the Father in spirit and truth; for such people the Father seeks to be His worshipers. (John 4:23)

The word for "follow me" in scripture is usually translated as "hunting, pursuing, even persecuting." So it could read, "Surely His goodness and steadfast love will pursue me relentlessly all the days of my life."

God refuses to give up on us—ever—even when we turn our backs on Him, on His church, or on each other. God pursues us relentlessly, all the days of our lives! He pursues us to return us to Himself, to the comfort and protection of His love and provision.

Sisters, this God Whom we pursue…is relentlessly pursuing us! He has known us since our conception. He knows us completely and perfectly. He will not stop loving us and drawing us to Himself… ever! He is NEVER far away or unaware. There is nowhere we can run or hide that God does not see us. There is nothing He cannot forgive. He is a God of restoration, healing, and peace! He is intimately involved in our lives…always! So, lean back in to His loving arms. They are never far from us!

JANUARY 10

Ask boldly, believingly, without a second thought. People who "worry their prayers" are like wind-whipped waves. Don't think you're going to get anything from the Master that way, adrift at sea, keeping all your options open. When down-and-outers get a break, cheer! And when the arrogant rich are brought down to size, cheer! Prosperity is as short-lived as a wildflower so don't ever count on it. You know that as soon as the sun rises pouring down its scorching heat the flower withers. Its petals wilt and, before you know it, that beautiful face is a barren stem. Well, that's a picture of the "prosperous life," At the moment everyone is looking on in admiration, it fades away to nothing. Anyone who meets a testing challenge head-on and manages to stick it out is mighty fortunate. For such persons loyally in love with God, the reward is life and more life. Don't let anyone under pressure to give in to evil say, "God is trying to trip me up." God is impervious to evil, and puts evil in no one's way. The temptation to give in to evil comes from us and only us. We have no one blame for the leering, seducing flare-up of our own lust. Lust gets pregnant, and has a baby; sin! Sin grows up to adulthood and becomes a real killer. So, my very dear friends, don't get thrown off course. (James 1:6–16, MSG)

But as for me, I watch in hope for the LORD, I wait for God my Savior; my God will hear me. (Micah 7:7)

The prayer of a righteous person is powerful and effective. (James 5:16)

The Lord is far from the wicked, but He hears the prayer of the righteous. (Proverbs 15:29)

Pray in the Spirit on all occasions with all kinds of prayers and requests. With this in mind, be alert and always keep on praying for all the Lord's people. (Ephesians 6:18)

Now to HIM Who is able to do immeasurably more than all we ask or imagine, according to His power that is at work within us, to HIM be glory in the church and in Christ Jesus throughout all generations, for ever and ever! Amen. (Ephesians 3:20–21)

Sisters, what is it that you believe about prayer? Do you believe that God hears you? Do you trust that He acts and intervenes on your behalf and on the behalf of those you are praying for? Do you believe that God is still active and at work even when His timing is not our timing? What we believe about prayer is a reflection of what we believe about GOD!

God's response to our prayers is not dependent on us…on how we pray, the words we use or the positions while doing so. The power comes from GOD! All-Wise, All-Knowing, All-Seeing, All-Understanding God!

In his book *Draw the Circle*, Mark Batterson writes, "Crazy begets crazy. If we want to see God do crazy miracles, sometimes we need to pray crazy prayers. Bold prayers honor God and God honors bold prayers!"

My dear soul sisters, may we become women who pray bold prayers while dreaming big dreams! May our new normal be expecting God to show up when we pray! May we wait patiently while God responds and effects generations yet to come with the bold, believing prayers of His children! God's GOT this! And God is in the details! ALWAYS and everywhere! So keep at it! Prayer is powerful! And the GOD we pray to…powerful beyond our wildest imaginings!

Have a great week!

JANUARY 11

But seek FIRST His Kingdom and HIS righteousness, and all these things will be given to you as well. (Matthew 6:33)

He says; "Be still, and know that I am God; I will be exalted among the nations, I will be exalted in the earth." (Psalm 46:10)

How can a young person stay on the path of purity? By living according to Your Word. (Psalm 119:9)

Come near to God and He will come near to you. Wash your hands, you sinners, and purify your hearts, you double-minded. (James 4:8)

Do your best to present yourself to God as one approved, a worker who does not need to be ashamed and who correctly handles the Word of truth. (2 Timothy 2:15)

But when you pray, go into your room, close the door and pray to your Father, Who is unseen. Then your Father, Who sees what is done in secret, will reward you. (Matthew 6:6)

Here I AM! I stand at the door and knock. If anyone hears My voice and opens the door, I will come in and eat with that person, and they with Me. (Revelation 3:20)

Truly my soul finds rest in God; my salvation comes from Him. (Psalm 62:1)

When we take time to pray to God and meditate on His word, do we expect to experience God? Do we step away from the busyness of our lives and enter in to a meaningful relationship with the Creator of the universe?

God knows us each intimately. He knows our intentions, our motivations, and our attitudes. He sees when we earnestly seek Him, and He hears us when we cry out to Him. I think the problem most of us have is that we don't see or hear HIM! God is present and actively working in each one of our lives, but because we can't see or hear Him, we doubt. Therein lies the whole issue of FAITH! Hebrews 11:1 says, "Now faith is confidence in what we hope for and assurance about what we do not see." Believing that the concerns we are bringing before God will be addressed by a loving and caring God. Resting assured that HE is acting and intervening on our behalf even when we cannot see or hear what HE is up to. The deep benefit that WE receive when we spend time alone, intentionally, with God is the peace that comes as our faith in our Father grows. The patience that accompanies that peace is patience to wait for God's timing and the assurance that God hears, acts, and understands. When I spend time in His presence, I am reminded that my plans are not always His, that my ways are often not the right way, that if I wait and trust God, all the parts and pieces of any concern will be molded and crafted in to a solution that brings glory to God.

There is no shortcut to spending time alone, intentionally, with God. No book, devotion, blog, or conversation can replace time spent alone...one on ONE with the Almighty Father. We may not feel like God is listening or speaking during our time with Him, but if we open our eyes and watch intently, God will speak. He will reveal Himself to us in a million different ways. Spending time with Him, frequently, purposefully, will open our spiritual eyes to see Him at work in our lives and in the lives around us! There have been moments in my life that have taken my breath away, when I have whispered through tears, "That was YOU, God...that was You!" Those moments are worth any inconvenience or schedule disruption. Spending time with Him allows our faith to grow and our trust to establish a firm foundation so that when trials come—as they surely will—we will be rooted in faith and trusting completely the Hand that is holding ours!

Have a great day! Love you, ladies!

JANUARY 12

The LORD is close to the brokenhearted and saves those who are crushed in spirit. (Psalm 34:18)

He heals the brokenhearted and binds up their wounds. (Psalm 147:3)

He will wipe every tear from their eyes. there will be no more death or mourning or crying or pain, for the old order of things has passed away. (Revelation 21:4)

Praise be to the God and Father of our Lord Jesus Christ, the Father of compassion and the God of all comfort, Who comforts us in all our troubles, so that we can comfort those in any trouble with the comfort we ourselves receive from God. (2 Corinthians 1:3–4)

Therefore, since we are surrounded by such a great cloud of witnesses, let us throw off everything that hinders and the sin that so easily entangles. And let us run with perseverance the race marked out for us, fixing our eyes on Jesus, the pioneer and perfecter of faith, For the joy set before Him He endured the cross, scorning its shame, and sat down at the right hand of the throne of God,. Consider Him Who endured such opposition from sinners, so that you will not grow weary and lose heart. (Hebrews 12:1–3)

This was a tough read today for me. I can only imagine how a friend of mine felt. Memories of her husband's diagnosis of ALS, and the pain and fear that followed, ran vividly through my mind! And the timing was interesting. I have been reading through an old journal that has my writing from the time in 2014 when our daughter really began to slide "downhill." She had just returned home from four weeks in rehab. My heart is heavy as I read it, and the pain comes back to haunt me once again. Yet I am so surprised that even in the midst of confrontation, confusion, pain, and uncertainty, my words also reveal a confidence in the Lord, and a surrender of my will to His Will. Let me share:

> Still lots of uncertainty here,…our grandchildren are with us,…our daughter is here often as well. I certainly don't see much progress or promise with her…sleep, sleep,…sleep, and laziness. So disheartening,…I am at a loss on how to motivate her, she won't help herself and is angry when confronted. My heart is heavy, I am weary of having to travel this same road over, and over,…and over again. Help us O Lord to stand firm, to not enable and to move forward with our lives,…fill us with joy, peace and laughter. I am on edge, frustrated, stumbling through my days. I surrender all of it to you Lord,…have your way with us, do what you will and restore us to a place of quiet trust and peace. (6/21/14)

So much pain, and it opens wounds, but I am dumbfounded that I still trusted God! I honestly don't remember that part. Yet, I read the word "trust" over and over as I read through my journal entries. The trust during that time was sheer gift. Looking back at our friends diagnosis and daughter's struggle, I am so VERY thankful that God held me, that He sustained my faith, that He put me back on my feet. My dear sisters, God is GOOD, all the time… God is good!

JANUARY 13

Y ou, Lord, are all I have, and You give me all I need; my future is in Your hands. How wonderful are your gifts to me; how good they are! Praise the Lord, because He guides me, and in the night my conscience warns me. I am always aware of the Lord's presence; He is near, and nothing can shake me. And so I am thankful and glad and I feel completely secure, because You protect me from the power of death. I have served you faithfully, and You will not abandon me to the world of the dead. You will show me the path that leads to life; Your presence fills me with joy and brings me pleasure forever. (Psalm 16:5–11)

The God who made the world and everything in it is the Lord of heaven and earth. He doesn't live in shrines made by human hands and He isn't served by people as if He needed anything. He Himself gives everyone life, breath, and everything else. (Acts 17:24)

I AM the vine, you are the branches. The one who abides in Me while I abide in her produces much fruit, because apart from ME you can do nothing. (John 15:5)

Almighty Father, today, we are reminded that you want to bring us to a point of total dependence on You, and You ALONE. So often in this life, we find ourselves broken, desperate, crying out to You for help! I remember the cry of my heart to You: "Father, I can't do this! Help me!" Lord, in Your wisdom and in Your time, You did indeed deliver us through that storm, but we have not come through it unscathed. We are scarred. Scarred by the understanding that we are not in control. That we are not able to save ourselves from trial, that we are completely insufficient to handle what life throws at us. Praise You, Lord, that YOU are sufficient! That You are able to handle anything that comes our way! That when we are no longer able to stand by our own strength, Your righteous right hand holds us, cradles us, strengthens us, and once again nudges us forward. How I wish, Lord, that we didn't have to be brought to our knees to remember WHO You are! Fill us with Your Holy Spirit, intercede for us... All the moments of our lives, remind us who we are... But more importantly, never let us forget who YOU are! Forgive our doubt, our worry, our ironclad determination to do things "our way" and let us willingly surrender our lives to You. YOU are the Potter, let us, as the clay, relax our grip and lean back in total dependence on You. Honestly, Father, I don't know why it is so hard to let go. To stop worrying and to trust that You are in the details of our lives. But it is hard. Somewhere in these little minds, we still think that we know best, that if YOU would just do things our way, life would work out. I am guilty of this, Lord, and I confess it now to You. I am truly sorry for my arrogance, my insistence on my own way, and my lack of trust. Please forgive me; renew me and set me on the path You have prepared for me. We love You, Lord. We need You, and we surrender to You. In Jesus's Holy name... Amen.

JANUARY 14

Sing to the LORD, all the earth; proclaim His salvation day after day. Declare His glory among the nations, His marvelous deeds among all peoples. For great is the LORD and most worthy of praise; He is to be feared above all gods. (1 Chronicles 16:23–25)

Sing for joy in the LORD, O you righteous ones; Praise is becoming to the upright. Give thanks to the LORD with the lyre; Sing praises to Him with a harp of ten strings. Sing to Him a new song; Play skillfully with a shout of joy. (Psalm 33:1–3)

But let all who take refuge in You be glad, Let them ever sing for joy; and may You shelter them, that those who love Your name may exult in You. (Psalm 5:11)

Sing for joy to God our strength; Shout joyfully to the God of Jacob. Raise a song, strike the timbrel, the sweet sounding lyre with the harp. (Psalm 81:1–2)

I will sing to the LORD as long as I live; I will sing praise to my God while I have my being. (Psalm 104:33)

I will sing to the LORD, because He has dealt bountifully with me. (Psalm 13:6)

But as for me, I shall sing of Your strength; Yes, I shall joyfully sing of Your lovingkindness in the morning, for You have been my stronghold and a refuge in the day of my distress. O my strength, I will sing praises to You; For God is my stronghold, the God Who shows me lovingkindness. (Psalm 59:16–17)

I am thankful for the power of music in our lives. I believe that music has the ability to lighten a mood, lift depression, and encourage reverence. I personally love Christian music and listen to it daily. There are songs that seem to speak to me with just the words I am in need of hearing.

When my brother died last year, my niece's husband called me and asked me to come right away. My brother was divorced; his wife had died a couple of years prior, and his two children, whom he had raised, were overwhelmed with planning a funeral. I left the day we found out and headed across the state to help them get things in order.

I spent the first night with my niece and her husband and then rented a hotel room nearby. As I was driving back and forth numerous times during the next five days, I kept hearing the same Christian song, saying that God was still God in the midst of the storm, with the words, "My only hope is to trust You." It was called "In the Eye of the Storm." I mentioned the song to my niece and nephew; they both listened to it and chose to play it at my brother's funeral service. There was comfort in that song, and my niece told me weeks later that she still continued to listen to that song every day.

After our daughter's funeral, I had a gentleman tell me that the songs that were played at the service had a great impact on him. It is interesting to me the influence music can and does have on lives.

When my husband and I serve at the minimum-security prison, the music and worship there is powerful! Off-key, yes, but powerful nonetheless because it is heartfelt and honest. How I wish you all could experience that with us! Seeing these inmates lift their hands and their voices in song, grasping the depth of God's lavish love and forgiveness, and feeling His presence! There is nothing like it!

Today, may you find the time to sing to our Lord and Savior. Reflect on His great and lavish love for you and fall back into the Arms that are holding you!

JANUARY 15

On the other hand I am filled with power—With the Spirit of the LORD—and with justice and courage to make known to Jacob his rebellious act, even to Israel his sin. (Micah 3:8)

"I have filled him with the Spirit of God in wisdom, in understanding, in knowledge, and in all kinds of craftsmanship." (Exodus 31:3)

And when they had prayed, the place where they had gathered together was shaken, and they were all filled with the Holy Spirit and began to speak the word of God with boldness. (Acts 4:31)

And the disciples were continually filled with joy and with the Holy Spirit. (Acts 13:52)

But it is the spirit in man, and the breath of the Almighty gives them understanding. (Job 32:8)

The Spirit of God has made me, and the breath of the Almighty gives me life. (Job 33:4)

Where can I go from Your Spirit? Or where can I flee from Your Presence? (Psalm 139:7)

The Spirit of the Lord will rest on Him, the spirit of wisdom and understanding. The spirit of counsel and strength, the spirit of knowledge and the fear of the Lord. (Psalm 139:7)

Christ's anointing teaches you the truth on everything you need to know about yourself and Him, uncontaminated by a single lie. Live deeply in what you were taught. (1 John 2:27, MSG)

Now He who establishes us with you in Christ and anointed us in God. (2 Corinthians 1:21–22)

Almighty God, we are all in need of a "fresh anointing," a fresh revelation of Your Spirit within us. Fill us with the power, justice, and courage of Your Spirit moving and breathing within us! Help us not to grow stagnant or weary in our walk of faith, but instead, renew, empower, establish us and fill us with Your spirit of wisdom and understanding. Apart from You, we can do no good thing. We need You; we need a continual outpouring of Your Spirit in our lives to free us from fear, from weariness, from focus on self. Thank You for Your great love, for Your continued provision, for Your Word, and for the anointing of Your Spirit on every one of our lives! Today, open our eyes to see You at work in and around us! Open our hearts to those You place in our path and our minds to receive Your wisdom and counsel. We love You, Lord...we need You, and we thank You today with sincere hearts. Amen.

JANUARY 16

Our people must learn to devote themselves to doing what is good, in order that they may provide for daily necessities and not live unproductive lives. (Titus 3:14)

Get wisdom, get understanding; do not forget My words or swerve from the. Do not forsake wisdom, and she will protect you; love her, and she will watch over you. Wisdom is supreme; therefore get wisdom. Though it cost all you have, get understanding. (Proverbs 4:5–7)

The plans of the diligent lead surely to abundance, but everyone who is hasty comes only to poverty. (Proverbs 21:5)

But if anyone does not provide for his relatives, and especially for members of his household, he has denied the faith and is worse than an unbeliever. (1 Timothy 5:8)

So whoever knows the right thing to do and fails to do it, for him it is sin. (James 4:17)

Know well the condition of your flocks, and give attention to your herds. (Proverbs 27:23)

Planning ahead, preparing for what lies ahead, taking care of the immediate and constant needs of our families—all these things are responsibilities that we all have. But have you considered the lasting implications these mundane, day-to-day responsibilities have in eternity? When the time comes and God delivers us home, He will examine our lives, how we lived, and what we did with what we were given.

After our daughter Kristin died she appeared to her younger sister in a dream. The two had a wonderful conversation where they talked about heaven and if it were possible for Kris to come and visit her again.

In the dream Kris appeared healthy and happy and full of life. The next morning after awaking what stood out the most for our daughter was the memory of Kris' insistence and the importance she placed on letting her know; that how we live our lives matters!

Our daughter called me the next morning to tell me about her dream. I asked her to write the details down and e-mail them to me so I could hang on to them. During the next couple of months, numerous times as I was reading various things, I read, "How you live your life matters." Seeing the same statement over and over, for me, was affirmation that it was a point to consider and remember.

Sometimes we see our situation or circumstances as insignificant, our lives mundane and unimportant. God tells us otherwise. He reminds us to care for what is right in front of us, to grow in our faith and trust in Him, and to keep our eyes open for what He is up to. My dear sisters, we are a work in progress! What we are dealing with today will not be what we will be dealing with a month or two from now! Perhaps our lives will change significantly, perhaps they will stay doggedly the same. Whatever God decides to do with us and through us is a work that is in His Hands. Let us prepare our hearts and our minds. May we seek the wisdom of Scripture, the faith of Mary, and the trust of David. "Father, my life and times are in Your Hands, do with me what will."

JANUARY 17

Do nothing from selfishness or empty conceit, but with humility of mind regard one another as more important than yourselves, do not merely look out for your own personal interests, but also for the interests of others. (Philippians 2:3–4)

Therefore, confess your sins to one another and pray for one another, that you may be healed. The prayer of a righteous person has great power as it is working. (James 5:16)

First of all, I urge that supplications, prayers, intercessions, and thanksgivings be made for all people. (1 Timothy 2:1)

And the Lord restored the fortunes of Job, when he had prayed for his friends. And the Lord gave job twice as much as he had before. (Job 42:10)

Likewise the Spirit helps us in our weakness. For we do not know what to pray for as we ought, but the Spirit Himself intercedes for us with groanings too deep for words. And He knows what is the mind of the Spirit, because the Spirit intercedes for the saints according to the will of God. (Romans 8:26–27)

Meanwhile, the moment we get tired in the waiting, God's Spirit is right alongside helping us along. If we don't know how or what to pray, it doesn't matter. He does our praying in and for us, making prayer out of our wordless sighs, our aching groans. He knows us far better than we know ourselves, knows our pregnant condition, and keeps us present before God. That's why we can be so sure that every detail in our lives of love for God is worked into something good. (Romans 8:26–27, MSG)

Do not be anxious about anything, but in everything by prayer and supplication with thanksgiving let your requests be made known to God. (Philippians 4:6)

Today, let us enter into God's presence, asking Him to help us meet the needs of those we encounter today. When the problems are too big or solutions not to be found, may we be reminded that nothing is too difficult for God. May we lift those we encounter up to our Lord in prayer. Asking Him to draw them to Himself as He draws us.

When I was younger, I was convinced that I could change my husband and raise my daughters pretty well on my own. I fixed, intervened, stood up for, disciplined, whined, cried, and cried and… cried. Turns out, even trying my hardest, I could not control or fix or change those I love the most! Sure, I would pray for them, for God to fix them in the way that I knew was best. My prayers seemed to fall on deaf ears (I wonder why?). It wasn't until I came to a point where I could surrender them to God, to deal with as HE saw fit, that I began to feel some peace. Looking back, I realize the more I prayed for Him to change them, the more He changed ME!

My dear friends, God is GOD! He KNOWS what HE is doing, ALL the time! He never says, "Oops, I never saw that coming" or "That's too difficult for Me." He can be trusted with those things and people nearest and dearest to your heart! He is a good Father, a loving Parent, a firm and fair Friend. Really, now is the time to let go and let God take over. Pray long and hard; surrender, over and over if you have to, and really trust the Hand that is holding yours. He knows and understands absolutely everything about anything we worry about. He is neither indifferent nor too busy. He is ready and able and supremely capable to take our worries and concerns and work them for His good! I am convinced that when we enter heaven and look back on our lives, we will wonder why we ever worried at all because we will see the loving, intimate, constant presence of our Heavenly Father throughout all the moments of our lives! And then we will fall to our knees, asking forgiveness for ever doubting!

You are LOVED!

JANUARY 18

Not by way of eyeservice, as men-pleasers, but as slaves of Christ, doing the will of God from the heart. (Ephesians 6:6)

Knowing that from the Lord you will receive the reward of the inheritance. It is the Lord Christ Whom you serve. (Colossians 3:24)

If anyone serves Me, she must follow me; and where I am, there will my servant be also. If anyone serves Me, the Father will honor her. (John 12:26)

For you were called to freedom, sisters. Only do not use your freedom as an opportunity for the flesh, but through love serve one another. (Galatians 5:13)

For even the Son of Man came not to be served but to serve, and to give His life as a ransom for many. (Mark 10:45)

This is how one should regard us, as servants of Christ and stewards of the mysteries of God. Moreover, it is required of stewards that they be found trustworthy. (1 Corinthians 4:1–2)

Being "slaves of Christ" is probably offensive to most of us. The word and the history with "slaves" is offensive, so how is it that we are to embrace "being slaves of Christ?" On many instances in the translated scriptures *slave* is translated *servant*. Either word certainly takes the attention from "us" and places it squarely on "Him." When we enter into relationship with Christ, we are no longer living for ourselves but for the will of the One we are in relationship with. Admittedly, that concept is foreign to us. We think of our relationship with Christ more as a quid pro quo: "I'll do this for You, Lord, then You do this for me." How our lives and our influence would change if we lived honestly as slaves of Christ. "Not MY will but YOUR will be done, today, tomorrow, and every moment of my life." If we truly are to live as "slaves of Christ," we must surrender our will and do whatever He places before us, depending on His strength and His endurance to run this race of faith well!

God is FOR us, HE always knows what He's doing and He can be trusted!

JANUARY 19

Therefore if you are presenting your offering at the altar, and there remember that your brother has something against you, leave your offering there before the altar and go; first be reconciled to your brother, and then come and present your offering. (Matthew 5:23–24)

Blessed are the peacemakers for they shall be called daughters of God. (Matthew 5:9)

But I say to you, love your enemies and pray for those who persecute you. (Matthew 5:44)

If possible, so far as it depends on you, be at peace with all men. (Romans 12:18)

So, as those who have been chosen of God, holy and beloved, put on a heart of compassion, kindness, humility, gentleness and patience; bearing with one another, and forgiving each other, whoever has a complaint against anyone; just as the Lord forgave you, so also should you. Beyond all these things put on love, which is the perfect bond of unity. Let the peace of Christ rule in your hearts, to which indeed you were called in one body; and be thankful. (Colossians 3:12–15, ESV)

So, chosen by God for this new life of love, dress in the wardrobe God picked out for you: compassion, kindness, humility, quiet strength, discipline. Be even-tempered, content with second place, quick to forgive an offense. Forgive as quickly and completely as the Master forgave you. And regardless of what else you put on, wear love. It's your basic all-purpose garment. Never be without it. Let the peace of Christ keep you in tune with each other, in step with each other. None of this going off and doing your own thing. Cultivate thankfulness. (Colossians 3:12–15, MSG)

Along this journey of life, we will all interact with multiple people that we find "difficult." Sometimes, they are in our own families.

The Bible makes it clear how we are to handle these challenging relationships: with compassion, kindness, humility (that one can be particularly hard when we just KNOW we are right). Scripture also encourages discipline, an even temper, and a willingness to forgive. But my favorite one listed is "quiet strength." The strength to do my best at reconciliation but the quiet trust to know that God is at work as well. When I don't fly off the handle, lose my temper, and just turn my back and walk away, God can use my words and my willingness to just be present to do His great and powerful work of restoration. Oftentimes, the best thing we can do in difficult relationships is "just show up" and be present. God is capable of the rest! Oh, may our God of hope fill our hearts with compassion and our minds with wisdom as we interact with the people He places in our path!

Have a great day. You are loved, you are called, and you are claimed by the Lord of heaven and earth! Walk through this day knowing Who's holding your hand and watching your back!

JANUARY 20

Love is patient, love is kind. It does not envy, it does not boast, it is not proud. It does not dishonor others, it is not self-seeking, it is not easily angered, it keeps no record of wrongs. Loves does not delight in evil but rejoices with truth. It always protects, always trusts, always hopes, always perseveres. Loves never fails. (1 Corinthians 13:4–8)

Love must be sincere. Hate what is evil; cling to what is good. Be devoted to one another in love. Honor one another above yourselves. (Romans 12:9–10)

"The most important one," answered Jesus, "is this: Hear O Israel; The Lord our God, the Lord is one. Love the Lord your God with all your heart and with all your soul and with all your mind ad with all your strength. The second is this; Love your neighbor as yourself. There is no commandment greater than these." (Mark 12:29–31, ESV)

Love the Lord God with all your passion and prayer and intelligence and energy…and love others as well as you love yourself. (Mark 12:29–31, MSG)

A friend loves at all times. (Proverbs 17:17)

And now these three remain: faith, hope and love. But the greatest of these is love. (Corinthians 13:13)

Above all, love each other deeply, because love covers over a multitude of sins. (Peter 4:8)

Real love is selfless, sacrificial, and loyal. My dear sisters, God is everywhere and always sees our heart. He sees it when it is breaking, when it is swelling with pride and when it is bruised and battered. He also understands our motivation—sometimes, even when we don't! There is nothing hidden in our lives from God. He alone is the One Who can change our hearts and our lives into lives of love. Taking away our own selfish motivations and replacing them with a love that deeply resembles His! As we continue to walk out our lives of faith, God continues to mold us and make us into women who ever more closely resemble Him! We come to a point when we realize that our love for others is genuine and sincere. That we truly desire the best for those around us and that we do indeed rejoice in truth! God is at work, friends, everywhere and always! Working, adjusting, changing, and encouraging us as we walk more and more in step with Him! The closer we are to Him, the brighter the reflection of His transforming light!

Shine bright! Love extravagantly, with all your passion, prayer, intelligence, and energy! Love transforms!

JANUARY 21

"I have heard the haunting sound of Jesus voice, I sense life and hope and adventure in the gospel! Help me be willing to speak up— to question the darkness around us, to express our deep desire for life—we must not keep quiet!" (From the book *Messy Spirituality*)

"We live our lives before the wild, dangerous, unfettered and free character of the Living God!" (Walter Bruggeman)

"I've been carrying you on my back from the day you were born, and I'll keep on carrying you when you're old. I'll be there, bearing you when you're old and gray. I've done it all and will keep on doing it, carrying you on My back, saving you. So to whom will you compare Me, the Incomparable? Can you picture me without reducing Me?" (Isaiah 46:3, 4, 5, MSG)

The words "Can you picture Me without reducing Me?" came to me like a hammer a few days ago when I was praying. I felt God asking me, "Why do you continually try to fit Me into a 'box' you can understand or control?" I felt for a second the sheer magnitude of God and was completely awed! My dear, dear sisters, the God we are reading about, the One we are seeking, is so much bigger than we can even get our little minds to fathom! He doesn't make mistakes, He always hears our prayers, He knows our hearts and every word out of our mouth before we speak it! He sees our brokenness, our doubts and fears and desires for us to trust Him. But regardless of if we do or not… He is STILL God! He is not waiting in some corner somewhere, hoping we will "accept" Him. He wants us to realize we need Him and throw off any notion of it being the other way around!

My personal resolution for this year is to stop reducing God into some form where I think I can understand Him! I resolve to embrace the wild, dangerous, unfettered, and free character of my God! I resolve to trust that God IS Who He says He is, whether I understand Him or not. I resolve to live my life in a spirited dance and not a religious plod. I resolve to let go and let our big, strong, passionate, wise God take control of my life! Will you join me?

I love you, ladies! But more importantly, this great big God I am talking about loves you even more! Let's expectantly look forward to what HE has in store for this new year! Have a great week!

JANUARY 22

It is clear to us, friends, that God not only loves you very much but also has put His Hand on you for something special. (1 Thessalonians 1:4)

Like a Father with a child, holding your hand, whispering encouragement showing you step-by-step how to live well before God, Who called us into His Own Kingdom, into this delightful life. (1 Thessalonians 2:12)

Because anyone who wants to approach God must believe both that He exists and that He cares enough to respond to those who seek Him. (Hebrews 11:6)

What do you expect from God? Do you expect Him to do a miracle in your life? How about many miracles? Honestly, I would have to say that most days, I don't expect God to show up in any "big" way. I am praying diligently for a miracle for my granddaughter in healing of her leg prior to us going to children's hospital. I am praying that by some miracle, I will find my rings. I am praying for a miracle in the healing of our nation, Syria, poverty, and injustice. But do I honestly expect a miracle?

No. Fortunately, it doesn't matter whether I "expect" something from God or not. God is God! He is going to do what He knows will bring Him Glory and serve His purpose!

We do well to remember that many times, the "miracles" we pray for are really nothing more than a temporary Band-Aid. God is working in ALL the backstage happenings; in ALL of the hearts, countries, minds involved; and in ALL of the minute details for His purpose and for His glory! What God is doing, unfortunately, most times, I cannot begin to understand. But I know in my heart it's going to be good! Why? Because God is good! Because God is more powerful than our enemy. Because God loves us, hears us, and responds to our prayers! So today, I'm going to trust Him for miracles in my life. And I'm going to move forward in a spirited dance, watching for what God is doing!

Because, my dear sisters, God IS alive and well! He is at work, in and around us! And He does indeed "love us very much and have His Hand on us!"

JANUARY 23

God, the Master, the Holy of Israel, has this solemn counsel. "Your salvation requires you to turn back to Me and stop your silly efforts to save yourselves. Your strength will come from settling down in complete dependence on Me—the very thing you've been unwilling to do." (Isaiah 30:15)

But God's not finished. He's waiting around to be gracious to you. He's gathering strength to show mercy to you. God takes the time to do everything right - everything. Those who wait around for Him are the lucky ones. (Isaiah 30:18, MSG)

Why is it so difficult for us to surrender to God? Is it because we don't trust Him? Or because we don't really believe that He has our best interests at heart? Or because we think we won't like how God answers our prayers? Or is it because we think we don't need Him?

I honestly don't know what holds people back from a surrendered life with Christ. I just marvel at the fact that God seeks us out. That He continually waits for us, even going so far as to relentlessly pursue us so that He can bless us and use us and fulfill us! God doesn't only know what is best for us and what will ultimately make us feel totally alive...but He wants for us to take the blessings He is extending to us! My dear sisters, God's love for us is wild, abandoned, freeing, and exciting! I truly believe He wants us to get up every morning and go to sleep every night overflowing with joy! So excited to be His daughters that our lives cannot help but leak His love on everyone we meet!

So today, throw off any lies of the devil that are holding you back and jump without fear into the arms waiting to catch you! You are greatly loved!

JANUARY 24

Why are you downcast, O my soul? Why so disturbed within me? Put your hope in God, for I will yet praise Him, my Savior and my God. (Psalm 42:11 and Psalm 43:5)

Why are you down in the dumps, dear soul? Why are you crying the blues? Fix my eyes on God - soon I'll be praising again. He puts a smile on my face. He's my God. (Psalm 42:11 and Psalm 43:5, MSG)

Ask and it will be given to you; seek and you will find; knock and the door will be opened to you. For everyone who asks receives; she who seeks finds; and to her who knocks, the door will be opened. (Matthew 7:7, 8)

Which of you, if her son asks for bread, will give him a stone? Or if he asks for a fish, will give him a snake? If you, then, though you are evil, know how to give good gifts to your children, how much more will your Father in heaven give good gifts to those who ask Him! (Matthew 7:9–11)

Evil forebodings and that feeling of dread. I think it is fair to say we have all experienced it from time to time. I would be very hesitant to camp there though! Sometimes, we just need to stop in our tracks and question what we are feeling…what has triggered that sense of "waiting for bad news." Anyone who has dealt with a wayward child can relate, I am certain. The middle-of-the-night telephone calls, the tearful conversations, the feeling of helplessness…we get into the mind-set of "waiting for the next shoe to drop." If we live in that state of anticipated bad news, it cannot help but destroy our joy! The psalm reminds us—not once, but twice—to "put our hope in God." He alone is our shield from the arrows that bring worry, dread, and evil foreboding! Hang in there, sisters, when you feel that arrow of fear. Call it what it is—an attack by the enemy—and move forward in faith. God's got this! And you!

JANUARY 25

Words have meaning. They can bring great joy and admonishment but they can also leave deep wounds where scars cannot be seen or easily be healed. One small word can do so much good but it can also do so much bad. The power of the human tongue is that it can make a child believe they'll never amount to anything or they'll feel encouraged by their parents and feel like they can amount to anything. The rudder of a great ship is so tiny compared to the vessel but that same tiny rudder can cause the whole vessel to sink. (Proverbs 18:21)

Whoever desires to love life and see good days, let her keep her tongue from evil and her lips from speaking deceit. (1 Peter 3:10)

Death and life are in the power of the tongue. And those who love it will eat its fruit. (Proverbs 18:21)

The tongue of the wise makes knowledge acceptable, but the mouth of fools spouts folly. (Proverbs 15:2)

Wise women store up knowledge, but with the mouth of the foolish, ruin is at hand. (Proverbs 10:14)

How long will you torment me and crush me with words? (Job 19:2)

They sharpen their tongues as a serpent; Poison of a viper is under their lips. (Psalm 140:3)

I know that we often underestimate the power of our words. It is so easy to lash out in anger and say something we regret. The big problem is, once spoken, the words cannot be taken back. I know I have hurt others with my words…even when my heart is really much more interested in encouragement. I have found that hurt people hurt people. When my heart is heavy, or feelings hurt, I am much quicker to use harsh words with someone else. My dear sisters, this day, we have the opportunity to be encouragers to the people God places in our path. But I pray, that we will also remember to use kind words (thoughts) about ourselves. Remember Whose you are and how crazy He is about you! Let's choose our words carefully and tame our thoughts as well as our tongues!

JANUARY 26

"Take captive every thought to make it obedient to Christ." (Romans 12:21)

Do not change yourselves to be like the people of this world, but be changed within by a new way of thinking. Then you will be able to decide what God wants for you; you will know what is good and pleasing to Him and what is perfect. (Romans 12:2)

Finally, brothers and sisters, whatever is true, whatever is noble, whatever is right, whatever is pure, whatever is lovely, whatever is admirable - if anything is excellent or praiseworthy - think about such things. (Philippians 4:8)

For the Spirit God gave us does not make us timid, but gives us power, love and self-discipline. (2 Timothy 1:7)

Have you ever heard the term "mind-bending spirits?" I came across that term from something I was reading once. I wasn't familiar with it, but I would go so far as to say that anytime someone decides that they want to follow Christ instead of the world, those spirits jump in. For example, we start believing that God does indeed love us, that He has a purpose for our being exactly where we are, and then...wham! Those ugly thoughts start bombarding us! "God didn't mean that! You better get your act cleaned up so God can use you... You don't know enough, haven't been to enough Bible studies...enough church services... God didn't really choose you... He will only love you when you deserve it."

The list goes on and on and is specific to wherever we feel the most vulnerable. Let me remind us all what God says to us...over and over and over: "I love you my daughters… I have a purpose for the place and time of your life. You matter greatly to Me… I am sufficient for anything and everything… I can use you for My Glory and for My Purpose if you will let Me… I can bring you joy, peace, and contentment…trust Me… I will make something beautiful from your life!" It seems to always go back to the same things: Trust God… Believe He is Who He says He is… Take every thought captive.

And say with authority: "I am a daughter of God Almighty!" Because, my dear, dear sisters, God's got you right where He wants you! And it's gonna be good!

JANUARY 27

And they said; "Believe in the Lord Jesus, and you will be saved, you and your household." (Acts 16:31)

But these are written so that you may believe that Jesus is the Christ, the Son of God, and that by believing you may have life in His name. (John 20:31)

And without faith it is impossible to please Him, for whoever would draw near to God must believe that He exists and that He rewards those who seek Him. (Hebrews 11:6)

That is why we labor and strive, because we have put our hope in the living God, who is the Savior of all people, and especially of those who believe. (1 Timothy 4:1)

Now faith is confidence in what we hope for and assurance about we do not see. (Hebrews 11:1)

Faith in Christ Jesus—our entire walk of faith is not a "one and done" experience. It is exactly the opposite! It is a day-by-day, step-by-step, decision-by-decision walk with the Creator of the universe! I oftentimes think of my walk with God as a small child walking with her dad. He holds her hand and keeps her close for a while, but He also lets her explore and wander off the path. He is never out of eyesight and always knows what she is up to. He longs to grab her by the hand again and put her on the path with Him, but because He is allowing her to discover and grow, He doesn't intervene unless He sees danger. Simplistic, but representative of our Heavenly Father with His children.

God loves us, more than our earthly fathers ever could. He knows us better, gave us our strengths and, yes, our weaknesses. He knows what we are capable of, and He knows what will throw us into a tailspin! He desires for us to grow in relationship with Him. But—and here's the kicker—He wants it to be our decision! He is reaching out to all of mankind, in every culture and every nation, and extending His hand. He repeats, "Come to Me." "I Am the way." "I Am able." And yet many, just like disobedient children, slap His hand and cry out, "NO!"

Joyce Meyer says, "The Spirit keeps reaching for your hands so He can pull you forward." I like that. Moving forward in faith! Not a religious plod, head down, feet dragging, shoulders slumped. But head held high, bouncing on eager toes of anticipation, asking, "What's next, Papa?" That's the kind of faith I want!

Have a great day, friends! You are greatly and eternally loved!

JANUARY 28

B e careful what you think, because your thoughts run your life (New Century version) (Proverbs 4:23)

Do not conform to the pattern of this world, but be transformed by the renewing of your mind. Then you will be able to test and approve what God's will is—His good, pleasing and perfect will. (Romans 12:2)

We fight with weapons that are different from those the world uses. Our weapons have power from God that can destroy the enemy's strong places. We destroy people's arguments and every proud thing that raises itself against the knowledge of God. We capture every thought and make it give up and obey Christ. (2 Corinthians 10:4 and 5)

Set your minds on things above, not on earthly things. (Colossians 3:2)

"As a woman thinks, so she is." Thoughts—did you ever realize that it matters so much to God what you think? Our thoughts set our mood, our mood sets our responses and our responses determine our day. God warns us in 2 Corinthians 10 to take every thought captive! To mull it over and consider where did it come from? Did it come from God or from our enemy? Is it life affirming, or life smoldering? It is helpful to remember when examining the source of our thoughts that God does not condemn us or belittle us or discourage us. Those thoughts are from the enemy camp. When your mind goes to that direction, tell Satan to "take a hike" and remind him Whose you are! The life-affirming thoughts the feeling of confidence and encouragement that comes to mind as well as the realization that someone much wiser than yourself is in control…those thoughts are from God!

My dear sisters, we are God's workmanship. He designed us, down to the smallest detail. He cares about how we perceive ourselves and how we present ourselves to the world in thought, word, and deed! He cares about our feelings, our bodies, our minds, and our souls! We will never, ever, ever find someone who knows us so intimately and loves us so ferociously! God created us to shine brightly in our dark world, to run wild into our culture, and to point the way to Jesus! May our lives glow so brightly that others cannot help but take notice and desire for themselves the Source of our Light!

YOU ARE LOVED!

JANUARY 29

Dear friend, listen well to my words; tune your ears to My voice. Keep My message in plain view at all times. Concentrate! Learn it by heart! Those who discover these words live, really live; body and soul, they're bursting with health. Keep vigilant watch over your heart; that's where life starts. (Proverbs 4:20–23, MSG)

My dear brothers and sisters, take note of this: Everyone should be quick to listen, slow to speak and slow to become angry. (James 1:19)

He replied, "Blessed rather are those who hear the word of God and obey it." (Luke 11:28)

Do not merely listen to the word, and so deceive yourselves. Do what it says. (James 1:22)

Call to Me and I will answer you and tell you great and unsearchable things you do not know. (Jeremiah 33:3)

Then you will call on Me and come and pray to Me, and I will listen to you. (Jeremiah 29:12)

I love the Lord, for He heard my voice, He heard my cry for mercy. Because He turned His ear to me, I will call on Him as long as I live. (Psalm 116:1, 2)

Almighty God, we ask you to help us to tune our ears to Your voice, our Hearts to Your Word, and our minds to Your thoughts. We desire to know you better and better...to trust You more and more and worry less and less! Help us! We admit that far too often, we listen and believe the words of our enemy... Help us to tune him out! Lord, we acknowledge that You alone are in control of all things, at all times! Forgive us when we try and take over or instruct You in the way things should be done. We are sorry. We are your daughters, and we ask that as such, You will be gentle and patient with us, forgiving us over and over, and gently nudging us again and again as we wander astray. We realize, Father, that You have not created us to be timid, afraid, or uncertain. But rather You are in the very process of making us more and more like You! You are forming us to be Your ambassadors, Your vessels for Your glory! Help us to grow in our knowledge of You, of Your Word, and of Your will for our lives. We love You, We thank You for the work You have begun in us, and We desire to worship you with our lives! So be it. Amen.

JANUARY 30

M ake a careful exploration of who you are and the work you have been given, and then sink yourself into that. Don't be impressed with yourself. Don't compare yourself with others. Each of you must take responsibility for doing the creative best you can with your own life. (Galatians 6:4, 5, MSG)

I ask the God of our Master, Jesus Christ, the God of glory— to make you intelligent and discerning in knowing Him personally, your eyes focused and clear, so that you can see exactly what it is He is calling you to do, grasp the immensity of this glorious way of life He has for His followers, oh, the utter extravagance of His work in us who trust Him—endless energy, boundless strength! (Ephesians 1: 8, 19)

Part of our responsibility as God's daughters is to keep our thought life healthy. What we think and how we speak matters to God. It affects us and the lives we interact with. Our actions originate in thought and what we believe about God, and consequently, what we believe about ourselves has a powerful, far-reaching influence on the world around us! If each one of us truly believed that we are who God tells us we are, and that God is everything He says He is, I think our lives as well as our thoughts would be healthy and strong! It's a daily battle against the evil forces of this world to reclaim our position as daughters of the King! But, my dear, dear sisters, it is worth the fight! I believe with my whole heart that God does indeed have a "glorious way of life" for each and every one of us! He has called us to be His ambassadors, to speak truth, love, forgiveness and grace into the broken lives around us! He calls us to a wild, free life through faith in Him! Freedom from pride, self-centeredness, and comparison with others. And instead turns our thoughts to embracing who He has created each one of us to be: helping us to truly examine the gifts He has given each of us and become comfortable and confident in our own identities. Then God is free to use us for His purposes and His glory! And not only will He use us, He will gift us with "endless energy and boundless strength!" Dear friends, God is in the process of giving each one of a "mind change," and it revolves around Him! God created us, gifted us, loves us, and continues to bring about His purposes for our lives. And you can believe it when I tell you, it's gonna be good!

JANUARY 31

Celebrate God all day, every day, I mean, revel in Him! Make it clear as you can to all you meet that you're on their side, working with them and not against them. Help them see that the Master is about to arrive. He could show up any minute. Don't fret or worry. Instead of worrying, pray. Let petitions and praises shape your worries into prayers, letting God know your concerns. Before you know it, a sense of God's wholeness, everything coming together for good, will come and settle you down. It's wonderful what happens when Christ displaces worry at the center of your life. Summing it all up, friends, I'd say you'll do best by filling your minds and meditating on things true, noble, reputable, authentic, compelling, gracious—the best, not the worst; the beautiful, not the ugly; things to praise, not things to curse. Put into practice what you learned from me (Paul) what you heard and saw and realized. Do that, and God, Who makes everything work together, will work you into His most excellent harmonies. (Philippians 4:4–9, MSG)

Living our lives in harmony with the people around us, I think we all want that. Did you notice that the scripture talks about letting others know "that you're on their side, working with them and not against them"? My dear sisters, we are all fighting a tough battle in our lives. Many of us have things going on that no one knows about but God. Many feel overwhelmed, ineffective, and frustrated in their relationships. Some of us are just plain tired! Others have fractured relationships, frustrating careers, and difficult marriages. I'm not just talking about our group here, but everyone around us!

Life is hard! Let's not make it more difficult for those around us! Let's let them know that we care about them, are praying for them, and are supportive of them! Let's remind ourselves to think about things to praise—beautiful, happy, noble, true things! About how very, very much we are loved and cared for! Let's think about the God Who placed us here in this time and in this place for His purposes! Let's give our enemy a reason to grumble when we get up every morning!

Let's be the light that transforms the dark around us! We can do it, ladies, through God's power working within us! He's coaching us forward! Telling us, "Get up, get moving…be My encourager today, be My ambassador!" Let's move forward in our day, leaking Jesus on everyone we meet!

FEBRUARY 1

Each one should test their own actions. Then they can take pride in themselves alone, without comparing themselves to someone else. (Galatians 6:4)

The LORD Almighty has a day in store for all the proud and lofty, for all that is exalted (and they will be humbled). (Isaiah 2:12)

But He gives us more grace. That is why Scripture says: "God opposes the proud but shows favor to the humble." (James 4:6)

Humble yourselves before the Lord, and He will lift you up. (James 4:10)

This is what the LORD says: "Let not the wise boast of their wisdom or the strong boast of their strength or the rich boast of their riches, but, let him who boasts, boast of this; that they know and understand Me." (Jeremiah 9:23)

Do nothing out of selfish ambition or vain conceit. Rather, in humility value others above yourselves. (Philippians 2:3)

When pride comes, then comes disgrace, but with humility comes wisdom. (Proverbs 11:2)

The LORD detests all the proud of heart. Be sure of this: They will not go unpunished. Pride goes before destruction, a haughty spirit before a fall. (Proverbs 16:5, 18)

Do you see a person wise in their own eyes? There is more hope for a fool than for them. (Proverbs 26:12)

The truth is that more damage has been done to the church by prideful, judgmental, arrogant Christians than those outside the church could ever do! OUCH!

We all realize it's true that looking down on others, judging them, and feeling superior are all the first steps of a major personal and spiritual crash! God hates the sin of pride! In fact, the Bible goes so far as to warn us that God will discipline the proud! That doesn't mean that we should live our lives in an "anything goes" fashion, accepting behaviors and beliefs that we know are contrary to scripture is sure to destroy us. But it is the sin that we should hate because of the damage it will do—and does—to the one who embraces it!

One of my biggest concerns with writing this devotional is that I will give the impression that I understand more than I do or that I am in some way "better" at this Christian thing than anyone else. Let me be the first and loudest to say, "I am a work in progress!" God continually convicts me of areas in my life that need improvement. I know that I cannot walk this life of faith apart from the Father. Daily, I confess, cry out, and beg for help in areas in which I struggle. Daily, I fail. But I know with a deep and abiding assurance that God will not leave me where I fell. He will once again pick me up, dust me off, and put me back on the path He has ordained for me. He does the same thing for each one of you every day! We may all be walking in different directions and experiencing different things, but the same Father is holding each one of us in His mighty hands. He is nudging, guiding, correcting, and encouraging every one of us, every day! May we tune our ears to hear His voice and understand His warnings. He will tell us HOW to live; we just need to LISTEN!

Have a great day! Never, ever, ever forget how fiercely loved and protected you are! The ONE Who watches over us is powerful beyond our wildest imaginings, and He NEVER lets us out of His sight!

FEBRUARY 2

Therefore, since we have these promises, dear friends, let us purify ourselves from everything that contaminates body and spirit, perfecting holiness out of reverence for God. (2 Corinthians 7:1)

He has saved us and called us to a holy life—not because of anything we have done but because of His own purpose and grace. This grace was given us in Christ Jesus before the beginning of time. (2 Timothy 1:9)

Search me, God, and know my heart; test me and know my anxious thoughts. See if there is any offensive way in me, and lead me in the way everlasting. (Psalm 139:23–24)

Do everything without grumbling or arguing, so that you may become blameless and pure, children of God without fault in a warped and crooked generation. Then you will shine among them like stars in the sky as you hold firmly to the Word of life. (Philippians 2:14–16a)

You are to be holy to Me because I, the Lord, am holy, and I have set you apart from the nations to be My own. (Leviticus 20:26)

Joel Scandrett writes about holiness this way: "God's call to be holy is a radical, all-encompassing claim on our lives, our loves and our identities. To be a disciple of Jesus Christ requires nothing less than death to our fallen, egocentric selves in order that we might live in and for Him. Holiness is not primarily about moral purity, it's about union with God in Christ and sharing in Christ's holiness."

Once again, how we live our lives matters!

We are called into relationship with Christ, we are forgiven through Jesus's blood on the cross for our sins, and we are called to be holy because the One we confess to believe is holy! Apart from Him, we can go through the outward motions of holiness, acting like we understand holiness, trying to put on an act of morality. But true holiness can only be obtained through relationship with Christ. First, God calls us and says, "Follow Me." Then He begins to work in us to will and to act according to His purpose. Holiness is a result of the Spirit's presence living within us. When we live out our lives in relationship with Christ everything else falls in to place.

Have a great day, friends! You are greatly and eternally loved!

FEBRUARY 3

How blessed is the woman who does not walk in the counsel of the wicked. Nor stand in the path of sinners, nor sit in the seat of scoffers! (Psalm 1:1–3)

Let the words of my mouth and the meditation of my heart be acceptable in Your sight, o LORD, my Rock and my Redeemer. (Psalm 19:14)

Let my meditation be pleasing to Him; as for me, I shall be glad in the LORD. (Psalm 104:34)

I have set the LORD continually before me; because He is at my right hand, I will not be shaken. (Psalm 16:8)

When I remember You on my bed, I meditate on You in the night watches. (Psalm 63:6)

I will meditate on Your precepts and regard Your ways. (Psalm 119:15–16)

Please receive instruction from His mouth and establish His Words in your heart. (Job 22:22)

Finally, brothers and sisters, whatever is true, whatever is honorable, whatever is lovely, whatever is of good repute, if there is any excellence and if anything worthy of praise, dwell on these things. (Philippians 4:8)

Where do your thoughts take you when faced with difficult situations? Is your "default setting" God's Word?

During different seasons in my life, different words of scripture have been my comfort. "I can do all things through Christ Who strengthens me." "You are my beloved." "Let the morning bring me news of your steadfast love." "Do not fear, I am your God." "When we trust in Him, we're free to say whatever needs to be said, bold to go wherever we need to go." One of my favorites is Psalm 147:11 *in the Message Translation:* "Those who fear God get God's attention, they can depend on His Strength!

There is a wealth of comfort, strength, and encouragement in God's Word. The importance of knowing it cannot be underestimated! God speaks to us through His Word, through people, circumstances, dreams, and a host of other ways. The best thing about hearing Him through His Word though is that there is never a doubt that it is HIS voice we are hearing and not our own! God desires to speak to us. He desires to know us intimately and to be known by us! A relationship with Him is worth any sacrifice or effort!

Love you, ladies! But more importantly, God loves you!

FEBRUARY 4

For all have sinned and fall short of the glory of God. (Romans 3:23)

If you do what is right, will you not be accepted? But if you do not do what is right, sin is crouching at your door; it desires to have you, but you must rule over it. (Genesis 4:7)

Put to death, therefore, whatever belongs to your earthly nature: sexual immorality, impurity, lust, evil desires and greed, which is idolatry. Because of these, the wrath of God is coming. (Colossians 3:5–6)

If anyone, then, knows the good they ought to do and doesn't do it, it is sin for them. (James 4:17)

You're cheating on God. If all you want is your own way, flirting with the world every chance you get, you end up enemies of God and His way. And do you suppose God doesn't care? The proverb has it that "He's a fiercely jealous lover." And what He gives in love is far better than anything else you'll find. It's common knowledge that "God goes against the willful proud, God gives grace to the willing humble." So let God work His will in you. Yell a loud NO to the devil and watch him scamper. Say a quiet yes to God and He'll be there in no time. Quit dabbling in sin. Purify your inner life. Quit playing the field. Hit bottom, and cry your eyes out. The fun and games are over. Get serious, really serious. Get down on your knees before the Master; it's the only way you'll get on your feet. (James 4:4–10, MSG)

So, what is sin? Why is it such an offense against God? Is it because its effects are toxic, or is it because sin is an affront to God's holy character? All sin is offensive to Him. Not just "big" sins—all sins!

In our culture, sin has become a joke. Literally! We laugh and make light of living in an "anything goes" culture. We have even gone so far as to say, "If it feels right, it's okay" or "God wants me to be happy." Actually, God wants us to be holy. Happiness is a result of inheriting His holiness. We laugh about sin, but sin is deadly! It destroys lives, homes, communities, bank accounts, marriages—and the list goes on and on. And why is it that the Bible is so clear about the consequences of sin? I believe it is because sin is what separates us from God. When we sin and demand our own way, we cannot expect to live in a way that is pleasing to God or in a lifestyle that He will bless with His peace and strength. I love the verse in James 4:5 of the Message translation that says, "He is a fiercely jealous lover!" God will not tolerate us living with one foot "in the world" and the other with Him. I have said it before, and I will say it again, God wants ALL of us! He wants access to every aspect of our lives—our personal lives, our sexual lives, our spiritual lives, our financial and material lives. We cannot live "lukewarm" lives and expect to experience all the blessings that God has in store for us. Sin does indeed have consequences, and one of the most severe, in my estimation, is separation from God. Sin causes division in our relationship that keeps us from hearing His voice and missing the mark of His guidance. God is indeed FOR us, but are we FOR Him?

You are fiercely loved, sisters! Believe it!

FEBRUARY 5

Looking at them, Jesus said, "With people it is impossible but not with God; for all things are possible with God." (Mark 10:27)

For nothing will be impossible with God. (Luke 1:37)

"I know that You can do all things, and that no purpose of Yours can be thwarted." (Job 42:2)

Can you discover the depths of God? Can you discover the limits of the Almighty? (Job 11:7)

For the Mighty One has done great things for me; and holy is His name. (Luke 1:49)

The LORD your God is in your midst, a victorious warrior He will exult over you with joy, He will be quiet in His love, He will rejoice over you with shouts of joy. (Zephaniah 3:17)

But You, O Lord, are a God merciful and gracious, slow to anger and abounding in steadfast love and faithfulness. (Psalm 86:15)

The steadfast love of the LORD never ceases; His mercies never come to an end; they are new every morning; great is Your faithfulness. (Lamentations 3 22–23)

But the LORD is faithful, He will establish you and guard you against the evil one. (2 Thessalonians 3:3)

He will cover you with His pinions, and under His wings you will find refuge; His faithfulness is a shield and buckler. (Psalm 91:4)

If we are faithless, He remains faithful—for HE cannot deny Himself. (2 Timothy 2:13)

"I ask the God of our Master, Jesus Christ, the God of glory— to make you intelligent and discerning in knowing Him personally, your eyes focused and clear, so that you can see exactly what it is He is calling you to do; grasp the immensity of this glorious way of life He has for His followers, oh, the utter extravagance of His work in us who trust Him - endless energy, boundless strength!... All this energy issues from Christ." (Ephesians 1:16–20, MSG)

My dear and faithful sisters; we have only just begun to dip our toes in to the depth of God's power, grace and faithfulness! He is soooo much bigger, stronger, fiercer than anything we can even imagine! NOTHING goes on in our lives that He doesn't know about—absolutely nothing! He is keenly aware of our problems, our frustrations, our shortcomings as well as our successes and what brings us joy! He is FAITHFUL, even when we are not! He guards us against our enemy, even when we let our guard down! He showers us with new mercies every morning, even when we are not grateful for the mercies of yesterday. He is our Shield and our Protector, guiding and protecting us from attacks we aren't even aware of! But the words that warm my heart most this morning are "God is in our midst" everywhere and always! HE is a victorious Warrior. He will exult over us with joy! He will rejoice over us with SHOUTS OF JOY! Wow, that humbles me! WHO are WE that God Almighty, ALL POWERFUL, should rejoice over US? That ALMIGHTY GOD should raise His voice in shouts of joy,... over us? My dear sisters, we are HIS beloved! HIS daughters! His love is inexhaustible, limitless, and immeasurable! How can we not be bouncing on eager toes of anticipation, asking, "What's next Papa?"

FEBRUARY 6

Whatever the LORD pleases, He does, in heaven and in earth, in the seas and in all deeps. (Psalm 135:6)

But our God is in the heavens; He does whatever He pleases. (Psalm 115:3)

For nothing will be impossible with God. (Luke 1:37)

I know that You can do all things, and that no purpose of Yours can be thwarted. (Job 42:2)

And looking at them Jesus said to them, "With people this is impossible, but with God all things are possible." (Matthew 19:26)

Now to Him Who is able to do far more abundantly beyond all that we ask or think, according to the power that works within us. (Ephesians 3:20)

And he said, "O LORD, the God of our fathers, are You not God in the heavens? And are You not ruler over all the kingdoms of the nations? Power and might are in Your hand so that no one can stand against You." (2 Chronicles 20:6)

Were He to snatch away, who could restrain Him? Who could say to Him, "What are You doing?" (Job 9:12)

Even from eternity I AM HE, and there is none who can deliver out of My hand; I act and who can reverse it? (Isaiah 43:13)

Woe to the one who quarrels with her Maker—an earthenware vessel among the vessels of earth! Will the clay say to the Potter, "What are you doing?" (Isaiah 45:9–10)

Let the heavens be glad, and let the earth rejoice, and let them say among the nations, "The LORD reigns." (1 Chronicles 16:31)

All the above scriptures (and there are many, many more) talk about God's sovereignty. But what does it mean to be sovereign?

If you were to look it up, you would find words and phrases like "superior," "greatest," "supreme in power and authority," "ruler," and "independent of all others." Simply put, God is in control! Everywhere and always, God is in control! There is absolutely nothing that happens in the universe that is outside of God's influence and authority. God has no limitations. He is immortal, present everywhere, and knows all things.

So once again, I am wondering why I spend so much of my time telling HIM what to do and how to run things! One would think that I would finally learn that God KNOWS what He is doing! That even when He allows or inflicts pain in my life that HE has a purpose and a reason that far exceeds anything I can understand. When will I learn that instead of arguing with God and demanding my own way, or at the LEAST an explanation of WHY things are not going along with my plan, I would just sit back and surrender my will to HIS WILL. After all, one of the earliest prayers we all learn reminds us, "Thy will be done." I guess we really don't mean those words. Perhaps what we are really thinking is; "Thy Kingdom come, MY will be done."

My dear sisters, believe me, I fully understand that this life can be difficult, extremely difficult! But as daughters of the King, we can rest assured that we are in good Hands…powerful Hands…wise and wonderful Hands that KNOW exactly what they are doing and why. The Hands that are holding us are stronger than anything our greatest enemy can throw at us. They are able to hold us safely until we arrive home. Understanding that the Hands holding us will determine when that will be. God is good, and He can be trusted!

FEBRUARY 7

For I know the plans I have for you declares the Lord, plans to prosper you and not to harm you, plans to give you hope and a future. (Jeremiah 29:11)

This is good, and pleases God our Savior, Who wants all people to be saved and to come to a knowledge of the truth. (1 Timothy 2:3–4)

If any of you lacks wisdom, you should ask God, Who gives generously to all without finding fault, and it will be given to you. (James 1:5)

Trust in the LORD with all your heart and lean not on your own understanding; in all your ways submit to Him and He will make your paths straight. (Proverbs 3:5–6)

For it is God's will that by doing good you should silence the ignorant talk of foolish people. (1 Peter 2:15)

YOUR kingdom come, YOUR will be done, on earth as it is in heaven. (Matthew 6:10)

Be very careful, then, how you live—not as unwise but as wise, making the most of every opportunity, because the days are evil. Therefore do not be foolish, but understand what the Lord's will is. Do not get drunk on wine, which leads to debauchery. Instead, be filled with the Spirit, speaking to one another with psalms, hymns, and songs from the Spirit. Sing and make music from your heart to the Lord, always giving thanks to God the Father for everything, in the name of our Lord Jesus Christ. (Ephesians 5:15–20)

He has shown you, O mortal, what is good. And what does the LORD require of you? To act justly and to love mercy and to walk humbly with your God. (Micah 6:8)

For you were formerly darkness, but now you are Light in the Lord, walk as children of Light. (Ephesians 5:8–10)

It is true that God created us to experience pleasure and joy, in fact God calls us to "be full of joy in the Lord."

Most of our days are spent in an endless pursuit of what we think will make us happy, or worrying about what could happen next. We may not even realize how we waste precious seconds of our life worrying about "how we will get out of the predicament we are in" or "how we will provide for tomorrow's needs" or "what will I do if this happens" or "what if this pain is something serious," or "what if I die!" We waste so much joy worrying about tomorrow that we forget to live today! We forget to look around at the beauty that surrounds us. To feel the love of a spouse or/and family, to delight in the rhythm of life. To rejoice in new life, and to reflect on death. We are oftentimes so overwhelmed with the "details" of life that we forget to embrace this precious, wonderful gift we have been given! Many years ago now, I read a book that spoke of being "fully alive" and "fully aware" of what was going on around us, in us, and because of us. How our moods, reactions, responses, and thoughts effected the people and environment around us. I realized then, as I realize now, that far too often, I go through the "motion" of life without enjoying life! I am so obsessed with "what's next" that I totally miss the moment!

TODAY is a day the LORD has made, let us REJOICE and BE GLAD IN IT! Scripture reminds us, "Don't worry about tomorrow, tomorrow has enough troubles of its own. Live fully in today!" (Paraphrase mine).

We don't need to chase after things that we think will make us happy or fulfill this need or that; we simply need to pause, take a deep breath, and lean in to the One that is holding us. He will direct our steps and fulfill every longing of our fickle hearts. And when, for that split second, we realize that we are truly happy and fulfilled and content, may we "rejoice before the LORD our God in everything we do!" The way we think, the way we walk and talk, and the way we live our lives, day in and day out!

As we walk out this life as daughters of the King, may His Light so brightly reflect off us that others cannot help but notice and in turn seek the source of our Light and Joy!

YOU are loved! YOU are called by the Father of Light…YOU are claimed and sealed and protected and instructed by Almighty God! There is no need for concern or worry…ever!

FEBRUARY 8

Blessed be the God and Father of our Lord Jesus Christ, Who has blessed us with every spiritual blessing in the heavenly places in Christ. (Ephesians 1:3–5)

Therefore if anyone is in Christ, she is a new creature; the old things passed away; behold new things have come. (2 Corinthians 5:17)

For you have not received a spirit of slavery leading to fear again, but you have received a spirit of adoption as daughters by which we cry out, "Abba, Father!" (Romans 8:15–17)

My sheep hear My voice, and I know them, and they follow Me; and I give eternal life to them, and they will never perish; and no one will snatch them out of My hand. "My Father, who has given them to Me, is greater than all; and no one is able to snatch them out of the Father's hand." (John 10:27–29)

Therefore there is now no condemnation for those who are in Christ Jesus. (Romans 8:1)

So, just what are spiritual blessings? And why would we desire them more than earthly blessings. I think that oftentimes, when I see or hear the word *blessing*, I put an "earthly spin" on it. Like being blessed with health, the love of family, or the "good" things of life.

And those are indeed blessings. But the "spiritual blessings" we receive when we become daughters of the King go far beyond earthly, temporal blessings. First of all, we are forgiven of our sin! The sin we know we committed as well as the sin of wanting what we don't have, envy, anger, jealousy, worry (the list goes on and on) that we struggle with every day of our earthly lives. We are not only forgiven but considered by God to be holy and without blemish! All through the sacrifice of Jesus on our behalf! But not only are we forgiven (which would be enough in itself), but we are adopted in God's very own family! We are no longer considered "outsiders," but we are pulled in and embraced by the loving arms of our Father, Who will never turn us away or abandon us! That being said, one of the "spiritual blessings" we are also privy to when we become daughters of the King is wisdom and insight through His Word to come to know and understand God and what He desires for our lives! God is no longer some big, vague, misunderstood cosmic cop who desires to punish and jail us but rather a kind and loving Father who desires the best for us—always! Who calls us by name, gently holds our broken hearts, pieces them back together, dusts us off, and puts us back on our feet! He challenges us, pushes us to be more than we ever thought we could be, gives us strength to endure when ours has failed, and rejoices over us! Our names are written on the palms of His hands and He is never, ever, far from us! Oh, my dear sisters, that we would be given eyes to see the magnitude of His love for us! That we could catch just a glimpse of His wisdom and power and intervention on our behalf! God is FOR us! Everywhere, every day, always! We are indeed blessed beyond measure!

FEBRUARY 9

She will give birth to a Son and will call Him Immanuel (which means God is with us.) (Isaiah 7:14)

The Lord your God is in your midst, a Mighty One Who will save; He will rejoice over you with gladness; He will quiet you by His love; He will exult over you with loud singing." (Zephaniah 3:17)

But He knows the way that I take; when He has tested me, I will come forth as gold. (Job 23:10)

Have I not commanded you? Be strong and courageous. Do not be frightened, and do not be dismayed, for the LORD your God is with you wherever you go. (Joshua 1:9)

Fear not, for I AM with you; be not dismayed, for I AM your God; I WILL strengthen you, I WILL help you, I WILL uphold you with My righteous right hand. (Isaiah 41:10)

Be strong and courageous. Do not fear or be in dread of them, for it is the Lord your God Who goes with you. He will not leave you or forsake you. (Deuteronomy 31:6)

Fear not, for I have redeemed you; I have called you by name, you are mine. When you pass through the waters, I will be with you; and through the rivers, they will not overwhelm you; when you walk through fire you shall not be burned, and the flame shall not consume you. For I AM the Lord your God, the Holy One of Israel, your Savior. (Isaiah 43:1–3)

Even to your old age and gray hairs I AM He, I AM He Who will sustain you. I have made you and I will carry you; I will sustain you and I Will rescue you. (Isaiah 46:4)

And surely I AM with you always, to the very end of the age…
(Matthew 28:20)

Throughout Scripture, we read God telling His followers, over and over again, "Do not fear, I will be with you."

I know from personal experience that when we are struggling in life with problems, pain, or uncertainty, we begin to think that God has withdrawn His presence from us. That for some reason He doesn't see us or, worse yet, doesn't care! We feel abandoned or somehow removed from His presence. We think that because we are struggling, God isn't there! But as much as we may wish it were so, God doesn't always take us around our problems. Sometimes, He leads us straight through. Into the darkness, into the fire, into the storm! But that being said, He is faithful to carry us through! We are not meant to stay stuck in the trial. For when we belong to Him, He has the power to define our days. To use the difficult for divine purpose! To refine and remake us into women of courage, strength, and light!

When I was younger, I thought that if I was devoted to God, my life would somehow avoid the trials and really difficult situations of life. That my kids would be beautiful, healthy, moral, kind, and loving! That my spouse would recognize me for the amazing treasure that I am (pun) and that I would sail through life with kindness, generosity (because God would give me material wealth), and health and great love and wisdom! As I age, I have realized that God does indeed provide. But in my experience, He has not provided through avoidance of problems but through strength to walk through them! I am learning that God's plans are very often entirely different than My plans. That God uses the troubles, temptations and trials of life to lead me to Himself. Reminding me that without Him, I am fragile, frightened and lost, tossed around by my latest thoughts or desires. I am learning that God more readily uses my tears and trials to encourage me or others that He is enough. He isn't impressed with "what I know" but with the tenderness of my heart. God is indeed molding me and stretching me and pushing me. He knows me well and knows that my first response is to "give up." You may think I am strong and able to withstand storms, but in all honesty, I am a wimpy, fragile woman whose first thought is to dissolve into a pile of tears and fear. God has His work cut out for Him with me, but glory to God! I am never alone, and He NEVER gives up!

FEBRUARY 10

He has not dealt with us according to our sins, not punished us according to our iniquities. For as the heavens are high above the earth, so great is His mercy toward those who fear Him; as far as the east is from the west, so far has He removed our transgressions from us. (Psalm 103:10–12)

I, even I, Am He Who blots out your transgressions for MY OWN sake; and I will not remember your sins. (Isaiah 43:25)

Let the wicked forsake her way, and the unrighteous woman her thoughts; let her return to the Lord, and HE will have mercy on her; and to our God, for He will abundantly pardon. (Isaiah 55:7)

For if you forgive men their trespasses, your heavenly Father will also forgive you. But if you do not forgive men their trespasses, neither will your Father forgive your trespasses. (Matthew 6:14–15)

Therefore I say to you, her sins, which are many, are forgiven, for she loved much. But to whom little is forgiven, the same loves little. (Luke 7:47–48)

I will rejoice greatly in the LORD, my soul will exult in my God; for He has clothed me with garments of salvation, He has wrapped me with a robe of righteousness. As a bridegroom decks himself with a garland, and as a bride adorns herself with jewels. (Isaiah 61:10)

It is difficult to imagine that when God says He will remember our sin no more or that He will remove our sin forever, that He really means it! How often do we as people remember people's sins, shortcoming, crimes, etc., for the rest of their lives? How frequently do we silently, or not so silently, continue to hold it against them? Forgiveness is not something that comes easily to us. And as far as forgetting altogether something that injured us, forget it! We are quick to call on God to forgive us when we fail, and He does. But we are certainly not as quick to forgive an offense against us. In Matthew, we are reminded that "if you do not forgive men their trespasses, neither will our Father forgive us ours!" Ouch!

There are so many scriptures in the Bible that speak of God's attributes, forgiveness being one. But there are also many verses in the Bible about our appropriate response to such grace! "Forgive others as God has forgiven you." "Be about doing the good work that God has prepared in advance for you to do." "Love patiently, with kindness."

My dear and faithful sisters, God is the source of all righteousness! God forgives, restores, renews, empowers, enables, guides, and goads us along. Our response is to follow HIS lead! Accept His forgiveness, His love, His guidance, and His discipline and clothe ourselves with His righteousness! When we do, we won't have to live out our lives in fear and trembling or shame and depression. Instead, we can walk boldly, eagerly through our days, bouncing on eager toes of anticipation. Knowing that our ABBA has whatever comes our way under HIS almighty control! God can be trusted to deal with our sin. He can be trusted to be more than we could ever ask or imagine! It's time to believe and embrace that God truly is WHO HE says HE is!

FEBRUARY 11

B ut avoid worldly and empty chatter, for it will lead to further ungodliness. (2 Timothy 2:16)

Do you not know that when you present yourselves to someone as slaves for obedience, you are slaves of the one whom you obey, either of sin resulting in death, or of obedience resulting in righteousness. Message - You know well enough from your own experience that there are some acts of so-called freedom that destroy freedom. Offer yourselves to sin, for instance, and it's your last free act. But offer yourselves to the ways of God and the freedom never quits. (Romans 6:16)

But your iniquities have made a separation between you and your God. And your sins have hidden His face from you so that He does not hear. (Isaiah 59:2)

Somewhere along the way and in a very short time, we as a country and a people have made a joke of sin. I remember being a little girl in church and understanding the importance of confession of sin, of asking God for forgiveness and admitting my sins. But my experiences in life have presented an entirely different picture. One that compares sins! "My sin is not as serious as 'her' sin." "That can't be sin!" "God doesn't understand the times we are living in." "That is outdated." "He/she has enough, they won't miss this." "It's just a little thing." "No one will know, so it doesn't matter." "Everyone does it."

Instead of admitting our sin and asking for forgiveness, we justify our sin. But that justification only works in our own minds. Every sin has consequence. The Bible is very clear that we will be asked to give an account of our sin. Thank GOD that He has made a way for us to be clear and clean of our sin. Through confession and forgiveness, the grace of God that we need on a daily basis!

Do you remember that we are called to give an account of even our thoughts? I will give you a very recent example of my own. An example I am not proud of but can be honest about. I heard through a friend that a woman was having significant emotional and physical problems. Now, I have always found this woman to be a "shove it down your throat" kind of Christian. I felt judged by her and always came up short. Now, my first and gut reaction was something like "Ha-ha, where is that great faith now?" But I knew that those thoughts were ugly and sinful and a disgrace to the faith that I confess. I had to wrestle with those thoughts and ask God for forgiveness and, not only that but a grace and compassion for her that I didn't initially feel.

ALL sin is detestable to God! Every sin against the body, another, or even a thought! Try as I might, I cannot think of one sin that does not have undesirable consequences. To the embezzler, the fear of being caught, of covering tracks, of wanting more and more. To the adulterer, the loss of family and marriage, to the liar, the fear of always being caught in that lie, and remembering what was said to whom—the list goes on and on. When I think of my own sin, I am ashamed and sorry. My times of defiance and justification of my sin are slowly going by the wayside. My heart is broken because I have broken the heart of God. Sin is ugly, self-perpetuating, destructive, and much more. But the worst of all of the consequences, in my view, is separation from God. Not being able to hear His voice, feel His hand in mine, or trust that He will guide and hold me.

Sisters, we cannot have it both ways. We cannot live with sin as our master and God. The choice is ours. As for me and my house (as much as it is up to me), we will choose the LORD!

FEBRUARY 12

And we all, who with unveiled faces contemplate the Lord's glory, are being transformed into His image with ever-increasing glory, which comes from the Lord, Who is the Spirit. (2 Corinthians 3:18)

Do not conform to the pattern of this world, but be transformed by the renewing of your mind. Then you will be able to test and approve what God's will is—His good, pleasing and perfect will. (Romans 12:2)

Therefore, if anyone is in Christ, she is a new creation. The old has passed away; behold, the new has come. (2 Corinthians 5:17)

Create in me a clean heart, O God, and renew a right spirit within me. Cast me not away from Your Presence, and take not Your Holy Spirit from me. Restore to me the joy of my salvation and uphold me with a willing spirit. (Psalm 51:10–12)

And I am sure of this, that He Who began a good work in you will bring it to completion at the day of Jesus Christ. (Philippians 1:6)

In the same way, let your light shine before others, so that they may see your good works and give glory to your Father Who is in heaven. (Matthew 5:16)

Who saved us and called us to a holy calling, not because of our works but because of His own purpose and grace, which He gave us in Christ Jesus before the ages began. (2 Timothy 1:9)

And by this we know that we have come to know Him, if we keep His commandments. Whoever says, "I know Him" but does not keep His commandments is a liar, and the truth is not in her, but whoever keeps His Word, in her truly the love of God is perfected. By this we may know that we are in Him; whoever says she abides in Him ought to walk in the same way in which she talked. (1 John 2:3–6)

Just as we do not think or reason today, as we did when we were thirteen or fourteen, or twenty or thirty. So do we continue to grow and stretch in our faith. We are all a work in progress. God is continually transforming us into His image through the trials, temptations, and victories of this life. Every one of us has a life individually ordered and guided by the hand of God. He allows the trials we will face, for HIS glory. He ordains the road we will travel, for HIS glory and He knows the "whats" and "whys" of each of our lives. Slowly but surely, God is piecing us together, weaving our earthly lives into a tapestry of phenomenal, everlasting beauty. We cannot see it from the vantage point we have now, but those cheering us on from the heavenly heights can see what God is up to. If we listen closely and tune out the noise of this world, I think we can hear them whisper, "It will all be worth it." "Worth every tear, every heartache, every challenge." "Something beautiful is happening. May we learn to trust the HAND doing it." Listen, sisters, can you hear it?

You are loved, you are called into His marvelous kingdom to live lives that matter. Lives that testify to the ability and love of the Hand molding them. Trusting that the Hand holding yours knows what He's doing. Trusting that no matter what, God will not discontinue or abandon the work He is doing in our lives. Little by little, stitch my stitch, piece by piece, we are being transformed into HIS likeness for HIS glory. Someday, when God brings us home, we will see the finished product and we will know with certainty, God's hand never left ours. The tapestry of our lives will take our breaths away. Let us not grow weary in the process.

FEBRUARY 13

Therefore I tell you, do not worry about your life, what you will eat or drink; or about your body, what you will wear. Is not life more than food, and the body more than clothes? Look at the birds of the air; they do not sow or reap or store away in barns, and yet your Heavenly Father feeds them. Are you not much more valuable than they? For the pagans run after all these things, and your Heavenly Father knows that you need them. But seek first His Kingdom and His Righteousness, and all these things will be given you as well. (Matthew 6:25–26, 32, 33)

I know what it is to be in need, and I know what it is to have plenty. I have learned the secret of being content in any and every situation, whether well fed or hungry, whether living in plenty or in want. I can do all this through Him Who gives me strength. (Philippians 4:12–13)

Keep your lives free from the love of money and be content with what you have, because God has said, "Never will I leave you; never will I forsake you." (Hebrews 13:5)

But godliness with contentment is great gain. For we brought nothing into the world, and we can take nothing out of it. (1 Timothy 6:6–7)

Then He said to them, "Watch out! Be on your guard against all kinds of greed; life does not consist in an abundance of possessions." (Luke 12:15)

Trust in the LORD and do good; dwell in the land and enjoy safe pasture. Take delight in the LORD and He will give you the desires of your heart. (Psalm 37:3–4)

For the love of money is a root of all kinds of evil. Some people, eager for money, have wandered from the faith and pierced themselves with many griefs. But you, woman of God, flee from all this, and pursue righteousness, godliness, faith, love, endurance and gentleness. (1 Timothy 6:10–11)

It has taken a while, but I am coming to realize that contentment is a choice. That joy is a choice and not a result of circumstances. I have forfeited joy because I bought into the lie of "if only!" "I will be happy, content, joyful if only I have this or that or achieve this or that or look like her".

No matter what, we can choose to dwell on the blessings we have received or the relentless desire for more or different or whatever it is that looks like a better option than what we have right now. We have the choice to allow our mind to dwell on possessions or "our image" or "what the neighbors think." Or we can choose to think thoughts that are glorifying God. Bringing our minds back to reflect on and remember the blessings that we already have. My dear friends, our lives are being orchestrated by the very hand of our Loving Father. He is fully aware of what He is doing. And, He promises us that when we delight in HIM, He will "give us the desires of our heart." It may be perhaps that He will change those desires, our desires may then reflect His character and HIS desires for us. But, either way, IT'S GONNA BE GOOD!

FEBRUARY 14

Do not be anxious about anything, but in everything, by prayer and supplication with thanksgiving, let your requests be made known to God. (Philippians 4:6)

Pray without ceasing. (1 Thessalonians 5:17)

Likewise, the Spirit helps us in our weakness. For we do not know what to pray for as we ought, but the Spirit himself intercedes for us with groaning too deep for words. (Romans 8:26)

And when you pray, do not heap up empty phrases as the Gentiles do, for they think that they will be heard for their many words. (Matthew 6:7)

Therefore, confess your sins to one another and pray for one another, that you may be healed. The prayer of a righteous person has great power as it is working. (James 5:16)

Continue steadfastly in prayer, being watchful in it with thanksgiving. (Colossians 4:2)

Then you will call upon Me and come and pray to Me, and I will hear you. (Jeremiah 29:12)

I don't know about all of you, but I know that sometimes, I do not know HOW to pray! Oh, I know how to pray for the things that I think are best, the things that I personally want for myself or others, but I am oftentimes at a loss for words when I simply don't know "what" to pray! For example, when I am sitting with a hospice patient who looks like they are very near the end of their life, do I pray that God would heal them? That God would "hurry" their departure? Sometimes, the patient doesn't want to die, then what? It really has been an issue for me, until I remember WHO I am praying to. I have found at times like those listed above and many, many others my "best" prayer has simply been "LORD, Your will be done. Give me the wisdom to ask according to Your will, and the grace to accept Your answer."

Lately, God has really been doing a work on my heart. Convicting me that He ALWAYS hears and ALWAYS acts when His children pray. I have been quick to say; "God CAN do this or that, but I am not sure that He will." And, I do believe that is an honest statement. But more recently I have come to believe that GOD ALWAYS acts! He acts with changes in lives that we can see, but oftentimes, He does things that we cannot see or even comprehend! When we pray for someone, I believe heaven hears, heaven responds and heaven intervenes. But because we are creatures of pride and self-centeredness, we often-times don't want to hear God's response or believe that God said, "NO!" We come back with statements like "God isn't responding, or answering" or "He is deaf, uncaring, unaware." When in reality, God may have heard, answered, and have an entirely different plan!

When we learn to pray God's will for our lives or for another's life, we can rest with perfect assurance that our prayers are heard. Proverbs 3:5, 6 comes with a promise that if we trust in God to work in our lives, He WILL make our paths straight. Or as the Message states it, "Trust GOD from the bottom of your heart; don't try to figure out everything on you own." Listen for God's voice in every-thing you do, everywhere you go, HE's the One Who will keep you on track.

You are loved, ladies! Remember that the very God who placed you here, in this time in history and in this very place, has a reason for doing so! You are of great importance in God's kingdom and in God's unfolding plan! Trust Him!

FEBRUARY 15

We will not hide these truths from our children; we will tell the next generation about the glorious deeds of the LORD, about His power and His Mighty wonders. (Psalm 78:4)

Let each generation tell its children of Your mighty acts; let them proclaim Your power. (Psalm 145:4)

So the next generation might know them—even the children not yet born—and they in turn will teach their own children. (Psalm 78:6)

Only take care, and keep your soul diligently, lest you forget the things that your eyes have seen, and lest they depart from your heart all the days of your life. Make them known to your children and your children's children... (Deuteronomy 4:9)

Fix these Words of Mine in your hearts and minds; tie them as symbols on your hands and bind them on your foreheads. Teach them to your children, talking about them when you sit at home and when you walk along the road, when you lie down and when you get up. (Deuteronomy 11:18–19)

The living, the living—they praise You, as I am doing today; parents tell their children about your faithfulness. (Isaiah 38:19)

When was the last time you examined your passion to follow hard after God? Do you contemplate that your example will set the tone for those who are watching and following after us?

These scriptures are a reminder of God's call upon our lives. A call to finish well and pass the faith on to those who will come after us. Bruce Wilkinson says that "the Christian race is like a relay race in which one generation passes the baton of God's truth to another generation." Now, that being said, we are not accountable for what people do with the truth given to them. Each person is ultimately responsible for their own response to God. But perhaps I am getting ahead of myself. Foundational to the beliefs we hope to pass on to our children/grandchildren is our own personal beliefs. What DO we believe about God? Are our beliefs important enough to us to purposely pursue? Are they foundational words or just incidental additions to our lives? Does what we believe effect how we live...each and every day? Only we can answer those questions.

God is a God of power, might, wisdom, and wonders! He has a track record recorded in books of antiquity, not just the Bible, and He can be trusted! He is worth living for! Then when our days on this earth are over and our memory takes their place, may the faith we profess have rung so true that those who follow after us will be encouraged and blessed!

FEBRUARY 16

Do not conform to the pattern of this world, but be transformed by the renewing of your mind. Then you will be able to test and approve what God's will is—His good, pleasing and perfect will. (Romans 12:2)

Finally, brothers and sisters, whatever is true, whatever is noble, whatever is right, whatever is pure, whatever is lovely, whatever is admirable—if anything is excellent or praiseworthy—think about such things. (Philippians 4:8)

For the Spirit God gave us does not make us timid, but gives us power, lover and self-discipline. (2 Timothy 1:7)

Call to Me and I will answer you and tell you great and unsearchable things you do not know. (Jeremiah 33:3)

Those who trust in themselves are fools, but those who walk in wisdom are kept safe. (Proverbs 28:26)

Above all else, guard your heart, for everything you do flows from it. (Proverbs 4:23)

We demolish arguments and every pretension that sets itself up against the knowledge of God, and we take captive every thought to make it obedient to Christ. (2 Corinthians 10:5)

Too often, we let our lives be dictated by our emotions. Our thoughts or feelings determine how we respond and interact with others. When we are angry or irritated our responses will make that clear.

We know that our faith is not a matter of how we are "feeling" at any particular moment, but from personal experience, I can tell you that when I am frustrated or disappointed, I blame God! Now, I am not proud of that, but I KNOW that God has the power to heal, to effect outcomes, to bless and discipline. But I want a "vending machine" God. A God whom I tell what to do and how to do it! I want to ask—and see results! I want to pray and immediately see an answer. I want God to act like I want Him to act! And when He doesn't (which is most of the time), I get mad at Him! Now, I fully realize that these are the exact thoughts that the scriptures above are talking about, "taking every thought captive" and exposing it for it really is—selfishness, self-centeredness, pride. All those things that, as God's child, I want to rid myself of! I truly wish that emotions and feelings had an on and off switch! That once I identified myself with Christ, I could turn off those emotions that tie me in knots and leave me blaming God!

We are told clearly in Isaiah 55:8 that God's thoughts are nothing like our thoughts...and God's ways are far beyond anything we can imagine. Yet I consistently feel that somehow, God owes me an explanation about WHAT He is doing and WHY!

Perhaps, that is exactly why we need to take every thought captive, honestly bring it to the light of Christ, and then make it obedient to Christ. I think we take our thoughts captive by realizing that we are emotional beings, that we only see a tiny sliver of the whole picture, that God is a God Who can be trusted. A God Who desires what is best for us, ALWAYS! A God Who knows what He is doing and why. A God Who is wiser and more capable than we could ever be! God does indeed have whatever we are going through in His hands! He is affecting outcomes, changing hearts, and healing lives. May we learn to trust that He knows what He's doing! May we learn to hand our emotions and fears and pain, depression, and anxiety over to Him and then leave it there!

FEBRUARY 17

For who has known the mind of the Lord that he may instruct Him? (1 Corinthians 2:16)

For the foolishness of God is wiser than man's wisdom, and the weakness of God is stronger than man's strength. (1 Corinthians 1:25)

Human wisdom is so tiny, so impotent, next to the seeming absurdity of God. Human strength can't begin to compete with God's "weakness." (1 Corinthians 1:25, MSG)

To God belong wisdom and power; counsel and understanding are His. (Job 12:13)

The fear of the Lord is the beginning of wisdom. (Proverbs 1:7)

The wise in heart accept commands, but a chattering fool comes to ruin. (Proverbs 10:8)

The way of a fool is right in her own eyes, but a wise woman listens to advice. (Proverbs 12:15)

Good morning, Heavenly Father! We thank you for this beautiful day, the sunshine, the very breath in our lungs. We thank you and pray for our nation, our leaders, our country, and the world. We admit that we cannot begin to fathom what You are up to in our hearts as well as the hearts of world leaders! We humbly acknowledge that "our first mistake is thinking we are smart enough to understand You." Forgive us. We have a tendency to think small because we are earthbound creatures, and we don't have the perspective to understand this life from Your viewpoint. Teach us the magnitude of this faith that we are confessing. Grant us wisdom, understanding, and patience in our day-to-day lives as well as in our world views. We confess that we scurry around before You, trying to "fix" and understand things, when in fact, we are merely getting in the way! Help us to step back in prayerful consideration of what You are doing around us. Open our eyes to Your constant intervention and action in the world and in our lives. Open our hearts to hear You speaking and guiding us and give us feet and conviction to move forward where You lead. We praise You for choosing us and our humble lives to witness to Your kingdom! We trust You to rule in our lives and in our world! We love you, Lord, we're all in! Teach us, guide us, and use us up for Your glory! So be it. Amen

FEBRUARY 18

No eye has seen, no ear has heard, no mind has conceived what God has prepared for those who love Him. (1 Corinthians 2:9)

What we read in Scripture is, "Abraham entered into what God was doing for him, and that was the turning point. He trusted God to set him right instead of trying to be right on his own." (Romans 4:3, MSG)

For My thoughts are not your thoughts, neither are your ways My ways," declares the Lord. As the heavens are higher than the earth, so are My ways higher than your ways and my thoughts than your thoughts. (Isaiah 55:8, 9)

"I don't think the way you think. The way you work isn't the way I work." God's decree. (Isaiah 55:8, 9, MSG)

I think it is fair to say we would all like to figure out what God is doing in the circumstances and events of our lives. I cannot begin to count the number of times that I have asked Him for answers or explanations as to "what He was up to?" I admit it is extremely difficult to step back from trying to figure things out…and simply trust.

In my own personal experience, when things haven't been going the way I think they should or could, I wonder if God is involved in the circumstance at all. I wonder if He simply doesn't care, is busy, or for some reason is ignoring me. I assume that because I cannot figure out what God is doing, that He must be doing nothing at all?! Sound familiar?

I find great encouragement in the verse "My thoughts are not your thoughts, neither are My ways, your ways." Thank goodness!

My dear sisters, we cannot begin to comprehend what God does! We cannot understand how He works in hearts and minds and heals bodies and spirits! We cannot see ten steps in front of us let alone the duration of our lives. God sees it all! He sees hearts, understands motives, and "works for the good of all who love Him." God is good! He has our best interests for our best lives in His thoughts at all times! Along with Abraham, our turning point is when we trust God to set us right instead of trying to be right on our own. When we get to the point that we trust God with the details of our lives and we approach Him with open hands and open hearts. When we finally abandon ourselves to complete and utter dependence on Him, believing with our whole heart that "God's got this!" Then we can sit back and be filled with the peace that comes with knowing that God is in control.

FEBRUARY 19

If any of you lacks wisdom, she should ask God, who gives generously to all without finding fault, and it will be given to her. But when she asks, she must believe and not doubt, because she who doubts is like a wave of the sea, blown and tossed by the wind. (James 1:5–6)

If you don't know what you're doing, pray to the Father. He loves to help. You'll get His help, and won't be condescended to when you ask for it. Ask boldly, believingly, without a second thought. People who "worry their prayers" are like wind-whipped waves. Don't think you're going to get anything from the Master that way, adrift at sea, keeping all your options open. (James 1:5–6, MSG)

My heart is steadfast, O God, my heart is steadfast. (Psalm 57:7) *Steadfast*—resolutely or dutifully firm and unwavering, loyal, committed, devoted, dedicated, dependable, reliable, steady, true, constant, staunch, solid, trustworthy.

Father, forgive me, in my frustration and weakness, I have allowed our enemy to cause me to question You! I have given in to the doubts and fear that I am not worth Your time. I never had considered that my doubt was opening a door for the enemy. Either I believe that God IS who He says He is and that His Word is true and relevant, or I don't! There is no "middle ground." I cannot choose to believe "part" because that discredits the "whole." Either God IS who He says or He is not. And if He is not, then our faith is useless and foolishness. "Choose this day Whom you will serve" (Joshua 24:15) and then do it with all your heart, mind, and soul! As for me and my house, we will serve the Lord!

FEBRUARY 20

Life is a journey you must travel with a deep consciousness of God. It cost God plenty to get you out of that dead-end, empty-headed life you grew up in. (1 Peter 1:18, MSG)

Keep a cool head. Stay alert. The Devil is poised to pounce, and would like nothing better than to catch you napping. Keep your guard up. You're not the only ones plunged into these hard times. It's the same with Christians all over the world. So keep a firm grip on the faith. The suffering won't last forever. It won't be long before this generous God who has great plans for us in Christ—eternal and glorious plans they are! - will have you put together and on your feet for good. He gets the last word, yes, He does! (1 Peter 5:8–11, MSG)

Every God-begotten person conquers the worlds ways. The conquering power that brings the world to its knees is our faith. The person who wins out over the world's ways is simply the one who believes Jesus is the Son of God. (1 John 5:4, 5, MSG)

Indeed, the enemy is ready to pounce! He wants to invade our thoughts, determine our actions and destroy our lives. If we live in fear of the enemy and his desire to destroy us, our lives become fearful, anxious, and anything but joyful and at peace! Instead of focusing our thoughts on the enemy, let us remember Who the enemy is trying to snatch us from. God, the God Who has great plans for us in Christ. The God of the universe who gets the last word. always! God, who paid the price for our souls through the death of His Son Jesus! God, Who has promised He will never leave us or forsake us!

It is our faith in Jesus Christ that brings the world to its knees and sends Satan fleeing in terror!

Let's remember Who's side we are on, or rather Who is on our side! Sisters, let us keep a firm grip on the faith that has brought us this far. let us keep our guard up and our prayer lives active! God has given us the weapons we need to fight our enemy. Let's use them for His glory! Because, my dear friends, God wins, and it's gonna be good!

Have a victorious day filled with peace, joy, and trust in then One Who loves you more than you can imagine!

FEBRUARY 21

Jesus said to them, "I Am the bread of life; she who comes to Me will not hunger, and she who believes in Me will never thirst." (John 6:35)

Jesus said to her, "I Am the resurrection and the life; she who believes in Me will live even if she dies." (John 11:25)

Jesus said to him, "I Am the way, and the truth, and the life; no one comes to the Father but through Me." (John 14:6)

"I Am the Alpha and the Omega," says the Lord God, "Who is and Who was and Who is to come, The Almighty." (Revelation 1:8)

But Jesus spoke to them at once. "Don't be afraid," he said. "Take courage. I am here!" (Matthew 14:27, NLT)

Almighty God, we come before your throne this morning, grateful for the life you have given us. We thank you for the beauty of creation that you have surrounded us with and for the desire for more of You that You have instilled in our hearts. Lord, You are all we will ever need. Help us to remember that all good and perfect gifts flow from Your hands! We pray that You would empower us to take the big steps of faith that in turn increase our faith! Lord, we want to walk on water! Help us to get out of the boat! Teach us to pray big, bold, believing prayers! For You, O Lord, are a BIG God! Help us to get past our preconceived notions of how You will or should act and wait in anxious anticipation for what You are going to do! We love You! We desire to know You more and more intimately! Grant us wisdom, perseverance, and an unyielding faith in not only Who You Are, but in who we are in You!

We love You, fill us with courage and remind us that You are here. Everywhere and always, You are with us. Amen.

FEBRUARY 22

Do not fear, for I am with you; do not be dismayed, for I Am your God. I will strengthen you and help you I will uphold you with My righteous right hand. (Isaiah 41:10)

Say to those with fearful hearts, "Be strong, do not fear, your God will come, He will come with vengeance, with divine retribution He will come to save you." (Isaiah 35:4)

Peace I leave with you, My Peace I give you. I do not give to you as the world gives. Do not let your hearts be troubled and do not be afraid. (John 14:27)

Have I not commanded you? Be strong and courageous. Do not be afraid, do not be discouraged for the Lord your God will be with you wherever you go. (Joshua 1:9)

Jesus encouraged His disciples on numerous occasions to "be strong and courageous." He reminded them, "Do not let your heats be troubled and do not be afraid." But honestly, how do we face our fear? Do we cower and hide or boldly ask God and step out in faith? Do we trust that God IS Who HE says He is? Do we believe that He can be trusted with our lives? When we are fearful, timid, and unsure of our faith in Jesus, we "hold back," not completely buying in to the idea of salvation, trust, and faith. As a result, our worship will not be heartfelt or wholehearted! We will walk through our lives with a timid, grave tending kind of faith. Jesus is calling us to the same kind of faith He called His disciples to! A daring, bold, adventurous, walking-on-water kind of faith! When we learn to trust God with our whole hearts and beings, the worship that results will be authentic and honest!

God is FOR us, my dear sisters! He tells us today, just as He did back then, "Take courage, I am here to take care of you!" "Do not be afraid, do not be discouraged, I am with you wherever you go!" God's got this!

FEBRUARY 23

Have I not commanded you? Be Strong and courageous. Do Not be afraid, do not be discouraged, for the LORD your God will be with you wherever you go." (Joshua 1:9)

Those who know Your name trust in You, for You, LORD, have never forsaken those who seek You. (Psalm 9:10)

But I trust in You, LORD: I say, "You are my God." (Psalm 31:14)

Trust in the LORD with all your heart and lean not on your own understanding; in all your way submit to Him and He will direct your steps. (Proverbs 3:5–6)

I realize that I have recently used the passage from Joshua 1:9 reminding us to; "be strong and courageous." But, I believe it deserves repeating. It is true that faith is a gift of God, but the choice to believe or doubt is ours!

I find it interesting that Jesus did not rebuke Peter for attempting too much, but for trusting too little! I think that is what our doubts do to us. We listen to the doubts in our heads, assume they are true and then give them merit; and soon, our faith in God is wavering! Doubting thoughts such as "God doesn't really love me" or "When I am better, wiser, more obedient, quieter, bolder, work harder— whatever—God will love me more!" Doubting thoughts about His love for us, His purpose for us, and even His gift of grace! All those lies of the enemy that need to be given a swift kick when they enter our thoughts! God did not give us a weak or unthinking mind. He equipped us before we were born with the wisdom we would need to discern the voice of the enemy if we will only examine our thoughts and hold them to the light of God's word. My dear, dear sisters, WE ARE God's chosen! Created by God, for HIS Glory and HIS great purpose! We need not worry about our value, our worthiness or our gifts. We need only listen to the voice of the One calling us forward in faith to bring light and encouragement to those He has placed around us. He's got the rest!

You are greatly and eternally loved! Believe it and give the enemy the boot!

FEBRUARY 24

"Believe me: I Am in my Father and My Father is in Me. If you can't believe that, believe what you see—these works. The person who trusts Me will not only do what I'm doing but even greater things, because I, on My way to the Father, am giving you the same work to do that I've been doing. You can count on it. From now on, whatever you request along the lines of Who I Am and What I Am doing, I'll do it. That's how the Father will be seen for who He is in the Son. I mean it. Whatever you request in this way, I'll do. (John 14:11–14, MSG)

"Are you tired? Worn out? Burned out on religion? Come to Me. Get away with Me and you'll recover your life. I'll show you how to take a real rest. Walk with Me and work with Me - watch how I do it. Learn the unforced rhythms of grace. I won't lay anything heavy or ill-fitting on you. Keep company with Me and you'll learn to live freely and lightly." (Matthew 11:28–30, MSG)

Oh, Father, we have to admit to You this morning that some-times, we feel overwhelmed with all we are learning about the battle going on for our minds. It makes us sad to realize that our unbelief is really disobedience! Help us to trust, help us to believe, help us to focus on You and what You are doing. We thank You that Your way is unforced, that You desire a life of freedom and a light heart for us. Help us to walk with You and work with You so that we may be able to complete all that You have called and anointed us to accomplish in this life. We're all in, Father, and we love You! Amen.

FEBRUARY 25

With Your very own Hands You formed me; now breathe Your Wisdom over me so I can understand You… Oh, love me—and right now!—hold me tight just the way You promised. (Psalm 119:73, 76 MSG)

We're depending on God; He's everything we need. What's more, our hearts brim with joy since we've taken for our own His Holy Name. Love us, God, with all You've got—that's what we're depending on. (Psalm 33:20–22 MSG)

God is in charge—everywhere and always, God is in charge! I don't know about you, but I am sooo very thankful that our salvation doesn't depend on how we are "feeling" at any given moment! I have been frustrated with some things in my life that don't seem to change regardless of how "hard" I pray and I have been arguing with God for a few weeks now.

My conversation has gone something like this: "God, it's me. I know You, I love You, I trust You (even though I find You extremely hard to understand), but I don't think You are holding up Your end of the deal! I can't see you responding to my prayers, I don't feel Your arms around me, and in fact, I feel like You have been noticeably absent and distant! What's up? Is it my fault? Do I need to pray harder? Read Scripture more? Take a vow of silence? Why am I not feeling the joy of my salvation? Why am I not feeling any joy at all?" Sound familiar?

Thankfully, regardless of how we feel, God is STILL God! He is still in control, still in love with us, and still directing the steps of our lives. So, for now, let's give ourselves a break, relax, breathe deep, and let the Lord of the universe hold us, keep us, and restore our joy! Because He's got this!

FEBRUARY 26

He reached down from on high and took hold of me; He drew me out of deep waters… He brought me out into a spacious place; He rescued me because He delighted in me! (Psalm 18:16, 19)

I have set the Lord always before me. Because He is at my right hand, I will not be shaken. (Psalm 16:8)

I will instruct you and teach you in the way you should go; I will counsel you and watch over you… Many are the woes of the wicked, but the Lord's unfailing love surrounds the woman who trusts in Him. (Psalm 32:8, 10)

Oh! May the God of green hope fill you up with joy, fill you up with peace, so that your believing lives, filled with the life-giving energy of the Holy Spirit will brim over with hope! (Romans 15:13, MSG)

My dear sisters, I fear we are becoming exhausted and discouraged because we are looking at ourselves and not our God! We are trying to be the women we think God has called us to be. To be the wives, mothers, workers, friends that we feel obligated to be; and frankly, I think we are wearing ourselves out! As hard as we try, we cannot change other people, fix their problems, or make lives run "smoothly." Perhaps we should take a step back (or a few steps back) and surrender it ALL to God! Our lives are in His very capable, loving hands! How about we lay them at His feet and whisper, "Your will be done"? Let's raise our voices in the prayer: "Oh, Mighty God of green hope, fill us up with joy, fill us up with peace and fill us up with the life giving energy of the Holy Spirit so that our lives will brim over with hope," and without even giving it a thought, we will leak Jesus on everyone in our paths! Today, let's remember that God called us and claimed us because He delights in us! Go figure!

FEBRUARY 27

D o not conform any longer to the pattern of this world, but be transformed by the renewing of your mind. Then you will be able to test and approve what God's will is—His good, pleasing and perfect will. For by the grace given me I say to every one of you: Do not think of yourself more highly than you ought, but rather think of yourself with sober judgment, in accordance with the measure of faith God has given you. (Romans 12:2, 3)

Be energetic in your life of salvation, reverent and sensitive before God. That energy is God's energy, an energy deep within you, God Himself willing and working at what will give Him the most pleasure. (Philippians 1:13, MSG)

I have heard a number of messages on the parable of the talents. The one that resonated the deepest with me was explaining that the talents can refer to the gifts that God has given each and every one of us! Every good and perfect thing that we have in our personalities is a gift from God. Some of us are organizers, some prayers, some workers, some thinkers. It doesn't matter what our talent is, just that we approach life with open hands before God, willing to let Him use us as He sees fit! And also recognizing God as the Giver of that talent! Some of us may feel short-changed in this department, but if we are honest, we must acknowledge that we have been given much! "Clutching what little we have won't allow us to fulfill God's plan. In fact, this kind of mind-set allows the devil to lie to us and cause us to give up on our dreams and God's plan for our lives" (J. Meyer).

I believe this parable simply means use what God has given us...to the best of our abilities...and leave the rest to Him!

Philippians 1:13 reminds us that the energy we use is God's energy, "an energy deep within you, God Himself willing and working at what will give Him the most pleasure."

So, my dear sisters, let's not bury it deep, stuff it down, or think our abilities insignificant. God doesn't make mistakes, nor does He make ineffective, incapable children! We have been given much! So today, unwrap your joy, sharpen up those talents, and let your light and life shine! It's gonna be good!

FEBRUARY 28

People with their minds set on You, You keep completely whole. Steady on their feet, because they keep at it and don't quit. (Isaiah 26:4, MSG)

Lord, You establish peace for us; all that we have accomplished You have done for us. (Isaiah 26:12)

Therefore I tell you, do not worry about your life, what you will eat or drink; or about your body, what you will wear. Is not life more important than food, and the body more important than clothes? Look at the birds of the air; they do not sow or reap or store away in barns, and yet your Heavenly Father feeds them. Are you not much more valuable than they? Who of you by worrying can add a single hour to her life? And why do you worry about clothes? See how the lilies of the field grow. They do not labor or spin. Yet I tell you that not even Solomon in all his splendor was dressed like one of these. If that is how God clothes the grass of the field, which is here today and tomorrow is thrown into the fire, will He not much more clothe you, O you of little faith? So, do not worry, saying, "What shall we wear? For the pagans run after all these things, and your Heavenly Father knows that you need them. But seek first His Kingdom and His Righteousness, and all these things will be given to you as well. Therefore do not worry about tomorrow, for tomorrow will worry about itself. Each day has enough trouble of its own." (Matthew 6:25–34)

Worry…how many of us have wasted valuable hours, minutes—heck, even months of our lives worrying? Many years ago, I read that "worry is sin," yet it is no easy thing to stop!

When worry invades our thoughts, interrupts our slumber, and ties us in knots, let's pause and take a moment and remember that worry is a tool of our enemy! Let's give the enemy a swift kick and remember Who is holding us! My dear sisters, we don't want to worry our lives away, always concerned about the next problem, the next disaster, the next "bad" thing! We tend to envision the worst case scenario in almost every situation instead of trusting God to handle any concerns of today AND tomorrow! Our worry, at best, is unproductive and distracting. At worst, obsessive and destructive! Let's give it a deliberate, decisive NO! Today, when worry creeps in, shout a loud NO to the devil and grab with both hands the peace that Christ is extending to us! God's got this! We need not worry about the details, the timing, or the way in which He will do it! Let's surrender our wills, our motivations, and our concerns to Him. Take a deep breath…and begin to bounce on eager toes of anticipation to see what He has in store! Because, my dear sisters, it's gonna be good!

FEBRUARY 29

And Jesus answered them, "Truly, I say to you, if you have faith and do not doubt, you will not only do what has been done to the fig tree, but even if you say to this mountain, "Be taken up and thrown into the sea," it will happen. (Matthew 21:21)

But they were startled and frightened and thought they saw a spirit. And he said to them, "Why are you troubled, and why do doubts arise in your hearts?" (Luke 24:37, 38)

Jesus immediately reached out His hand and took hold of him, saying to him, "O you of little faith, why did you doubt?" (Matthew 14:31)

Immediately the father of the child cried out and said, "I believe; help my unbelief!" (Mark 9:24)

"I believe, Lord! Help my unbelief!" I think it is fair to say that all of us struggle with doubt and questions regarding our faith. Even those in leadership and authority face doubt and uncertainty. I can say that personally, I don't think I doubt the authority of God, but I doubt His goodness. When we see suffering, addiction, depression, injustice around us, I think we have all entertained the thought, "Where are you, God?" We are so limited in our thinking and in our ability to see the "whole" picture that we are certain that God is absent or unavailable. These are the times when we are encouraged to trust God and ask Him to "help us in our unbelief!"

My dear sisters, there is so very much we will not understand this side of heaven. But Almighty God asks us to believe and trust anyway! It may require a "leap of faith," but instead of worrying about the "leap," let's focus on the loving arms outstretched to catch us! God IS good!. God is FOR us! He ALONE is worthy of our trust!

LET'S LEAP!

MARCH 1

Trust in the Lord with ALL your heart, and do not lean on your own understanding. In ALL your ways acknowledge Him, and He will make straight your paths. (Proverbs 3:5–6)

And those who know Your Name put their trust in You, for You, O LORD, have not forsaken those who seek You. (Psalm 9:10)

Therefore, my beloved, as you have always obeyed, so now, not only as in my presence but much more in my absence, work out your salvation with fear and trembling, for it is God Who works in you, both to will and to work for His good pleasure. Do all things without grumbling or questioning, that you may be blameless and innocent, children of God without blemish in the midst of a crooked and twisted generation, among whom you shine as lights in the world, holding fast to the Word of life, so that in the day of Christ I may be proud that I did not run in vain or labor in vain. (Philippians 2:12–16)

HE must increase, but I must decrease. (John 3:30)

Submit yourselves therefore to God. Resist the devil, and he will flee from you. (James 4:7)

"Woe to the one who quarrels with her Maker—An earthenware vessel among the vessels of earth!" Will the clay say to the Potter, "What are you doing?" Or the thing you are making say, "He has no hands?" (Isaiah 45:9)

Lately, I have had a profound aha moment! I have been wrestling with questions asking God why He doesn't seem to respond when we pray. Why we can cry out to Him over and over and over, and He doesn't seem to "fix" things. Why He oftentimes seems so distant and unconcerned or even unaware of our pain and problems.

I was beginning to question my beliefs about Him... I was beginning to wonder if I didn't have Him labeled and boxed up as a god that I could control! Then Sunday's message in church literally opened my eyes! I have been thinking of little else since.

We are oftentimes disappointed with God because we have made God in our own image. We have determined how, when, and why He should act and we stamp our feet like petulant children when we don't get our way. Sisters, I have been humbled to my knees finally realizing that God is GOD! He isn't the least bit concerned about disappointing us because HE KNOWS what He is doing! We have it all wrong! Instead of approaching God's throne and ASKING... asking...asking what would happen in all our lives if we prayed like this: "Here I am God. I thank You for salvation, for life. I surrender my life to you today, to be used how you see fit (regardless of how I feel, or what I want). Use me for Your good purpose and for Your glory. Amen!"

Just something to think about! God has promised us He will NEVER leave or forsake us. He doesn't promise us that we can call the shots! My desire is to let HIM direct the day-to-day course of my life and abandon my doubts and concerns at His feet. If I'm surrendered, and HE's leading...it's gonna be good!

Have a great day! May you glimpse the POWER and purpose of the Hand holding yours!

MARCH 2

When he (the Holy Spirit) comes, He will convict the world of guilt in regard to sin and righteousness, and judgment. NIV

God's Spirit beckons. There are things to do and places to go! This resurrection life you received from God is not a timid, grave-tending life. It's adventurously expectant, greeting God with a childlike "What's next Papa?" God's Spirit touches our spirits and confirms who we really are. We know Who He is, and we know who we are: Father and children. And we know we are going to get what's coming to us—an unbelievable inheritance! We go through exactly what Christ goes through. If we go through the hard times with Him, then we're certainly going to go through the good times with Him! (Romans 8:14–17, MSG)

Instead, speaking the truth in love, we will in all things grow up into Him who is the Head, that is, Christ. - Ephesians 4:15 NIV - MSG God wants us to grow up, to know the whole truth and tell it in love.

It is obvious what kind of life develops out of trying to get your own way all the time; repetitive, loveless, cheap sex; a stinking accumulation of mental and emotional garbage; frenzied and joy-less grabs for happiness, trinket gods; magic-show religion; paranoid loneliness; cutthroat competition; all consuming-yet-never-satisfied wants; a brutal temper; an impotence to love or be loved; divided homes and divided lives, small-minded and lopsided pursuits; the vicious habit of depersonalizing everyone into a rival, uncontrolled and uncontrollable addictions; ugly parodies of community. I could go on. (Galatians 5:19–21 MSG)

But what happens when we live God's way? He brings gifts into our lives, much the same way that fruit appears in an orchard—

things like affection for others, exuberance about life, serenity. We develop a willingness to stick with things, a sense of compassion in the heart and a conviction that a basic holiness permeates things and people. We find ourselves involved in loyal commitments, not needing to force our way in life, able to marshal and direct our energies wisely. (Galatians 5:22 MSG)

I started out this morning looking for scriptures on the guidance of the Holy Spirit. I was heading in the direction of obeying the promptings of that Spirit. As is normal for me, I headed to the problem many of us may deal with. Control issues! Who is in control of our lives? Are we willing to follow the Spirit's promptings when we don't want to? I have found that very often, the Holy Spirit asks me to do exactly what my stubborn heart does not want to do! He asks me to forgive when I've sincerely been wronged, to reach out in love to someone that has rejected and hurt me, to be committed to a relationship that may be feeling very one-sided! He asks that I quit reaching for more and more and be content with what I have. He nudges me to speak when I don't want to! Or to be silent when I think I have much to say! The Spirit demands loyalty in the midst of pain and disloyalty. He asks me to spend my time wisely, to worship sincerely, and to love extravagantly! This Spirit, the Holy Spirit, asks a lot of us! In fact, when we respond in one area, the Spirit points out another! And why? Why should we respond when we feel convicted to do so? It is oftentimes much easier to just ignore the promptings. I think we respond because somewhere deep inside of us, we KNOW that God desires the best for us. Yet, when we surrender, saying "yes Lord" it is the hardest thing we do! But, if we listen, we can hear the whisper; "Trust Me, it will be worth it!

This relationship with the Living God that we are all walking through is a continual struggle of wills! Will we surrender and let God call the shots? Or will we continue to demand our own way? Will we trust the Hand holding ours and act on the promptings of His Spirit within us? Take a minute? Listen…what is God, through

His Spirit, prompting you to do? Forgive? Reach out? Tell someone about this hope you have? Ask forgiveness from someone you have wronged? Give up something? Trust?

My dear sisters, God is alive and active in each one of our lives. What He is doing in your life, He may not be doing in mine. He meets each one of us exactly where we are and says, "Follow Me." How we respond is up to us! Never forget how deeply you are loved!

MARCH 3

I f you are really wise, you'll think this over—it's time you appreciated God's deep love. (Psalm 107:43)

God is higher than anything and anyone, outshining everything you can see in the skies. Who can compare with God, our God, so majestically enthroned, surveying His magnificent heavens and earth? (Psalm 113:4, 5)

God is gracious—it is He Who makes things right, our most compassionate God. God takes the side of the helpless; when I was at the end of my rope, He saved me. (Psalm 116:5, 6)

When they arrive at the gates of death, God welcomes those who love Him. Oh, God, here I am, Your servant, Your faithful servant: set me free for Your service. (Psalm 116:15, 16)

Thank God because He's good, because His love never quits. vs 6 - God's my strong champion; I flick off my enemies like flies. (Psalm 118:1)

God's my strength, He's also my song, and now He's my salvation. (Psalm 118:15)

(All scriptures from the Message Translation)

My dear sisters, if God has enough wisdom to manage the boundaries of the sea, the motions of the heavens, and the instincts of the animals, He has more than enough wisdom to run your life! To Whom can we compare Him? That being said, as we celebrate the grace of God in our lives, the forgiveness of sins, the access to His Throne, the deliverance from our enemies, we would do well to remember that as Jesus lavishly makes us recipients of His grace,

He calls us to be conduits of His grace as well. As we extend grace to others the kindness of God is dispersed to a broken and messy world. In his book *Dirty God*, Johnnie Moore writes, "Each of us has the power to spread within OUR world an extra layer of the grace of God. We must not take this opportunity for granted. We should grab this chance so tightly our knuckles turn white. Grace calls us to turn the everyday into the miraculous. Every act of kindness is a parting of someone's Red Sea."

May we run this race of faith so well that others cannot help but take notice and glorify our Father in heaven! Have a great week! You are loved, called, claimed and blessed! Return the favor, extend the grace!

MARCH 4

Finally, brothers and sisters, whatever is true, whatever is noble, whatever is right, whatever is pure, whatever is lovely, whatever is admirable—if anything is excellent or praiseworthy—think about such things. (Philippians 4:8)

Since, then, you have been raised with Christ, set your hearts on things above, where Christ is, seated at the right hand of God. Set your minds on things above, not on earthly things. (Colossians 3:1–2)

My daughter, do not forget my teaching, but keep my commands in your heart, for they will prolong your life many years and bring you peace and prosperity. Let love and faithfulness never leave you; bind them around your neck, write them on the tablet of your heart. Then you will win favor and a good name in the sight of God and man. (Proverbs 3:1–4)

Rejoice always, pray continually, give thanks in all circumstances; for this is God's will for you in Christ Jesus. Do not quench the Spirit. (1 Thessalonians 5:16–19)

Above all else, guard your heart, for everything you do flows from it. Keep your mouth free of perversity; keep corrupt talk far from your lips. Let your eyes look straight ahead; fix your gaze directly before you. Give careful thought to the paths for your feet and be steadfast in all your ways. Do not turn to the right or the left; keep your foot from evil. (Proverbs 4:23–27)

A cheerful heart is good medicine, but a crushed spirit dries up the bones. (Proverbs 17:22)

Good leaders abhor wrongdoing of all kinds; sound leadership has a moral foundation. (Proverbs 16:12)

A good leader motivates, doesn't mislead, doesn't exploit. (Proverbs 16:10)

Good tempered leaders invigorate lives; they're like spring rain and sunshine. (Proverbs 16:15)

A wise person gets know for insight; gracious words add to one's reputation. (Proverbs 16:21)

Gracious speech is like clover honey - good taste to the soul, quick energy for the body. (Proverbs 16:24)

Fools care nothing for thoughtful discourse; all they do is run off at the mouth. (Proverbs 18:2)

The words of a fool start fights; do him a favor and gag him. (Proverbs 18:6)

Listening to gossip is like eating cheap candy; do you really want junk like that in your belly?(Proverbs 18: 8)

Words kill, words give life; they're either poison or fruit—you choose. (Proverbs 18:21)

Lots of scriptures today, and in fact, I had a hard time stopping where I did. I enjoy Proverbs in the Message translation.

Today's reading reminded me of a *Saturday Night* skit with a character named Debby Downer. It was a humorous spin on negative people! Face it; we all know negative people. People who love to complain and whine about just about everything! We have probably even been that person ourselves on occasion! But scripture is clear that we are to keep our conduct free of arguing and complaining. Now, I understand, and God knows that when our lives are difficult we may cry out with words of complaint and despair, but we don't want to stay there, living our lives in a constant state of ingratitude, with a disgruntled spirit! We do have the power to choose our attitude. Every moment of every day. And if we want our lives to draw others to the bright light of Christ in us, we do well not to darken our light with a downcast, negative, complaining attitude!

May our speech invigorate the lives of those around us, "like spring rain and sunshine." May our speech be gracious and our words give life! And in those times when we feel depressed and discouraged, may we seek the source of ALL good and perfect gifts! May He renew our strength, infuse our souls with His energy and restore the joy of our salvation!

Love you, ladies! And God is absolutely crazy about you!

MARCH 5

Do not merely look out for your own personal interests, but also for the interests of others. (Philippians 2:4)

Bear one another's burdens and thereby fulfill the law of Christ. (Galatians 6:2)

Be devoted to one another in brotherly love, give preference to one another in honor. (Romans 12:10)

So then, while we have opportunity, let us do good to all people, and especially to those who are of the household of faith. (Galatians 6:10)

But if anyone does not provide for her own, and especially for those of her household, she has denied the faith and is worse than an unbeliever. (1 Timothy 5:8)

She who shuts her ear to the cry of the poor will also cry herself and not be answered. (Proverbs 21:13)

Pure and undefiled religion in the sight of our God and Father is this: to visit orphans and widows in their distress, and to keep oneself unstained by the world. (James 1:27)

One who is gracious to a poor man lends to the Lord, and He will repay her for her good deed. (Proverbs 19:17)

Be kind to one another, tender-hearted, forgiving each other, just as God in Christ also has forgiven you. (Ephesians 4:32)

The King will answer and say to them, "Truly I say to you, to the extent that you did it to one of these brother of Mine, even the least of them, you did it to Me." (Matthew 25:40)

Years ago, our oldest daughter and her husband took in a young man that was struggling at home. He remained with them for years and today is still a dear, much-loved member of our family. He always will be. I think that is exactly what today's scriptures are talking about. We are all members of God's family, regardless of our birth parents. So, dear friends, that makes you and I sisters in Christ! I don't know about you, but that excites me! We have so much to learn from one another, so much to share together, and so much adventure yet ahead of us all! May we be quick to lend a hand, share a burden, and extend love to our brothers and sisters. Those who were born into our family as well as those who have been adopted alongside of us into the family of God!

MARCH 6

Honor the Lord from your wealth and from the first of all your produce. (Proverbs 3:9)

Whether, then, you eat or drink or whatever you do, do all to the glory of God. (1 Corinthians 10:31)

For you have been bought with a price: therefore glorify God in your body. (1 Corinthians 6:20)

O magnify the Lord with me, and let us exalt His name together. (Psalm 34:3)

O Lord, You are my God; I will exalt and praise Your name, for in perfect faithfulness, You have done marvelous things, things planned long ago. (Isaiah 25:1 NIV)

You shall love the Lord your God with all your heart and with all your soul and with all your might. (Deuteronomy 6:5)

Do you not know that you are God's temple and that God's Spirit dwells in you? (1 Corinthians 3:16)

We honor God's word by the way we live and respond to life's trials and tribulations. But do we respond out of gratitude or a sense of "should"? We "should" respond in this way or that way; our lives "should" honor God's Word. In response, I feel guilt for all those times my response was less than "God honoring!" Don't get me wrong, I strongly feel that Christians should be identifiable by just looking at their lives, even when they don't say a word; but when our sense of "duty" outweighs our relationship, our faith is taking a step in the wrong direction! Ideally, we want to become "Christlike" because we are so in love with Who Christ is! We are infatuated with

His kindness, overwhelmed by His love and provision, and we automatically live out His Word because it has come to define us! Not out of duty or a sense of "I should feel this way!" We are being changed from within! The Holy Spirit continues to convict and refine us. Not just our thoughts but our feelings and our actions. Our most important part in this transformation is relationship! Staying connected, purposely and intentionally and consistently, with the Source of this transformation!

In Johnnie. Meyer's book *Dirty God*, he writes, "Our pursuit of holiness could be a celebration—a joyous celebration of God's relentless grace, rather than a long and arduous walk up a mountain of righteousness that we know we'll never summit… When we keep grace at an arm's length, religion will always deconstruct into duty motivated by obligation. Even worse, we'll drain the fun out of our faith." God's GRACE is the action that is at work within us! "Grace accepts us as we are but is too powerful and too transformative to leave us where we are."

My dear sisters, IF we remember WHO is doing the work in us… if we remember that we are NEVER on this journey alone, and IF we stay connected to the Source of this transformative power, we simply cannot help but leak Jesus!

Have a great week! You are powerfully, fiercely, unconditionally loved by the greatest Game Changer in the world! Hang on! It's going to be a wild ride!

MARCH 7

Therefore no one will be declared righteous in God's sight by the works of the law; rather, through the law we become conscious of our sin. But now apart from the law the righteousness of God has been made known, to which the law and the prophets testify. This righteousness is given through faith in Jesus Christ to ALL who believe. There is no difference between Jew and Gentile, for all have sinned and fall short of the glory of God, and all are justified freely by HIS grace through the redemption that came by Christ Jesus. (Romans 3:20–24)

Paul, a servant of Christ Jesus, called to be an apostle and set apart for the gospel of God. (Romans 1:1)

Now Stephen, a man full of God's grace and power, performed great wonders and signs among the people. (Acts 6:8)

But to each one of us grace has been given as Christ apportioned it. (Ephesians 4:7)

For it is by grace you have been saved, through faith—and this is not from yourselves, it is the gift of God—not by works, so that no one can boast. (Ephesians 2:8–9)

Friends, we were chosen by God! Take a fresh look at Romans 1:1 and place your name there—Sherryl, Michelle, Marilyn, Sharon, Evelyn, Carmen—a servant of Jesus Christ, called to be an apostle and set apart for the gospel of God. Or "Now, Becky, Margie, Barb, Kim, Laura, Leslie, Lori, etcetera, women full of God's grace and power, performed great wonders and signs among the people."

Sisters, the Words spoken in scripture are still alive, well, and relevant today! WE are God's chosen people! Set apart by Jesus Christ for the Gospel of God! We have a great and awe-inspiring commission! GO! Live life boldly, confidently in the power of the ONE who chose us! Reflect the light of Christ brightly and extravagantly! Fear no one—but God! Believe wholeheartedly, with great confidence in the One Who calls and equips for everything HE places in our paths. Trust that He always knows what HE is doing and enjoy every moment of life that He blesses us with!

When the time comes and we meet Jesus face-to-face, may we confidently say, "I have run the race you gave me to run with all that I had... I left nothing undone or unsaid." And, in return, may we hear those words I am so longing to hear... "Well done, good and faithful servant!"

MARCH 8

Bear with each other and forgive one another if any of you has a grievance against someone. Forgive as the Lord forgave you. (Colossians 3:13)

Get rid of all bitterness, rage and anger, brawling and slander, along with every form of malice. Be kind and compassionate to one another, forgiving each other, just as in Christ God forgave you. (Ephesians 4:31–32)

Make a clean break with all cutting, backbiting, profane talk. Be gentle with one another, sensitive. Forgive one another as quickly and thoroughly as God in Christ forgave you. (Ephesians 4:31–32, MSG)

"Come now, let us settle the matter," says the LORD, "Though your sins are like scarlet, they shall be as white as snow; though they are red as crimson, they shall be like wool." (Isaiah 1:18)

Therefore, if anyone is in Christ, the new creation has come; the old has gone, the new is here! (2 Corinthians 5:17)

In Him, we have redemption through His blood, the forgiveness of sins, in accordance with the riches of God's grace. (Ephesians 1:7)

The Lord our God is merciful and forgiving, even though we have rebelled against Him. (Daniel 9:9)

"It is finished!" As we approach Easter once again, we are reminded of a truth that many believers take for granted… Jesus Christ suffered and died on our behalf. Sin is detestable to God, and without the saving blood of Jesus, we would NEVER be able to approach His Throne, appeal for HIS help or accept His love. Sin always was—and still is—a BIG deal! I know that I need this annual reminder of the sacrifice Jesus made on my behalf. I need to dwell on the nails, the beatings, the blood, anguish, and pain that He suffered for me and for you. And then with a repentant heart, I can cry; "Hallelujah" on Easter morning. "It is finished! I am forgiven!" GOD WINS!

MARCH 9

Your arm is endowed with power, Your hand is strong, your right hand exalted. Righteousness and justice are the foundation of Your throne; love and faithfulness go before You. Blessed are those who have learned to acclaim You, who walk in the light of Your presence, LORD. (Psalm 89:13–15)

It was MY HAND that laid the foundations of the earth, MY RIGHT HAND that spread out the heavens above. When I call out the starts, they all appear in order. (Isaiah 48:3)

ALL things were made through Him, and without Him was not anything made that was made. (John 1:3)

AH, LORD GOD! It is YOU Who have made the heavens and the earth by YOUR great power and by YOUR outstretched arm! Nothing is too hard for You! (Jeremiah 32:17)

Which of all these does not know that the HAND of the LORD has done this? In HIS HAND is the life of every creature and the breath of all mankind. (Job 12:9–10)

FEAR NOT, for I am with you; be not dismayed, for I Am your God; I will strengthen You, I will help you, I will uphold you with My Righteous Right Hand. (Isaiah 41:10)

Your Right Hand, O LORD, glorious in power, Your Right Hand, O LORD, shatters the enemy. (Exodus 15:6)

With a mighty Hand and outstretched arm: His love endures forever. To HIM Who divided the Red Sea asunder His love endures forever. (Psalm 136:12–13)

Our lives, just like the life of Jesus, are in the hands of God! And, scripture promises us that no one can snatch us from His hands!

"His life (Jesus)—like ours—is in the *hands* of God." As children of God, saved by His perfect sacrifice, our lives are in the safe care and keeping of our heavenly Father, and NO ONE is able to "snatch" us away from those hands! Sit and think on the words of promise listed there. WE, OUR LIVES—our walking around, going to work, cleaning house, doing laundry— are in the very HANDS of GOD! There are so many scripture references about God's hands and the POWER contained in those Hands, and yet we worry, stew, whine, complain, and connive to figure out "what's going on?" We doubt God's ability to care for us, our loved ones, our very lives! Yet as His children, He has promised us over and over, "I will uphold you with My righteous right hand." "My love endures forever." "No one can snatch you from MY hand." "I will strengthen you, I will help you." His hand is the hand of life. NOTHING is too hard for God or for the righteous right hand that is holding ours! What a glorious reason for celebration! For lives that leak the joy of Jesus! God's GOT THIS! And God's got the next thing, and the next thing, and the next thing!

He is risen! He is ALIVE and WELL and fully aware and capable to handle whatever we may be facing! God is FOR us!

HALLELUJAH!

MARCH 10

All that God is and does is good. "You are good, and what You do is good; teach me Your decrees." (Psalm 119:68)

God's goodness and love last forever. Give thanks to the LORD, for He is good; His love endures forever. (Psalm 107:1)

God is good to everyone. The LORD is good to all; He has compassion on all He has made. (Psalm 145:9)

God has goodness stored up for us. How abundant are the good things that You have stored up for those who fear You, that You bestow in the sight of all, on those who take refuge in You. (Psalm 39:19)

All things that are good are from God. Every good and perfect gift is from above, coming down from the Father of the heavenly lights, Who does not change like shifting shadows. (James 1:17)

For the LORD God is a sun and shield; the LORD bestows favor and honor; no good thing does He withhold from those whose walk is blameless. (Psalm 84:11)

We are blessed through God's goodness. Taste and see that the LORD is good; blessed is the woman who takes refuge in Him. (Psalm 34:8)

The LORD is good, a stronghold in the day of trouble, and HE knows those who take refuge in Him. (Nahum 1:7)

When life is difficult and laden with troubles, do we see God's goodness? Okay, how about when things are going smoothly and we are happy, do we attribute it to God's goodness? It seems to me that when things are hard, we blame God; and when things are good, we don't give Him a thought! How would it change our attitude if we truly believed and embraced the fact that God is in the details of the lives of those He knows? Of the men and women who confess Jesus as their Lord and Savior. How would it affect your thinking if you remembered that God can and will work ALL things for good and for His purpose in the lives of those who love Him?

My dear sisters, there is much more going on in our lives of faith that we can see or even imagine! God is working through the details of our lives for His purpose. Now, we may not understand the what and why's but as His daughters, we can know that God is working all things for our good! He can be trusted! May we learn to pray for patience in the trial so that we may come out shining on the other side! God is FOR us! God is good! May we say with confidence, "Yes, Lord, not my will but Thine be done!"

You are greatly and eternally loved, and God isn't finished with you yet!

MARCH 11

So Christ Himself gave the apostles, the prophets, the evangelists, the pastors and teachers, to equip His people for works of service, so that the body of Christ may be built up until we all reach unity in the faith and in the knowledge of the Son of God and become mature, attaining to the whole measure of the fullness of Christ. (Ephesians 4:11–13)

Bear with each other and forgive one another if any of you has a grievance against someone. Forgive as the Lord forgave you. And over all these virtues put on love, which binds them all together in perfect unity. (Colossians 3:13–14)

How good and pleasant it is when God's people live together in unity. (Psalm 133:1)

Finally, all of you, be like-minded, be sympathetic, love one another, be compassionate and humble. (1 Peter 3:8)

Iron sharpens iron; so a woman sharpens the countenance of her friend. (Proverbs 27:17)

Bear you one another's burdens, and so fulfill the law of Christ. (Galatians 6:2)

Let the peace of Christ keep you in tune with each other, in step with each other. None of this going off and doing your own thing. And cultivate thankfulness. Let the Word of Christ—the Message—have the run of the house. Give it plenty of room in your lives. Instruct and direct one another using good common sense. And sing, sing your hearts out to God! Let every detail in your lives—words, actions, whatever—be done in the name of the Master, Jesus, thanking God the Father every step of the way. (Colossians 3:15–17, MSG)

What this adds up to, then, is this; no more lies, no more pretense. Tell your neighbor the truth. In Christ's body we're all connected to each other, after all. When you lie to others, you end up lying to yourself. (Ephesians 4:25, MSG)

I want you to get out there and walk—better yet, run!—on the road God called you tor travel. I don't want any of you sitting around on your hands. I don't want anyone strolling off, down some path that goes nowhere. And mark that you do this with humility and discipline—not in fits and starts, but steadily pouring yourselves out for each other in acts of love, alert at noticing differences and quick at mending fences. (Ephesians 4:2, 3)

My dear sisters, we are ALL a work in progress, all weak and ineffective in our faith, all in need of accountability and confession! There is not ONE dear woman in this group that cannot be trusted to understand and sympathize with the struggles that every one of us faces! The walk of faith is nothing if not a walk of humility! Admitting we don't "get" everything! That we stumble and fail! Heck, I do it on a daily basis! Life can be difficult, problems relentless! Loss, pain, confusion can overwhelm us and leave us buckled at the knees, uncertain of the goodness of God. Feeling abandoned and perpetually "not good enough"—ALL these emotions are the work of our enemy! The deceiver so wants us to turn our back on God, to blame Him for every struggle and every bit of pain we feel. He works hard to impress us with thoughts that we are "unworthy," "shameful," "overlooked," "ignored," "misunderstood," and that our God is "unavailable," "not trustworthy," "uninterested," "unconcerned," and "angry." We NEED each other to remind us that God IS FOR us! That GOD loves us, intervenes in ways we see and in ways we don't see. That God calls, claims, and equips us, EVERY day! And that we are called to live lives of anxious anticipation, not weary, sad, ineffective lives!

This Jesus, that suffered and died for us, extends grace that overwhelms! Grace that heals, restores, builds up, and encourages! We are FORGIVEN! We are ENOUGH! We are LOVED!

I need to be reminded often and loudly that there is more to this life than just making it through another day, that our lives of faith and love matter and are a fragrant offering to the world around us and to God! How we live matters! At death, we will be called to give an account of how we lived our lives. Offering each other compassion, understanding, and grace will embolden our steps and strengthen our faith! We were not meant to live alone or walk this journey of faith without the support of a church and family of faith! I challenge you to "be the rock of faith" for someone else and, in so doing, abound in trust in the Lord!

MARCH 12

Praise be to the God and Father of our Lord Jesus Christ, the Father of compassion and the God of all comfort, who comforts us in all our troubles, so that we can comfort those in any trouble with the comfort we ourselves receive from God. (2 Corinthians 1:3, 4)

And the God of all grace, Who called you to His eternal glory in Christ, after you have suffered a little while, will Himself restore you and make you strong, firm and steadfast. (1 Peter 5:10)

I consider that our present sufferings are not worth comparing with the glory that will be revealed in us. (Romans 8:18)

The righteous person may have many troubles, but the Lord delivers her from them all. (Psalm 34:19)

For our light and momentary troubles are achieving for us an eternal glory that far outweighs them all. (2 Corinthians 4:17)

I have said these things to you, that in Me, you may have peace. In the world you will have tribulation. But take heart; I have overcome the world!" (John 16:33)

When you pass through the waters, I will be with you; and through the rivers, they shall not overwhelm you; when you walk through fire you shall not be burned, and the flame shall not consume you. (Isaiah 43:2)

They stripped Him and put a scarlet robe on Him, and then twisted together a crown of thorns and set it on His head. They put a staff in His Right Hand. Then they knelt in front of Him and mocked Him, "Hail, King of the Jews!" they said. (Matthew 27:28–29)

Suffering—no one likes it, looks forward to it, or rejoices in it without divine intervention! Yet in our walk on this planet, we will ALL suffer at one point or another, even on numerous occasions. I have a friend that lost her husband to ALS, another who had breast cancer, yet another who lost her child. All of these things are examples of suffering, and all of the beautiful women involved spoke (maybe not intentionally) about the "growth" they experienced walking through that suffering.

I think it is probably fair and honest to say that everyone reading this has suffered through something that was overwhelming, painful, and unpleasant. I imagine that every one of you would agree that there was a "lesson learned" or "new appreciation given" that wasn't there before.

No matter the cause of our suffering, if it is a "chastening" a "pruning" or a "result of living in a fallen world," it is painful AND God can and will use it for HIS glory! Our Lord Jesus suffered and died in a horrific way because of our sin. He did that so that we would be acceptable and pure and able to approach His Fathers throne. Jesus suffered for us. Although it would be wonderful if we learned life lessons through the suffering of others, personal experience has taught me that I learn best and remember better by experiencing my own pain.

Through the suffering I have endured in my own life I have learned not to judge others. I have learned compassion for the addicted, the lost, and the confused. I have learned that the scars that suffering leaves are beautiful in their own way and don't need to be hidden. I have learned that there is strength and comfort from one who has experienced similar circumstances. I have learned to speak up for those not able to speak for themselves, and I have learned to pray long and hard for the souls of those I love. Honestly, my personal suffering has changed me. For the better! Life is hard. God never promised us otherwise. Will we trust Him anyway?

MARCH 13

I pray also that the eyes of your heart may be enlightened in order that you may know the hope to which He has called you, the riches of His glorious inheritance in the saints, and His incomparably great power for us who believe. That power is like the working of His mighty strength. (Ephesians 1:18,19, NIV)

Rejoice in the Lord always. I will say it again: Rejoice! Let your gentleness be evident to all. The Lord is near. Do not be anxious about anything, but in everything, by prayer and petition, with thanksgiving present your requests to God. And the peace of God, which transcends all understanding, will guard your hears and your minds in Christ Jesus. (Philippians 4:4–7, NIV)

Don't fret or worry. Instead of worrying, pray. Let petitions and praises shape your worries into prayers, letting God know your concerns. Before you know it, a sense of God's wholeness, everything coming together for good, will come and settle you down. It's wonderful what happens when Christ displaces worry at the center of your life. Summing it all up friends, I'd say you'll do best by filling your minds and meditating on things true, noble, reputable, authentic, compelling, gracious - the best, not the worst, the beautiful, not the ugly, things to praise, not to curse. (Philippians 4:6–8, MSG)

What if we trained our thinking to ponder all the "good things" that God has placed in our lives instead of rehashing all the things and people that have hurt us! Honestly, sisters, I have been in a season of depression and mourning "what could have been." I have once again believed the lie of our enemy that "I have it more difficult than

I should, that I have been hurt and am wounded!" I desperately need to be reminded to think about all the good things God has brought into my life! Because, there are MANY! It is so easy to dwell on the words and events in our lives that have wounded us and forget about the faithfulness of God! We can recall hurtful words in a millisecond but have to sit and think about the true, noble, lovely, admirable things in our lives. How can that be? I am praying for all of us that the pure, noble, right, true, lovely, admirable thoughts will be our constant mind-set! That instead of focusing on the painful, pitiful, weak, wounded moments, our thinking shifts to the best!

Romans 8:31 says, "If God is for us, who can be against us?" The Message says, "With God on our side like this, how can we lose? If God didn't hesitate to put everything on the line for us, embracing our condition and exposing Himself to the worst by sending his own Son, is there anything else He wouldn't gladly and freely do for us?" And then, as I have quoted before, "And, who would dare tangle with God by messing with one of God's chosen? Who would dare even to point a finger? The One who died for us—Who was raised to life for us!—is in the presence of God at this very moment sticking up for us. Do you think anyone is going to be able to drive a wedge between us and Christ's love for us? There is no way! Not trouble, not hard times, not hatred, not hunger, not homelessness, not bullying threats, not backstabbing, not even the worst sins listed in Scripture."

Absolutely nothing can get between us and God's love because of the way that Jesus our Master has embraced us!

My dear sisters, this week, let's erect a monument in our homes and our hearts to all the wonderful things that God has done for us! Let's purposely and frequently reflect on the true, noble, authentic, beautiful things, things to praise Him for! Let's shout a loud NO to the devil and watch him run!

Because with God being FOR us, the enemy doesn't stand a chance!

You are greatly and eternally loved! Believe it! Embrace it! And Claim it!

Have a great week!

MARCH 14

But seek first His Kingdom and His Righteousness, and all these things will be given to you as well. (Matthew 6:33)

Cast your cares on the Lord and He will sustain you: He will never let the righteous fall. (Psalm 56:22)

And Jesus came and said to them, "All authority in heaven and on earth has been given to Me." (Matthew 28:18, ESV)

Submit yourselves therefore to God. Resist the devil, and he will flee from you. (James 4:7)

Righteous are You, O LORD, and upright are Your judgments. (Psalm 119:137)

Clouds and thick darkness surround Him; Righteousness and justice are the foundation of His throne. (Psalm 97:2)

In Mark Betterson's book *The Grave Robber*, he writes "We commit intellectual idolatry creating God in our own image. So instead of living a life that resembles this Super natural standard set in Scripture, we follow an abridged version of the Bible that looks an awful lot like us!"

Somewhere along the days and weeks of our lives, it seems to me that we quit looking for God and His plan and purposes and started trying to fit Him into ours. I for one am guilty of this. Many times, my chief intent is to seek His gifts, His healing, His peace, His intercession. I come before His throne with a list of requests. More times than not, I don't get around to worshiping Him, let alone praising Him. I have an agenda! Our nation, our city, our schools, our families need His touch, His healing, and so I constantly beg Him to act. In fact, I had just been having this conversation with God. Admitting to Him that I always seem to want something from Him. Admitting that I was not content to just let Him be God but rather, wanting Him to follow "my lead" and my agenda! I had been convicted that I was seeking God more like one uses a vending machine. I had and have forgotten that when we pray, we are coming before the throne of ALMIGHTY GOD! God is righteous! He doesn't need to be told how to respond! God is well aware of what is going on. He sees it all and understands it far better than we do. Habakkuk 2:20 says, "But the Lord is in His Holy Temple; let all the earth be silent before Him." He goes on in chapter 3 verse 2 to say, "Lord, I have heard of your fame, I stand in awe of your deeds, O Lord. Renew them in our day, in our time make them known, in wrath remember mercy."

Today's reminder to "seek God" is as timely today as it was years ago. Dear sisters, today, let us seek God with all our hearts and minds and leave the details up to Him!

Let's remember WHO He is and Whose we are! He's got this!

MARCH 15

God's Spirit is right alongside helping us along. If we don't know how or what to pray, it doesn't matter. He does our praying in and for us, making prayer out of our wordless sighs, our aching groans. He knows us far better than we know ourselves, knows our pregnant condition, and keeps us present before God. That's why we can be so sure that every detail in our lives of love for God is worked into something good. (Romans 8:26–28, MSG)

All we're saying is that God has the first word, initiating the action in which we play our part for good or ill. (Romans 9:18)

Because instead of trusting God, they took over. They were absorbed in what they themselves were doing. They were so absorbed in their "God Projects" that they didn't notice God right in front of them. (Romans 9:32, MSG)

Good morning, Lord! We lift our prayers before You. we praise You, and we acknowledge that You alone are the Author and Perfector of our faith! We thank you that you care about the people we care about, about the problems we face, and about the direction our faith is taking in our walk with You. We boldly ask this morning that You will strengthen us both in body and in spirit. That Your Mighty hand will guide us and lead us on whatever path You have ordained for each one of us. We acknowledge that oftentimes, we get "hung up" in the details. Questioning if we are "doing it right,"—"doing enough," and even worthy of Your calling on our lives. Please, Lord, help us leave those thoughts where they belong. At Your feet! We are Your daughters! You have called us, you have claimed us and we are yours!

Today and every day, may we walk in the freedom that comes with walking with You. May we not get hung up on the details but live our lives and our faith in a state of anticipation! For You are good! You are for us! You know us completely and love us anyway! Thank You, thank You! We claim our identity as Your daughters! May we learn to run unfettered into our world living out the joy of our salvation! We love You!

So be it! Amen!

MARCH 16

Humble yourselves, therefore, under God's mighty hand, that He may lift you up in due time. Cast all your anxiety on Him because He cares for you. (1 Peter 5:6–7)

So be content with who you are, and don't put on airs. God's strong hand is on you, He'll promote you at the right time. Live carefree before God, He is most careful with you. (1 Peter 5:6–7, MSG)

Cast your cares on the Lord and He will sustain you; He will never let the righteous fall. (Psalm 55:22)

Pile your troubles on God's shoulders—He'll carry your load, He'll help you out. He'll never let good people topple into ruin. (Psalm 55:22, MSG)

God calls our lack of faith "sin." We all hold on to things that hinder our walk with Christ. We try mightily to handle things on our own, pridefully refusing to surrender our lives to God! I challenge you to give God whatever issues are hindering you from walking in the fullness of His love. We are called to lives of endurance! I encourage you to be faithful to God and confident in your faith through the trials and difficulties of life. Enduring the hard times with a determined faith. Not giving into doubts and fears about God's presence, purpose, or provision during those times of struggle and uncertainty. Instead, focusing on God's promises, believing that He is with us ALWAYS! Then when we have endured, we will come through on the other side—tested, strong, and faithful! My dear sisters, God is FOR us. He will walk us through anything we are going through. He will mold and refine us until we come forth as gold! Reflecting His light so brightly that darkness doesn't stand a chance!

We are greatly and eternally loved! Let your light shine sisters!

MARCH 17

So do not fear, for I Am with you, do not be dismayed, for I Am your God. I will strengthen you and help you; I will uphold you with My Righteous Right Hand. (Isaiah 41:10)

For I Am the Lord, your God, Who takes hold of your right hand and says to you, Do not fear; I will help you. (Isaiah 42:13)

"Fear not, for I have redeemed you; I have summoned you by name; you are Mine. When you pass through the rivers, they will not sweep over you. When you walk through the fire, you will not be burned; the flames will not set you ablaze. For I AM the Lord, YOUR GOD, the Holy One of Israel, your Savior." (Isaiah 43:1–3)

The Lord is my light, and my salvation—whom shall I fear? The Lord is the stronghold of my life—of whom shall I be afraid? (Psalm 27:1)

Have I not commanded you? "Be strong and courageous. Do not be terrified; do not be discouraged, for the Lord your God will be with you wherever you go." (Joshua 1:9)

My dear friends, we live in enemy territory. To say anything less would be a lie! Our enemy, Satan, prowls around, waiting for us to let our guard down and our faith waiver.

That being said—and with the realization that we will indeed be tested, discouraged and under attack in this life—instead of cowering in fear, it is the time to take to heart the promises listed in Scripture.

"I Am with you, I Am your God, I will strengthen you and help you—I will uphold you—I will equip you and give you strength and courage!" I have a sign in my house that reads, "The will of God will never take you where the grace of God will not protect you." I believe that with my whole heart! God has proven Himself faithful to each one of us. Think about the times when you were defeated, overcome with anxiety, overwhelmed, and unable to make a move. Then reflect on where your strength and determination came from?

Maybe you believe you "pulled yourself up by your bootstraps?" Perhaps you believe no one came through for you? But I can promise, God was right there with you. He never left your side, He upheld you with His Righteous Right Hand, and He delivered you to the other side. The only way over these difficult seasons in our lives is through them. God promises that He will be with us every step of the way!

Have a wonderful, strong, and courageous day! Leak Jesus on everyone you meet and relax in the love of a Savior that will never let you go!

MARCH 18

Therefore, since we are surrounded by so great a cloud of witnesses, let us also lay aside every weight, and sin which clings so closely, and let us run with endurance the race that is set before us, looking to Jesus, the founder and perfecter of our faith, who for the joy that was set before Him endured the cross, despising the shame, and is seated at the right hand of the Throne of God. (Hebrews 12:1–2)

Lord, make me to know my end and what is the extent of my days; let me know how transient I am. (Psalm 39:4)

Yet you do not know what your life will be like tomorrow. You are just a vapor that appears for a little while and then vanishes away. (James 4:14)

My days are like a lengthened shadow, and I wither away like grass. (Psalm 102:11)

Scripture reminds us that in the scheme of things, our lives are "but a breath." We are literally "here today and gone tomorrow." Now, sisters, I don't say that to depress you but rather to embolden you to "live big lives." Our time here is short let's not waste a moment of it! Let's grab with both hands the wonders, joys and adventure this life offers and live out our days with a grateful heart Let go of the constant nag of worry. Live dependent on God and His provision! We all know His promises. Our part is to trust; His part is to provide! I love the idea of being "surrounded by a great cloud of witnesses!" Those who have gone before us, cheering us on, encouraging us to "press on to reach the end of the race and receive the heavenly prize for which God, through Christ Jesus is calling us" (Philippians 3:14). The storms of this life are temporary!

There is so much in life to look forward to. There are places to go, things to do and blessings to give and receive. So, pick up your step and lift up your head—It's gonna be good!

MARCH 19

Therefore, since we are surrounded by such a great cloud of witnesses, let us throw off everything that hinders and the sin that so easily entangles, and let us run with perseverance the race marked out for us. (Hebrews 12:1)

I have fought the good fight, I have finished the race, I have kept the faith. (2 Timothy 4:7)

You were running a good race. Who cut in on you to keep you from obeying the truth? (Galatians 5:7)

But those who hope in the Lord will renew their strength. They will soar on wings like eagles; they will run and not grow weary, they will walk and not be faint. (Isaiah 40:31)

I run in the path of Your commands, for You have broadened my understanding. (Psalm 119:32)

Do you not know that in a race all the runners run, but only one gets the prize? Run in such a way as to get the prize. Everyone who competes in the games goes into strict training. They do it to get a crown that will not last, but we do it to get a crown that will last forever. Therefore, I do not run like someone training aimlessly; I do not fight like a boxer beating the air. No, I strike a blow to my body and make it my slave so that after I have preached to others, I myself will not be disqualified for this prize. (1 Corinthians 9:24–27)

Holding fast to the word of life, so that in the day of Christ I will have reason to glory because I did not run in vain nor toil in vain. (Philippians 2:16)

Good morning, friends! I do not know what particular race each one of you is running today, but I do know that the race set before us often wears us out. Sometimes, it's the monotony of the same ole, same old. Sometimes, it's the frustration of obstacles that trip us up and slow us down. And other times, it's the feeling of defeat before we even begin!

I love the Scripture from Hebrews 12 that reminds us that we are surrounded by a "great cloud of witnesses," cheering us on, encouraging us to "stick with it." To pursue righteousness and relationship with Jesus. I fear that oftentimes, instead of listening to the voices that encourage us, we instead listen to the voices of defeat! The voices that tell us, "You'll never get it right," "You'll never be fast enough, strong enough, courageous enough" to win this race. Those voices are lying to you! Pay them no attention. Instead, focus your attention on Christ. Listen, instead, to His words of encouragement. Words like: "I will be your confidence and will keep your foot from being snared" (Proverbs 3:26) or, "I will strengthen you with My own great power so that you will not give up when trouble comes, but you will be patient" (Colossians 1:11). God is FOR us! He fights for us; He delights in us! My dear sisters, never give up, and never give in to the lies of our enemy. Fight the good fight, finish this race of faith and purpose! I promise you, it will be worth it!

Have a great day, remembering always, you are fiercely loved!

MARCH 20

Finally brothers/sisters, whatever is true, whatever is noble, whatever is right, whatever is pure, whatever is lovely, whatever is admirable—if anything is excellent or praiseworthy—think about such things. (Philippians 4:8)

Above all else, guard your heart, for everything you do flows from it. (Proverbs 4:23)

What goes into someone's mouth does not defile them, but what comes out of their mouth, that is what defiles them. (Matthew 15:11)

Do not conform to the pattern of this world, but be transformed by the renewing of your mind. Then you will be able to test and approve what God's will is—His good pleasing and perfect will. (Romans 12:2)

Almighty God, good morning! We thank You for this journey of faith that each one of us has been on. We thank You for Your constant provision and constant protection that we admittedly, take for granted. We thank You for Your intervention in our lives and in the lives of our loved ones. We thank You for Your Word, Your Holy Spirit, and Your Son. We acknowledge that without You as the center of our lives, we are lost and broken people. We ask You this morning to renew our minds by Your power. May we always be aware of our thoughts, our attitude toward others, our judgment of others and every word we speak. May we navigate this broken world with a kindness and a gentleness that comes from Your Spirit within us. Keep us from willful sin, from critical minds, and critical speech. You remind us in 1 Thessalonians 5:11 to "encourage one another and build each other up," not tear down and discourage! Help us to live what we profess to believe, living in such a way that our action speaks louder than our words. Free us from the things that ensnare us and give us a boldness and energy to speak truth in love!

Father, You love us, You guide us and protect us. May we begin to live lives worthy of Your calling! We love You, and we thank You! Amen.

MARCH 21

Live creatively friends. If someone falls into sin, forgivingly restore her, saving your critical comments for yourself. YOU might be needing forgiveness before the day's out. Stoop down and reach out to those who are oppressed. Share their burdens and so complete Christ's law. If you think you are too good for that, you are badly deceived... Don't be misled No one makes a fool of God. What a person plants, she will harvest. The person who plants selfishness, ignoring the needs of others—ignoring God—harvests a crop of weeds. All she'll have to show for her life is weeds. But the one who plants in response to God, letting God's Spirit do the growth work in her, harvests a crop of real life, eternal life. (Galatians 6:1–3 and 7–8, MSG)

These words I speak to you are not incidental additions to your life, homeowner improvements to your standard of living. They are foundational words, words to build a life on. (Matthew 7:24, MSG)

Accountability! People that "walk the walk, not just talk the talk." I think that is foundational to living the "good life!" Living a life that follows what we confess to believe.

I like the Message translation of the verse in Galatians because it reminds us not to be judgmental, critical, or prideful. "WE might be needing forgiveness before the day's out!"

My dear sisters, God loves us—right here, right now! In the middle of whatever mess we might be in! But He loves us too much to leave us there! The whole purpose of this devotional is to draw us near to God! To encourage us to build a relationship with the Lord of the universe who wants so much more than our attendance at church on Sunday morning! He wants a vibrant, intimate, honest relationship with every one of us! He wants to hear our concerns, our frustrations, and share our joys! He wants us to know He is right beside us in the difficult moments of life, but also in the joyful, exciting ones! He wants us to live fully! To live boldly confident in HIM! To "run and not grow weary, to walk and not faint!" He promises to strengthen us, to sustain us, and uphold us with His mighty right hand! No wonder we want to "pick up" our sisters and brothers when they stumble in faith! God's plan for our lives is one that I promise you, you don't want to miss out on! When I think about God's hand on every one of us—wow! I honestly cannot help but bounce on eager toes of anticipation to see what He has got in store! I know in the depths of my soul that it's gonna be good!

MARCH 22

So where does that leave you when you criticize a brother? And where does that leave you when you condescend to a sister? I'd say it leaves you looking pretty silly—or worse. Eventually, we're all going to end up kneeling side by side in the place of judgment facing God. Your critical and condescending ways aren't going to improve your position there one bit. Read it for yourself in Scripture: "As I live and breathe," God says, "every knee will bow before Me; Every tongue will tell the honest truth that I and only I am God." - So tend to your knitting. You've got your hands full just taking care of your own life before God. Forget about deciding what's right for each other. Here's what you need to be concerned about: that you don't get in the way of someone else, making life more difficult than it already is. (Romans 14:10–14, MSG)

So friends, take a firm stand, feet on the ground and head high. Keep a tight grip on what you were taught, May Jesus Himself and God our Father, who reached out in love and surprised you with gifts of unending help and confidence, put a fresh heart in you, invigorate your work, enliven your speech. (2 Thessalonians 2:15–17, MSG)

I do believe that God is working in the details of the lives of His children. I am not certain what He is doing, but I do know that God alone changes hearts, heals, and restores and has better info and a better vantage point that we do!

As far as passing judgment goes, I agree with Paul in that "I've got my hands full just taking care of my own life before God!" My mother always said, "Don't judge another until you've walked a mile in their shoes." The sobering fact about judgment is this: God alone is the One, True, Judge. We will all be called to give an account of how we lived our lives, what we did with the faith He instilled in us, and how well we lived in this short span called our life. Thank Jesus that He took the guilty verdict for our sin and paid the penalty so that our sin will not be held against us! Life is far too short and precious to be wasted judging others! Once again, I'm asking God to "put a fresh heart in me, invigorate my work, and enliven my speech," keeping me out of the way of what He is doing in and around me. May we continue to lift others before the throne of God and leave Him to the details. Then we will be free to live confidently, boldly, and joyfully in this blip of eternity. Live BIG, BOLD BEAUTI-FUL lives before God, sisters! Enjoy the days He gives us, and come sliding into death with a smile and the words, "Ooooh, what a ride!" Because... He's got this!

MARCH 23

And do not grieve the Holy Spirit of God, with whom you were sealed for the day of redemption. Get rid of all bitterness, rage and anger, brawling and slander, along with every form of malice. Be kind and compassionate to one another, forgiving each other, just as in Christ God forgave you. (Ephesians 4:30–32)

Don't grieve God. Don't break His heart. His Holy Spirit, moving and breathing in you, is the most intimate part of your life, making you fit for Himself. Don't take such a gift for granted. Make a clean break with all cutting, backbiting, profane talk. Be gentle with one another, sensitive. Forgive one another as quickly and thoroughly as God in Christ forgave you. (Ephesians 4:30–32, MSG)

Do not merely look out for your own personal interests, but also for the interests of others. (Philippians 2:4)

She who shuts her ear to the cry of the poor will also cry herself and not be answered. (Proverbs 21:13)

But whoever has the world's goods, and sees her brother in need and closes her heart against him, how does the love of God abide in her? Little children, let us not love with word or with tongue, but in deed and truth. (1 John 3:17, 18)

I have heard it said that our form of hatred today is more like indifference. We don't really dislike people, but we don't really care either! OUCH! That one hit home with me. I am quick to explain why it might be inconvenient for me to help someone or even to rationalize that "surely, someone else will take care of them." It is painful to realize that that inaction is considered hatred! Sure, we are quick to help out our families and friends, but how about our Christian brothers and sisters around our community and around the globe in need of our loving compassion and assistance? I think so often, we are overwhelmed by the magnitude of the problems around us. We understand that we cannot solve the problem, so we do nothing. My dear sisters, we may not be able to help everyone, but we can help one! And if each one helps one, the problem will begin to get much smaller and more manageable!

Have a great day, ladies! You are greatly and eternally loved!

PS: I love the promise in this scripture from Ephesians: "You were sealed for the day of redemption." I think about that often. God has sealed my mind, my soul, and my spirit from fatal attack of the enemy. He has claimed, called, and sealed each one of us for HIS PURPOSE and HIS GLORY! Satan has no power over us that we cannot overcome through the Holy Spirit!

MARCH 24

Above all else, guard your heart, for it is the wellspring of life. (Proverbs 4:23)

My daughter, preserve sound judgement and discernment, do not let them out of your sight; they will be life for you, an ornament to grace your neck. Then you will go on your way in safety, and your foot will not stumble; when you lie down, you will not be afraid; when you lie down, your sleep will be sweet. Have no fear of sudden disaster or the ruin that overtakes the wicked, for the Lord will be your confidence and will keep your foot from being snared. (Proverbs 3:23–26)

Almighty God, we come before Your throne with humble, thankful hearts. Humble because we get of glimpse of the cost of our salvation and thankful because we realize that Your hand has held us, guided us, protected us, and brought us this far. Thank You! We need Your help, Lord. We need Your protection for our hearts. As your daughters, sometimes, we are fickle, led astray by our own desires, the ideas of the world, and just plain stubbornness! Honestly, Father, sometimes we don't "feel" Your presence, and we tell ourselves "You aren't there," "You don't care," "You don't understand." ALL lies of the enemy! Please remind us during those times that our "feelings" are not reality. That You are faithful to Your promise to never leave us or forsake us! Help us to "guard our hearts." To remember Your promises. To yell a loud "NO" to the enemy and watch him run! In Your constant care and provision, we have no reason to fear. Help us believe it and live it! We love You, we boldly take our place as Your daughters, and we wait with anxious anticipation to see what You have in store for us. Please be with those we love, those in need of healing and strength; and may Your will be done in our churches, nation, and homes. Thank You for Who You are, for what You have already done, and for what You are going to do. Amen.

MARCH 25

Do not be conformed to this world, but be transformed by the renewal of your mind, that by testing you may discern what is the will of God, what is good and acceptable and perfect. (Romans 12:2)

Give your servant therefore an understanding mind to govern your people, that I may discern between good and evil, for who is able to govern this your great people? (1 Kings 3:9)

But solid food is for the mature, for those who have their powers of discernment trained by constant practice to distinguish good from evil. (Hebrews 5:14)

And it is my prayer that your love may abound more and more, with knowledge and all discernment, so that you may approve what is excellent, and so be pure and blameless for the day of Christ. (Philippians 1:9–10)

Commit your way to the Lord; trust in Him and He will act. (Psalm 37:5)

Trust has certainly been a consistent topic of this devotional since we started! Today, I listed a number of scriptures on discernment as well. How DO we discern God's voice? How can we trust if we aren't sure we are hearing from Him?

We probably would all agree that we would love to be good at discerning God's voice as well as His will for our lives. How often do we wonder, "Is that coming from my head, or is it God's voice?" We can talk about ways to test the prompting, to try and determine the source, but I think the scripture makes it pretty clear. Discerning God's voice takes the power of the Holy Spirit, constant practice, and a willingness to learn! Whether we are aware of it or not, God is continually transforming us as we build relationship with Him. He is transforming our minds to resemble His, softening our hearts to hurt for what hurts Him, and filling us with wisdom, understanding, and discernment through His Holy Spirit. Yep, ladies… I hate to be redundant, but "God's got this too!" He, by the power of His Holy Spirit within us, is molding us into the mighty women of faith He has called and created us to be! We just need to hang in there and hang on! Because, IT'S GONNA BE GOOD!

You are loved!

MARCH 26

Whoever keeps her mouth and her tongue keeps herself out of trouble. (Proverbs 21:23)

Let no corrupting talk come out of your mouths, but only such as is good for building up, as fits the occasion, that it may give grace to those who hear. (Ephesians 4:29)

There is one whose rash words are like sword thrusts, but the tongue of the wise brings healing. (Proverbs 12:18)

Set a guard, O Lord, over my mouth, keep watch over the door of my lips. (Psalm 141:3)

If anyone thinks she is religious and does not bridle her tongue but deceives her heart, this person's religion is worthless. (James 1:26)

Ever notice how some friends and family LOVE to talk about other friends and family who are not present? Have you ever engaged in those conversations and walked away feeling awful? I sincerely hope that we do feel awful, or even better yet, not engage in the conversation at all. Even getting to the point of being bold enough to say, "Enough! That person isn't here to defend themselves and I wouldn't want you talking about me that way." The scriptures are FULL of verses reminding us to "guard our tongue." To be gentle in speech...to keep our mouths closed! The saying my mom used to tell me when I was speaking ill of someone was, "If you don't have something nice to say, don't say anything at all!" To this day, I try and take that to heart!

As far as being wounded by something someone else has report-edly said about us, first, examine the source. There are those among us who love to "stir the pot!" If the source isn't reliable, don't give it a second thought. Remember, friends, the only opinion of us that really matters is God's! And we already know what He thinks about us!

Have a great day, "soul sisters!"

MARCH 27

A word fitly spoken is like apples of gold in a setting of silver… A word spoken at the right time is like gold apples on a silver tray. (Proverbs 25:11)

Words from a wise woman's mouth are gracious, but a fool is consumed by her own lips. At the beginning her words are folly' at the end they are wicked madness—and the fool multiplies words. (Ecclesiastes 10:12–14)

The words of a wise person are gracious. The talk of a fool self-destructs—He starts out talking nonsense and ends up spouting insanity and evil. Fools talk way too much, Chattering stuff they know nothing about. (Ecclesiastes 10:12–14, MSG)

I will bless the Lord at all times; His praise shall continually be in my mouth. (Psalm 34:1)

Watch the way you talk. Let nothing foul or dirty come out of your mouth. Say only what helps, each word a gift. (Ephesians 4:29, MSG)

It honestly never ceases to amaze me that no matter what we are talking about, there are scriptures for that! There are many scriptures on speech. Too many to list! The verse that follows one we have been talking quite a bit about, "Keep vigilant watch over your heart; that's where life starts," is immediately followed by "Don't talk out of both sides of your mouth, avoid careless banter, white lies, and gossip" (Proverbs 4:23, 24, MSG). Scripture has much to teach us about the way we are to live out our lives of faith. Even down to the smallest details.

Don't be misled sisters; how we speak and interact with others matters greatly to God. We are cautioned not to gossip, not to speak ill of another, and not to babble on and on. We are also advised not to use foul language. When others overhear our conversations, will they think they are "gracious and wise?" If we learn to communicate the way the Scripture instructs us to, they will. May we be encouragers this day, and may our words be well-spoken and kind.

I imagine we can all think of a time when we have been encouraged by someone's words. I know personally that there are many who have encouraged me time and time again. Our kind, honest words of encouragement have more power than we realize. God calls us as His children to "build each other up," "encourage one another." Heaven knows life is difficult, and kind words, honestly spoken, are indeed points of light in our dark world and in our day! So today, my challenge to you is to speak a kind word of encouragement to someone God places in your path. Or someone He puts on your heart. Maybe with a call, a note, or just a word in passing. And if you want to get really crazy, how about speaking a kind word to your husband? Just a thought!

You are loved, you are light. And with Jesus in your life, you are a gift to this world!

MARCH 28

Seize life! Eat bread with gusto, drink wine with a robust heart. Oh yes—God takes pleasure in your pleasure! - Dress festively every morning. Don't skimp on colors and scarves. Relish life with the spouse you love. Each and every day of your precarious life. Each day is God's gift. It's all you get in exchange for the hard work of staying alive. Make the most of each one! Whatever turns up, grab it and do it! and heartily! This is your last and only chance at it, for there's neither work to do nor thoughts to think in the company of the dead, where you're most certainly headed. (Ecclesiastes 9:7–10, MSG)

Passive minds—passive lives! I love this scripture because it talks about seizing life! Living life to the full! Living BIG, BOLD lives where ever God has placed us! I know I have probably overused the phrase, but I fear too many Christians live "grave tending," careful, fearful lives. And I believe with ALL my heart that God has called us to live abundant, brave, carefree lives before Him! Whatever God has placed before you, wherever He has you, do it well! Do it with joy, do it with gusto! Every single day we get on this earth is a sheer gift! We cannot go back and do any moment over. So, dear sisters, grab on to this day with both hands…keep your heart open to whatever God has placed in your path and life big! Boldly speak words of love and life to those around you! No regrets! No "would have, should have, could haves" today!

You are wildly loved by the Creator! Let's live like it!

MARCH 29

Be imitators of God, therefore, as dearly loved children and live a life of love, just as Christ loved us and gave Himself up for us as a fragrant offering and sacrifice to God. (Ephesians 5:1, 2)

Watch what God does, and then you do it, like children who learn proper behavior from their parents. Mostly what God does is love you. Keep company with Him and learn a life of love. Observe how Christ loved us. His love was not cautious but extravagant. He didn't love in order to get something from us but to give everything of Himself to us. Love like that. (Ephesians 5:1, 2, MSG)

Almighty, All-knowing, Everlasting God, we come before You on this beautiful morning with grateful, humble hearts. We earnestly thank You for the work You have begun in us and acknowledge that all the good things we have in our lives come from Your loving hands. We are humbled by the love You have for us; we recognize our weaknesses and sin, and we lay them before You now. Forgive us, cleanse us, renew us for Your service. Remove any wrong thinking from our minds, any stubbornness from our hearts, and any laziness from our hands. Put us to use for Your service, O Lord! We ask for Your presence in the lives of those mourning from loss. We ask Your mighty hand of healing and comfort for those ill and in treatment. Please bring Your wisdom to the doctors and nurses as you strengthen and heal their bodies. Grant Your peace that surpasses human understanding. Father, there is such great need in our communities, and so many in need of Your help. We ask that You will be with all of those we love, all of those in need, all of those in trials of every kind. We need You, Lord, so desperately! Make Your presence known, expose the deeds of darkness, and raise Your people up to do Your work in this world! I pray to You today that we, as your daughters and children of light, will move forward in courage and live lives of extravagant love! No regrets, no good word unspoken! Thank You for loving us so well. Thank You for what You have already done and for what You are going to do. We love You, and we trust You! Amen.

MARCH 30

And He answered, "You shall love the Lord your God with all your heart and with all your soul and with all your mind, and your neighbor as yourself." (Luke 10:27)

For to set the mind on the flesh is death, but to set the mind on the Spirit is life and peace. (Romans 8:6)

Do not be conformed to this world, but be transformed by the renewal of your mind, that by testing you may discern what is the will of God, what is good and acceptable and perfect. (Romans 12:2)

For who has understood the mind of the Lord so as to instruct him? But we have the mind of Christ. (1 Corinthians 2:16)

And the peace of God, which surpasses all understanding, will guard your hearts and your minds in Christ Jesus. (Philippians 4:7)

Just as our children pick up our attitudes, habits, and even patterns of speech, so do we as daughters of the King. As we spend time with God in His Word, in prayer and in our thought life, we are transformed by His Spirit living within us. We begin to think like Him, speak like Him, and even mourn the hurt, hate, and injustice of this world like Him.

Honestly, sometimes, it's hard when our hearts break for the magnitude of the poverty, pain, and injustice we see in this world. It feels so overwhelming, but as we live and grow in Christ, I don't think we can help but be broken by what breaks the very heart of God! But and here's the good news, God is transforming us by the power of His Spirit living within us! We are being equipped with His power, His strength and His joy in the very depths of our heart! We cannot help but be so filled to overflowing by His transforming presence that, unbeknownst to us, we "leak Jesus" on those we encounter every day!

My dear, dear friends, it is God's Spirit that does this wonderful transformation within us. Our part is to be willing to let Him take up residence in our lives, to spend time talking and learning about Him, and by surrendering whatever He tells us we need to let go of! He does the work; our part is to let Him!

You go, God! Take our lives and transform them in Your image for Your glory!

He's got this! Have a great day!

MARCH 31

Enter His gates with thanksgiving, and His courts with praise! Give thanks to Him; Bless His Name! For the Lord is good; His steadfast love endures forever, and His faithfulness to all generations. (Psalm 100:4, 5)

Let your roots grow down into Him, and let your lives be built on Him. Then your faith will grow strong in the truth you were taught, and you will overflow with thankfulness. (Colossians 2:7)

So, my very dear friends, don't get thrown off course. Every desirable and beneficial gift comes out of heaven. The gifts are rivers of light cascading down from the Father of Light. There is nothing deceitful in God, nothing two-faced, nothing fickle. He brought us to life using the true Word, showing us off as the crown of all His creatures. (James 1:16–18, MSG)

Almighty God, Father of Light, we come before Your throne this morning with humble, thankful hearts. We are overwhelmed by Your love for us and to imagine that we are "the crown of your creation," that You love us immeasurably, that You "show us off," and that Your love for us endures forever, even to our children's children… and beyond! It is more than our little minds can fathom! Lord, we know that all of this is not because of us…but is sheer gift to us given to us by Your Son's death on the cross. We are humbled. Humbled that You have chosen us, humbled that You choose to use us to do Your work in this world, to be Your light reflecting in the darkness. Humbled that You call us friends, daughters, and holy! Humbled that You CHOOSE to walk beside us, encourage us, strengthen us, and empower us to do Your will. Help us, Lord, to be worthy of the calling. Help us keep our focus on You, on what You have done, and on what you are doing at this moment. Looking forward with anticipation to what You will do! Help us to remember that every good and perfect gift flows from Your hands! Our families, our health, our country, our homes, our friends, our gifts and abilities—all sheer gift! We thank You, Father! We Love You, and we ask in Jesus's name that You will hold us close, turn us around if we wander, and fill us with the light of Your presence! So be it! Amen!

APRIL 1

And one called out to another and said, "Holy, Holy, Holy, is the LORD of hosts. The whole earth is full of His glory." (Isaiah 6:3)

There is no one Holy like the LORD, indeed, there is no one besides You, Nor is there any rock like our God. (1 Samuel 2:2)

To whom then will you liken Me that I would be his equal? Says the Holy One. (Isaiah 40:25)

Be glad in the Lord, you righteous ones, and give thanks to His holy name. (Psalm 97:12)

For the Mighty One has done great things for me, and holy is His name. (Luke 1:49)

God reigns over the nations, God sits on His holy throne. (Psalm 47:8)

And He said; "My presence will go with you, and I will give you rest." (Exodus 33:14)

You make known to me the path of life; in Your Presence there is fullness of joy; at Your Right Hand are pleasures forevermore. (Psalm 16:11)

"Holy, Holy, Holy is the LORD, the whole earth is full of His glory!"

Many turn to God because they want God to DO something for them. Heal, mend relationships, find jobs, grant wishes. Few turn to God realizing that without Him, they are simply incomplete! We were created for relationship with God. Without this emotional, spiritual, and dependent relationship with our Creator, we will never find happiness and never feel complete. God calls us to Himself because He knows that is the safest, most fulfilling place to be! He doesn't promise us that our lives will be easy or trouble-free, but He does promise us victory! Reminding us that for a while, we may have troubles, but HE has overcome the world! He will walk with us always, strengthen us for what lies ahead, and sustain us through the trial! The best is yet to come! May we remain faithful in the trial and confident in the Hand holding ours! We are daughters of the King! Let's let God be God and trust that He knows what He is doing!

Have a great week!

APRIL 2

Praise the LORD! How blessed is the woman who fears the Lord, who greatly delights in His commandments. (Psalm 112:1)

He will bless those who fear the LORD, the small together with the great. (Psalm 115:13)

The fear of the Lord prolongs life, but the years of the wicked will be shortened. (Proverbs 10:27)

The fear of the Lord leads to life, so that one may sleep satisfied, untouched by evil. (Proverbs 19:23)

The reward of humility and the fear of the Lord are riches, honor and life. (Proverbs 22:4)

Behold the eye of the Lord is on those who fear Him, on those who hope for His lovingkindness. (Psalm 33:18–19)

The angel of the Lord encamps around those who fear Him, and rescues them. (Psalm 34:7)

Who is the woman who fears the Lord? He will instruct her in the way she should choose. (Psalm 25:12)

For as high as the heavens are above the earth, so great is His lovingkindness toward those who fear Him. (Psalm 103:11)

To fear the Lord is to hate evil; I hate pride and arrogance, evil behavior and perverse speech. (Proverbs 8:13)

Let those who love the Lord hate evil, for He guard the lives of His faithful one and delivers them from the hand of the wicked. (Psalm 97:10)

I tell you, my friends, do not be afraid of those who kill the body and after that can do no more. But I will show you whom you should fear: Fear Him who, after your body has been killed, has authority to throw you into hell. Yes, I tell you, fear Him. (Luke 12:4–5)

If you address as Father the One who impartially judges according to each one's work, conduct yourselves in fear during the time of your stay on earth. (1 Peter 1:17)

I have been wrestling with this issue of "fearing the Lord" for some time. I wonder, "do I fear Him?" We all know that God is good, kind, loving, right? But I fear we have emasculated Him to the point of irrelevance! I ask you sincerely, do you fear God? Do you HATE evil? Fitz Cherry writes, "Do you tremble at His Word? Are you sorry for your sins against a holy God? Do you cry out to the Lord? When you fear the Lord, sin deeply affects you. Sin breaks your heart. You hate it. It was your sin that put Christ on the cross. You know your need for a Savior; you have no self-righteousness because you know your only hope is in Jesus Christ." When we fear God, when we approach His throne with sincere and honest hearts, He begins a transformation in us. He begins to change us from the inside out. He gives us a strong moral code, a deep-seated compassion for others, and a hatred of evil! Our heart begins to break for the things that break God's heart. We fear for the ones separated from Him, for those who deny Him. Fits Cherry continues, "We have lost the fear of God in the church. Pastors are sending the most people to Hell. These preachers today are the reason for the massive false conversions that are going on in the church today. No one preaches against sin. No one is convicted anymore. No one talks about reverence for God. No one talks about God's hatred and judgment. All we talk about is love, love, love. He is also holy, holy, holy! He is a consuming fire and He is NOT mocked. Do you fear God? Do you fear that you may hurt God by the way you live?"

Heavy words, but words we all need to ponder. Do we live in fear of hurting this God of consuming fire that we confess to belong to? Do we tremble at His commands? Do we understand that HE alone is righteous, above reproach? Do we even get it a little bit that we are in absolutely NO position to question, negotiate, or demand of God?

My dear sisters, God does not owe us an explanation! He is infinitely wise and beyond comprehension! There is so much more that we have yet to discover about this God! And that is precisely why I have been questioning myself on my "fear of the Lord." I want to know MORE about God, about His heart of hearts. I want more of His wisdom, His guidance, His strength. I want MORE of HIM! The scripture is clear that "fear of the Lord is the beginning of knowledge." So that is where I must start!

Do you want to join me in pursing this holy fear? This radical pursuit of the heart of God? Come on!

You are loved, called, and claimed by a holy, righteous God!

APRIL 3

For I know the plans I have for you, declares the Lord, plans to prosper you and not to harm you, plans to give you hope and a future. (Jeremiah 29:11)

Now may the God of peace, Who through the blood of the eternal covenant brought back from the dead our Lord Jesus, that great Shepherd of the sheep, equip you with everything good for doing His will, and may He work in us what is pleasing to Him, through Jesus Christ, to Who be glory for ever and ever Amen. (Hebrews 13:20–21)

If any of you lacks wisdom, you should ask God, Who gives generously to all without finding fault, and it will be given to you. (James 1:5)

Trust in the Lord with all your heart and lean not on your own understanding; in all your ways submit to Him, and He will make your paths straight. (Proverbs 3:5–6)

For it is God's will that by doing good you should silence the ignorant talk of foolish people. (1 Peter 2:15)

He has shown you, O mortal, what is good. And what does the Lord require of you? To act justly and to love mercy and to walk humbly with your God. (Micah 6:8)

The Lord work out everything to its proper end—even the wicked for a day of disaster. (Proverbs 16:4)

You need to persevere so that when you have done the will of God, you will receive what He has promised. (Hebrews 10:36)

"Your will be done." I think oftentimes, we mumble those words as an afterthought. After we have already asked God for what we need or want, done in a time frame of our ordaining! But when we humbly and honestly say those words to our Father in Heaven and trust that He knows what He is doing, we unleash HIS powerful and perfect will for our lives and the lives of those we love!

My dear sisters, God does indeed have a "will" for our lives. There are plans for our growth, plans to refine and perfect our faith. There are divine reasons for what God allows in our lives. He does not always rescue us immediately from the consequences of our own sin, but when we repent and turn away from it, He will use even those consequences for our good! God is indeed a good Father, but He is not soft; nor is He deaf, dumb, or blind!

His will is to draw us closer to Him; to envelope us with His love, strength, and power; and then to send us out as His hands and His feet to spread the Word to a world that is hurting. Encouraging those we meet to "come along with us, our God is good, and He loves you more than you can imagine!" May we use our lives of love as witness to His goodness. May He use us to reflect His light and dispel the darkness around us!

Your will, O Lord, be done. Not my will but Yours—today, tomorrow and forever. Use us up for Your glory and bring us home!

We love You, we need You, and we trust You! So be it, Amen!

APRIL 4

But whoever hates his brother or sister is in the darkness and walks in the darkness, and does not know where she is going, because the darkness has blinded her eyes. (1 John 2:10)

"In their case the god of this world has blinded the minds of the unbelievers, to keep them from seeing the light of the gospel of the glory of Christ, who is the image of God." (2 Corinthians 4:4)

The natural person does not accept the things of the Spirit of God, for they are folly to her and she is not able to understand them because they are spiritually discerned. (1 Corinthians 2:14)

Again Jesus spoke to them, saying; "I Am the light of the world. Whoever follows Me will not walk in darkness, but will have the Light of Life!" (John 8:12)

But YOU are a chosen race, a royal priesthood, a holy nation, a people for His own possession, that you may proclaim the excellencies of Him Who called you out of darkness into His Marvelous Light! (1 Peter 2:9)

There is an old worship song that goes, "Open the eyes of my heart, Lord, open the eyes of my heart, I want to see You, I want to see You." I think that is an honest, intelligent prayer to use.

Lord, open our eyes, let us witness firsthand Your presence in our lives, in the lives of those we are praying for…in our homes and communities. We do want spiritual eyes to see You at work!

You may have noticed that I love the scriptures that speak of believers as "light" In Corinthians, it says, "I Am the Light of the World and whoever follows Me will have the Light of Life!"

Dear sisters, as followers of Christ, our eyes and minds have been opened to the ways of Christ. We are no longer stumbling around in darkness, but we are surrounded by a brilliant, blinding light! I read a story once about a woman walking downtown NYC one evening after leaving a restaurant for dinner with friends. She was being followed and hurried to safety. She came across a policeman on the sidewalk who stopped the two following her. He asked them what they were doing, and one admitted, "We were going to grab her purse and run, but we were frightened by the light surrounding her." Now, whether that is true or not, I don't know. But I do believe that the "light of Christ" that reflects off all of God's children CAN be seen by unbelievers and our enemy, and that light frightens and aggravates them!

My dear friends...we have been called out of the darkness to walk in the marvelous light of God's love! He is calling and equipping us to live out our lives boldly and extravagantly in His presence and for His glory! Shine on, sisters!

APRIL 5

Whoever conceals her transgressions will not prosper, but she who confesses and forsakes them will obtain mercy. (Proverbs 28:13)

The soul who sins shall die. The son shall not suffer for the iniquity of the father, nor the father suffer for the iniquity of the son. The righteousness of the righteous shall be upon himself, and the wickedness of the wicked shall be upon himself. (Ezekiel 18:20)

Arise, for it is your task, and we are with you; be strong and do it. (Ezra 10:4)

So whoever knows the right thing to do and fails to do it, for her it is sin. (James 4:17)

Beloved, never avenge yourselves, but leave it to the wrath of God, for it is written, "Vengeance is min, I will repay, says the Lord." (Romans 12:19)

A fool's mouth is her ruin, and her lips are a snare to her soul. (Proverbs 18:7)

Do not be deceived: God is not mocked, for whatever one sows, that will she also reap. (Galatians 6:7)

Let no corrupting talk come out of your mouths, but only such as is good for building up, as fits the occasion, that it may give grace to those who hear. And do not grieve the Holy Spirit of God, by Whom you were sealed for the day of redemption. Let all bitterness and wrath and anger and clamor and slander be put away from you, along with all malice. Be kind to one another, tenderhearted, forgiving one another, as God is Christ forgave you. (Ephesians 4:29–32)

There is so much wisdom and insight in these scriptures! First, and I think extremely important for us, is to take full and total responsibility for the way we think, act, and live out our lives. It is so easy to blame others for our attitudes, our emotions, and even our actions when, honestly, we all have the power to choose every day of our lives how we will live and how we will react to situations that affect us. One of the problems with always playing the "blame game" is that we suck other people into this game by bemoaning the point that "we were taken advantage of, mistreated, or slandered." So now, those we love are angry, depressed, hurting, and discouraged as well! As parents, we call all relate to this! Our kids come home from school and say, "So-and-so were mean to me today." What do our hearts do? They break! And our instant response is to get angry at "those" kids, to think less of them, even feeling vengeful! The blame game is contagious and spreads like a plague! Pretty soon, we are living our lives out of a place of resentment, unforgiveness, and a victim mentality!

Sure people hurt us, say mean things, undermine or falsely accuse us, but we are given the power to forgive, to move forward and turn the hurt over to God. God can then in turn release us from the pain so that we can live our lives in expectant hope for what is coming ahead! The remarks and things that hurt us don't have to hold us down or entrap us in victim mode. We are more than conquerors through HIM who loved and loves us! It's time to get up, dust off the lies of entrapment and move forward in joyful anticipation of life! There is much, much more ahead! Beauty to be witnessed, love to be felt, hope to be embraced, and adventure to be had! LET GO of whatever is holding you back and, in faith, begin to bounce on joyful toes of anticipation, asking, "What's next Papa!" Because I promise, it's going to be good!

You are loved! Live free, bold, beautiful lives, full of extravagant love and endless hope and overflowing joy! Have a wonderful week!

APRIL 6

Evil words destroy one's friends; wise discernment rescues the godly. (Proverbs 11:9)

It is foolish to belittle a neighbor; a person with good sense remains silent. (Proverbs 11:12)

Your own soul is nourished when you are kind; but you destroy yourself when you are cruel. (Proverbs 11:17)

A gentle answer turns away wrath, but hard words stir up anger. (Proverbs 15:1)

Gentle words bring life and health; a deceitful tongue crushes the spirit. (Proverbs 15:4)

Kind words are like honey-sweet to the soul and healthy for the body. (Proverbs 16:24)

A person's words can be life-giving water; words of true wisdom are as refreshing as a bubbling brook. (Proverbs 18:4)

Wise speech is rare and more valuable than gold and rubies. (Proverbs 20:15)

Telling lies about others is as harmful as hitting them with an ax, wounding them with a sword, or shooting them with a sharp arrow. (Proverbs 25:18)

For whoever would love life and see good days must keep their tongue from evil and their lips from deceitful speech. (1 Peter 3:10)

Let your conversation be always full of grace, seasoned with salt, so that you may know how to answer everyone. (Colossians 4:6)

Words. We all love to speak, few like to listen, and fewer still consider every word they say! Yet our words have incredible power.

With words, we can lift up, encourage and spur to action. With that same tongue, we can shame, hurt and degrade.

No wonder the Bible is full of so many scriptures on the power of the tongue! I have only listed a few above, but there are many, many more. In Ephesians 4, we are warned to "not let any unwholesome talk come out of our mouths," but encouraged to speak "what is helpful for building others up according to their needs." We are warned not to gossip, not to lavish others with false praise, and ultimately to guard our tongues and think before we speak! I believe more harm has been done with our words than we can imagine!

I know, personally, there have been many things I have said or not said that I wish I could do over!

I think there is also a need to avoid giving false praise or lavishing praise for mediocre performance. When we measure our words, ALL of our words, they will have more influence. And if we want our words to contain influence, we had better be sure they are wise!

Wisdom alone would be an excellent reason to seek God! Job 12:13: "To GOD belong wisdom and power, counsel and understanding are His." Proverbs 1:7: "The fear of the Lord is the beginning of wisdom."

Love you, ladies!

Our God is wise beyond our wildest imagining and more powerful than anything we may be struggling with. As we seek Him today, may we be blessed with a gentle heart and a wise tongue! Have a great day! You are greatly and eternally loved!

APRIL 7

The Lord is near to the brokenhearted and saves the crushed in spirit. (Psalm 34:18)

The sacrifices of God are a broken spirit; a broken and contrite heart, O God, you will not despise. (Psalm 51:17)

He heals the brokenhearted and binds up their wounds. (Psalm 147:3)

But He gives more grace. therefore it says, "God opposes the proud, but gives grace to the humble." (James 4:6)

All these things My Hand has made, and so all these things came to be, declares the Lord. But this is the one to whom I will look; she who is humble and contrite in spirit and trembles at My word. (Isaiah 66:2)

"A Message from the high and towering God, who lives in Eternity, whose name is Holy; I live in the high and holy places, but also with the low-spirited, the spirit-crushed, and what I do is put new spirit in them, get them up and on their feet again." (Isaiah 57:15, MSG)

Blessed are the poor in spirit, for theirs is the kingdom of heaven. Blessed are those who mourn, for they shall be comforted. (Matthew 5:3–4)

You're blessed when you're at the end of your rope. With less of you there is more of God and His rule. You're blessed when you feel you've lost what is most dear to you. Only then can you be embraced by the One most dear to you. (Matthew 5:3–4, MSG)

You're blessed when you're content with just who you are - no more, no less. That's the moment you find yourselves proud owners of everything that can't be bought. (Matthew 5:5, MSG)

No one likes the subject of brokenness. Because no one likes to be broken! Yet brokenness and restoration are a constant theme in scripture. Notice that after brokenness comes healing, binding of wounds, grace, and redemption! Personally, I think that if we weren't such a hardheaded, hard-hearted people, God wouldn't need to break us! Unfortunately, the devil's tool of pride has many of us in its grip, and those that have been blessed with a comfortable, healthy life even more so! When things are going good, we rarely feel a need to "call out to God." We are content with handling things on our own. Often repeating the mantra, "I've got this!" But through this prideful path in life, God sees the soul, the heart of His children, and sees how desperately we need Him. He sees us chasing after things that don't matter, injuring others, and hardening our hearts on the way. He sees His children in pursuit of fame, money, importance instead of the things He created us for. Things like worship, serving others, helping those in need, advocating for those with no voice, caring for the sick and elderly. On our own, we head off on a path of the totally wrong direction!

Ever wonder why so many wealthy, famous people are depressed, addicted, and angry? Perhaps it is because they have spent their lives in the pursuit of things that can never make them happy or fulfill them! They have followed the lies of the enemy and now wonder how they ended up where they are!

God breaks us because He loves us! He knows that the pain of brokenness will produce a dependence on Him. A relationship with Him, and only there is where we will find true happiness and fulfillment and peace! My dear sisters, God is FOR us always! Even when it hurts! You are incredibly loved and pursued by the Commander of the angel armies. He can be trusted!

APRIL 8

So do not fear, for I am with you; do not be dismayed, for I am your God. I will strengthen you and help you; I will uphold you with My Righteous Right Hand! (Isaiah 41:10)

When I am afraid, I put my trust in You. (Psalm 56:2)

Don't fret or worry. Instead of worrying, pray. Let petitions and praises shape your worries into prayers, letting God know your concerns. Before you know it, a sense of God's wholeness, everything coming together for good, will come and settle you down. It's wonderful what happens when Christ displaces worry at the center of your life. (Philippians 4:6, 7, MSG)

For God HAS NOT given us a spirit of fear, but of power and of love and of a sound mind. (1 Timothy 1:7)

And one more... But now, this is what the Lord says... FEAR NOT, for I have redeemed you; I have summoned you by name; YOU ARE MINE! (Isaiah 43:1)

So very many scriptures on fear... I just don't know how many you want to read! God's word from 1 Timothy that says God has not given us a spirit of fear! Once again, the word *spirit* is used, not *emotion*, not *feeling*, not *reflex*—*spirit*. Fear is a spirit!

It is a spirit that I don't think any one of us want to claim! Instead, let's claim God's promise that He has "given us a spirit of power, love and a sound mind!"

So the next time fear knocks on your door, send faith to answer!

Starting today, lets "armor up!" Face life's challenges head-on, with an on-fire, Bible-believing spirit, and watch our enemy run in terror! God has chosen to leave us here in this life for now. Let's make the most of it and leak Jesus on anyone in our path!

APRIL 9

The Spirit of the Lord is on Me, because He has anointed Me to preach good news to the poor. He has sent Me to proclaim freedom for the prisoners and recovery of sight for the blind, to release the oppressed, to proclaim the year of the Lord's favor. (Luke 4:18–19)

Bless the LORD, O my soul, and forget none of His benefits; Who pardons all your iniquities, Who heals all your diseases. (Psalm 103:2, 3)

Because of the sacrifice of the Messiah, His blood poured out on the altar of the Cross, we're a free people—free of penalties and punishments, chalked up by all our misdeeds. And not just barely free, either. Abundantly free! (Ephesians 1:7, MSG)

If we claim that we're free of sin, we're only fooling ourselves. A claim like that is errant nonsense. On the other hand, if we admit our sins—make a clean breast of them—He won't let us down, He'll be true to Himself. He'll forgive our sins and purge us of all wrongdoing. If we claim that we've never sinned, we out and out contradict God—make a liar out of Him. A claim like that only shows off our ignorance of God. (1 John 1:8–10, MSG)

Jesus's death on the cross freed us from the consequences of our sins. The Bible is very clear that sin is abhorrent to God, and all the sacrifices of blood in scripture and even in history reveal that even ancient man seemed to understand that to appease the "gods," blood had to be shed. Jesus is saying in Luke 4, "I Am that sacrifice! I have come to set you free, to restore you, to release you from the power of sin and death!"

My dear sisters, God has forgiven us, when we lay our sins before Him. He removes them from His memory. Why then is it so difficult for us to let go of them? I think that is one of the enemy's favorite games—whispering, "You're not really forgiven," "You need to clean up your act before God loves you," "You'll never be good enough for God." All LIES!

Trust God enough to believe His Word and begin to live the free, abundant life He has for each of us! We are made in Christ's image! Called to be His ambassadors to bring the good news of salvation and forgiveness to our friends, families, and neighbors! Let's go BOLDLY into our lives believing that God, Who created us, knew exactly what He was doing when He placed us in this place, at this time! Because you know friends, HE DID!

You are loved, forgiven, empowered masterpieces of God! Live like you believe it!

APRIL 10

This Book of the Law shall not depart from your mouth, but you should meditate on it day and night, so that you may be careful to do according to all that is written in it. For then you will make your way prosperous, and then you will have good success. (Joshua 1:8)

I will meditate on Your precepts and fix my eyes on Your ways. (Psalm 119:15)

Let the word of Christ dwell in you richly in all wisdom. (Colossians 3:16)

For the Word of God is living and active, sharper than any two-edged sword, piercing to the division of soul and of spirit, of joints and of marrow, and discerning the thoughts and intentions of the heart. And no creature is hidden from His sight, but all are naked and exposed to the eyes of Him to whom we must give account. (Hebrews 4:12–13)

When we study and contemplate God's Word, He illumes our souls with His Light! I love that illustration. Probably because I embrace the idea that we, as God's children, reflect His light! Remember the scripture: "God is Light. In Him there is no darkness at all"? God's word, God's promises, God's warnings will, over time and with meditation, become our default thoughts. Here's what I mean. When we hear about a trial or misfortune of someone else, instead of "being glad it isn't us," our hearts will instead be filled with compassion and a desire to help. When we see another lost to depression, addiction, or lawlessness, we will, instead of judgment, be filled with compassion and genuine fear and sadness for their soul. As we read, study, and contemplate the words of God, God does something only He can do: He gently, yet persistently, changes us!

It never ceases to amaze me that how, while reading God's Word, a verse or sentence will speak directly to my heart, oftentimes bringing me to tears!

My dear sisters, there is POWER in God's word. There is POWER in memorizing it, thinking about it, sharing it, and meditating on it! God has so much to say to us; may we learn to listen!

You are loved, you are light! Your light and love are both desperately needed in this world! Today, remember the words of the Sunday school song from way back when: "This little light of mine, I'm gonna let it shine, this little light of mine, I'm gonna let it shine, let it shine…" And then let it shine!

APRIL 11

Don't grumble against each other, sisters, or you will be judged. The Judge is standing at the door! (James 5:9)

Do not let any unwholesome talk come out of your mouths, but only what is helpful for building others up according to their needs, that it may benefit those who listen. (Ephesians 4:29)

Be cheerful no matter what; pray all the time; thank God no matter what happens. This is the way God wants you who belong to Christ Jesus to live. (1 Thessalonians 5:16–18, MSG)

Do everything without complaining or arguing, so that you may become blameless and pure, children of God without fault in a warped and crooked generation. Then you will shine among them like stars in the sky as you hold firmly to the word of life. And then I [Paul] will be able to boast on the day of Christ that I did not run or labor in vain. (Philippians 2:14–16)

We have become experts at complaining! So caught up with what is wrong that we have no energy to notice what is good! Come on, ladies, we all know some of these kind of people! Heck, we try to avoid them and will go out of our way to not have to interact with them! My prayer this morning is that we are not one of them! It is easy to get caught up in thinking about what is "wrong" in our lives. It takes a conscious effort to concentrate on what is "good" in them! But as "light bearers," we are called to shine like stars in our generation and to do everything without grumbling, complaining, or arguing! As far as the scripture from Thessalonians on "being cheerful no matter what," that's a hard request to follow; but it is in God's Word, so it is a request we need to take seriously! There is that old line, I think I am misquoting it but it goes something like "When times are tough, the tough get going." In any event, I think that God would be pleased if that described His daughters, if He could watch us go through our difficult times and trials with a spiritual and mental "toughness" instead of gritted teeth and a grimace on our face. What if we exhibited a willful determination and silent strength? With no complaining or arguing, but a cheerful expectation of what God will do in and through the trial at hand!

Life is hard! Oh, how I wish it wasn't! But we do know the One Who understands everything! And He has promised to walk with us every step of the way! So shine on, sisters! The world needs your light!

APRIL 12

M ake a careful exploration of who you are and the work you have been given, and then sink yourself into that. Don't be impressed with yourself. Don't compare yourself with others. Each of you must take responsibility for doing the creative best you can with your own life. (Galatians 6:4, 5, MSG)

Don't be misled. No one makes a fool of God. What a person plants she will harvest. The person who plans selfishness, ignoring the needs of others—ignoring God—harvests a crop of weeds. All she'll have to show for her life is weeds! But the one who plants in response to God, letting God's Spirit do the growth work in her, harvests a crop of real life, eternal life. (Galatians 6:6, 7, 8)

So be content with who you are, and don't put on airs. God's strong hand is on you, He'll promote you at the right time. Live carefree before God, He is most careful with you. (1 Peter 5, 6, MSG)

Get serious, really serious. Get down on your knees before the Master, it's the only way you'll get on your feet. (James 4:10)

Responsibility...what is our responsibility and what is God's? Over the years, I have had many conversations on this very question! What is my part in all of this? I think the scripture in Galatians lays it out for us. We are to "do the creative best we can with our own lives" and then "let God's Spirit do the growth work in us." What do you LOVE to do? What gets your creativity flowing or your heart racing? I would dare say God designed you to pursue that! He wired us with gifts and abilities that He intended us to use. These gifts not only bring us joy and make time fly by but bring Him glory as well! I don't think we need to get tripped up with the idea of being responsible to God's call on our lives. I think instead, we just need to keep "putting one foot in front of the other," getting up when we mess up or turn away, and get back on our knees and on with our lives!

God will work out the details. He who called us is faithful. If He has called us, His grace will protect us.

Where is God calling you? What do you love to do and how can you use that for His glory? In case you are drawing a blank, I have some areas that many of you are already engaged in: using your gift to make beautiful quilts and throws then giving them to those with cancer or as gifts. How about using your gifted voice to sing at funerals or events?

Maybe you've given your time and gifted design "eye" to shop with a friend or decorate an event hall? Maybe God has used your compassionate heart to care for newborn calves and children and friends and strangers! Get my point? God can use us for His glory, and we may not even realize it! My dear sisters, just do the best you can with your life and leave the rest to God! He's got this, and He's got you in His strong hands! Today, feel free to live carefree and boldly before God! We were created to let out light shine!

APRIL 13

O Lord, You have searched me and You know me. You know when I sit and when I rise; You perceive my thoughts from afar. You discern my going out and my lying down; You are familiar with all my ways. Before a word is on my tongue You know it completely, O Lord. (Psalm 139:1, 2)

Search me, O God, and know my heart; test me and know my anxious thoughts. See if there is any offensive way in me, and lead me in the way everlasting. (Psalm 139:23)

The heart of the discerning acquires knowledge, for the ears of the wise seek it out. (Proverbs 18:15)

My daughter, if you accept My words and store up My commands within you, turning your ear to wisdom and applying your heart to understanding, and if you call out for insight and cry aloud for understanding, and if you look for it as for silver and search for it as for hidden treasure, then you will understand the fear of the Lord and find the knowledge of God. For the Lord gives wisdom and from His mouth come knowledge and understanding. (Proverbs 2:1, 6)

"Who do YOU say I AM?" As we contemplate Easter and celebrate Jesus's resurrection during the month of April, take a minute and give some thought to the question; "Who is Jesus to me?" Is He just a historical figure? A symbol of the Christian faith? Or is it more personal than that? Only you can answer that. Personally, just asking myself these questions makes me want to find out more about this Jesus I profess as my Savior! I want to know Him more...trust Him more…and grow up in my faith. I want to hear those words, "Well done, good and faithful servant" when my life here is done. I want to live my life boldly and expectantly as a "child of God" and not just go through the motions! I want my life to ring so true "my neighbor will be blessed!"

APRIL 14

But those who hope in the Lord will renew their strength. They will soar on wings like eagles; they will run and not grow weary, they will walk and not be faint. (Isaiah 40:31)

There is a time for everything, and a season for every activity under the heavens. (Ecclesiastes 3:1)

But do not forget this one thing, dear friends: With the Lord a day is like a thousand years, and a thousand years are like a day. (2 Peter 3:8)

He said to them; "It is not for you to know the times or dates the Father has set by His own authority." (Acts 1:7)

He has made everything beautiful in its time. He has also set eternity in the human heart; yet no one can fathom what God has done from beginning to end. (Ecclesiastes 3:11)

The Lord is good to those who hope is in Him, to the one who seeks Him; it is good to wait quietly for the salvation of the Lord. (Lamentations 3:25–26)

I have heard it said, "If we wait for perfect conditions, we will never do anything!" Friends, we can ALWAYS find reasons NOT to do what we know we should do! That statement reminds me of many people I have known and talked to over the years. People who have said, "Someday…" they would think about their faith. People that said, "I want to live a little before I follow Christ." People that believed having a "good time" and believing in Christ Jesus were mutually exclusive. Dear friends, I DO believe that God continues to pursue us throughout our entire life, but I also believe that the time to build a relationship with Him is NOW! Every single breath we take is from Him; every day we are given—pure gift. We are not promised tomorrow. Our estimation of time is nonsense to God. As the scripture reminds us, "NO ONE can fathom what God has done" …is doing…and will do!

God is calling us now, in this time and in this place, to commit our lives to Him. To pursue relationship with Him, to walk in the way He has prepared for us. To do the things "He has prepared in advance for us to do." Our lives have great meaning and unimaginable purpose when lived in the will of God!

What is He calling you to do today? Grab His hand and trust Him to lead you. He knows what He is doing!

APRIL 15

Lead me in Your truth and teach me, for You are the God of my salvation; for You I wait all the day. (Psalm 25:5)

The eyes of all look to You, and You give them their food in due time. You open Your hand and satisfy the desire of every living thing. (Psalm 145:15–16)

Therefore, be patient, sisters, until the coming of the Lord. The farmer waits for the precious produce of the soil, being patient about it, until it get the early and late rains. You too be patient; strengthen your hearts, for the coming of the Lord is near. (James 5:7, 8)

He said to them: "It is not for you to know the times or dates the Father has set by His own authority." (Acts 1:7)

He has made everything beautiful in its time. He has also set eternity in the human heart; yet no one can fathom what God has done from beginning to end. (Ecclesiastes 3:11)

"For You, I wait all the day." "You give them food in due time." "Therefore be patient."

These lines from today's scriptures spoke to and encouraged me. For any of you that know me, you know that I am impatient! I am not proud of the fact and have been asking God for some time to help me with this character flaw (one among many). It is a conscious effort on my part, but when I find myself waiting in line, in traffic, or waiting for someone, I have learned to ask, "God, show me someone or something to pray for in my waiting." I have been known to pray for the harried clerk that looks like a "new hire," a mom with screaming children on the airplane, the older couple three cars up that is holding up the whole line, the woman with the overflowing cart in the express lane. When I pray, my impatience immediately subsides! I am NOT a good "waiter"! I think it is also fair to say that I am not the only one who hates to wait! Because of that mind-set of instant gratification, it is particularly difficult to wait for God's timing. In fact, I would go so far as to say that when we pray for something or someone and don't see or feel that God is responding in a particular time frame, we immediately believe that God isn't listening! That God doesn't care, that what is important to us isn't important to God! My dear sisters, those thoughts are all lies! Scripture is very clear about the power of prayer! In fact in Revelation, scripture refers to our prayers as "incense" ascending to the altar of God! A fragrant offering to God! When we think of prayer in that light, we learn to realize that God does INDEED hear every prayer we utter or think; every cry of our soul ascends to the very throne of God! So, if that is the case, and scripture is clear that it is...if we can learn to believe that God hears every prayer, works on every heart involved, and understands the eternal consequences of our requests, we can rest assured that waiting for God's timing is the best possible outcome for anything we pray! My dear friends, God loves us too much to give us everything we want. He knows what is best for us, all the time. He asks us to trust His wisdom, His purpose, and His plan for ourselves and our loved ones. Let's lift them in prayer and surrender them to HIS care and His authority! He's got this!

APRIL 16

Be joyful in hope, patient in affliction, faithful in prayer. (Romans 12:2)

Being strengthened with power according to His glorious might so that you may have great endurance and patience, and giving joyful thanks to the Father, Who has qualified you to share in the inheritance of His Holy People in the Kingdom of Light. (Colossians 1:11–12)

Let us not become weary in doing good, for at the proper time we will reap a harvest, if we do not give up. (Galatians 6:9)

Blessed is the woman who perseveres under trial because having stood the test, that person will receive the crown of life that the Lord has promised to those who love Him. (James 1:12)

And as for you, brothers and sisters, never tire of doing what is good. (2 Thessalonians 3:13)

Put on the full armor of God, so that you can take your stand against the devil's schemes. (Ephesians 6:11)

There is a memory that has left a powerful impression on me. A couple of years ago, when we were preparing a group to go to the Philippines with Trash Mountain Project, we had a telephone (Skype) meeting with some of the staff from TMP. We had a bunch of questions and were going to be leaving from the United States shortly. We finished our conversation and asked Brett Durbin (the Founder) to pray for us. Although I don't remember his prayer word for word, it went something like this: "Father, we are Yours. You created us for Your glory and to do the work You have prepared for us. I ask that we will be about doing what You have for us to do. I do not ask for safety. I know You will be with us. I ask instead that in our time here, You would use us up for Your glory and then bring us home!" It blew me away! And made me stop and think… "Am I willing to be used up for God?" Following this vein of thought, here is my prayer for this Holy day:

Almighty, All-powerful, All-knowing God, we come before Your throne in humble gratitude, deeply thankful for Jesus sacrifice on our behalf. We are no longer condemned by our sin but set free into glorious, forgiven life! How can we ever repay You? My prayer for myself and my sisters today is that You will free us from a "whiny" spirit, free us from complaining and the mind-set of "victory without battle, triumph without effort, and ease without labor." Instead, we ask that You strengthen us for the battles ahead, clothe us with "great endurance and patience" use us up for Your glory, and then bring us home into Your kingdom of light! We love You. We thank You. And we are all in! So be it. Amen.

APRIL 17

In the same way, let your light shine before others, that they may see your good deeds and glorify your Father in Heaven. (Matthew 5:16)

The light shines in the darkness, and the darkness has not overcome it. (John 1:5)

When Jesus spoke again to the people, He said, "I Am the Light of the world. Whoever follows Me will never walk in darkness, but will have the light of life." (John 8:12)

Your eye is the lamp of your body. When your eyes are healthy, your whole body also is full of light. But when they are unhealthy, your body also is full of darkness. See to it, then, that the light within you is not darkness. (Luke 11:34–35)

For you were once darkness, but now you are light in the Lord. Live as children of light. (Ephesians 5:8)

Look to the Lord and His Strength; seek His face always. (1 Chronicles 16:11)

If My people, who are called by My name, will humble themselves and pray and seek My face and turn from their wicked ways, then I will hear from heaven, and I will forgive their sin and will heal their land. (2 Chronicles 7:14)

I pray that the eyes of your heart may be enlightened in order that you may know the hope to which He has called you, the riches of His glorious inheritance in His holy people. (Ephesians 1:18)

I ask—ask the God of our Master, Jesus Christ, the God of glory—to make you intelligent and discerning in knowing Him personally, your eyes focused and clear, so that you can see exactly what it is He is calling you to do, grasp the immensity of this glorious way of life He has for His followers, oh, the utter extravagance of His work in us who trust Him—endless energy, boundless strength! (Ephesians 1:18, 19, MSG)

Then you will call on Me and come and pray to Me, and I will listen to you. (Jeremiah 29:12)

My prayer is not that you take them out of the world but that you protect them from the evil one. (John 17:15)

Prayer…our conversation with the God of the universe! It is difficult to imagine that just by uttering the name of "Jesus," heaven hears! Max Lucado puts it this way:

> "One call and heaven's fleet appears. Your prayer on earth activates God's power in heaven.
>
> You are the "someone" of God's kingdom. Your prayers move God to change the world. You may not understand the mystery of prayer. You don't need to. But this much is clear: Actions in heaven begin when someone prays on earth. What an amazing thought!
>
> When you speak, Jesus hears.
>
> And when Jesus hears, the world is changed. All because someone prayed."

Almighty, All-powerful, All-knowing God, empower us to come boldly before Your throne, seeking Your wisdom, Your direction, and Your strength to go through our days. We need YOUR LIGHT, LORD! On our own, we smolder and die. Remind us, Father, of Who YOU are and Whose WE are! We are Your beloved daughters, the children of the King! Let us claim our inheritance and remember the "utter extravagance of Your work in us!" Lord, make us "intelligent and discerning in knowing You." Keep our eyes focused and clear so that we can understand what You are calling us to do. Help us grasp the immensity of the glorious way of life you have for us as Your people. Let us never grow weary or discouraged in our conversations with You. I ask that You would fill us with Your joy, strengthen us by Your power, and use us for Your glory!

In the name of Your precious Son, Jesus, so be it. Amen!

APRIL 18

Be cheerful no matter what, pray all the time; thank God no matter what happens. This is the way God wants you who belong to Christ Jesus to live. (1 Thessalonians 5:16–18, MSG)

Trust God from the bottom of your heart; don't try to figure out everything on your own. Listen for God's voice in everything you do, everywhere you go, He's the one who will keep you on track. (Proverbs 3:5, 6, MSG)

Rejoice in hope, be patient in tribulation, be constant in prayer. (Romans 12:12)

Do not be anxious about anything, but in everything by prayer and supplication with thanksgiving let your requests be made known to God. (Philippians 4:6)

But when you pray, go into your room and shut the door and pray to your Father who is in secret. And your Father who sees in secret will reward you. (Matthew 6:5)

Continue steadfastly in prayer, being watchful in it with thanksgiving. (Colossians 4:2)

The Bible tells us to "pray without ceasing." I used to wonder how that was even possible, but over the years, I have noticed that it is really not that difficult. First thing in the morning, my thoughts turn to God, thanking Him for a good-night's sleep, a beautiful morning, the smell of coffee (if Dennis is up before myself). Next, I read devotions, and of course my thoughts turn to God. During the day, I catch my thoughts drifting to God, "Thanks, God, for the money to buy groceries, for a car that runs, for children that stay in touch, for good friends, stimulating conversations, happy grandkids." Then as problems come up or concerns are realized, I pray for guidance, wisdom, and the right words. Before I even realize it, night has fallen; and the prayer on my lips is, "Good night, Father," and we start all over again!

We will find Him, sisters, when we seek Him with all our hearts! God is jealous for our attention and promises to "keep us on track" in our relationship with Him! Have a fantastic week remembering always that you are a child of the King!

APRIL 19

Be still before the Lord, all mankind, because He has roused Himself from His holy dwelling. (Zechariah 2:13)

For the eyes of the Lord range throughout the earth to strengthen those whose hearts are fully committed to Him. (2 Chronicles 16:9)

He makes me lie down in green pastures, He leads me beside quiet waters, He restores my soul. He guides me in the paths of righteousness for His name's sake. (Psalm 23:2–3)

The Lord your God is with you, He is mighty to save He will take great delight in you, He will quiet you with His love, He will rejoice over you with singing. (Zephaniah 3:17)

Take heart, friends. Our effort to draw closer to God is not going unnoticed in the heavenly realms! In fact, scripture tells us the Lord Himself searches the earth to find those who are earnestly seeking Him! Our moments spent with God are never in vain!

Today at the hospital, I met an amazing woman. I delivered a couple of packages to her that had come in the mail. She was ashen in color, and I could tell she was in quite a bit of pain. She asked me to open the packages for her because she didn't have the strength. She went on to tell me that she was "terminal" and "only would be alive for a couple more days." She was pleased with her gifts but wondered why someone would send her something since she "would be dying soon." She asked me to take a small white kitten that had been sent to her a few days prior since she "couldn't take it with her." I opened her gifts, helped her read the cards, and then asked if there was anything else I could do for her. She asked me to "pray with her." We held hands, and she began, "Lord, thank You for all the wonderful people that are working so hard to take care of me…bless them, I ask. Thank You for giving me such a wonderful life. I don't know why You blessed me so, but I thank You… Thank you for the kindness of everyone here. Amen." I finished in prayer for God to bring her home to His glory and asked Him to give her peace. We held hands for a bit, and she said, "Everything good we have comes from Him, you know?"

I left the room reminded of what a blessing it is when the Lord brings one of His home and what a fantastic gift it is for this woman to know where she was headed!

In His peace and power, He will guide us and bring us home! In the meantime…live fully and thankfully because everything good comes from Him!

APRIL 20

But we have this treasure in jars of clay to show that this all-surpassing power is from God and not from us. (2 Corinthians 4:7)

This is what the Sovereign Lord, the Holy One of Israel, says: "In repentance and rest is your salvation, in quietness and trust is your strength, but you would have none of it." (Isaiah 30:15)

"Come to Me, all you who are weary and burdened, and I will give you rest. Take my yoke upon you and learn from Me, for I am gentle and humble in heart, and you will find rest for your souls. For My yoke is easy and My burden is light." (Matthew 11:28–30)

In vain you rise early and stay up late, toiling for food to eat—for He grants sleep to those He loves. (Psalm 127:2)

I have always loved this verse from Isaiah: "In quietness and trust is your strength"! It seems completely opposite from where we would expect to find strength. The world tells us we find strength through training, pushing ourselves to our physical limits, brute-strength workouts! Society teaches us do not show weakness, overpower our adversaries—go, go, go! The Lord tells us, "In quietness and trust is your strength." I LOVE that! Because once again, it isn't about us! It's about Him! The Sovereign Lord provides us with a rock-solid strength when we need it, a strength that we never had a clue we possessed! A strength that He supplies when we have exhausted our own!

The heavenly gifts that the Lord wants to fill us with are ALL things that I believe each one of us would love to have—love, joy, peace, patience, kindness, goodness, faithfulness, gentleness self-control and strength, and trust!

We want to have these gifts—God wants to give them to us! It's a win-win!

My dear sisters, may we strive to become all that God desires for us to be! May we not be included with those who "would have none of it." May we go gently, with quietness and trust through this day. Reflecting the great love of the Father.

APRIL 21

Y et, O Lord, You are our Father. We are the clay, you are the potter, we are all the work of Your hand. (Isaiah 64:8)

My heart says of you, "Seek His face!" Your face, Lord, I will seek. (Psalm 27:8)

"Can I not, O house of Israel, deal with you as this potter does?" declares the LORD. "Behold, like the clay in the potter's hand, so are you in My hand, O house of Israel." (Jeremiah 18:6)

You turn things around! Shall the potter be considered as equal with the clay, that what is made would say to its maker, "He did not make me" 'Or what is formed say to Him who formed it, "He has no understanding?" (Isaiah 29:16)

Are you pliable in the hands of the Potter? The Bible uses many names for God's people. We are called clay, sheep, children, and brides of Christ. I don't know why, but I have always related best to a lump of clay! There are days when I feel like God is indeed molding me into a vessel of use for His purpose. And then there are the days when I feel like I have been pounded flat again, and God is starting over! But the good news is… I am NOT the potter! And if I surrender my life daily to His hands, God will indeed bring to pass His plan and purpose for my life! I may not understand what it is this side of eternity, but I know I will never regret surrendering to the will of the Master Potter.

Have a great moldable day! The hands that are shaping you have gifted you with exactly what you need for the purpose intended for you! Trust Him!

APRIL 22

Moses led Israel from the Red Sea on to the Wilderness of Shur. They traveled for three days through the wilderness without finding any water. They got to Marah, but they couldn't drink the water at Marah, it was bitter That's why they called the place Marah (Bitter). And the people complained to Moses, "So what are we supposed to drink?" So Moses cried out in prayer to God, God pointed him to a stick of wood. Moses threw it into the water and the water turned sweet. (Exodus 15:22–25, MSG)

But I trust in you, O Lord; I say "You are my God." My times are in your hands. (Psalm 31:14)

God appointed Moses with the task of leading the Israelites from captivity. He led the way and told Moses what direction to take them. So, then, why are there still major bumps and turns along the way? God KNEW the Israelites would be thirsty, He KNEW the water at Marah was bitter so why there? Seems to me He did it to bring the point of today's devotional home. "TRUST ME moment by moment!" Sure, He could have smoothed out the path along the whole way BEFORE the people arrived, but my guess is they would have done exactly what we do when things are running along smoothly—forget about God! Or even begin to believe that we don't need God's help with life. We are indeed a fickle creation. When things are going well, we take the credit; and when things begin to unravel or become difficult, we blame God!

We find ourselves back at the starting point of our discussions: trust...trust...trust!

Today, moment by moment, I choose to live this day in thankfulness and trust!

Have a wonderful day, remembering always Who is doing the leading! He loves you with a fierce passion and promises to be with us whatever comes our way, bitter water or long lines of traffic!

You are greatly and eternally loved, friends!

APRIL 23

Whatever you do, work at it with all your heart, as working for the Lord, not for men. (Colossians 3:23)

I am the vine; you are the branches. If a woman remains in Me and I in her, she will bear much fruit; apart from Me you can do nothing. (John 15:5)

Look to the Lord and His strength; seek His face always. (Psalm 105:4)

Do your best to present yourself to God as one approved, a worker who has no need to be ashamed, rightly handling the word of truth. (2 Timothy 2:15)

Therefore, my beloved brothers (and sisters) be steadfast, immovable, always abounding in the work of the Lord, knowing that in the Lord your labor is not in vain. (1 Corinthians 15:58)

For we are God's fellow workers. You are God's field, God's building. (1 Corinthians 3:9)

I think sometimes, as Christians, we feel like we should be "working" for the Lord. We should be teaching Sunday school, heading Bible studies, leading prayer teams, etc., but scripture is clear that God is most interested in our walking around—eating, sleeping, working—everyday lives! The verses today remind us that we are to continually seek His face, continually remember His presence, and trust Him to be with us and guide us through our day. Nothing hard, nothing requiring superhuman effort or strength, just a moment-by-moment process of bringing our hearts and minds to focus on Him throughout the day. God is interested in all the details of our lives. He desires us to remember Him because when we do, we reflect Him! We shine His light on those we encounter at work, in the grocery store line, or at home. HIS presence is LIGHT, and when we draw near to Him, we reflect light into the everyday, ordinary hours that make up our lives!

Blessings to you this day!

APRIL 24

Y ou are the salt of the earth, but if the salt has lost its flavor, with what will it be salted? It is then good for nothing, but to be cast out and trodden under the feet of men. (Matthew 5:13)

For this world is not our permanent home; we are looking forward to a home yet to come. (Hebrews 13:14)

Now this is the message we have heard from Him and declare to you: God is light; in Him there is no darkness at all. If we claim to have fellowship with Him yet walk in the darkness, we lie and do not live by the truth. But if we walk in the light, as He is in the light, we have fellowship with one another, and the blood of Jesus, His Son, purifies us from all sin. (1 John 1:5–7)

Go therefore and make disciples of all nations, baptizing them in the name of the Father and of the Son and of the Holy Spirit. (Matthew 28:19)

We who have run for our very lives to God have every reason to grab the promised hope with both hands and never let go. It's an unbreakable spiritual lifeline, reaching past all appearances right to the very presence of God where Jesus, running on ahead of us has taken up His permanent post as high priest for us. (Hebrews 6:18-20, MSG)

There have been times in my life when I have prayed, "Lord, bring me home. I don't want to be here anymore." That may sound like "suicidal ideology," but somewhere deep in my soul, I realize that earth is not my home. Something deep within my heart reminds me that I am just visiting! Or as scripture says "tenting" here. We are visitors here. We have been placed here by God, for His purpose, to impact (or not) the people in this time and in this place. We are called to be "salt of the earth," "light that dispels the darkness," and "disciples to share the good news of Jesus Christ." That is why we are here! I beg you not to get too attached to the trappings of this place because NOTHING can compare to where our next destination takes us! My little mind cannot grasp heaven, but I know it gonna be good!

Have a light-filled, salty day! Remember always how fiercely loved you are!

APRIL 25

She will have no fear of bad news; her heart is steadfast, trusting in the Lord. (Psalm 112:7)

So do not fear, for I am with you; do not be dismayed, for I am your God. I will strengthen you and help you; I will uphold you with My righteous right hand. (Isaiah 41:10)

Say to those with fearful hearts, "Be strong, do not fear; your God will come, He will come with vengeance; with divine retribution He will come to save you." (Isaiah 35:4)

Peace I leave with you; My peace I give you. I do not give to you as the world gives. Do not let your hearts be troubled and do not be afraid. (John 14:27)

Have I not commanded you? Be strong and courageous. Do not be afraid; do not be discouraged, for the LORD your God will be with you wherever you go." (Joshua 1:9)

Illness, aging parents, cancer, children, grandchildren, pets, accidents, jobs—these are all things we deal with on a daily basis! So how come scripture tells us, "Do not fear"? Or "Do not be dismayed"? Doesn't heaven realize how difficult life on this planet can be? Just a second, did you catch it, sisters? We are not alone! The Lord of the universe says, "I AM WITH YOU! I will strengthen and help you, and I will uphold you with My righteous right hand!"

Friends, we waste our lives consumed with worry! Heads down, feet dragging, shoulders slumped dread! We spend precious hours of our lives worrying about things that will NEVER happen! We worry about things we cannot control, people we cannot control, circumstances we cannot control, and—for what? We KNOW the ONE Who knows! We know the One who CAN control all things! Let's turn our concerns over to Him, trust that He knows what He's doing, and take a deep breath! He's GOT this! So, today I encourage you to jump into His outstretched arms and face with excited expectation whatever this day holds!

APRIL 26

I have loved you with an everlasting love; I have drawn you with loving-kindness. (Jeremiah 31:3)

I delight greatly in the Lord; my soul rejoices in my God. For He has clothed me with garments of salvation and arrayed me in a robe of righteousness, as a bridegroom adorns his head like a priest, and as a bride adorns herself with her jewels. (Isaiah 61:10)

Let Your face shine on Your servant; save me in Your unfailing love. (Psalm 31:16)

Let them give thanks to the Lord for His unfailing love and His wonderful deeds for men. (Psalm 107:8)

Good morning, sisters! Did you catch the theme this morning? "I love you with an everlasting love! I robe you in righteousness! My love is unfailing! I love you no matter what!" Whew! That sure takes the pressure off, doesn't it? It doesn't matter if we feel we don't measure up. God loves us anyway! If we doubt His grace, His ability to heal, His almighty power or presence... He loves us anyway! He is walking with us! He is gently but firmly preparing us for the path ahead. He sees the future, knows our pasts, and loves us anyway!

Today, I am giving thanks for God's unfailing love that lifts, strengthens, and sustains us through the good days and the bad days.

You are greatly and eternally loved with an everlasting love!

APRIL 27

He got up, rebuked the wind and said to the waves, "Quiet, be still!" Then the wind died down and it was completely calm. (Mark 4:39)

Be strong and courageous. Do not be afraid or terrified because of them, for the Lord your God goes with you; He will never leave you nor forsake you. (Deuteronomy 31:6)

Therefore we will not fear, though the earth give way and the mountains fall into the heart of the sea. (Psalm 46:2)

Yet I am always with you; You hold me by my right hand. You guide me with Your counsel, and afterward you will take me into glory. (Psalm 73:23–24)

"Do not be afraid or terrified." I thought of a friend of mine when I read this verse this morning. Her son is in the hospital, gravely ill, and I imagined her helpless feeling of not being able to do anything about it. Then my mind raced to another friend whose husband was facing the end of his life due to ALS. Immediately thoughts of multiple friends facing cancer diagnosis crowded in. And then, finally back to the memories of our own daughter; missing, and found dead.

Face it, friends, life can be full of terrifying moments! But—and this is HUGE—"the Lord your God goes with you!" Remember, sisters, this is the same Guy that spoke to the raging sea and told it to "knock it off, be still!" ...AND IT OBEYED! I am convinced that we underestimate the POWER of God on a daily basis! We might throw up a "Hail Mary," but do we really stop and contemplate just how great His power and strength is for those who seek Him? And that's us, dear friends! Wow, I can understand why the disciples were afraid when they witnessed Jesus's power. It is beyond our comprehension! I don't know about you, but today, I am going to grasp tight that right hand that is holding me and HANG on!

We are greatly loved and never abandoned by the Hand that clings tightly to ours! We can trust His guidance for our lives.

APRIL 28

So if the Son sets you free, you will be free indeed. (John 8:36)

Many are the plans in a woman's heart, but it is the Lord's purpose that prevails. (Proverbs 19:21)

"My sheep listen to my voice; I know them, and they follow Me." (John 10:27)

Therefore, confess your sins to one another and pray for one another, that you may be healed. The prayer of a righteous person has great power as it is working. (James 5:16)

Do not be anxious about anything, but in everything by prayer and supplication with thanksgiving let your requests be known to God. And the peace of God, which surpasses all understanding, will guard your hearts and your minds in Christ Jesus. (Philippians 4:6–7)

And this is the confidence that we have toward Him, that if we ask anything according to His will He hears us. (1 John 5:14)

My dear friends, there is soo much power in prayer! When we pray for friends, family, and even strangers, the Lord of the universe hears us! He sees, understands the whole situation, and responds in the way that He knows is best! I think one of the saddest groups of people for me is those that don't even know they need prayer! They have no clue that they NEED God to fill the aching void in their life! Our time here is short. The Bible says we are "but a mist"! In the timeline of creation, we are but a blip! So, I encourage you, make your "blip" count! Listen for God's voice, follow Him, and pray with all your might for the people and situations around you! Then when we breathe our last, may we hear the words we long to hear: "Well done, good and faithful servant!"

Remember always the Hand that hung the stars and calmed the waves is holding yours! He loves you with a fierce passion!

APRIL 29

Let us fix our eyes on Jesus the author and perfecter of our faith, who for the joy set before Him endured the cross, scorning its shame, and sat down at the right had of the throne of God. (Hebrews 12:2)

Keep your eyes on Jesus, who both began and finished this race we're in. Study how He did it. Because He never lost sight of where He was headed - that exhilarating finish in and with God - He could put up with anything along the way; Cross, shame, whatever. And now He's there, in the place of honor, right alongside God. (Hebrews 12:2, MSG)

But from everlasting to everlasting the Lord's love is with those who fear Him; and His righteousness with their children's children. (Psalm 103:17)

The finish line...it's where we are all headed. Beyond the finish line is where we will experience a joy, peace, and satisfaction that exists that we now cannot comprehend! I believe deep in my heart that this place called heaven will be a place of adventure and beauty and unimaginable joy! But in the meantime, the race is long, full of detours (illness, fires, deaths, floods, anger, shame, frustrations, and questions), and we easily lose sight of the finish line. For that reason, I believe the scripture tells us to "fix our eyes upon Jesus." Heaven knew we would struggle at times, and Jesus reminds us during those difficult steps to keep our eyes on Him, not on the struggles. There will and have also been times where we run easily, with purpose and confidence. We are reminded to "keep our eyes on Him" during those times as well so that we don't run off the course and head off in the wrong direction of our personal choosing.

We are all at different "mile markers" on this race. Some of us much closer to the finish than others! Some of us may think we have a long way to go before we finish, but unfortunately, none of us can be completely sure where the actual finish line is for us. So, once again, the words of scripture are our best coach: "Keep your eyes upon Me!"

May you run your race this week with a quick step, an easy smile, and an unshakable confidence in your Coach!

APRIL 30

T herefore we do not lose heart. Though outwardly we are wasting away, yet inwardly we are being renewed day by day. For our light and momentary troubles are achieving for us eternal glory that far outweighs them all. So we fix our eyes not on what is seen, but on what is unseen. For what is seen is temporary, but what is unseen is eternal. (2 Corinthians 4:16–18)

Blessed are those who have learned to acclaim You, who walk in the light of your presence O Lord. (Psalm 89:15)

The people living in darkness have seen a great light; on those living in the land of the shadow of death a light has dawned. (Matthew 4:16)

The light shines in the darkness, and the darkness has not overcome it. (John 1:5)

When Jesus spoke again to the people, He said, "I am the light of the world. Whoever follows Me will never walk in darkness, but will have the light of life." (John 8:12)

"The most important part of our task will be to tell everyone who will listen that Jesus is the only answer to the problems that are disturbing the hearts of men and nations. We shall have the right to speak because we can tell from our experience that His Light is more powerful than the deepest darkness... How wonderful that the reality of His Presence is greater than the reality of the hell about us" (Betsie ten Boom).

(Betsie ten Boom, sister of author and speaker Corrie ten Boom, died in a Nazi concentration camp during World War II.)

We have a great commission! We are directed by the Lord of the universe to reach a lost and frightened world! We are asked to be the hands and feet of Christ to a world that is hurting. To bring HIS light to dispel the darkness around us. There is much to be done, and as we were reminded yesterday, so little time! So, get moving, friends!

Almighty God, equip us for the work You have ordained for us. Use us for Your glory, Your purpose, and Your will. We surrender our lives to You. Help us to keep our gaze always upon You. When we wander off track, pull us back, Lord, redirect our steps, strengthen our resolve. We love You. We surrender our lives to You. So be it. Amen.

MAY 1

Look to the Lord and His Strength; seek His Face always. (1 Chronicles 16:11)

Be prepared. You're up against far more than you can handle on your own. Take all the help you can get, every weapon God has issued, so that when it's all over but the shouting you'll still be on your feet, Truth, righteousness, peace, faith, and salvation are more than words. Learn how to apply them. You'll need them throughout your life. God's Word is an indispensable weapon. In the same way, prayer is essential in this ongoing warfare. Pray hard and long. Pray for your brothers and sisters. Keep your eyes open. Keep each other's spirits up so that no one falls behind or drops out. (Ephesians 6:13–18, MSG)

The Lord will give strength to His people; the Lord will bless His people with peace. (Psalm 29:11)

I am strong in the Lord and in the power of His might. (Ephesians 6:10)

I have put on the complete armor of God. (Ephesians 6:11)

God gives power to the weak. And to those who have not might, He increases strength. (Isaiah 40:29)

Almighty God, we come before Your throne this bright, beautiful morning to bask in Your presence! Thank you for this day, for our health, for new beginnings, second chances, family, friends, and community. Thank You for Your hand of protection and guidance that guards our every step. Thank You for grace, for salvation, and for never giving up on us. Thank you for friendships, new and old, for laughter and healing tears. Help us never to doubt Your tremendous love for us. Please equip us for Your service, strengthen our resolve to follow You, and give us hearts for our fellow man. We love You, Lord; we desire truth, righteousness, peace and faith in our lives. We desire to leave a legacy of kindness, love, peace, joy, patience, goodness, and gentleness in our wake. Fill us to overflowing with Your strength and with Your power so that we make leak Jesus on everyone we come in contact with. Forgive us for our sin, our impatience, and our self-centeredness. Mold us and make us more and more like Jesus and use us up for Your glory!

In Jesus's holy name. Amen.

MAY 2

For God gave us a spirit not of fear but of power and love and self-control. (2 Timothy 1:7)

You make known to me the path of life; in Your Presence there is fullness of joy, at Your right hand are pleasures forevermore. (Psalm 16:11)

The heart of a woman plans her way, but the Lord establishes her steps. (Proverbs 16:9)

Whatever you do, work heartily, as for the Lord and not for men. (Colossians 3:23)

And I am sure of this, that He who began a good work in you will bring it to completion at the day of Jesus Christ. (Philippians 1:6)

This resurrection life you received from God is not a timid, grave-tending life. It's adventurously expectant, greeting God with a childlike "What's next Papa?" God's Spirit touches our spirits and confirms who we really are. We know Who He is, and we know who we are; Father and children. (Romans 8:15, MSG)

What would walking in radical obedience look like for you? For me, I think it would be trusting God more. Realizing that every detail of my life is in accordance with His will for me. I would worry less, speak the truth in kindness and love, and only be concerned about God as my audience of one! My dear sisters...our lives matter! They matter to the people around us, and they matter to God! We are here, in this time and in this place, for God's purpose and by God's design! There are places to go, things to be done, and hope to be shared! Let's not life our lives in a "half-dead" state or in a "timid, grave-tending" way! Let us live BIG, BOLD, BEAUTIFUL, FULL lives before God and upon our deaths come sliding home with the words, "Whew, what a ride!" on our lips.

Have a great week, friends, remembering you are loved, blessed, and empowered by the Lord of the universe! Let's put our big-girl panties on and get out there! Time is short, the need is great! Go! Leak Jesus!

MAY 3

For I know the plans I have for you, declares the Lord, "plans to prosper you and not to harm you, plans to give you hope and a future." (Jeremiah 29:11)

Trust in the Lord with all your heart and lean not on your own understanding; in all your ways submit to Him, and He will make your paths straight. (Proverbs 3:6–7)

For it is God's will that by doing good you should silence the ignorant talk of foolish people. (1 Peter 2:15)

But you are the ones chosen by God, chosen for the high-calling of priestly work, chosen to be a holy people, God's instruments to do His work and speak out for Him, to tell others of the night-and-day difference He made for you - from nothing to something, form rejected to accepted. (1 Peter 2:9, 10, MSG)

My dear children, let's not just talk about love, let's practice real love. This is the only way we'll know we're living truly, living in God's reality. It's also the way to shut down debilitating self-criticism, even when there is something to it. For God is greater than our worried hearts and knows more about us than we do ourselves. (1 John 18–20, MSG)

"You're My handpicked servant So that you'll come to know and trust Me, understand both THAT I am and WHO I am…yes, I am God. I've always been God and I always will be God." (Isaiah 43:11 and 13, MSG)

Lysa Terkeurst writes: "God must feel the same way when we miss the surprise parties (divine appointments) that await us each day. How it must disappoint Him when we don't hear or don't listen to Him redirecting us to the front door. How it must grieve Him when we walk through our lives oblivious of His activity all around us. How it must break His heart when we brush aside something that not only would make us feel special and noticed by God, but also would allow us to join Him in making life a little sweeter for others."

My dear friends... I believe wholeheartedly that God does indeed have "divine appointments" for us all the time! That there are people He puts in our path for His specific purposes. That there are moments of heaven inspired beauty around us. That we get a glimpse of God at work daily! My continued prayer for all of us is that He will give us eyes to see it! Hearts to believe it and strength to live it! We ARE His handpicked servants! His beloved children! His instruments! His holy people!

I don't know about you, but I am bouncing on eager toes of anticipation and straining to see where He is leading us! Because as you already know; It's gonna be good!

MAY 4

If it is disagreeable in your sight to serve the Lord, choose for yourselves today whom you will serve: whether the gods which your fathers served which were beyond the river, or the gods of the Amorites in whose land you are living; but as for me and my house, we will serve the LORD. (Joshua 24:15)

Barricade the road that goes nowhere; grace me with Your clear revelation. I choose the true road to somewhere, I post your road signs at every curve and corner. I grasp and cling to whatever you tell me; God, don't let me down! I'll run the course You lay out for me if You'll just show me how. God teach me lessons for living so I can stay the course. Give me insight so I can do what you tell me—my whole life one long, obedient response. (Psalm 119:25–33, MSG)

Point out the road I must travel I'm all ears, all eyes before You. Save me from my enemies, God - You're my only hope! Teach me how to live to please You. (Psalm 143:9, 10, MSG)

When our situations are beyond our abilities… Jesus is the way through. When we lack patience, wisdom, or insight…lean on Jesus. He's the way, the truth, and the light that we need to see the next step ahead of us. He promises to never leave or turn His back to us. Life can be extremely difficult, but remember, friends, we don't have to do it alone! Someone much, much wiser, stronger, and more insightful has got our backs! He's not concerned with our comfort but with the condition of our hearts! His desire is to guide us, to direct our steps, to "barricade the road that goes nowhere!" He does indeed post "road signs" for the heart that is seeking!

Lord, open our eyes to see You at every bend in the road. At every crossroad, and in every moment You choose to give us breath! We are ALL in! We love You, and we boldly ask for Your direction for our lives! Amen.

MAY 5

This is the confidence we have in approaching God; that if we ask anything according to His Will, He hears us. (1 John 5:14)

Then you will call on Me and come and pray to Me, and I will listen to you. (Jeremiah 29:12)

Is anyone among you in trouble? Let them pray. Is anyone happy? Let them sing songs of praise. (James 5:13)

Watch and pray so that you will not fall into temptation. The spirit is willing, but the flesh is weak. (Matthew 26:41)

The Lord detests the sacrifice of the wicked, but the prayer of the upright pleases Him. (Proverbs 15:8)

May my prayer be set before You like incense; may the lifting up of my hands be like the evening sacrifice. (Psalm 141:2)

Sometimes, God says *no*...sometimes, *wait*...sometimes He laughs!

Heavenly Father, Almighty, All-knowing God, we lift our prayers before Your throne today. We ask that our words and hearts might be pleasing to You, a fragrant offering to You this day. We acknowledge our desire to understand Your thoughts toward us. To understand why You, at so many times during our lives, seem so distant, so uninterested.

Forgive us for doubting Your authority over our lives, forgive us for thinking that we know what is best for ourselves and our loved ones, forgive us for our arrogance. Help us always to remember that "even hell holds no secrets from You" (Proverbs 15:11). We are prideful in believing even for an instant that You cannot read and understand human hearts! You, o LORD are GOD! We are not. Help us to get that through our thick skulls! Help us to trust You during those times we don't understand. To remember that sometimes, You answer prayer best by saying *no* or *wait* or *Trust Me*. Give us patience to wait for Your good and perfect answer. We know in the depths of our hearts that You do indeed hear us when we pray. The Bible is clear about that. Help us to believe that You hear us and respond to us in the way best for us, for those involved, and for Your purposes. We love you, Lord, and we know that You love us! Sometimes we forget just how much You do indeed care for all the details in our lives, big and small!

We ask that you will continue to guide and encourage us along this journey of faith. We ask your hand of protection and provision on our lives and the lives of our loved ones. We pray earnestly now for our communities, our nation, and our world. We ask that You would use our lives for Your glory. That You would continue to shape us in the image of Your Son and strengthen our resolve to trust You at all times and in all situations. We love you, Lord. We are lost, broken, and hopeless without You! Have Your way with us. Use us and fill us with the joy of knowing that You have "got" whatever it is that is binding us up. Thank You, Father, for what you have done for us and for what You have in store. Amen!

MAY 6

"Because you're not taking God seriously," said Jesus. "The simple truth is that if you had a mere kernel of faith, a poppy seed, say, you would tell this mountain, "Move" and it would move! There is nothing you wouldn't be able to tackle." (Matthew 17:20, MSG)

Be brave. Be strong. Don't give up. Expect God to get here soon, (Psalm 31:24, MSG)

We're depending on God; He's everything we need. What's more, our hearts brim with joy since we've taken for our own His Holy Name, Love us, God, with all You've got - that's what we're depending on. (Psalm 33:20–22, MSG)

God is strong, and He wants you strong. So take everything the Master has set out for you, well-made weapons of the best materials. And put them to use so you will be able to stand up to everything the Devil throws your way. This is no afternoon athletic contest that we'll walk away from and forget about in a couple of hours. This is for keeps, a life-or-death fight to the finish against the devil and all his angels. Be prepared. You're up against far more that you can handle on your own. Take all the help you can get, every weapon God has issued, so that when it's all over but the shouting you'll still be on your feet. Truth, righteousness, peace, faith, and salvation are more than words. Learn how to apply them. You'll need them throughout your life. (Ephesians 6:10–14, MSG)

These scriptures are calling us friends, encouraging us, spurring us on! The Bible is full of verses reminding us to get out there and fight! Fight for our beliefs, for our families, communities, friends, and marriages! Fight against apathy, indifference, and inaction. Fight for truth, righteousness, peace, faith, and salvation for others! God has laid before us the weapons we will need. He reminds us that He's everything we need! That He is strong! That He is dependable! Don't you see, sisters, nothing is impossible for God!

There is no marriage beyond repair, no wayward child forever lost, no God-inspired dream too difficult! God is bigger, bolder, stronger, and wiser than any obstacle the enemy may put in our path! Friends, God reminds us in Isaiah 41:10, "Don't fear! I AM WITH YOU; do not be dismayed, for I AM YOUR GOD. I WILL strengthen you and help you; I will uphold you with MY righteous right hand!" God's got whatever "impossible" we may be looking at today! Let's get out there and actively fight against whatever is in the way!

You are loved, empowered, and held by the righteous right hand of God! Live like it! Have a great day, friends!

MAY 7

That they would seek God, if perhaps they might grope for Him and find Him, though He is not far from each one of us. (Acts 17:27)

Seek the Lord and his strength; seek His face continually. (1 Chronicles 16:11)

The Lord has looked down from heaven upon the daughters of men to see if there are any who understand, Who seek after God. (Psalm 14:2)

"I love those who love Me; and those who diligently seek Me will find Me." (Proverbs 8:17)

You will seek Me and find Me when you search for Me with all your heart. (Jeremiah 29:13)

These scriptures are near and dear to my heart, and I want to take a minute to talk about them. Our private, quiet times are so important to our relationship with God that I want to reinforce what scripture tells us. Take the time, friends, to read other author's books along with your Bible. (There are so many great authors out there!) I have found it really helpful over the years to read a chapter of a Christian book I was interested in then continue in prayer and conversation with God about what I just read. I also love to journal or highlight things in the book that spoke to me. Just an idea, but I just want to encourage you to spend time alone with God, being honest about what you are feeling, any questions or confusion, anything on your heart. Bring it all to God, talk it over with Him. I promise you, you will never regret the time you spend seeking His wisdom, His strength and relationship with Him. For He promises that we will find Him, when we search for Him with our whole heart.

MAY 8

Blessed is the one who perseveres under trial because, having stood the test, that person will receive the crown of life that the Lord has promised to those who love Him. (James 1:12)

Anyone who meets a testing challenge head-on and manages to stick it out is mighty fortunate. For such persons loyally in love with God, the reward is life and more life. (James 1:12, MSG)

Trust in the Lord with all your heart and lean not on your own understanding; in all your ways submit to Him, and He will make your paths straight. (Proverbs 3:5, 6)

Now it is God who makes both us and you stand firm in Christ. He anointed us. (2 Corinthians 1:21)

Put on the full armor of God so that you can take your stand against the devil's scheme. (Ephesians 6:11)

So take everything the Master has set out for you, well-made weapons of the best materials. And put them to use so you will be able to stand up to everything the devil throws your way. (Ephesians 6:11, MSG)

Stand firm, and you will win life. (Luke 21:19)

Staying with it—that's what is required. Stay with it to the end. You won't be sorry, you'll be saved. (Luke 21:19, MSG)

My dear friends, we are called to a life of radical obedience! Wait, I know that has some of you shaking in your slippers! But a spiritual battle is raging around us and our enemy HATES it when we jump the fence of complacency and run eagerly toward the will of God! God never promised us easy lives but He did promise to help us every step of the way! As we draw nearer to God, our enemy, the devil, reaches deeper into his bag of tricks to find something new and more challenging to throw us off course with God. I wholeheartedly understand that the enemy hates the radically obedient! Our enemy would love to keep us in a constant state of complacency, caring little, loving little and living small, scared, insignificant lives. However—and this is (in my thinking, anyway) extremely important—God is bigger, wiser, and on to anything the devil throws at us! He will give us a way of escape, a way to overcome, and the tools we need to stand up against anything our enemy throws our way! We may be in for the fight of our lives against our enemy, but I promise, it will be worth it! Personally, I would much rather fight the enemy with every breath, thought, and action within me than settle for a complacent, wishy-washy, insignificant version of life!

Sisters, God has called and equipped us to live BIG, BOLD, BEAUTIFUL lives before Him! To witness to others through our faith, actions and perseverance! To stand strong in the face of adversity, to grab on to the belief, with both hands! Believe it, GOD IS FOR US! Embrace lives of hope, joy, and anticipation of what lies ahead!

Give life your "best shot" today and don't forget to listen for the applause of heaven!

MAY 9

"These things I have spoken to you, so that in Me you may have peace. In the world you have tribulation, but take courage; I have overcome the world." (John 16:33, MSG)

I've told you all this so that trusting Me, you will be unshakable and assured, deeply at peace. In this godless world you will continue to experience difficulties. But take heart! I've conquered the world."

"Peace I leave with you; My Peace I give to you; not as the world gives do I give to you. Do not let your heart be troubled, nor let it be fearful." (John 14:27)

Wait for the Lord; be strong and let your heart take courage; Yes; wait for the Lord. (Psalm 27:14)

I'm sure now I'll see God's goodness in the exuberant earth. Stay with God! Take heart. Don't quit. I'll say it again: Stay with God. (Psalm 27:13, 14, MSG)

"Do not let your heart be troubled," "In Me you may have peace." "But take courage; I have overcome the world." These scriptures do not sugarcoat the fact that we will indeed need courage! We will be frightened and weak. God reminds us to "take heart," to "take courage," to not quit! Friends, God has GOOD things in store for His children! Do we believe it? Do we embrace it and joyfully anticipate the "good things"? One of my biggest frustrations is the dogged religious plod, feet dragging, shoulders slumped, head down walk of many Christians. GOD IS FOR US! He FIGHTS for US! HE EMPOWERS us! Let's dance through the days He ordains for us! Let us remain radically obedient in the small things. Steadfast in trust when the "big" things come. From my perspective, it seems like life is MOSTLY filled with the "small things." Sure, there might be moments in our lives when we know that we have experienced something exceptional, but mostly life just seems to be a series of "small things." Most we don't even take note of. But if we are living our lives trying to be obedient to the Spirit's promptings, trying to listen and respond to God's voice, then we are instruments in the hands of God! What we may see as insignificant in our lives of obedience may be used by God to accomplish His purposes! What a thought! So, dear sisters, take heart! Don't quit! Don't worry about the opinion of others. Stay with God! He promises to make us unshakable and courageous, and He promises us peace! God's got this!

MAY 10

"As the Father has loved Me, so have I loved you. Now remain in My love." (John 15:9)

We demolish arguments and every pretension that sets itself up against the knowledge of God, and we take captive every thought to make it obedient to Christ. (2 Corinthians 10:5)

The world is unprincipled. It's dog-eat-dog out there! The world doesn't fight fair. But we don't live or fight our battles that way - never have and never will. The tools of our trade aren't for marketing or manipulation, but they are for demolishing that entire massively corrupt culture. We use our powerful God-tools for smashing warped philosophies, tearing down barriers erected against the truth of God, fitting every loose thought and emotion and impulse into the structure of life shaped by Christ. Our tools are ready at hand for clearing the ground of every obstruction and building lives of obedience into maturity. (2 Corinthians 10:3–5, MSG)

This calls for patient endurance on the part of the people of God who keep His commands and remain faithful to Jesus. (Revelation 14:12)

And this is love; that we walk in obedience to His commands. As you have heard from the beginning, His command is that you walk in love. (2 John 1:6)

"Patience endurance"—a painful reminder of the experience we had in "trusting God's plan" with our daughter's life and ultimately death. Trusting that He could use ALL of it somehow, in some way, for good. Surrendering our broken, hurting child into God's hands and saying, "Your will be done." Remembering and believing that He loved her even more than we did. We didn't experience a miracle that we could see, but it was only by the power of God that we were able to withstand it all without giving in, giving up, and abandoning our faith. God is good and strong and faithful when we are overwhelmed, weak, and stumbling. Scriptures call to remain faithful is the battle cry we all need to remember when life gets hard.

Almighty God, Commander of the angel armies, Loving Father, we come before Your very throne this morning, asking for Your power to stand strong in the face of adversity. To listen to Your call for radical obedience. We know that it is Your love that compels us, Your power that enables us, and Your Spirit that protects and guides us as we do what You've called us to do. Father, sometimes I think we get so caught up in wondering what You have called us to do that we overlook Your command to love. "Love the Lord thy God with all your heart, soul and mind and love your neighbor as yourself." Love, love of You, loving ourselves, and loving those you have placed around us. It sounds simple when we look at this as being what You have "called us to do" …help us to not make it more difficult than it has to be. Draw us deeper and more intimately in love with You. Help us to be kinder and forgiving with ourselves and to love our family, friends, and neighbors with a love that reflects You, a love of compassion, strength, and truth. Let us not stumble or turn away from this walk of faith we are on. Give us the perseverance, desire, and fortitude it will take to live lives of radical obedience! We love You, Lord! We thank You that You love us, that You guide and protect us, that You know us completely and love us despite flaws, weaknesses, and pride. We surrender it all to You. Use us for Your glory, for Your purpose, and equip us for what lies ahead! We're all in. Fill us so completely with Your love, Your light, and Your wisdom that we cannot help but "leak Jesus" on everyone You put in our path today! Amen.

MAY 11

I'm not saying that I have this all together, that I have it made. But I am well on my way, reaching out for Christ, Who has so wondrously reached out for me. Friends, don't get me wrong; by no means do I count myself an expert in all of this, but I've got my eye on the goal, where God is beckoning us onward—to Jesus. I'm off and running, and I'm not turning back. (Philippians 3:12–14, MSG)

I want you to get out there and walk—better yet, run!—on the road God called you to travel. I don't want any of you sitting around on your hands. I don't want anyone strolling off, down some path that goes nowhere. And mark that you do this with humility and discipline—not in fits and starts, but steadily, pouring yourselves out for each other in acts of love, alert at noticing differences and quick at mending fences. (Ephesians 4:2, 3, MSG)

God knew what He was doing from the very beginning. He decided from the onset to shape the lives of those who love Him along the same lines as the life of His Son. (Romans 8:29, 30, MSG)

So, don't you see that we don't owe this old do-it-yourself life one red cent. There's nothing in it for us, nothing at all. The best thing to do is give it a decent burial and get on with your new life. God's Spirit beckons. There are things to do and places to go! (Romans 8:12–14, MSG)

Our lives are lived out in a series of "small steps." Being kind, compassionate, loving in the day-to-day moments that make up our lives. Sisters, that's radical obedience! We don't know where this obedience will lead; we don't know where God will lead us next. But we can only be obedient in the specific things that He puts in front of us every day! Sometimes, He chooses to lead us out of our "comfort zones"; sometimes, He calls us to be obedient in the mundane, same stuff! No matter where or how God calls us to obedience, His purpose is the same: He desires us, as His daughters, to rely on Him. Always!

I cannot imagine what God has in store for each one of you, my friends. But I am confident that He is indeed beckoning you forward! His Spirit nudging your spirit, reminding you "there are things to do and places to go!" I love Paul's words in Philippians 3. Friends, I'm no expert on all of this, but I've got my eye on the goal… I'm off and running and not turning back! God doesn't call us to be perfect or an expert! He calls us to "get moving," "keep pressing on," to trust that God will reveal His call on our lives as we walk daily in obedience to Christ in the little things! My dear sisters, this life we are called to live is no sprint! It is a marathon! It's time to get our running shoes on and arm ourselves with the tools that God has given each one of us. Wrapping ourselves in love, joy, peace, patience, kindness, goodness, faithfulness, gentleness, and self-control! Only God knows where our obedience will take us. But we can all know, it's gonna be good!

MAY 12

For where your treasure is, there your heart will be also. (Matthew 6:212)

Whoever loves money never has enough; whoever loves wealth is never satisfied with their income. This too is meaningless. (Ecclesiastes 5:10)

Better the little that the righteous have than the wealth of many wicked, for the power of the wicked will be broken, but the Lord upholds the righteous. (Psalm 37:16–17)

Less is more and more is less. One righteous will outclass fifty wicked, for the wicked are moral weaklings but the righteous are God-strong! (Psalm 37:16–17, MSG)

Keep your lives free from the love of money and be content with what you have, because God has said, "Never will I leave you; never will I forsake you." (Hebrews 13:5)

Don't be obsessed with getting more material things. Be relaxed with what you have. Since God assured us, "I'll never let you down, never walk off and leave you," we can boldly quote: God is there, ready to help, I'm fearless no matter what. Who or what can get to me? (Hebrews 13:5–6, MSG)

No one can serve two masters. Either you will hate the one and love the other, or you will be devoted to the one and despise the other. You cannot serve both God and money. (Matthew 6:24)

Even if someone lived a thousand years—make it two thousand—but didn't enjoy anything, what's the point? Doesn't everyone end up in the same place? We work to feed our appetites; Meanwhile our souls go hungry. (Ecclesiastes 6:6, 7, MSG)

Everything we own, manage, and desire comes from God! Everything is His! We live in a money, status, power-obsessed culture! Oftentimes, the "measure of a woman" is her wealth, what she has obtained. How large her house is, how fast her car is, how in fashion her clothes are. King Solomon refers to this as "chasing the wind" or "meaningless.". Our love of money—and oftentimes, fear of losing it—is one of the most powerful weapons in the enemy's arsenal! Everything we are, everything we have, everything we propose and plan, is first in the hands of God. He is the One who gifts us with good things. Things like health, mental abilities, and physical abilities. He has placed us in the United States, a country of opportunity, freedom, and resources. We are blessed beyond measure, to start with, all gifts! I am sure you have heard it said, "What you are is God's gift to you, what you become is your gift to God" (Hans Urs von Bathasar). Yet somewhere along the line, we have twisted it to sound like "Everything I have is because of what I have done!" or "Mine, mine, mine!" It is a constant battle to live before the Lord with open hearts and open pockets! I don't have the answer, friends. I think managing our money, like managing our lives, comes down to obtaining wisdom from God. I have read it written this way (in among the Message introductions): "Wisdom has to do with becoming skillful in honoring our parents and raising our children, handling our money and conducting our sexual lives, going to work and exercising leadership, using words well and treating friends kindly, eating and drinking healthily, cultivating emotions within ourselves and attitudes toward others that make for peace. Threaded through all these items is the insistence that the way we think of and respond to God is the most practical thing we do. In matters of everyday practicality, nothing, absolutely nothing, takes precedence over God." So, there you have it! It's ALL God's! He gave it to us, and He can take it away! May our hands be open before Him and our souls be whole and healthy!

MAY 13

W hat marvelous love the Father has extended to us! Just look at it—we're called children of God! That's who we really are. But that's also why the world doesn't recognize us or take us seriously, because it has no idea who He is or what He's up to. But friends, that's exactly who we are: children of God. And that's only the beginning. Who knows how we'll end up! (1 John 3:1–2, MSG)

Before I formed you in the womb I knew you, before you were born I set you apart; I appointed you as a prophet to the nations. (Jeremiah 1:5)

So if you're serious about living this new resurrection life with Christ, act like it. Pursue the things over which Christ presides. Don't shuffle along, eyes to the ground, absorbed with the things right in front of you. Look up, and be alert to what is going on around Christ - that's where the action is. See things from His perspective. (Colossians 3:1–3, MSG)

Where does your sense of identity stem from? Does it rest on the accomplishments of your husband, your kids, yourself? Or do we find our identity in our communities, offices, our moods? Do we have our noses "to the grindstone" and our eyes firmly fixed on the tasks in front of us, so engrossed in the details that we forget to "look up"? Do we daily pause and consider God's perspective? I think as humans, we keep looking for our identity in the people and world around us. Thinking, "Who does the world think I am?" or "What do the people around me think of me?" when in truth, our identity is found in Christ. Our thinking should instead default to "Who does God say I am?"

Sisters, God reminds us, we are children of God. We are a branch of the True Vine and a conduit of Christ's life. A friend of Jesus. We are justified and redeemed. We are chosen, holy, and blameless before God! We don't need to build our identity on anyone or anything else! Christ in me is enough!

Much love to you today, my dear, busy, kind, faithful sisters! Keep your eyes open today to what God is up to… He has surprises in store!

MAY 14

You intended to harm me, but God intended it for good to accomplish what is now being done, the saving of many lives. (Genesis 50:20)

He [the Holy Spirit] knows us better than we know ourselves, knows our pregnant condition and keeps us present before God. That's why we can be so sure that every detail in our lives of love for God is worked into something good. God knew what He was doing from the very beginning. He decided from the onset to shape the lives of those who love Him along the same lines as the life of His Son. (Romans 8:27–29, MSG)

God knew what He was doing from the very beginning. He is shaping our lives, He is working in the details. So, what is our part? Personally, I would say it is the reminder to live authentic lives before God. It is being gut-level honest with Him about the condition of our hearts and lives. I relish the idea that God knows us better than we know ourselves. He understands our fear, insecurities, and motives even better than we do! We are free as His daughters to lay it all on His lap, lift our tearstained faces and walk—no, better yet, run—forward in faith! God's got us! He is bigger, wiser and more powerful than absolutely anything that has or will trip us up! Our enemy's desire is to trip us and tangle us up in our mistakes and failures. God's desire is to untangle and restore! So, "tell me, what is it you plan to do with your one wild and precious life?" (Mary Oliver).

Today, may we be pliable, teachable, and willing in the hands molding our lives! Have a great day!

MAY 15

This is the confidence we have in approaching God: That if we ask anything according to His Will, He hears us. (1 John 5:14)

Look to the Lord and His strength; seek His face always. (1 Chronicles 16:11)

If My People, who are called by My Name, will humble themselves and pray and seek My face and turn from their wicked ways, then I will hear from heaven, and I will forgive their sin and will heal their land. (2 Chronicles 7:14)

I pray that they eyes of your heart may be enlightened in order that you may know the hope to which He has called you, the riches of His glorious inheritance in His Holy people. (Ephesians 1:18)

Then you will call on Me and come and pray to Me, and I will listen to you. (Jeremiah 29:12)

What an awesome privilege it is for us, as Christ's daughters, to bring anything and everything to the very throne of God! Prayer is not just "shooting a wish" or "hoping for the best," but it is an open wave of communication between us and heaven! Scripture promises us that God hears us when we pray! Whether it is a prayer whispered in private, shouted from the hilltops, or prayed in earnestness in our minds. God hears us…always! God is not a vending-machine God. He very often doesn't give us what we ask for. Sometimes for our own good, sometimes for the good of others, and other times for reasons we cannot and will not understand this side of heaven. But we can rest assured, my dear sisters, GOD HEARS!

I believe that God speaks to each and every one of us…every day! Oftentimes, many times throughout the day. My prayer for all of us is that we will be better able to recognize His voice in our day-to-day experiences and then to react and respond to Him in a way that brings Him glory! That we will learn to rely on HIS strength, seek HIS wisdom, and believe that we are HIS beloved children!

Prayers for grieving hearts, for healing bodies, for our nation, our world, our families and our friends, for the lost, the broken, and the stubborn. May our light so shine that the darkness scatters! May we live this day with confident belief and trust in the Hand holding ours!

MAY 16

Call to Me and I WILL Answer you, and will tell you great and hidden things that you have not known. (Jeremiah 33:3)

I will instruct you and teach you in the way you should go: I will counsel you with My eye upon you. Be not like a horse or a mule, without understanding, which must be curbed with bit and bridle, or it will not stay near you. (Psalm 32:8–9)

And your ears shall hear a word behind you, saying, "This is the way, walk in it" when you turn to the right or when you turn to the left. (Isaiah 30:21)

My sheep hear My voice, and I know them, and they follow Me. (John 10:27)

For it is God who works in you, both to will and to work for His good purpose. (Philippians 2:13)

Okay, so maybe you do believe that God is speaking to you, but you think you are not hearing because the whole idea of God—Who is in heaven, speaking to us, who are definitely earthbound—seems too absurd to be true! Yet you are intrigued, and you don't want to miss out. Let's hash it out. Scripture speaks over and over and over again about God conversing with His people. The scriptures above are more than just verses—they are promises! God tells us in Jeremiah that when we call to Him, He will answer! In Psalms, He promises to instruct and teach us in the way we should go, to counsel us and keep His eye upon us. In Isaiah, He promises that our ears SHALL HEAR Him speak; and then in Philippians, He goes one step further and promises that He HIMSELF is working within us so that we will desire to work for His purposes!

So just in these few passages (and there are many more), God makes it clear that He does indeed speak to His people! The scriptures don't say that God USED to speak to His people, but that God continues to do so. How exciting is that! The Lord God of the universe, God Almighty, Leader of the angel armies, wants to communicate with us!? Wow!

I am excited that we are learning to "hear" to actively listen for God's voice in our lives. Take a minute; think of a time when you heard from God. Think about it! Don't be embarrassed or shy about sharing it. Someone will be blessed by your courage! I believe that sometimes, God speaks to us in a simple, gentle way. For example, yesterday early morning, I was hemming a pair of dress slacks that my grandson wanted to wear. I felt a voice whisper, "This is an act of love… I love you." I knew it was from God. How did I know? Because I have heard and acknowledged His voice before, and it is becoming familiar to me, the voice of a friend!

MAY 17

T hen God said, "Let us make man in our image, in our likeness and let them rule over the fish of the sea and the birds of the air, over the livestock, over all the earth, and over all the creatures that move along the ground." So God created man in His own image, in the image of God He created him: male and female He created them. (Genesis 1:26–27)

Those who live according to the sinful nature have their minds set on what that nature desires; but those who live in accordance with the Spirit have their minds set on what the Spirit desires. The mind of sinful man is death, but the mind controlled by the Spirit is life and peace. (Romans 8:5–6)

We destroy arguments and every lofty opinion raised against the knowledge of God, and take every thought captive to obey Christ. (2 Corinthians 10:5)

You keep her in perfect peace whose mind is stayed on You, because she trusts in You. (Isaiah 26:3)

Every morning when we wake up, we make a choice. Do we choose to think about reasons to be thankful for, or do we focus our thoughts on the problems and worries the day presents? I don't believe that even one of us would say, "I just love it when my thoughts are in turmoil and my emotions follow on their heels!" But so often, that is the road we let our minds take us down. The Bible warns us to "take every thought captive" …to set our minds on what the Spirit desires. So today, when thinking about your "to-do list," invite God's peace and wisdom into the process, ask for guidance to understand what the Spirit desires, and take a deep breath and remember that the hand that calmed the waves is grasping yours and is willing and exceedingly able to calm you anxious thoughts and give you peace!

MAY 18

You did not choose me, but I chose you and appointed you so that you might go and bear fruit—fruit that will last—and so that whatever you ask in My Name the Father will give to you. (John 15:16)

And we know that in all things God works for the good of those who love Him, who have been called according to His purpose. (Romans 8:28)

The One Who calls you is faithful, and HE WILL DO IT. (1 Thessalonians 5:24)

Do not repay evil with evil or insult with insult. On the contrary, repay evil with blessing, because to this you were called so that you may inherit a blessing. (1 Peter 3:9)

He has saved us and called us to a holy life—not because of anything we have done but because of His Own Purpose and grace. This grace was given us in Christ Jesus before the beginning of time. (2 Timothy 1:9)

Through Him we received both the generous gift of His life and the urgent task of passing it on to others through this gift and call of Jesus Christ! (Romans 1:4, 5, MSG)

God is kind, but He's not soft. In kindness He takes us firmly by the hand and leads us into a radical life change. (Romans 2:4, MSG)

God's calling. You realize that each and every one of our lives has God's calling on it? Sometimes that calling looks like visiting a friend in hospice, sometimes it looks like caring for and loving our family, friends, and strangers. And sometimes it looks like simply putting one foot in front of the other, not sure where God is leading but being willing and faithful in going anyway! The Bible does give us a lot of clues on what to expect God's calling on our lives will look like. It may look like turning the other cheek and forgiving when we have been hurt because God asks us "not to repay evil with evil or insult with insult." It may look like stepping outside of our comfort zone and speaking words of life and encouragement to someone in need—knowing that on our own, we will fail miserably. It may look like picking up after the family one more time (for the fiftieth time) and not giving up. God calls. God equips, and God uses our every-day, ordinary acts of obedience for His purpose and for His glory.

Sometimes, God calls us to do some really hard things that we really, really do not want to do. But by trusting Him even in the midst of trial and upheaval, He continually provides the strength and stamina we need to persevere. And then He promises to use every dif-ficult and painful thing for His glory! I firmly believe that God is not so concerned about our comfort in this life but about the state of our souls. And the souls of those He surrounds us with. God is always able, and He calls on us to rely on His strength, His ability, and His wisdom for whatever is at hand. He desires to equip us for whatever He has in store for us…we just have to be willing to say, "I'll go."

MAY 19

No one can serve two masters. Either she will hate the one and love the other, or she will be devoted to the one and despise the other. You cannot serve both God and money. (Matthew 6:24)

Yet I hold this against you: You have forsaken your first love. (Revelation 2:4)

I pray that out of His glorious riches He may strengthen you with power through His Spirit in your inner being, so that Christ may dwell in your hearts through faith. And I pray that you, being rooted and established in love, may have power, together with all the saints to grasp how wide and long and high and deep is the love of Christ. (Ephesians 3:16–17)

You have made known to me the path of life; You will fill me with joy in Your presence. (Psalm 16:11)

I believe heaven calls us to be mirrors, reflectors of what we are learning and experiencing through our intimate relationship with Jesus. God doesn't ask us to "shine brightly" or "generate light," merely reflect it! In fact, as a Christian, I think it would be impossible for us not to "shine." We are only a prayer, thought, or whisper away from the Creator of the universe! God, who hung the stars, ordered the heavens, calmed the seas, raised the dead, and created us in our mother's wombs! THAT power, that authority! Our God is glorious and shines with brilliance and blinding light! The closer we get, the brighter we shine! So, friends, grab your sunglasses! You are loved with the unfathomable love of Christ!

MAY 20

Ascribe to the Lord the glory due His name; worship the Lord in the splendor of His holiness. (Psalm 29:2)

Bravo, God, bravo! Gods and all angels shout, "Encore!" In awe before the glory, in awe before God's visible power. Stand at attention! Dress your best to honor him! (Psalm 29:1–2, MSG)

Though you have not seen Him, you love Him; and even though you do not see Him now, you believe in Him and are filled with an inexpressible and glorious joy, for you are receiving the goal of your faith, the salvation of our souls. (1 Peter 1:8–9)

You never saw Him, yet you love Him. You still don't see Him, yet you trust Him—with laughter and singing. Because you kept on believing, you'll get what you're looking forward to: total salvation. (1 Peter 1:8–9, MSG)

Now if you obey Me fully and keep my covenant, then out of all nations you will be my treasured possession. Although the whole earth is mine. (Exodus 19:5)

We demolish arguments and every pretension that sets itself up against the knowledge of God, and we take captive every though to make it obedient to Christ. (2 Corinthians 10:5)

"Lord, take me where you want me to go,
Let me meet who You want me to meet.
Tell me what you want me to say.
And keep me out of Your way!"
(often prayed by Father Michael Judge who was
killed at the World Trade Center on 9/11/2001)

Almighty God, guide us today to be Your people who walk in Your will and are obedient to Your ways. May we be filled with inexpressible gratitude and glorious joy as we step out in faith, determined to listen for Your voice and humbled by Your Presence in our lives. Please give us the words to say as well as the wisdom to know when to be silent. We are genuinely thankful that it is not up to us to save the world, but help us to do our part to bring You glory with our lives. You have placed us here, in this time and in this place, for Your purposes. May we be women of faith who reflect brightly, speak wisely, and love extravagantly! We love You, Lord, we surrender our lives to You, and we thank You for Your goodness toward us. Amen.

MAY 21

You will keep in perfect peace her whose mind is steadfast, because she trusts in You. (Isaiah 26:3)

Lord, You establish peace for us; all that we have accomplished You have done for us. (Isaiah 26:12)

So we fix our eyes not on what is seen, but on what is unseen, For what is seen is temporary but what is unseen is eternal. (2 Corinthians 4:18)

Let us hold fast the confession of our hope without wavering, for He who promised is faithful. (Hebrews 10:23)

Therefore, my dear brothers and sisters, stand firm. Let nothing move you. Always give yourselves fully to the work of the Lord, because you know that your labor in the Lord is not in vain. (1 Corinthians 15:58)

May the Lord direct your hearts to the love of God and to the steadfastness of Christ. (2 Thessalonians 3:5)

Steadfast—firm and unwavering. Loyal, faithful, committed, devoted, dedicated, dependable, reliable, steady, true, constant, staunch, solid, trusty, determined, relentless, single-minded, unchanging, unwavering, unyielding, unflinching.

Lord, my mind is steadfast! Steady and true, I will strive to put one step ahead of the other in faith. Determined and relentless, I will seek You. With single-minded, unchanging, unwavering trust, I will praise You, and seek Your will for my life. For You, Father, determine our steps. Whatever we have accomplished, You have done for us. Whatever blessings we enjoy, they have come from Your hand.

Our salvation is a gift of pure grace. You know us better than we know ourselves, even the hair on our heads are numbered! Help us, we pray, to never take a single moment for granted. Every morning, when we wake up, may praise be the first thing on our lips, and as we close our eyes in slumber, may we be thanking You for the blessings of the day. For You alone are worthy of praise! You are our God, and we are Your daughters. We love You, and thank You. Amen

MAY 22

And we know that in all things God works for the good of those who love Him, who have been called according to His purpose. (Romans 8:28)

But as for me, I watch in hope for the Lord, I wait for God my Savior, my God will hear me. (Micah 7:7)

But the wisdom from above is first pure, then peaceable, gentle, open to reason, full of mercy and good fruits, impartial and sincere. (James 3:17)

I have said these things to you, that in Me you may have peace. In the world you will have tribulation. But take heart; I have overcome the world. (John 16:33)

A while back, I had the conversation with a couple of friends about having the chance to "do it all over." After giving it a little thought, I decided I would not want to start my life over even if I could. As I looked back over the events of my life, I was overwhelmed by how difficult so many of the times have been. I could clearly see where I had been, but there is still mystery left to where I am going! Of course if I did things over, I considered the possibility that I could change some of the mistakes I have made. Perhaps even affecting the outcome, but even if I could "redo" some of my decisions, there is still no guarantee of a change. So, reflecting on Romans 8:28, I will be content with how things have transpired and leave the results in God's hands. I will quit being so hard on myself and remember the words of Mother Teresa: "God doesn't call us to be perfect, just faithful." Perfection has not been, nor will it ever be, within my grasp!

But I can be faithful to the One who can fit all the pieces of my life, and yours, into a life of beauty and meaning that can be used for His purpose and His glory! So "shine on," friends, God's got this!

Have a great week remembering the fierce love of the Father that placed us here, in this time and in this place, for His purposes!

MAY 23

Let us come before Him with thanksgiving and extol Him with music and song. (Psalm 95:2)

This is the message we have heard from him and declare to you. God is light; in Him there is no darkness at all. (1 John 1:5)

This is the confidence we have in approaching God: that if we ask anything according to His will, He hears us. (1 John 5:14)

Look to the LORD and His strength; seek His face always. (1 Chronicles 16:11)

If my people, who are called by My name, will humble themselves and pray and seek My face and turn from their wicked ways, then I will hear from heaven, and I will forgive their sin and will heal their land. (2 Chronicles 7:14)

Reading the scripture in 1 John 5:14, my mind instantly went to times in my life when I felt God did not hear or answer my prayers. The first was many years ago in 1987 when God did not heal the daughter of a dear friend of mine of cancer, and she died at the age of two and a half! I was sooo angry at God! It was a real time of searching and questioning for me. And then my mind went over all the years of prayers for healing and restoration for our daughter and for a friend with ALS, again, I wondered many times, "Where are you, God? Don't you care? Am I praying wrong, living wrong? Why won't you answer?" So, this morning, when I was reminded "God is light; in Him there is no darkness," I remembered my ways are NOT His ways, and my thoughts are not His thoughts! We are all going to die someday. Most of us imagine we have seventy, eighty, ninety years, but, my friends, the number of our days is written in God's book before we are born. Some live days, some months, some die at two, some at thirty-two. God isn't deaf, nor is He cruel. Every day is a gift. We may not understand or like how this life plays out, but we can relax in the knowledge that God is not missing a thing. He is not uninterested, uncaring, or unable. We can approach His throne with confidence, knowing that He sees what is going on in our lives and in the lives of those we love. We can ask that His will be done and that we may have strength for whatever outcome is in store. Because, my dear sisters, God is good, He is light, in Him we find courage, encouragement and strength because He can be trusted! You are loved, called, and claimed by the Lord God Almighty! Nothing is impossible!

MAY 24

Do not be anxious about anything, but in everything by prayer and petition, with thanksgiving, present your requests to God. And the peace of God, which transcends all understanding will guard your hearts and your minds in Christ Jesus. (Philippians 4:6, 7)

Peace I leave with you; My peace I give you. I do not give to you as the world gives. Do not let your hearts be troubled and do not be afraid. (John 14:27)

Casting all your anxieties on Him, because He cares for you. (1 Peter 5:7)

But seek first the kingdom of God and His righteousness, and all these things will be added to you. Therefore, do not be anxious about tomorrow, for tomorrow will be anxious for itself. Sufficient for the day is its own trouble. (Matthew 6:33–34)

Humble yourselves, therefore, under the mighty hand of God so that at the proper time He may exalt you, casting all your anxieties om Him, because He cares for you. (1 Peter 5:6–7)

"Do not let your hearts be troubled"—now, that's a tall order! Is it even possible? I have to admit that many of the things—heck, the majority of the things I stew and fuss and worry about are completely out of my hands! Now, remembering that most of the things we worry about won't come to pass, and I am left with a sinking feeling that I have spent a large portion of my life worrying about problems I have NO control over or problems that may not even become problems if left where they belong—in the future! What a freeing reminder that "God's got this!" "My peace I give you, do NOT let your hearts be troubled!" It always seems to circle back to trust! Trust that God sees and cares for us, trust that He knows what is going on. He can handle people and situations we have no control over, and He will give us the strength and wisdom we need to see them through. I think sometimes we want so badly to spare our children or loved ones from life's pain that we forget to think about the strength and beauty of character that develops from trial and struggle. Many years ago, I read something to the effect, "Don't worry about other people's journeys, that is their journey and their life." God will use circumstances and people other than ourselves to mold them into the people He intends them to be. He's got them! Our part is to pray and encourage and, you know it, TRUST in the God who knows us—and them—better than we do!

So, take a deep breath, sisters. Hand your concerns over to God and trust in the One who is faithful, wise, all powerful, and all knowing. Let His peace guard our hearts and our minds! He's crazy about you!

MAY 25

The Lord replied, "My Presence will go with you, and I will give you rest." (Exodus 33:14)

Come to Me, all you who are weary and burdened, and I will give you rest. Take my yoke upon you and learn from Me, for I am gentle and humble in heart and you will find rest for your souls. For My yoke is easy and my burden is light." (Matthew 11:28–29)

"Are you tired? Worn out? Burned out on religion? Come to Me. Get away with Me and you'll recover your life. I'll show you how to take a real rest. Walk with Me and work with Me - watch how I do it. Learn the unforced rhythms of grace. I won't lay anything heavy or ill-fitting on you. Keep company with Me and you'll learn to live freely and lightly." (Matthew 11:28–29, MSG)

I love the message translation of Matthew 28–29! "Learn the unforced rhythms of grace...learn to live freely and lightly." My dear friends, sometimes we "try" so hard to do, say, even think the right things that our lives are anything but freely and joyously lived! Somewhere in this whole "religion" thing, we shift the focus from what God is doing to what we are doing! It doesn't have to be that way! Just as we are not created to be light "bearers" but rather light reflectors, we are also created by God to be filled, equipped, and renewed by God! Think of our lives as jars (not an original thought; you will find it in 2 Corinthians); we are made to be filled! In order to be of use, we must have something to give! God fills us with His love, His compassion, His wisdom, His joy, His energy, and His thoughts; and then He places us wherever He sees fit! We simply brim or spill over from the continual flow of His Spirit in our lives! Wearing or burning out is actually a result of "drying" out! We need to be filled, dear sisters! Every moment, every day, with the continual reminder of His love, concern, and intimacy in our lives so that He can fill us to overflowing with what He has for us! He is not asking us to give anything out of our own supply but rather out of the abundance He continually pours into our hearts, minds, and lives! So, quit trying so hard! Open your hearts to what God has for you and just be you! God will do the rest!

Have a wonderful day! You are greatly and eternally loved!

MAY 26

Humble yourselves therefore, under God's mighty hand, that He may lift you up in due time. Cast all your anxiety on Him because He cares for you. (1 Peter 5:6–7)

So be content with who you are, and don't put on airs. God's strong hand is on you, He'll promote you at the right time. Live carefree before God, He is most careful with you. (1 Peter 5:6–7, MSG)

Be joyful always; pray continually; give thanks in all circumstances, for this is God's will for you in Christ Jesus. (1 Thessalonians 5:18)

We plan the way we want to live, but only God makes us able to live it. (Proverbs 16:9 MSG)

My dear sisters, rest assured that God is indeed at work in your life. We may not always recognize Him or think He is fast enough, but He is there! That unexpected joy you feel at the oddest moments—God! That patience you find you have that is totally out of character for you—God! The compassion you feel for someone you don't even know—God! The desire to live a life pleasing to God—well, that too comes from God! The fruits of the spirit are: love, joy, peace kindness, gentleness, self-control, patience, and goodness. As we walk with God, He begins to do a number on our hearts, changing us from the inside out, making us more like Him! So, go ahead, live carefree before God, remembering that He is carefully, tenderly molding you into the woman He intends you to be! And He loves you like crazy!

MAY 27

And my God will meet all your needs according to His glorious riches in Christ Jesus. (Philippians 4:19)

We live by faith, not by sight. (2 Corinthians 5:7)

Jesus said to him, "if you can believe, all things are possible to him who believes." Immediately the father of the child cried out and said with tears, "Lord, I believe; help my unbelief!" (Mark 9:23–25)

I have spread out My hands all day long to a rebellious people, who walk in the way which is not good, following their own thoughts. (Isaiah 65:2)

Yet, with respect to the promise of God, he did not waver in unbelief but grew strong in faith, giving glory to God. (Romans 4:20)

Good morning! One of the most reassuring scriptures I have read is the one in the New Testament when the man asks Jesus to heal his daughter. Jesus asks, "Do you believe?" The man replies, "I believe, heal my unbelief." And get this, Jesus heals the man's daughter! The man basically admits he wants to believe, and does believe to some extent. In fact, he has tracked Jesus down to ask for the miracle, yet he still harbors some doubts and questions in his mind! Jesus knew this man's heart just as He knows ours! He knows our faith is a work in progress, that we sometimes question, wonder, and speculate about the goodness of God as we see the struggles and difficulties and downright unfairness of this life! It got me thinking, is my faith proportional to my willingness to surrender my unbelief? I immediately thought of the doubts of this man! Ladies, I want EVERYTHING God has for us—not only that, I want us to have EVERY-

THING God has in store for us! All the faith, strength and wisdom He has in supply. We serve a God of abundance! He is not giving out of a limited storehouse. He has gifts and surprises for us that we can't even imagine! So, today, my prayer will be, "Lord, I believe, please heal my unbelief!"

Have a great day! You are fiercely loved!

MAY 28

"Love the Lord your God with all your heart and with all your soul and with all your mind." (Matthew 22:37)

To shine on those living in darkness and in the shadow of death, to guide our feet into the path of peace. (Luke 1:79)

No longer do I call you servants, for the servant does not know what her master is doing; but I have called you friends, for all that I have heard from my Father I have made known to you. (John 15:15)

You are my friends if you do what I command you. (John 15:14)

To God belong wisdom and power; counsel and understanding are His. (Job 12:13)

Teach us to number our days, that we may gain a heart of wisdom. (Psalm 90:12)

As much as we may like the imagery of Jesus as our Friend and Lover of our soul, we must also recognize Him as King of kings and Lord over all! God is almighty, all-knowing, and all-powerful; and ultimately, what God wills for our lives will come to pass. I believe that scripture teaches us that God is more interested in where we will spend eternity than our comfort or ease in this life. I believe He is more interested in having us trust Him through the trial than removing our trials and problems.

Our God is indeed a God of great love and compassion, but let us not forget He is ultimately wise and in control of absolutely everything! So this week, let us hang on "loosely" to the things of this world and grasp tightly the hand of the Sovereign Lord who leads us and upholds us with His mighty right hand! I understand that there are many trials that I will not be able to face on my own, but I know the One who cannot only face but conquer anything we come up against in this life! It reminds me of a song I learned in my youth. "Many things about tomorrow, I can't begin to understand, but I know Who holds tomorrow, and I know He holds my hand!"

Hang on tightly, sisters, to the Hand holding yours!

MAY 29

God is spirit, and His worshipers must worship in spirit and in truth. (John 4:24)

"It's who you are and the way you live that count before God. Your worship must engage your spirit in the pursuit of truth. That's the kind of people the Father is out looking for; those who are simply and honestly themselves before Him in their worship. God is sheer being itself—Spirit. Those who worship Him must do it out of their very being, their spirits, their true selves, in adoration." (John 4:23–24)

For my thoughts are not your thoughts, neither are your ways My ways declares the Lord, As the heavens are higher than the earth, so are My ways higher than your ways and My thoughts higher than your thoughts. (Isaiah 55: 8–9)

Have you ever spent time with someone that you knew wanted something from you? Someone that was hanging around you for some ulterior motive? If you have, you have probably felt that frustration of being "used." I think that is what the scripture in John 4 is talking about. Jesus doesn't want some superficial "in it for what we can get out of it" type of followers. He wants our authentic selves. He wants our honest, heartfelt questions as well as our genuine praise and worship! He wants us to be genuinely open and sincere before Him. He isn't interested in hearing practiced prayers that have no connection to our hearts. He wants our tears, our frustrations, and our laughter! He wants ALL of us! And then He wants our lives to reflect what we believe! Oh, my dear friends, may we be known as women who "walk the walk," along with the talk! And may we enter into worship with sincere hearts and true adoration.

Remember that our thoughts are not God's thoughts, nor are our ways always His way! We are deeply loved, but, we are not in charge!

MAY 30

Now we see but a poor reflection as in a mirror; then we shall see face to face. Now I know in part; then I shall know fully, even as I am fully known. (1 Corinthians 13:12)

We don't yet see things clearly. We're squinting in a fog, peering through a mist. But it won't be long before the weather clears and the sun shines bright! We'll see it all then see it all as clearly as God sees us, knowing Him directly just as He knows us! (1 Corinthians 13:12, MSG)

What no eye has seen, what no ear has heard, and what no human mind has conceived" - the things God has prepared for those who love Him. (1 Corinthians 2:9)

You know the anticipation you feel when you are looking forward to a trip, exciting event, or a special recognition? I read somewhere that when planning a trip with your family, you will enjoy it more if you let everyone know well ahead of time so you can discuss, plan, and anticipate the journey together! It makes sense to me! Many, many years ago, we took our then very young daughters to Disney World. We let them know at Christmastime, and the next three months were spent in preparation and excited conversation about what we would experience. It was glorious! We were ALL so excited the night before we left for the trip that we could hardly sleep!

As for heaven, there are times when I think about what awaits us that I get that same feeling! In fact, one time, my granddaughter said to me, "Gramma, I don't want you to go" (somewhere, can't remember where I was going), and I asked her what she was afraid of.

She responded, "I don't want you to die." I went on to explain that I believe that if it is "my" time, I will die, regardless of where I am at. "When my time is up, it's up!" To which she replied, "I know, but you will probably be saying to God—take me now!" I chuckled and thought, "If you only knew, honey, how many times I have thought that very thought!"

I am curious what you think heaven will be like. Have you given it any serious thought? Let's begin to anticipate the destination together.

Have a wonderful day in the presence, protection, and love of our Father!

MAY 31

My purpose is that they may be encouraged in heart and united in love, so that they may have the full riches of complete understanding, in order that they may know the mystery of God, namely, Christ, in Whom are hidden all the treasures of wisdom and knowledge. (Colossians 2:2–3)

I'm a long way off, true, and you may never lay eyes on Me, but believe Me, I'm on your side, right beside you. I am delighted to hear of the careful and orderly ways you conduct your affairs, and impressed with the solid substance of your faith in Christ. (Colossians 2:5)

He will be the firm foundation for your times, a rich store of salvation and wisdom and knowledge; the fear of the Lord is the key to this treasure. (Isaiah 33:6)

I am with you and will watch over you wherever you go, and I will bring you back to this land. I will not leave you until I have done what I have promised you. (Genesis 28:15)

I will instruct you and teach you in the way you should go; I will counsel you with my loving eyes on you. (Psalm 32:8)

A couple of things spoke to me today in the scriptures, first of all that God sees us clearly. He sees how we handle our lives on a daily basis. He sees us on our best days and at our worst. He orders our days for what He is doing in our lives. A dose of trial to bring our minds back to the source of our strength (Jesus). And then on a daily basis He showers us with signs of His love. He surrounds us with beauty and then blesses us with the health and breath to enjoy it all! He challenges us through Scripture and through friends to consider what it is we believe and then He continuously gives us opportunity to live our faith out! The second thing that stood out for me in the scripture was that He watches us to see how we "conduct our affairs"—how we grow (or stagnate) in our faith, and He continues to prod us on, forward in our walk of faith, always mindful of the goal of our lives: love for God and love for others!

"The fear of the Lord is the key to this treasure." Any scriptures that speak of "fear of the Lord" have always thrown me for a loop! Why does God want us to fear Him? Doesn't it go against us "loving and trusting" Him? I am going to make an observation here that makes sense to me; take it for what it is worth. I think the fear referred to is intended to invoke reverence, submission, and utmost respect for God. I believe it is to remind us that God—in no way, shape, or form—needs us, but that without HIM, we are lost! I think it is a stern warning to take Him at His word! To take His authority and His word seriously, without putting our own "spin" on things. It is an admonishment to come to know Him in ALL His wisdom, Authority, and power and then to offer Him our heartfelt worship and praise—heck, even our lives as a response! After all, if God IS Who He says He is; and if HE can do what He says He can do, He is worthy of all praise, honor, and glory.! And if He is not, if His Word is outdated, old-fashioned, or in error, then, my sisters, we are fools!

Have a great day remembering to keep your eyes and hearts open for what God has in store for you today and be mindful always that you are greatly and eternally loved!

JUNE 1

For I Am the Lord your God, who takes hold of your right hand and says to you, Do not fear; I will help you. (Isaiah 41:13)

As for God, His Way is perfect; the word of the Lord is flawless. He is a shield for all who take refuge in Him. (Psalm 18:30)

Trust in the Lord with all your heart, and do not lean on your own understanding. In all your ways acknowledge Him, and He will make straight your paths. (Proverbs 3:5, 6)

I will instruct you and teach you in the way you should go; I will counsel you with my eye upon you. (Psalm 32:8)

Almighty God, as You led Your people in days of old, lead us today, we pray. Keep us mindful always of Your authority, power, and control over all the difficult and confusing detours we encounter on the way. Help us to remember that You are with us always. We need only to pause and bring our hearts back to You to enjoy the light of Your presence throughout our day.

Take hold of our right hands and lead us into a life of compassion, kindness, and service that You have prepared for us in advance. Protect us with the shield of Your love so that the arrows of this life are deflected from doing any damage to our faith and bring us home, wrapped in Your loving arms! Let us never forget the price that You paid for each and every one of us. As we stumble and misstep, forgive us, Lord. Nudge us back into the way You have intended for us. Pick us up, dust us off, and send us on our way again so that our lives may bring You honor and glory! Thank you for the gifts along the way; the beauty of this day, the laughter of friends and families, food, shelter, and health to enjoy it all! We love You, Lord. Help us to never take You, or Your gifts for granted! Amen.

JUNE 2

Don't let the wise brag of their wisdom. Don't let hero's brag of their exploits. Don't let the rich brag of their riches. If you brag, brag of this and this only: That you understand and know Me. I'm God, and I act in loyal love. I do what's right and set things right and fair, and delight in those who do the same things. These are my trademarks"—God's Decree. (Jeremiah 9:23–24, MSG)

Be still, and know that I am God; I will be exalted among the nations, I will be exalted in the earth. (Psalm 46:10)

Dear friends, now we are children of God, and what we will be has not yet been made known. But we know that when He appears, we shall be like Him, for we shall see Him as He is. (1 John 3:2)

This is eternal life, that they may know You, the only true God, and Jesus Christ whom You have sent. (John 17:3)

We become more like God the more we develop our intimate relationship with Him. After all these years, it still amazes me that God wants to know me intimately, and that He wants me to know Him intimately! This relationship we are in with our Heavenly Father is not intended to be a casual one. He wants our devotion, our secrets, our repentance, and our very hearts! He never intended to be our "Sunday Friend" but rather our Confidant, our Teacher, our LORD! He walks with us every—catch it—*every* step of our lives and gently calls to us, "Here I am…lean on Me… I've got this"

Today, cease striving and lean into the loving arms of the Father! He's got you and He will never leave you!

JUNE 3

Love must be sincere. Hate what is evil; cling to what is good. (Romans 12:9)

Love from the center of who you are; don't fake it. Run for dear life from evil, hold on for dear life to good. Be good friends who love deeply, practice playing second fiddle. (Romans 12:9, 10, MSG)

Loves does no harm to a neighbor. Therefore love is the fulfillment of the law. (Romans 13:10)

And now these three remain; faith, hope and love. But the greatest of these is love. (1 Corinthians 13:13)

Be completely humble and gentle; be patient, bearing with one another in love. (Ephesians 4:2)

Above all, love each other deeply, because love covers over a multitude of sins. (1 Peter 4:8)

There is no fear in love. But perfect love drives out fear, because fear has to do with punishment. The one who fears is not made perfect in love. (1 John 4:18)

There is no room in love for fear. Well-formed love banishes fear. Since fear is crippling, a fearful life—fear of death, fear of judgment - is one not yet fully formed in love. (1 John 4:18, MSG)

A friend loves at all times, and a brother is born for a time of adversity. (Proverbs 17:17)

I imagine it is fair to say we have all wanted to "run away" on occasion! If I am honest, I will admit that there have been many, many times when I have uttered "I can't do this God…" Running away from everything in my life seemed like a good option! But I think it was love that kept me where I was. Love for my family and a desire to persevere, to walk through whatever was going on, so I could get to the other side. I will admit that life sometimes feels less like a normal "ebb and flow" and more like a tidal wave! Holding fast to God in those times is like holding on to a life preserver, holding on for dear life because you fear the next wave is the one that is going to drown you. And silently hoping that maybe it will! Dark, hard times. We ALL experience them. They are, after all, a part of this life on earth. The good news—heck, great news—is that we don't have to run away! God gives us the strength and wisdom to "hold on," to persevere, to rise again to victorious living! God is good, dear sisters, even in the midst of the most difficult of times. We just need to trust that He has a plan. To trust that He is working things out for good— that there is more to what is going on than we can see. When we hold on, even with shaking hands and broken hearts, God is glorified; and if we listen, we can hear, "Well done, good and faithful servant!"

Never forget, sisters, that God has our backs! He loves us, encourages us, and directs our steps! Don't waiver—the world needs your light!

JUNE 4

We demolish arguments and every pretension that sets itself up against the knowledge of God, and we take captive every thought to make it obedient to Christ. (2 Corinthians 10:5)

We use our powerful God-tools for smashing warped philosophies, tearing down barriers erected against the truth of God, fitting every loose thought and emotion and impulse into the structure of life shaped by Christ. (2 Corinthians 10:5, MSG)

Set your minds on things above, not on earthly things. (Colossians 3:2)

Don't shuffle along, eyes to the ground, absorbed with the things right in front of you. Look up, and be alert to what is going on around Christ—that's where the action is. See things from HIS perspective. (Colossians 3:2, MSG)

More than anything you guard, protect your mind, for life flows from it. (Proverbs 4:23)

Do not be conformed to this world, but be transformed by the renewing of your mind, so that you may prove what the will of God is, that which is good and acceptable and perfect. (Romans 12:2)

As a woman thinks...so she is. If we focus on our inadequacies, our weaknesses, our flaws, we begin to think that those things define us. We believe that the world sees those blaring defects in us when they look at us. We begin to carry ourselves in a way that states, "Don't look at me, I'm nothing special." When in fact, if we listen, the Bible tells us something completely different! God calls us "His children," "His beloved," "heirs to His kingdom," "His ambassadors"!

Of course we can all admit to thoughts that are not God pleasing in regard to someone else (our husbands, our circumstances). But personally, most of the negative thoughts I have are aimed squarely at myself! I can belittle myself so severely before I even step out of the house in the morning that my thoughts are anything but pleasing to God. "I am so heavy, out of shape, dumb, unmotivated," the list goes on and on. Destructive, negative thoughts—lies of the enemy!

I think that if we could begin to view ourselves at God sees us, if we would begin to believe that we ARE indeed who HE says we are, if we would grab on with both hands to the truth about our identity in Christ, we would become the "light" that overcomes the darkness in and around us!

My dear sisters, those annoying and destructive cussing thoughts are only that—thoughts! They need to be swatted away like an annoying insect! A serious refocus is called for when those thoughts come flooding in! God is light! In HIM there is no darkness at all! No dark thoughts, no dark moods, and no dark unforgiveness of ourselves or others! Let's move forward this week and choose to live the legacy that God has given us as His children! Children of Light! Have a great week!

JUNE 5

Y et to all who did receive Him, to those who believed in His Name, He gave the right to become children of God. (John 1:12)

But you are a chosen people, a royal priesthood, a holy nation, God's special possession, that you may declare the praises of Him who called you out of darkness into His wonderful light. (1 Peter 2:9)

But you are the ones chosen by God, chosen for the high calling of priestly work, chosen to be a holy people, God's instruments to do His work and speak out for Him, to tell others of the night-and-day difference He made for you—from nothing to something, from rejected to accepted. (1 Peter 2:9)

No longer do I call you servants, for a servant does not know what his master is doing; but I have called you friends, for all things that I heard from My Father I have made known to you. (John 15:15)

See, I have inscribed you on the palms of My hands. (Isaiah 49:16)

Put on the new woman which was created according to God, in true righteousness and holiness. (Ephesians 4:24)

I imagine we have all felt the rejection and the hurt that followed when we "weren't invited, weren't chosen" weren't given the athletic uniform, the cheerleader uniform, etc. Unfortunately, many of us have, at least for a moment, hung our identity on that rejection. "I'm not accepted, good enough, not liked." My dear sisters, our identity is in WHOSE we are, not in how we "feel" at any given moment.

"The world may tell us we're too much and never enough."

"But we can walk wildly in who God created us to be and rest freely in the work Jesus did for us."

"We do not have to be confined or conformed by cultural expectations."

"We choose compassion over comparison."

"We love without condition, without reserve."

"Our eyes are on God; we hold nothing back; we run fast and strong; we do not hide our light."

"We aren't wild and free for our sake alone; rather we sing life, hope, and truth over the world with abandon - just as God sings over us."

"We are wild and free."

"And we are poised to do mighty things, in Christ alone."

from Wild and Free by Jess Connelly and Haley Morgan.

When we buy into the lies of the enemy, we shrink back from who God created us to be. "We have been given great authority through Christ! We're called to action! Ladies, you are not called to sit on your hands in silence. You are called by our great God to run wild into our culture, calling out an incredible message of life: God loves you! World! God loves you and made a way for you! Come with me! You don't have to live lost and alone! My Dad has a place for you! He sees you as His ultimate treasure!" From Wild and Free.

Dear friends, let your light shine and your life leak Jesus on anyone in your path!

JUNE 6

Do you not know that those who run in a race all run, but only one receives the prize? Run in such a way that you may win. (1 Corinthians 9:24)

I press on toward the goal for the prize of the upward call of God in Christ Jesus. (Philippians 3:14)

Therefore, since we have so great a cloud of witnesses surrounding us, let us also lay aside every encumbrance and the sin which so easily entangles us, and let us run with endurance the race that is set before us. (Hebrews 12:1)

I have fought the good fight, I have finished the course, I have kept the faith. (2 Timothy 4:7)

Our lives here are not a sprint! They are a marathon! We need to refuel, refresh, and rest if we are to run well the race set before each and every one of us! I have found throughout the years that when I focus on my exhaustion and my fatigue, I become really weary and tired! I have often heard myself repeating to myself, "I am exhausted, I am tired." You know the feeling that resulted? Weariness! Instead, I have begun to train myself to repeat, "This too shall pass, I can continue, I can do this!" As we think, so very often we feel and become! I know, sisters, that this race of life can be exhausting! I know that you grow weary and tired, that you feel at times you can't take another step! But YOU CAN! Life is short! Run hard! We may be imperfect, and our race may look more like a run through a maze than a straight run to the finish line, but I can promise you, God has run with you every step of the way, no matter what your personal race looks like!

With our last breath, may we all utter, "I have fought the good fight, I have finished the course, I have kept the faith."

JUNE 7

B ut You, O Lord are a God merciful and gracious, slow to anger and abounding in steadfast love and faithfulness. (Psalm 86:15)

The steadfast love of the LORD never ceases; His mercies never come to an end; they are new every morning; great is Your faithfulness. (Lamentations 3:22–23)

But the Lord is faithful. He will establish you and guard you against the evil one. (2 Thessalonians 3:3)

Let us hold fast the confession of our hope without wavering, for He who promised is faithful. (Hebrews 10:23)

For am I now seeking the approval of man, or of God? Or am I trying to please man? If I were still trying to please man, I would not be a servant of Christ. (Galatians 1:10)

But just as we have been approved by God to be entrusted with the gospel, so we speak not to please man, but to please God who tests our hearts. (1 Thessalonians 2:4)

The fear of man lays a snare, but whoever trusts in the Lord is safe. (Proverbs 29:25)

The fear of human opinion disables, trusting in God protects you from that. (Proverbs 29:25, MSG)

For they loved the glory that comes from man more than the glory that comes from God. (John 12:43)

Whatever you do, work heartily, as for the Lord and not for men. (Colossians 3:23)

Now faith is the assurance of things hoped for, the conviction of things not seen. (Hebrews 11:1)

And without faith it is impossible to please Him, for whoever would draw near to God must believe that He exists and that He rewards those who seek Him. (Hebrews 11:6)

If we are honest, I think we would all admit that there have been moments in our lives when we have simply felt underqualified and insufficient for the tasks at hand. In those moments in my own life, when things were spinning out of control and my faith felt weak, small, and dying, I simply cried out, "Help, God!" It was all I could muster! Just "HELP!" Watching as a dear friend holds her two and a half year old daughter dying of Leukemia... "Help, God!" Sitting alone with my dad as he lay dying, gasping for breath, "HELP, GOD!" Upon hearing a dear friend's diagnosis... "Help, God!" Our daughter's multiple disappearances, crying phone calls and hospitalizations... "Help, God!" I had nothing to give, nothing to offer! I felt the world chaotically spinning around me and felt myself slipping into the abyss. I was not strong. I was being held by the hand of the Father. Because of these experiences and more not mentioned, I can honestly say, "God is faithful!" I remember crying out at one point to God, "I don't know who you think I am, but You are giving me more than I can handle!" I remember being embraced by the thought, "I know YOU can't, but I can!"

My dear sisters, I wish I knew why life has to be so incredibly hard for so many. I don't have any answer other than it is because we live in a fallen world. God doesn't promise us anywhere in scripture that our lives will be easy. But He does promise us that He will give us strength when we have none. That He will be with us always...and reward us for our faithfulness. The thing is, in my peanut logic anyway, life is difficult whether you are a Christian or not! But without the mighty hand of God guiding, nudging, and holding us, I can't imagine making it through this life with any sense of sanity left! God is good! God is FOR us! Life is hard, but praise God! We don't have to do it alone!

God's got this, friends! He will see us through and hold us when we cannot stand on our own! Hang in there, don't abandon your faith... It's gonna be good! The best is yet to come!

JUNE 8

Lord, You are my God; I will exalt You and praise Your name, for in perfect faithfulness You have done wonderful things, things planned long ago. (Isaiah 25:1)

Let everything that has breath praise the Lord. Praise the Lord. (Psalm 150:6)

Praise the Lord, my soul; all my inmost being, praise His Holy Name. (Psalm 103:1)

Give thanks to the Lord, for He is good; His love endures forever. (1 Chronicles 16:34)

I say to the Lord, "You are my Lord; apart from You I have no good thing." (Psalm 16:2)

Now to Him who is able to do immeasurably more than all we ask or imagine, according to His power that is at work within us, to Him be glory in the church and in Christ Jesus throughout all generations, for ever and ever! (Ephesians 3:20–21)

God, don't let me down! I'll run the course You lay out for me if You'll just show me how. God, teach me lessons for living so I can stay the course. Give me insight so I can do what You tell me—my whole life one long, obedient response. (Psalm 119:32–34, MSG)

Almighty Lord, Commander of the angel armies, Heavenly Father, forgive our stubbornness and our desire to live life on our terms.

We confess that "our flesh seeks the approval of others, is swayed by Satan's voice of condemnation, and looks for the comfortable way out." We acknowledge that more often than not, we listen to this voice of condemnation telling us we will "never be good enough" or "worthy" to be called Your children. Remind us, Lord, that "none of this is about us—it's all about You!" May our lives so reflect Your light, Your goodness, and Your faithfulness that others cannot help but notice and give You the glory! Give us hearts of worship, Lord! Hearts filled with praise and thanksgiving for all you have done for us. Hearts that anxiously await what You have in store for us! Hearts that believe that You are up to something that is far greater than all we ask or imagine! Hearts that grasp, if even for an instant, this incredible powerful Spirit that is at work within us! Lord, we love You! We admit we do not always understand Your ways or Your timing; but we desire Your insight, Your wisdom, Your counsel to run well the course you have laid before us! Help us not neglect where You have placed us so that in doing so, we miss why You have placed us there. We need You to do this life well...to become all that You intended us to be! Help! We surrender our lives to You! Use us for Your glory, and when our assignment here is done, bring us home! So be it. Amen.

You are loved more than you can imagine... God does indeed have a plan in all of the things going on in your lives and the lives of those you love! He is surrounding you, working in the details. Trust Him!

JUNE 9

For am I now seeking the approval of man, or of God? Or am I trying to please man? If I were still trying to please man, I would not be a servant of Christ. (Galatians 1:10)

But just as we have been approved by God to be entrusted with the gospel, so we speak not to please man, but to please God who tests our hearts. (1 Thessalonians 2:4)

The fear of man lays a snare, but whoever trusts in the Lord is safe. (Proverbs 29:25)

The fear of human opinion disables, trusting in God protects you from that. (Proverbs 29:25, MSG)

For they loved the glory that comes from man more than the glory that comes from God. (John 12:43)

Whatever you do, work heartily, as for the Lord and not for men. (Colossians 3:23)

There have been more times in my life than I would care to admit when I have been caught up in "people pleasing." Times when I misspoke, spoke too much, or did something stupid when I worried "they must think I am such an idiot!" Honestly, there are still times when I get caught up in others' opinions of me…but slowly, I am coming to the realization that what my heart craves more than the approval of my peers is the approval of my Father. My prayer on most days is, "Lord, may I speak today what is pleasing to You. May my words lift up and encourage today… May my thoughts be light and life today." Of course I fail. I stumble, lose my temper, get frustrated. That's when I need to refocus. Actually pray for direction, seek counsel from scripture, and remember Who I represent on a daily basis! Scripture reminds us that we are Christ's "ambassadors!" Called to reflect Jesus in our daily walking around, going to work lives! We need to stay "plugged in" to the Source of this light in order to be effective in the dark, stumbling world!

Shine on, sisters! We reflect a most amazing, spectacular, almighty God! It's HIS opinion that matters! He loves us, guides us, and protects and empowers us to live lives that please Him!

JUNE 10

For you were formerly darkness, but now you are Light in the Lord; walk as children of Light (for the fruit of the Light consists in all goodness and righteousness and truth), trying to learn what is pleasing to the Lord. (Ephesians 5:8–10)

You groped your way through that muck once, but no longer. You're out in the open now. The bright light of Christ makes your way plain. So no more stumbling around. Get on with it! The good, the right, the true—these are the actions appropriate for daylight hours. Figure out what will please Christ, and then do it. (Ephesians 5:8–10, MSG)

Therefore we also have as our ambition, whether at home or absent, to be pleasing to Him. (2 Corinthians 5:9)

Cheerfully pleasing God is the main thing, and that's what we aim to do, regardless of our conditions. Sooner or later we'll all have to face God, regardless of our conditions. We will appear before Christ and take what's coming to us as a result of our actions, either good or bad. (2 Corinthians 5:9, 10, MSG)

So that you will walk in a manner worthy of the Lord, to please Him in all respects, bearing fruit in every good work and increasing in the knowledge of God. (Colossians 1:10)

But just as we have been approved by God to be entrusted with the gospel, so we speak, not as pleasing men, but God who examines our hearts. (1 Thessalonians 2:4)

Hard as we may try, dear sisters, we can never be enough for everyone in our lives. We cannot "fix" their problems, determine their steps, or "give" them faith in God. As a parent, believe me, I have tried! We are ALL given free will to live our lives however we want to. That "will" drastically changes, however, when we come to Christ and claim Him as our Lord and Savior! Slowly, over time and trial and error, God changes "our" will into "His" will for our lives. We may not realize that it is happening, but the Holy Spirit convicts, corrects, and directs our thoughts and motives to look more and more like Christ's! As we grow closer to Christ through relationship with Him, we do indeed begin to "walk in a manner worthy of the Lord, pleasing to Him, bearing fruit and increasing in knowledge." Our individual "walks" may not look like a straight line, but praise God, He is patient with us and diligent in His pursuit of us! God loves us, friends… He has a purpose for placing us here, in this time and in this place! We have places to go, people to meet, and light to share! Walking in a manner pleasing to God has a positive effect on everyone around us! Shine on, sisters!

JUNE 11

Love is patient, love is kind, it is not envious. Love does not brag, it is not puffed up, it is not rude, it is not self-serving, it is not easily angered or resentful. It is not glad about injustice, but rejoices in the truth. It bears all things, believes all things, hopes all things, endures all things. (1 Corinthians 13:4–7)

To sum up, all of you be harmonious, sympathetic, brotherly, kindhearted, and humble in spirit. (1 Peter 3:8)

Summing up; Be agreeable, be sympathetic, be loving, be compassionate, be humble. That goes for all of you, no exceptions. No retaliation. No sharp-tongue sarcasm. Instead bless—that's your job, to bless. You'll be a blessing and also get a blessing. (1 Peter 3:8, MSG)

But I say to you who listen; Love your enemies, do what is good to those who hate you, bless those who curse you, pray for those who mistreat you. (Luke 6:27, 28)

Instead of being motivated by selfish ambition or vanity, each of you should, in humility, be moved to treat one another as more important than yourself. Each of you should be concerned not only about your own interests, but about the interests of others as well. (Philippians 2:3, 4)

There have been a number of occasions when I have been asked to work with a woman that I find difficult. This woman openly admits and speaks poorly about other women. She comments that "American women are so judgmental and critical"

She is extremely intelligent and educated and an asset to working in global missions, so she has much to add to a missions board.

On one occasion, I had a chance to sit and talk with her, one on one. I saw the hurt that motivated her feelings and was able to say to her, "I don't know the women you are speaking about, the women I know and love are not anything like the women you describe. My women friends are kind, compassionate, generous, and strong!" Now, I do know that there are a lot of judgmental people around us, causing many to believe our churches are filled with self-righteous, judgmental folks. But, my dear sisters, I believe that we are ALL broken and in need of a Savior! We are all a "work in progress," and frankly, life is too short to spend our time judging and second-guessing others! Let's let God judge and give Him time to mold us into the women He intended us to be!

Almighty God, we come before Your throne of mercy, grace, and forgiveness with anxious anticipation. Thankful that You are not finished with us yet! Thankful that You can mend what is broken, bent, and out of place in our lives and transform us into women of Proverbs 31 proportions! We freely acknowledge that on our own, we are lost and frightened. We become quick to judge and condemn. But oh, Father, when we keep our eyes on You alone, we no longer feel the need to judge or be critical because our eyes are no longer focused inward but looking toward You, the Author and Perfecter of our faith! Forgive us of our "cattiness" our "smirks" our unkind remarks and instead help us grow in love, joy, peace, patience, kindness, faithfulness, thankfulness, goodness, and self-control and leave the rest to You. Thank You for never giving up on us! We love You, and we need You. In Jesus's holy, powerful name, so be it. Amen!

JUNE 12

Behold, the eye of the Lord is on those who fear Him, on those who hope in His steadfast love, that He may deliver their soul from death and keep them alive in famine. (Psalm 33:18, 19)

For I know the plans I have for you, declares the Lord, plans for welfare and not for evil, to give you a future and a hope. (Jeremiah 29:11)

But those who hope in the Lord will renew their strength, they will soar on wings like eagles; they will run and not grow weary, they will walk and not be faint. (Isaiah 40:31)

May the God of hope fill you with all joy and peace as you trust in Him, so that you may overflow with hope by the power of the Holy Spirit. (Romans 15:13)

The world's hope is a "hope-so," but the Christian's view of hope is a "know-so." The scriptures are full of verses on hope. These verses remind us over and over and over again that God is FOR us! That He wants us to turn to Him with any and all of the things that bother, upset, confuse, or exasperate us. Personally, I think that God wants us to turn our attention to Him so that He can turn our attention away from ourselves! We can become so consumed with the "problem of the day" that we are blinded to everything else going on in and around us. God is constantly at work. He is working in our circumstances even when we don't see it. God uses everything in the lives of His children for His purposes and for the good of His people. That being said, disappointment with our circumstances—whether it is our relationships, our finances, our jobs—goes on. Disappointment, very often, overshadows the joy and peace that God promises for those who trust in Him. I think that perhaps one of the reasons we become disappointed is because we don't believe that God really is in the details, that He really has our best interests at heart.

My dear friends, God is FOR us! Everywhere and every day, God is for us!

JUNE 13

Oh yes, You shaped me first inside then out; You formed me in my mother's womb. I thank You, High God—you're breathtaking! Body and soul, I am marvelously made! I worship in adoration—what a creation! You know me inside and out, You know every bone in my body; You know exactly how I was made, bit by bit, how I was sculpted from nothing into something. Like an open book, You watched me grow from conception to birth; all the stages of my life were spread out before You, the days of my life all prepared before I'd even lived one day. (Psalm 139:13–16, MSG)

You made me; You created me. Now give me the sense to follow Your commands. May all who fear You find in me a cause for joy, for I have put my hope in Your word. (Psalm 119:73, 74)

Yet You, LORD, are our Father. We are the clay, You are the potter; we are all the work of Your hand. (Isaiah 64:8)

For we are His workmanship, created in Christ Jesus for good works, which God prepared beforehand, that we should walk in them. (Ephesians 2:10)

You know when I sit down or stand up. You know my thoughts even when I'm far away. You see me when I travel and when I rest at home. You know everything I do. You know what I am going to say even before I say it, LORD. (Psalm 139:2–4)

I enjoy the writing of Max Lucado. One of the books that gave me a lot of things to think about was *Cure for the Common Life*.

In that book, Max writes about our children. Paraphrasing, he writes, "Our children come hard-wired from God. We have eighteen years to figure out who they are, and then encourage them on that path." My dear sisters, WE have all been delivered to this world "hard-wired" by the Hand of God! We have each been given strengths, passions, and gifts. Things that we love to do, things that excite us and get our creative thoughts going. God knew what He was doing when He knit each one of us together in our mother's wombs. The desires and skills He gave you aren't necessarily the ones He gave me! We are each uniquely made. Crafted by the Potter's hands for His purposes. We all have places to go, things to do, and people to meet. God's "wisdom has to do with becoming skillful in honoring our parents and raising our children, handling our money and conducting our sexual lives, going to work and exercising leadership, using words well and treating friends kindly, eating and drinking healthily, cultivating emotions within ourselves and attitudes toward others that make for peace. Threaded through all these items is the insistence that the way we think and respond to God is the most practical thing we do. In matters of everyday practicality, nothing, absolutely nothing, takes precedence over God" (Eugene Peterson).

So, in closing, if you have one of those "strong-willed" children or grandchildren or if you are wondering about what God's purpose for your own life is, examine your (or your child's) strengths, the things that get your hearts racing and toes tapping—God "wired" those things into you. I would bet that His will for you or your child has something to do with what He has already placed within you! God is in the details. He desires for our children as well as for each of us to rise to the potential of all He created us to be! To grow in HIS wisdom to live lives that reflect Him! Be unique! Be all you were created to be! As it is often said, "Be yourself! Everyone else is already taken!" Have a great day! You are deeply loved by the God Who placed you here, in this time and place, for His purposes!

JUNE 14

All Scripture is God-breathed and is useful for teaching, rebuking, correcting and training in righteousness, so that the servant of God may be thoroughly equipped for every good work. (Timothy 3:16, 17)

We have different gifts, according to the grace given to each of us. If your gift is prophesying, then prophesy in accordance with your faith; if it is serving, then serve; if it is teaching, then teach; if it is to encourage, then give encouragement; if it is giving, then give generously; if it is to lead, do it diligently; if it is to show mercy, do it cheerfully. (Romans 12:6–8)

Before I was afflicted I went astray, but now I obey Your work. You are good, and what You do is good; teach me your decrees. (Psalm 119:67, 68)

But the Advocate, the Holy Spirit whom the Father will send in My name, will teach you all things and will remind you of everything I have said to you. (John 14:26)

The heavens declare the glory of God; the skies proclaim the work of His Hands. Day after day they pour fourth speech; night after night they reveal knowledge. (Psalm 19:1, 2)

God speaks through whatever or whomever He chooses but never in disagreement with the Bible. (Job 33:14)

I think it is fair to say that every one of us wants to hear from God. We want to be able to discern His voice and respond with a whole-hearted "Yes, Lord!" The six scriptures above tell us six ways God uses to communicate with us: (1) God speaks to us through scripture. (2) God speaks through gifted teachers whose source is the Bible. (3) God speaks to us through difficulties. (4) God speaks through impressions of the Holy Spirit. (5) God speaks through His creation. (6) God speaks through whatever or whomever He chooses but never in disagreement with the Bible.

My dear sisters, God continues to speak today, just as He did in Scripture. He speaks, guides, and protects now, just as He did then!. God is at work among us! In our circumstances, in our hearts and our minds, He is continually moving, molding, protecting, and guiding! He is moving in community, our churches, and our relationships. My prayer is that He will open our eyes to see and our minds to believe that God is with us, that He is FOR us, and that He is good! You are loved! Believe it!

JUNE 15

But if anyone loves God, she is known by God. (1 Corinthians 8:3)

So now that you know God (or should I say, now that God knows you), why do you want to go back again and become slaves once more to the weak and useless spiritual principles of this world? (Galatians 4:9)

O Lord, You have searched me and known me. (Psalm 139:1)

But the LORD said to Samuel, "Do not look at his appearance or at the height of his stature, because I have rejected him; for God sees not as a man sees, for man looks at the outward appearance, but the LORD looks at the heart." (1 Samuel 16:7)

That I may know Him and the power of His resurrection and the fellowship of His sufferings, being conformed to His death. (Philippians 3:10)

"I Am the good shepherd, and I know My own and My own know Me." (John 10:14)

One of my favorite books is *Not a Fan*. It talks about being a fan or follower of Jesus Christ and goes into detail about the difference. A "fan" might know all about someone, their stats, accomplishments, likes and dislikes, etc. But a follower knows the person themselves. A follower has a relationship with this person. I think these scriptures are referencing the same vein of thought. Jesus says in John 10:14, "I know My own and My own know Me."

I have coveted over the years the solid faith I have witnessed in others. I remember when I was a very young wife and mother, listening to the women in my church's women's group (Sunshine

Circle) and wondering, "How did they get where they are in their relationship with Jesus? How can they be so sure in their faith and trust?" What resulted was a desire to spend time with Jesus, to study scripture and learn more about God. I started out in 1982 thinking, "I will read the Bible and pray fifteen minutes a day," figuring that if I did, in one week, I would have spent one hour and forty-five minutes alone with God, learning His word. It didn't sound like much at fifteen minutes a time, but I liked the thought of almost two hours a week! It was hard; I failed often, was distracted frequently, and struggled to fit the fifteen minutes into my day. Sometimes, my fifteen minutes was in the middle of the night! Our oldest had croup, and nights were looooong! She could sleep being held, so hold her I did. When she would fall off in fitful slumber, I would continue to hold her, read a chapter of Scripture, and pray. Eventually, early mornings became my 15-minute prayer time. Over time, it became a routine. Early morning it was. That was what worked best for me. I remember praying as I would fall asleep on busy or long days, "Lord, wake me up for my time with You if it is important to You." I will never cease to be amazed that—without fail—God woke me up! My fifteen minutes became thirty, forty-five, sixty, and sometimes even longer. My time with God literally flew by, and my relationship with the Living God grew! That being said, I know that I will never know all there is to know about God, not even close! But I also consider God my friend, confidant, and Savior! I realize how utterly dependent I am on Him to lead, guide, and encourage me in my faith. We are on a journey together, and I sincerely bounce on eager toes of anticipation thinking about the day I get to meet Him face-to-face!

My dear sisters, God is pursuing you!! He wants relationship, closeness, friendship with His children. He wants to be the first person you turn to in any situation and the last person on your mind as you fall asleep! He loves us more than our little minds can comprehend! To paraphrase Matthew 7:24, 25, the words of God are not incidental additions to my life or simple improvements to my standard of living. They are foundational words! Words to build a life on!

JUNE 16

W ho is it that overcomes the world? Only the one who believes that Jesus is the Son of God. (1 John 5:5)

Yet to all who did receive Him, to those who believed in His Name, He gave the right to become children of God. (John 1:12)

Whoever believes in the Son has eternal life, but whoever rejects the Son will not see life, for God's wrath remains on them. (John 3:36)

Whoever believes in Me, as Scripture has said, rivers of living water will flow from within them., (John 7:38)

I pray that out of His glorious riches He may strengthen you with power through His Spirit in your inner being, so that Christ may dwell in your hearts through faith. And I pray that you, being rooted and established in love, you'll be able to take in with all followers of Jesus the extravagant dimensions of Christ's love. (Ephesians 3:16, 17)

When we trust in Him, we're free to say whatever needs to be said, bold to go wherever we need to go. (Ephesians 3:12, MSG)

"Faith is not just a small part of our life; it is central to all that we do" (author unknown).

Almighty God, here we are again, standing in Your presence, seeking to grow in faith, in trust, and in obedience. When we read stories of those that are radically obedient to You, we are encouraged, strengthened, and grow bolder in our own faith walk. Lord, we desire to grow in obedience, even to the point of radical obedience, whatever that may look like in each of our lives! May we learn to ask the question, "What would it look like to trust You in this situation?" Whether we need trust with a difficult time in our marriage, for challenges with our children, our coworkers, our family, or with our relationships. What if we trust You to first develop us into the women of faith you called us to be and then released the timing of all the other situations to You? What if we trusted You to mold us, sustain us, stretch us into more than we ever imagined we could be? What if we truly believed that You alone are more than we will ever need. What if we surrendered with open hands everything You have entrusted to us? What if...what if we trusted You, surrendered our doubts when they arose, squashed our fears, focused our minds on You, and believed that You are ALL You say You are? Help us, Father. On our own, we will fail, but You are sufficient! You desire to draw us closer and closer to Yourself. Hold us, guide us, strengthen us to move forward in faith. Use us, Lord, for Your purposes and for Your glory! We love you, we need you, and we praise You! Thank You for how You are moving in our lives. Be with those we love, with our nation and our world. May Your light shine so brightly through Your children that the world cannot help but notice and be drawn to You! So be it. Amen!

JUNE 17

Now may the Lord of Peace Himself give you peace at all times and in every way. The Lord be with all of you. (2 Thessalonians 3:16)

Submit to God and be at peace with Him; in this way prosperity will come to you. (Job 22:21)

Be still before the LORD, all mankind, because He has roused Himself from His holy dwelling. (Zechariah 2:13)

Be still and know that I am God! I will be honored by every nation. I will be honored throughout the world. The Lord of Heaven's Armies is here among us; the God of Israel is our fortress. (Psalm 46:10–11)

The LORD will fight for you while you keep still. (Exodus 14:14)

The LORD is in His holy temple. All the earth be quiet in His presence. (Habakkuk 2:20)

Being still is what the scriptures this morning are about. There is a quote by Ram Dass that goes, "The quieter you become, the more you can hear."

Many, many years ago, when I started with morning devotions, being still was the hardest part of what I did. It took me ages to get to a point where I could "still" my mind and focus on just being in God's presence. Now, I realize we are always in God's presence, but bringing my mind and thoughts to focus just on Him and His Word was the hard part! There are always distractions, a "to do" list that looms large, and sitting in silence and prayer seems time consuming! But the rewards—ahhh…the rewards! I have found strength when I had none. I have found patience when mine was spent. I have felt loved and forgiven when I have not deserved it, and I have discovered that the Lord of the universe has a sense of humor! And that He desires for me to live fully, freely, and joyfully for however long I have on this earth. He has given me a family who loves me. Friends who bring me great joy…and work to do that engages my mind, body, and soul! So now, if there are mornings when I don't have time for prayer and to sit in His presence, I find that He either wakes me up really early (sometimes 4:00 or 5:00 a.m.). If I don't take the time, I feel deprived of something that has become very important to me. Being "still" in the presence of my Lord, listening for His voice, His promptings, and feeling His comfort, love, and presence! I promise you, it is worth any lack of sleep or sacrifice you need to make to make it happen! God loves us, sisters, with a HUGE, FIERCE passion! He wants ALL of us, not just our Sunday morning best! He wants us at our lowest, ugliest, and most unhappy times as well. He promises to transform us by the renewing of our minds! Who wouldn't want that!

JUNE 18

Look to the Lord, and His strength; seek His face always. (Psalm 105:4)

The heavens declare the glory of God; the skies proclaim the work of His hands. Day after day they pour forth speech; night after night they display knowledge. (Psalm 19:1–2)

See, darkness covers the earth and thick darkness is over the peoples, but the Lord rises upon you, and His glory appears over you. (Isaiah 60:2)

Thus says the LORD, Who gives the sun for light by day and the fixed order of the moon and the stars for light by night. Who stirs up the sea so that its waves roar; the LORD of hosts is His name. (Jeremiah 31:35)

To Him who made the great lights, For His lovingkindness is everlasting; the sun to rule by day, for His lovingkindness is everlasting, The moon and stars to rule by night, for His lovingkindness is everlasting. (Psalm 136:7–9)

The scripture in Psalm 19 says, "Day after day (the heavens) pour forth speech; night after night they display knowledge." I have wondered about this particular scripture before. This morning, it seemed to me that what this might mean is as Christians, we look at the heavens, stars, sun, and moon and acknowledge their beauty and thank God their creator; but as scientists, we want to know, "What's out there? How does it work?" We are blown away by the sheer vastness of space, and we realize that we cannot begin to comprehend it in its entirety. Yet day after day, after day, after day, great minds are uncovering the speech of the heavens; and day after day, they are learning more and more of the Creative Force behind the heavens! I don't believe for a second that God wants us to have a blind faith! A faith that "follows" without question. I believe God wants us to be diligent in figuring out what we believe, and why we believe it! He is not afraid or intimidated by our questions. He speaks to the great minds of our time by pouring forth "speech and knowledge" from the heavens so that scientists can study and understand. And He speaks to us! Sometimes in a whisper, sometimes with a shout! He speaks in a way that we can understand, and says to anyone who will listen, "I AM GOD! There is no one else like Me! Test Me, search Me out! Try and find fault with Me! Then, when you have done your 'due diligence,' trust Me and lean on Me, and I will be with you always!"

Have a great week remembering that the Hand that hung the stars is holding you!

JUNE 19

Don't fuss about what's on the table at mealtimes or if the clothes in your closet are in fashion. There is far more to your inner life than the food you put in your stomach, more to your outer appearance than the clothes you hang on your body. Look at the ravens, free and unfettered, not tied down to a job description, carefree in the care of God. And you count far more. Has anyone by fussing before the mirror ever gotten taller by so much as an inch? If fussing can't even do that, why fuss at all? Walk into the fields and look at the wildflowers. They don't fuss with their appearance—but have you ever seen color and design quite like it? The ten best-dressed men and women in the country look shabby alongside them. If God gives such attention to the wildflowers, most of them never even seen, don't you think He'll attend to you, take pride in you, do His best for you? What I'm trying to do here is get you to relax, not be so preoccupied with getting so you can respond to God's giving. People who don't know God and the way He works fuss over these things, but you know both God and how He works. Steep yourself in God-reality, God-initiative, God-provisions. You'll find all your everyday human concerns will be met. Don't be afraid of missing out. You're my dearest friends! The Father wants to give you the very kingdom itself. (Luke 12:22–32, MSG)

"I have told you these things so that in Me you may have peace. In this world you will have trouble. But, take heart! I have overcome the world." (John 16:33)

I have been aware for quite some time that worry is contrary to scripture. That we are warned about worry and advised not to worry but to trust...but really? How can we NOT worry? When things spiral out of control, when loved ones are sick, when marriages fall apart, how can we avoid worry? Honestly, I don't know! I worry, fret, and stew till my stomach hurts! I KNOW God says He will take care of me. I KNOW He says don't worry, but it is almost a default setting in my head! Bad news—worry!

So, today, the reminder not to worry but trust that God will take care of even the ordinary, everyday things in my life is encouragement to me. A reminder that God is faithful even in the smallest details! If He is concerned about the clothes on my back and the hairs on my head, then I can trust that He's got the big, scary stuff as well!

Have a wonderful, stress-free, worry-free day! You are loved!

JUNE 20

Above all, love each other deeply, because love covers over a multitude of sins. (1 Peter 4:8)

There is no fear in love. But perfect love drives out fear, fear has to do with punishment. The one who fears is not made perfect in love. (1 John 4:18)

Yet I hold this against you: You have forsaken your first love. (Revelation 2:4)

If I speak in the tongues of men or of angels, but do not have love, I am only a resounding gong or a clanging cymbal. If I have the gift of prophecy and can fathom all mysteries and all knowledge, and if I have a faith that can move mountains, but do not have love, I am nothing. If I give all I possess to the poor and give over my body to hardship that I may boast, but do not have love, I gain nothing. (1 Corinthians 13:1–3)

Charles Spurgeon said, "We believe in the providence of God, but we do not believe half enough of it."

What if we are worried, frightened, and fearful and there is absolutely no reason to be? What if we assume the worst and live accordingly? What if God "helps those who help themselves"? What if we are on our own and there is no such thing as divine intervention? What if God really isn't interested in the details of our lives, our problems, or our souls? What if it is all up to us? Then, my dear sisters, we are in trouble with a capital T! But PRAISE GOD that is NOT the case! God's word is full of evidence to the contrary! Philippians 4:5, 6: "The Lord is near. Do not be anxious about anything…"

Isaiah 65:24: "I will answer them before they even call to Me, while they are still talking about their needs. I will go ahead and answer their prayers."

We serve a God who is present, interested, and involved in the details of our lives! He calls us to live in the light of His love, to reflect His glory and to light the way for those who may follow us! So get out there, torchbearers! This world is in desperate need of love and light!

Have a great day! And watch for God at work! He is ordering our circumstances. His unseen hand is guiding, guarding, arranging, and rearranging circumstances! Can you see Him?

JUNE 21

"I have loved you with an everlasting love; I have drawn you with loving kindness." (Jeremiah 31:3)

I delight greatly in the Lord; my soul rejoices in my God. For He has clothed me with garments of salvation and arrayed me in a robe of righteousness, as a bridegroom adorns his head like a priest, and as a bride adorns herself with her jewels. (Isaiah 61:10)

But you are a chosen people, a royal priesthood, a holy nation, a people belonging to God, that you may declare the praises of Him who called you out of the darkness into His wonderful light. (1 Peter 2:9)

I love the scriptures that speak of God's "ownership" of us.

"I have loved you, Becky, Sherryl, Evelyn, Kim, Carmen, with an everlasting love... Before time began, I knew you, Marilyn, Margie, Lori, Barb, Leslie. I knit you together in your mother's wombs... I prepared the date and times of your birth...and of your death. I see you struggles, your success's and your joy! I weep when you weep and celebrate with you in your happiness! I AM ever present, ever watchful, and all knowing! Nothing, absolutely nothing takes Me by surprise or is too difficult for Me! You are My chosen, My beloved, My daughters! I have called you each by name into My wonderful light so that your lives might be lived close to Me and for My glory!"

You are not a happenstance, accident, or incident but a wonderful work of art signed by the Creator Himself! Don't settle for an ordinary life; you were created to be extraordinary!

Embrace this day... You are fiercely loved!

JUNE 22

So we fix our eyes not on what is seen, but on what is unseen. For what is seen is temporary, but what is unseen is eternal. (2 Corinthians 4:18)

And they were calling to one another: "Holy, holy, holy is the Lord Almighty; the whole earth is full of His glory." (Isaiah 6:3)

I wait for the Lord, my soul waits; and in His word I put my hope. (Psalm 130:5)

I will give them a heart to know Me, for I am the LORD; and they will be My people, and I will be their God, for they will return to Me with their whole heart. (Jeremiah 24:7)

Because she has focused her love on Me, I will deliver her. I will protect her because she knows My name. When she calls out to Me, I will answer her. I will be with her in her distress. I will deliver her, and I will honor her. (Psalm 91:14–15)

Hebrews 12:1 is one of my favorite scriptures: "Therefore, since we are surrounded by such a great cloud of witnesses, let us throw off everything that hinders and the sin that so easily entangles, and let us run with perseverance the race marked out for us…let us fix our eyes on Jesus, the author and perfecter of our faith."

Hard to get this little mind around the fact that there is much going on around us each and every day that we cannot see with our mortal eyes. The Bible refers to a great cloud of witnesses watching our steps, cheering us on! So then, how DO we fix our eyes on what is unseen? Is it even possible? I think that is exactly what "faith" is about. Believing that God sees each situation, each problem, each person and not only knows what's going on, but understands the hidden motives, the fear, brokenness, and reasoning behind every thought. He sees the condition of our hearts, and, dear sisters, He cares! He calls out to us to "come to Me, take every thought captive, search for Me, and you will find Me!" He alone is the "author and perfecter" of our faith. In Him, we have "eyes to see and ears to hear." In Him we place our hope!

JUNE 23

In the same way, let your light shine before others, so that they may see your good works and give glory to your Father who is in heaven. (Matthew 5:16)

What good is it, my brothers (sisters), if someone says they have faith but does not have works? Can that faith save them? If a brother or sister is poorly clothed and lacking in daily food, and one of you says to them, "Go in peace, be warmed and filled," without giving them the things needed for the body, what good is that? So, also faith by itself, if it does not have works, is dead. (James 2:14–17)

For we are God's workmanship, created in Christ Jesus to do good works, which God prepared in advance for us to do. (Ephesians 2:10)

He has showed you O man, what is good. And what does the Lord require of you? To act justly and to love mercy and to walk humbly with your God. (Micah 6:8)

Did you catch it? The verse in Ephesians 2 comes directly after one of the most quoted scriptures in the Bible!

Verses 8–9: "For it is by grace you have been saved, through faith - and this not from yourselves, it is the gift of God—not by works, so that no one can boast." Then verse 10 goes on to say that we have been created to do good works! Seems to me that somewhere along the way, we have taken in, stopped at, and concluded with "For it is by grace you have been saved!" We have chosen to stop there and not continue on to our part that speaks of doing what God has prepared in advance for us to do. Now, I know this is a slippery slope, so to speak; we need to be so careful not to get caught up in "good works" and "earning salvation" (which by the way is clearly impossible!). But these scriptures today leave me with the distinct impression that God DOES expect something from us? In fact, Micah asks the question, "What does the Lord REQUIRE of you?" Thinking about this makes my heart jump and my pulse race! My first thought being, what do I need to do? Then I calm back down and remember, all that is required of me is to put my heart where my mouth is. God will do the rest. If we continue to live in relationship with God and seek His direction and wisdom for our lives, HE will work within us to desire His "will and to act according to His good purposes." After all, He is the Director of this show that we call our lives. God is the One who arranges circumstances and directs our steps. Our part is to stay close to Him. I think of it like this: when we were children, our parents took us by the hand and led us where they wanted us to go they "directed" us, so to speak. God does the same...if we don't pull our hand away and throw a tantrum! He will take us where He wants us for His purpose and for His glory. Our part is to hang on to the Hand that is holding ours! Hang on tight, friends! It's going to be quite the adventure! You are loved!

JUNE 24

Let the morning bring me word of your unfailing love, for I have put my trust in You. Show me the way I should go, for to You I lift up my soul. (Psalm 143:8)

I am with you and will watch over you wherever you go, and I will bring you back to this land. I will not leave you until I have done what I have promised you. (Genesis 28:15)

The Spirit of the Lord God is upon me, because the LORD has anointed me to bring good news to the afflicted; He has sent me to bind up the brokenhearted, to proclaim liberty to captives and freedom to prisoners; to proclaim the favorable year of the LORD and the day of vengeance of our God; to comfort all who mourn. (Isaiah 61:1–2)

Behold, My servant, whom I uphold; My chosen one in whom My soul delights I have put My spirit upon her; she will bring forth justice to the nations. (Isaiah 42:1)

Good morning, friends! Isn't it good to know that God will equip us with exactly WHAT we need WHEN we need it? He won't load us down with everything we need for the journey (days) ahead, but rather, He will supply what we need at exactly the right moment, when we need it! Remember, He is traveling right beside us throughout our days. In fact, I can't help but think He is already looking ahead to all of our tomorrows, packing our bags, knowing exactly what we will need!

Psalm 143:8 has long been one of my favorite verses in Psalms and one I committed to memory long ago. For me, it shifts the focus of my thoughts and days to Him. For in the morning, I lift my thoughts heavenward, putting my trust in Him and asking for direction on the way I should go.? Then reminding Him (and myself) that I am His, for to Him alone I surrender my soul; my steps are in His Hands!

Have a great week, ladies! As for me, I am bouncing on eager toes of anticipation waiting to see what God has in store for this week!

Never, ever, ever forget Whose you are and how fiercely He loves you! Guard your hearts from anything or anyone who tells you otherwise! Have a great day!

JUNE 25

In the morning, O Lord, You hear my voice; in the morning I lay my requests before You and wait in expectation. (Psalm 5:3)

O God, You are my God; earnestly I seek You; my soul thirsts for You, in a dry and weary land where there is no water. (Psalm 63:1)

I can do everything through Him who gives me strength. (Philippians 4:13)

Look to the LORD and His strength; seek His face always. (1 Chronicles 16:11)

God did this so that they would seek Him and perhaps reach out for Him and find Him, though He is not far from any one of us. (Acts 17:27)

And without faith it is impossible to please God, because anyone who comes to Him must believe that He exists and that He rewards those who earnestly seek Him. (Hebrews 11:6)

Good morning, lovely ladies! God has certainly proven to me that once again, He will take care of things! He has answered prayers concerning my mother. She is getting "up there" in years and needs a little additional assistance, so some changes had to be made. Not only did my mother agree to leave her home of over fifty-five years and move across the state to where I could help. But God, in a weekend, found a place for us to buy for her to live! All that stressing I did, worrying about what we were going to do—WHAT A WASTE!

The scripture today in Psalm 63 where it says, "My soul thirsts for You, in a dry and weary land where there is no water" makes me question, "do I thirst for God like that?" Do I desire Him so desperately that I can compare it to looking for water in the desert? There have been times in my life (during crisis) where I have desperately cried out to Him to intervene, but on a day-to-day basis? The walking around, eating, going to work, daily everydayness of life, do I seek Him with that kind of passion? With that kind of desperation? No. I don't. And it is to my detriment! God desires ALL of us, my dear sisters, on our "good" days as well as our "bad." He desires our laughter as well as our sorrows! So this morning, I am inviting Him along with me every moment of my day! Who knows where we may venture together?

Have a great day! You are greatly and eternally loved!

JUNE 26

Therefore, since we are receiving a kingdom that cannot be shaken, let us be thankful, and so worship God acceptably with reverence and awe, for our "God is a consuming fire." (Hebrews 12:28–29)

Message translation; Do you see what we've got? An unshakable kingdom! And do you see how thankful we must me? Not only thankful, but brimming with worship, deeply reverent before God. For God is not an indifferent bystander. He's actively cleaning house, torching all that needs to burn, and He won't quit until it's all cleansed. God Himself is Fire!

Your word is a lamp to my feet and a light for my path. (Psalm 119:105)

For the LORD your God is a consuming fire, a jealous God. (Deuteronomy 4:24)

"Our God is a consuming fire!" Not exactly what I particularly like to think of Him as! I like loving, watchful, protective, saving God! But, dear sisters, we must not blind ourselves to the truths in the Bible. The truths that can be uncomfortable! God alone is worthy of praise! The Bible says that "every knee WILL bow and EVERY tongue will confess that He ALONE is God!" It reminds us that our God is a jealous God. He will not tolerate our worship of things or idols other than Himself. He will not be mocked, and we WILL reap what we sow! Sobering thoughts this morning, but also a reminder that God has chosen to give us each another day to pick ourselves up, look to Him, and seek His will for our lives. There are places to go and things to do before we rest our heads! Let us be mindful always that the Lord of the universe, God, who hung the moon and flung the stars into space, goes with us! We are never abandoned or forgotten. This God of the consuming fire is fiercely jealous of our souls! And He loves us with a passion we cannot begin to understand! So step out boldly, friends! Our God is FOR us and WITH us!

JUNE 27

I'm praying not only for them but also for those who will believe in Me because of them and their witness about me. The goal is for all of them to become one heart and mind—just as you, Father, are in Me and I in You. So they might be one heart and mind with us. Then the world might believe that You, in fact, sent Me. The same glory You gave me, I gave them, so they'll be as unified and together as We are—I in them and You in Me. (John 17:20–23, MSG)

For even young people tire and drop out, young folks in their prime stumble and fall. But those who wait upon God get fresh strength. They spread their wings and soar like eagles, they run and don't get tired, they walk and don't lag behind. (Isaiah 40:29–31, MSG)

He has filled the hungry with good things; and sent away the rich empty-handed. (Luke 1:53)

When you set her free, you shall not send her away empty-handed. (Deuteronomy 15:13)

So, I have been thinking this morning about what it means to come to God with "empty hands." What I have come up with thus far is no agenda of my own, no hidden motives (I'll worship you if...), no conditions, and no expectations of what God is going to do. Either I trust God completely and believe that He knows all things, understands all things, and addresses all things, or I hang on to the details that I think I can control or manipulate and divide up the things I am carrying. "I'll take this issue, God, you take this one," etc. To be honest, very rarely do I come before God with "empty"

hands! I generally come to Him with my carefully crafted "list!" Today, my prayer will be, "Father, you see us, and know us completely! You know when we wake up, wash our faces, have our coffee and go about our day. You know the words out of our mouth before we speak them. You know the intent of our heart and the weariness of our bodies. You go before us and know everyone and everything we will experience today. You go behind us to encourage us on. So, today, we surrender this day to you—all of it! May we live in a way that is pleasing to you, and may we so reflect Your light that the people you place in our paths cannot help but notice. Amen.

May you walk through your day remembering always that you are fiercely loved!

JUNE 28

And surely I am will you always, to the very end of the age. (Matthew 28:20)

O Lord, you have searched me and you know me. You know when I sit and when I rise; you perceive my thoughts from afar. You discern my going out and my lying down; you are familiar with all my ways. Before a word is on my tongue you know it completely, O Lord. (Psalm 139:1–4)

Psalm 139 has always been one of my favorite chapters in the Psalms. It goes on in verse 23 to say "Search me, O God, and KNOW my heart; test me and know my anxious thoughts." I have always wondered about the fear that some feel about confessing sin and mistakes to God. I don't understand it. He knows it all anyway! He even knows WHY we did what we did, said what we said, or didn't do what we should have. So, why then is there hesitation to lay our sins and failures before Him? I think it has more to do with us. I remember thinking, "If I surrender all to Him, that includes everything I have, right? What if He wants me to give it all away? What if He gets tired or angry with me always messing up? What if I am of no use to God?" The list goes on.

My dear sisters, God created you in your mother's womb. He placed you here, in this time, in this place, for HIS purpose, for His glory. And, we can relax in the knowledge that God DOESN'T make mistakes!

So, today, ask God to search you heart, to bring to your mind what you are afraid of, what you are holding on to, what you need to ask forgiveness for, and surrender it to Him. Then, sit back with your mind and heart open to God's healing, and restoring power; allow Him to work miracles in your life! He knows all about you anyway and loves you more than you can imagine!

JUNE 29

I have told you these things, so that you might have peace. In this world you will have trouble. But, take heart! I have overcome the world. (John 16:33)

I've told you all this so that trusting me, you will be unshakable and assured, deeply at peace. In this godless world you will continue to experience difficulties. But, take heart! I've conquered the world! (John 16:33, MSG)

She will have no fear of bad news; her heart is steadfast, trusting in the Lord. (Psalm 112:7)

Even in darkness light dawns for the upright, for the gracious and compassionate and righteous woman. (Psalm 112:4)

I have always loved the prosperity gospel taught from many a pulpit! The only problem is, it really isn't Biblical! I would LOVE to think that once we become a Christian, our lives would be easy. No family issues, no money issues, no marital issues—smooth sailing! Right? Why wouldn't God remove all the trouble and heartache from our lives when we turn to Him? As much as I love that idea, I think He is too good a "Father" for that. I have come to believe that this life is a test, a journey under God's watchful guidance. He allows things in our life that are difficult. He stands beside us through every trial; He cheers us on; He encourages us through His word, friends, family; but He allows us to "think" we are on our own. Only when we shift our focus from ourselves to Him do we see that we are NEVER alone. God is ahead of us preparing a way, encouraging us forward, nudging us from behind. But why does it have to be so hard? I sometimes wonder. That, dear friends, I honestly don't know. But I rest in the assurance that God does! Nothing, absolutely nothing, He does is ever wasted! I have been moved to tears in my life by the reassurance and comfort of friends in difficult times, by the kindness of strangers who have heard our story, by the doors opened with others by admitting our struggles and frustrations. I don't know what God is up to, but I know the One who has allowed the trials, and that is enough!

Have a great day! May you remember always the One who walks beside, ahead, and behind you in great love!

JUNE 30

Let the peace of Christ rule in your hearts, since as members of one body you were called to peace. And be thankful. (Colossians 3:15)

Immediately, something like scales fell from Saul's eyes, and he could see again. He got up and was baptized. (Acts 9:18, NIV)

And again they shouted: "Hallelujah! The smoke from her goes up for ever and ever." The twenty-four elders and the four living creatures fell down and worshiped God, who was seated on the throne. And they cried: "Amen, Hallelujah!" Then a voice came from the throne, saying: "Praise our God, all you His servants, you who fear Him, both small and great!" Then I heard what sounded like a great multitude, like the roar of rushing waters and like loud peals of thunder, shouting: "Hallelujah! For our Lord God Almighty reigns." (Revelation 19:3–6, NIV)

Enter his gates with thanksgiving and his courts with praise; give thanks to him and praise his name. For the Lord is good and his love endures forever, his faithfulness continues through all generations. (Psalm 100:4, 5, NIV)

Have you heard the phrase "attitude of gratitude"? It is a call to action on our part. I don't believe *worship* is a passive word, but rather a call to engage! A call for us as believers to get off our duffs and praise and thank our God for what he has done, is doing, and is going to do in our lives and in the lives of our families, friends, and even the women reading this devotional!

Do you have the faith to believe that God IS who He says He is? Do you believe that He can DO what He says He can? If you can wrap your mind around the fact that He IS precisely Who He says He is…there is nothing that is too hard for Him or goes unnoticed by Him…there is cause for celebration (a.k.a. praise and worship)! I will be the first to admit that many times, I haven't a clue what He is up to; or how He is going to work in the details, but, by returning my thoughts to the fact that God knows precisely the what and why, and when I remember that He can use anything for good, I can relax!

Enjoy your day, friends, remembering that Jesus died for you, intercedes for you along with the Holy Spirit, and loves you deeply and eternally!

JULY 1

Trust in the Lord with all your heart and do not lean on your own understanding. In all your ways acknowledge Him and He will make your paths straight. (Proverbs 3:5, 6)

Delight yourself in the Lord and He will give you the desires of your heart. Commit your way to the Lord, trust also in Him and He will do it. (Psalm 37:4, 5)

Now to Him who is able to do far more abundantly beyond all that we ask or think, according to the power that works within us. (Ephesians 5:20)

For God has not given us a spirit of fear, but of power, love and sound mind. (1 Timothy 1:7)

I can do all things through Him who strengthens me. (Philippians 4:13)

My dear sisters, I don't honestly know what God has in store for each one of you. Heck, I have no idea what God has in store for me either! However, I do know that our lives have a profound effect on the lives around us. We each hold a circle of influence and affect others in a way we may be unaware of. Even our "mood of the day" has an effect on the people around us! We can daily choose how we want to live this life that God has gifted us with. I fully understand that it is no easy task to juggle all the things going on in our lives and still have the time and desire to live our life intentionally and with forethought. But honestly, I think that is what a lot of scripture asks us to do. It reminds us to think about the attitude that we will bring with us into our day. It asks us to trust in God with ALL our hearts and not try to figure everything out. It asks us to "delight" in the Lord, to be pleased with what He is doing in and around us, to commit our ways, words, actions and thoughts to Him. To live our lives openly and with joyous expectation before Him! I don't know if you noticed, but the scriptures above also were filled with responses from God when we live in the way mentioned. "And, He will make your paths straight." He will work out the details. "He will give you the desire of your heart." "He will do it." "He is able to do far more than we can imagine, plan or conceive!" "He who is able to do far more abundantly beyond all that we ask or think." "He has given us a spirit of power, love and a sound mind!"

My dear friends, we can indeed do ALL things God lays in front of us through His power that strengthens us! Dream big! Live bold, carefree lives before God! When we surrender to Him, He is in the details and promises to "direct our steps! "Let's live our lives every day so empowered by God's Spirit within us that the enemy dreads the moment we wake! Shine bright and dream BIG! God's power and wisdom is beyond anything we can imagine, and He is FOR us!

JULY 2

I can do all this through Him who gives me strength. (Philippians 4:13)

He gives strength to the weary and increases the power of the weak. (Isaiah 40:29)

My soul is weary with sorrow; strengthen me according to Your word. (Psalm 119:28)

Finally, be strong in the LORD and in His Mighty Power! (Ephesians 6:10)

But those who hope in the LORD will renew their strength. They will soar on wings like eagles; they will run and not grow weary, they will walk and not be faint. (Isaiah 40:31)

God is our refuge and strength, an ever-present help in trouble. (Psalm 46:1)

I fear that we have spent so much time and energy trying to become the women the world calls us to be that we have misplaced our authentic selves. The selves that God called and created us to be. We are trying so hard to master the steps to a dance that we were never called to dance. I don't believe that God is asking us to "run the show" or "drive the car" of our lives. Rather, I believe He is asking us to "catch the wind"—more like a sailboat. "The last resort in a sailboat is to row it." I think God is calling us to show up each day and align our lives with the Wind-Giver! It's about dropping the oars and opening ourselves up to where God is moving in our lives. It's about keeping our eyes focused solely on Him, through the triumph, the tears, the missteps and trips! Friends, God is FOR us! Our lives are empowered by HIS love and imagination! His dreams are way better than anything we can dream up on our own! We don't need to try so hard to "perform" or fit some mold that we think would be pleasing to God! The best way to please God is to do the things He sets before us each and every day! The ordinary, uneventful things that make up our daily lives. In the book *Wonderlife* (where this vein of thought stems from) Mike Foster writes, "The ministry of guacamole making, warm hug giving and packing kids lunches is just as significant as fighting the evils of human trafficking. You may not think so, but God does. He never called us to be famous, only faithful."

This week, moment by moment, lock your eyes on the eyes of our Savior. Feel His love surrounding you, His power protecting you, and His Arms wrapped around you! He's got whatever is going on in your life. Honestly, I don't think He is nearly as concerned about our happiness as about our wholeness!

JULY 3

Let the peace of Christ rule in your hearts, since as members of one body you were called to peace. And be thankful. (Colossians 3:15)

Make every effort to live in peace with everyone and be holy; without holiness no one will see the Lord. (Hebrews 12:14)

Work at getting along with each other and with God. Otherwise you'll never get so much as a glimpse of God. (Hebrews 12:14, MSG)

They must turn from evil and do good; they must seek peace and pursue it. (1 Peter 3:11)

Peacemakers who sow in peace reap a harvest of righteousness. (James 3:18)

Real wisdom, God's wisdom, begins with a holy life and is characterized by getting along with others. It is gentle and reasonable, overflowing with mercy and blessings, not hot one day and cold the next, not two-faced. You can develop a healthy, robust community that lives right with God and enjoy its results only if you do the hard work of getting along with each other, treating each other with dignity and honor. (James 3:17–18, MSG)

The LORD gives strength to His people; the LORD blesses His people with peace. (Psalm 29:11)

Almighty God, we come before Your throne this morning offering our hearts, minds, and bodies for Your service. Father, we want Your peace. The peace that flows over the obstacles and difficulties in our lives and grows stronger, more purposeful, and gains determined direction as it flows along! We love You, we thank You, and we worship You today with our thoughts and with our lives.

May we shine so bright in the reflection of Your love that others cannot help but take notice and worship You! Without You, Lord, we are lost, wandering aimlessly through this life. Our lives amounting to nothing more than chaff blowing in the wind. Ahh, but with You, O LORD, our lives become purpose-driven, powerful, and useful in Your hands! Use us up for Your glory, and when our work here is done, bring us home to Your wonderful presence! In Jesus's holy name. Amen.

Well, friends, tomorrow is the Fourth of July! A day for fireworks and BBQs! I encourage you to do something fun! Something happy and silly and memorable! Life is short, live BIG!

JULY 4

Walk with the wise and becomes wise, for a companion of fools suffers harm. (Proverbs 13:20)

Whatever you do, work at it with all your heart, as working for the Lord, not for human masters. (Colossians 3:23)

And let us consider how we may spur one another on toward love and good deeds. not giving up meeting together, as some are in the habit of doing, but encouraging one another - and all the more as you see the Day approaching. (Hebrews 10:24–25)

One who has unreliable friends soon comes to ruin, but there is a friend who sticks closer than a brother. (Proverbs 18:24)

Humble yourselves, therefore, under God's mighty hand, that He may lift you up in due time. Cast all your anxiety on Him because He cares for you. (1 Peter 5:6, 7)

Sisters, this daily practice of scripture readings and notes from me is for nothing if it doesn't draw us closer to God! As pleased as it makes me to think that something I wrote encourages you, it doesn't matter one little bit if it doesn't draw you deeper in relationship with your Lord and Savior!

I don't know about you, but I KNOW that I NEED reliable friends, friends that stick "closer than a sister" that "spur me on toward love and good deeds," that encourage me in my faith and in my relationship with God. It is much too easy for me to put "all things God" on the back burner of my life for another time or another day. The enemy is constantly telling us that there are other things far more pressing, urgent, or important than our time with God. But honestly, friends, there is absolutely nothing more important than our relationship with Christ. Not only because of where we will spend eternity (which is HUGE) but also because of how we will spend our day-to-day lives, our walking around, going to work, eating and drinking, laughing, and crying lives! Through relationship is how God molds and morphs us into the women He called us to be! Here and now, in this exact time in life, in whatever place He has placed you! That's where God wants you and me. I cannot say that I "get it," but my prayer is that we all will "press on toward the goal to which God has called us heavenward in Christ Jesus." Or as the Message translation puts it in Philippians 3:12–14: "I'm not saying that I have this all together, that I have it made. But I am well on my way, reaching out for Christ, Who has so wondrously reached out for me. Friends, don't get me wrong; by no means do I count myself an expert on all of this, but I've got my eye on the goal, where God is beckoning us onward—to Jesus. I'm off and running, and I'm not turning back!"

Join me?!

JULY 5

For where your treasure is, there your heart will be also. (Matthew 6:21)

Whoever loves money never has enough; whoever loves wealth is never satisfied with their income. This too is meaningless. (Ecclesiastes 5:10)

Keep your lives free from the love of money and be content with what you have, because God has said, "Never will I leave you; never will I forsake you." (Hebrews 13:5)

"No one can serve two masters, Either you will hate the one and love the other, or you will be devoted to the one and despise the other. You cannot serve both God and money." (Matthew 6:24)

Tell those rich in this world's wealth to quit being so full of themselves and so obsessed with money, which is here today and gone tomorrow. Tell them to go after God, who piles on all the riches we could ever manage - to do good, to be rich in helping others, to be extravagantly generous. If they do that, they'll build a treasury that will last, gaining life that is truly life. (1 Timothy 6:17–19, MSG)

Money...OUR money! We can talk about a lot of things, but don't talk about how we spend our money! Actually, the Bible is full of scriptures about money. Money and possessions are mentioned more than eight hundred times in the Bible. My dear friends, everything we have is a gift from our Lord, Savior, and Provider! The air we breathe—gift! The lungs, body, health, minds, abilities—gift! Absolutely everything we have, enjoy, or take for granted has been provided for us by our God! God is in the details. I have to honestly admit that it was easier for me to say to God, "Lord I surrender my life to You," than it was for me to say, "Lord, where do you want me to spend Your money?" Did you catch the shift in thinking? Until I was finally able to realize that "my" money was actually "God's" money I hung on with clenched fists. When I finally understood that the money in my pocket and bank accounts was God's, it was much easier to surrender! Believe me, I am still a work in progress just as much as anyone else, but a turning point came for me years ago when a friend and I took a bunch of kids to Acquire the Fire in Denver. One of the speakers said, "God has a lot of money, we just need to figure out whose pockets it's in" (when talking about raising money.) I remember thinking, "Is the money in MY pocket God's?"

My dear sisters, God doesn't need our money. He wants our hearts! Heck, He wants ALL of us, not our leftovers, and He knows that wealth, security, and "things" stand in the gap between Him and our total surrender to Him. Don't even get me started on this topic! But...since I am... God also wants us to surrender our children/grandchildren/loved ones to HIM! No STRINGS ATTACHED! It's a lot to take in! And first, we need to come to the point in our faith where we believe that God does indeed love us and have our best lives in mind for us when He tests, pushes, and convicts us. We have to get to a point when we can say honestly, "Lord, I believe You are Who You say You are! I believe that You can do what You say You can do! Heal my unbelief!"

Friends, God is FOR us! Who could dare stand against!

JULY 6

It is absolutely clear that God has called you to a free life. Just make sure that you don't use this freedom as an excuse to do whatever you want to do and destroy your freedom. Rather, use your freedom to serve one another in love, that's how freedom grows. (Galatians 5:13–14)

Love from the center of who you are; don't fake it. Run for dear life from evil, hold on for dear life too good. Be good friends, who love deeply; practice playing second fiddle. Don't burn out; keep yourselves fueled and aflame. Be alert servants of the Master, cheerfully expectant. Don't quit in hard times; pray all the harder. Help needy Christians; be inventive in hospitality. (Romans 12:9–10, MSG)

"If any of you wants to serve Me, then follow Me. Then you'll be where I am, ready to serve at a moment's notice. The Father will reward anyone who serves Me." (John 12:26, MSG)

"Don't pick on people, jump on their failures, criticize their faults - unless, of course, you want the same treatment. Don't condemn those who are down; that hardness can boomerang. Be easy on people, you'll find life a lot easier. Give away your life; you'll find life given back, but not merely given back—given back with bonus and blessing. Giving; not getting, is the way. Generosity begets generosity." (Luke 6:37, 38, MSG)

So, sisters, how do we grasp the concept of eternity when living on this planet, this life is all we have ever known? The only answer or idea I have on that one is "through the power of the Holy Spirit living, breathing, moving and molding our hearts and minds." Ecclesiastes 3:11 says, "He has made everything beautiful in its time. He has also set eternity in the human heart; yet no one can fathom what God has done from beginning to end." So much of what God wants to do in and through us is done through HIS SPIRIT working in us. God wants to use us for His Glory and His purposes. I believe our only part is to be willing! He will do the rest! He will place us where He wants us, put the people in our paths He chooses, use the circumstances around us to strengthen, test and refine us, and ultimately mold us into the women of God He called us to be! Sometimes, we may be "along for the ride" kicking and screaming, whining, complaining and questioning. But when we say "yes" to God, He claims us as His children; and He will discipline, comfort, and encourage us as any loving parent would!

God is FOR us! He wants the very best lives for us as His children! He calls us to live free, authentic lives, lives filled with genuine love and service and compassion! Lives that bring encouragement and gifts into the lives of others. Generous, giving lives that overflow with blessings, both in this life and the next!_Now, those lives may not be exactly what we were envisioning when we said yes to God, but make no mistake, as God's much-loved daughters, He is constantly in the details. Working, moving, empowering, and encouraging as we go through our days, sometimes totally unaware of what is going on in and around us. God is at work within us. His Spirit is living, breathing, and working through you! You may not see or "feel" the effect your faith has on those around you, but because of "Whose" you are, you cannot help but leak Jesus on those you come in contact with! Leak away! I promise you won't run dry! You are being continually filled with the love, blessings, and pleasure of Jesus as He looks upon His much-loved daughters!

JULY 7

Bear with each other and forgive one another if any of you has a grievance against someone. Forgive as the Lord forgave you. (Colossians 3:13)

For if you forgive other people when they sin against you, your heavenly Father will also forgive you. But if you do not forgive others sins, your Father will not forgive your sins. (Matthew 6:14, 15)

Get rid of all bitterness, rage and anger, brawling and slander, along with every form of malice. Be kind and compassionate to one another, forgiving each other, just as in Christ God forgave you. (Ephesians 4:31–32)

Make a clean break with all cutting, backbiting, profane talk. Be gentle with one another, sensitive. Forgive one another so quickly and thoroughly as God in Christ forgave you. (Ephesians 4:31–32, MSG)

If we confess our sins, He is faithful and just and will forgive us our sins and purify us from all unrighteousness. (1 John 1:9)

Come now, let us settle the matter, says the LORD. Though your sins are like scarlet, they shall be as white as snow; though they are red as crimson, they shall be like wool. (Isaiah 1:18)

Forgiveness—everyone wants it for themselves when they screw up, but not very many of us are so willing to extend it. In my experiences there are 3 in my life who I struggle with forgiving. The first is God. So often I have found myself blaming God for the circumstances in my life. Not the pleasant ones, mind you, the difficult ones. "God, why don't You…? You could have…?" Myself: "Man, I am such a screw-up," "I can't believe I said…did…didn't…do that!" And finally, others who have hurt me, either willingly or unwillingly.

Over the years in the grocery store, we were robbed on a number of occasions. In one instance, we were vandalized as well. A gun was used to shoot anything that would make a mess. Honey jars, ketchup, syrup, the freezer and cooler doors, etc. It was a huge mess and a tremendous amount of money in damages! I was so angry and felt violated! They found the young men who robbed us and the hardware store that night, and I was seething with anger! "Those little ——! How could they?" I knew from the Word and from the depths of my heart that God wanted me to forgive them, even before, or even if they didn't ask. So, unwillingly, I began to pray. "Father, help me forgive them." I prayed this prayer daily through clenched teeth. I prayed it every time the anger welled up in me. I prayed it through the cleaning up, the insurance mess, and the court appearances. Slowly, I began to feel less and less anger toward these young men. Slowly, I felt forgiveness replacing the hurt and anger. Forgiveness wasn't an overnight fix for me; it took time, patience, and constant surrender of the feelings; but ultimately, forgiveness was a gift that benefited me, not them! I learned a lot through that experience. And I learned the difficult work of surrendering our pain and frustration over and over and over again to the only One Who can do anything about it!

My dear sisters, God calls us to forgive one another. God also calls us to confess our sin and then forgive ourselves, just as He forgives us. The work of forgiveness can be time-consuming and painful, but I urge you to do it! I can imagine you have pain that you have "stuffed down" over the years deep into your hearts. Giving it a shove back down anytime it showed it's ugly head. I encourage you to bring whatever pain you are carrying into the light of Jesus's presence. Unforgiveness for ourselves or others is like a festering wound that we can bandage over and over again but cannot heal on our own. Only God has the power to heal, restore, and rebuild. Expose it to His presence! Sure, life will leave us bloody and bruised at times. We may enter heaven with a multitude of scars someday. But God wants to restore our joy, our peace, and our anticipation for life! Let's leave the stuff that is dragging us down and slowing us up at the foot of His throne and move forward! God is FOR us, He is a great and mighty Healer! We may not understand why life is so hard, but this I know. Nothing, absolutely NOTHING is beyond God's watchful eye or His ability to heal and restore! Let God restore your joy and give you peace!

Have a great day, remembering always Who goes before, behind, and alongside you! You are loved beyond measure!

JULY 8

Trust in the LORD with all your heart and lean not on your own understanding; in all your ways submit to Him, and He will make your paths straight. (Proverbs 3:5, 6)

For it is God's will that by doing good you should silence the ignorant talk of foolish people. (1 Peter 2:15)

Your kingdom come, Your will be done, on earth as it is in heaven. (Matthew 6:10)

For I KNOW the plans I have for you," declares the LORD, "plans to prosper you and not to harm you, plans to give you hope and a future." (Jeremiah 29:11)

Do not be conformed to this world, but be transformed by the renewal of your mind, that by testing you may discern what is the will of God, what is good and acceptable and perfect. (Romans 12:2)

As moms, we are "fixers." We are also, by nature, protectors! We protect our babies from the time we know we are pregnant, we kiss away "boo-boos," wipe away tears, and listen for long hours to crying, whining teenagers and young adults who are finding out life is hard! We want with every ounce of our being to "fix" the problems and to make life easier for those we so desperately love! Now, that being said, think about this for a minute. Don't you think that's how God feels? He sees our struggle, He understands our confusion, sorrow, and disappointment; and yet He is allowing or perhaps even orchestrating the events in our lives or the lives of our loved ones. The Bible tells us that "Jesus wept" when He heard of His friends' death. He understands the pain. I think that He looks at His children in their struggles, and instead of swooping in and rescuing them (which He also does on occasion), He instead quietly encourages them and whispers, "Hold on, it's gonna be good! There is a reason I am allowing this. I am using this to grow you into the woman I created you to be. This is for My glory! You will see things differently when you get through this. I am with you." This example comes to my mind this morning. You know the uberrich who swoop in and get their kids out of trouble any time they screw up? It might be DUI, it might be theft and has even been murder. What happens to those kids? Are the parents really doing them any favors? These children grow up with a sense of entitlement, a sense of being superior to the laws of society, with no accountability and no sense of needing forgiveness and a change of direction. They don't (unless something happens) become the wiser for their problems, their faith isn't increased, and they don't even know they need God! Yet, I believe, they will continue to feel the "emptiness" within them that drives them to acquire more and more, feel more—anything to fill the void that only God can fill!

My dear sisters, God is FOR us! He is FOR those who we love! He has plans to prosper us, to give us a future and a hope! These temporary struggles are necessary for our development and our growth as His children. And they are necessary for our loved ones as well! So, let's sit back (tape our mouths and hands if necessary) and let God be God. God wants us to trust Him with everything and everyone in our lives. Let's get out of His way and watch Him work!

JULY 9

But the Lord is faithful, and He will strengthen you and protect you from the evil one. (2 Thessalonians 3:3)

Be strong and courageous. Do not be afraid or terrified because of them, for the LORD your God goes with you; He will never leave you nor forsake you. (Deuteronomy 31:6)

So do not fear, for I am with you, do not be dismayed, for I am your God. I will strengthen you and help you; I will uphold you with My righteous right hand. (Isaiah 41:10)

But let all who take refuge in You be glad; let them ever sing for joy. Spread Your protection over them, that those who love Your name will rejoice in You. (Psalm 5:11)

Many are the afflictions of the righteous, but the LORD delivers them from them all! (Psalm 34:19)

The term *bundled up* is not really a term we are using today. But the picture that comes to mind when we think of bundling something up is grabbing a sheet, putting our most treasured belongings in the middle of it then tying up the corners so we can make a sack out of it and take whatever is inside with us. In the event of a fire threatening our property, we would bundle up our most precious things and protect them from danger.

Now envision God doing that with our lives, protecting our souls and our bodies from danger, from attack from the evil one. I am convinced that, when we finally arrive in heaven, we will be brought to our knees by the sheer number of times God has intervened in our lives and protected us and our loved ones from dangers that we didn't even see. We will finally see all the moments in our lives when God strengthened us, protected us and delivered us from evil. Then Ephesians 1:13 scripture tells us that when we believe, we are marked with a seal, a seal of ownership by the Lord God Almighty! Now, on earth, we cannot see this seal, but the spiritual world sees it. The enemy knows those who belong to God, and it pisses him off!

My dear sisters, God has called you. He has claimed you, and He is commissioning you to tell the people He has placed in your path. "Come with me! My Father loves you, and He made a way for you!"

Our almighty God has sealed us with His Holy Spirit, and He promises to protect us! We are indeed in good hands!

May we live our lives in such a way that, when we step out of bed in the morning, the enemy shouts, "DAMN, SHE'S UP!"

Have a great week, friends! God's got you in His powerful, protective, empowering hands!

JULY 10

Do nothing from selfish or empty conceit, but with humility of mind regard one another as more important than yourselves; do not merely look out for your own interests, but also for the interests of others. (Philippians 2:2–3)

For where jealousy and selfish ambition exist, there is disorder and every evil thing. (James 3:16)

But realize this, that in the last days difficult times will come. For men will be lovers of self, lovers of money, boastful, arrogant, revilers, disobedient to parents, ungrateful, unholy. (2 Timothy 3:1–2)

Work willingly at whatever you do, as though you were working for the Lord rather than for people. (Colossians 3:23)

But as for you, be strong and do not give up, for your work will be rewarded. (2 Chronicles 15:7)

Work hard, but not just to please your masters when they are watching. As slaves of Christ, do the will of God with all your heart. Work with enthusiasm, as though you were working for the Lord rather than for people. (Ephesians 6:6)

Don't just do what you have to do to get by, but work heartily, as Christ's servants doing what God wants you to do. And work with a smile on your face, always keeping in mind that no matter who happens to be giving the orders, you're really serving God. (Ephesians 6:6 MSG)

And also that every man should eat and drink, and enjoy the good of all his labor, it is the gift of God. (Ecclesiastes 3:13)

The scriptures listed above are just a few of the many verses in the Bible about work. The first three I listed were about working for ourselves in selfish ambition. The second set of verses are about the attitude the Bible encourages us to have regarding our work. There are *so* many more!

"I have brought You glory on earth by completing the work You gave me to do." (John 17:4, NIV). "He (she) who has been stealing must steal no longer, but must work, doing something useful with his (her) own hands, that he (she) may have something to share with those in need" (Ephesians 4:28, NIV). "May the favor of the LORD our God rest on us; establish the work of our hands for us - yes, establish the work of our hands" (Psalm 90:17, NIV).

Like it or not, the scriptures are clear about how God feels about work. God blesses the work of our hands when we work with the right motives. Not for personal gain (although that is definitely a byproduct), but rather with an attitude of "working for the Lord" doing everything we do to the best of our abilities. Whether that means cleaning the tub and toilets of our home or overseeing multi-million dollar deals.

We need to be aware of becoming so focused on the outcome of our work, that we disregard the relationships that are key to a happy, healthy life. We can become so obsessed with our own personal agenda's that we disregard or ignore the needs and concerns of others. That can happen at work or at home. Personally, I love a clean house. Left to my own agenda my house would always be clean! Everything would be picked up and put away, floors clean and beds made. But that makes for a boring and sterile place for my grandchildren to play! When everyone is at the height of happiness and laughter abounds in my house, it is when there is an obstacle course in the middle of my living room! A chaotic chorus of children and dogs (and dog hair) running and jumping and squealing with joy. My house looks like a war zone, but relationships are strengthened and enjoyed.

Friends, God encourages us to work to the best of our ability, but He reminds us that the people He places in our path are not just incidental distractions to our lives but important to Him and to our own personal happiness.

So today, when we think about the family and friends that God has gifted us with and the jobs that pay our bills and bring us fulfillment, may we rejoice in the goodness of our Lord, who blesses us with so many good things! God is good! He is for us! And He loves us!

JULY 11

O Sovereign LORD! You have made the heavens and earth by Your great power. Nothing is too hard for You! (Jeremiah 32:17)

Where can I go from Your Spirit? Where can I flee from Your presence? If I go up to the heavens, You are there. If I make my bed in the depths, You are there. If I rise on the wings of the dawn, if I settle on the far side of the sea, even there Your hand will guide me, Your right hand will hold me fast. If I say, "Surely the darkness will hide me and the light become night around me," even the darkness will not be dark to You; the night will shine like the day, for darkness is as light to You. (Psalm 139:7–12)

He determines the course of world events; He removes kings and sets others on the throne. He give wisdom to the wise and knowledge to the scholars. (Daniel 2:21)

All the people of the earth are nothing compared to Him, He has the power to do as He pleases among the angels of heaven and with those who live on earth. No one can stop Him or challenge Him, saying, "What do You mean by doing these things." (Daniel 4:35)

You are truly My disciples if you keep obeying My teachings. And you will know the truth, and the truth will set you free. (John 8:31–32)

I must confess that, over the years, I have been guilty of having a faulty view of God. When God didn't answer my prayer in a way I could see or understand, I believed He didn't care. When problems kept coming up and no solution was at hand, I believed

He was impotent, weak, unable. When I saw the suffering and poverty in America and around the globe, I believed God was harsh and uncaring. I was quick to blame God for all the difficulties in life and write Him off as absent from the scene! Father, forgive me for such ignorance!

My dear sisters, God the Father is at work everywhere and always! Nothing, absolutely nothing escapes His notice! I believe He always answers prayer. Our part is to trust His timing and His authority. When we don't see a solution at hand, we can trust that He is in the details, "working all things for good for those who love Him." God grieves over the condition of our hearts and of our world. God commissions and sends His people, His "hands and feet," into the world to do amazing things around the world and in the hearts and lives of others.

We may not begin to understand what God is up to in the world around us, and in our very own lives, but rest assured, our God never grows tired or weak or uncertain. The heavens and earth jump to respond to His commands! There is absolutely nothing weak, uncaring, or uncertain about the personality of God. God is ALL powerful, ALL knowing, ALL wise, and ALL seeing. The scriptures tell us, "The Lord thy God is a consuming fire." Nothing and no one has the power to stand in His way or thwart His plans!

Sisters, do you realize the power, authority, and strength of the hands that are holding you? At HIS NAME, the "mountains quake and tremble"! At HIS NAME, the "oceans roar and rumble"! AT HIS NAME, demons flee and heaven responds!

Let's clean off those lenses and pray for God to restore our sight so that we may see and believe that God is indeed WHO He says He is and let's live in such a way that our lives demonstrate the power and authority of God. May we be filled this day to overflowing so that we cannot help but "leak Jesus" on those in our path!

JULY 12

But seek first His kingdom and His righteousness, and all these things will be given to you as well. (Matthew 6:33)

He says, "Be still, and know that I AM God; I WILL be exalted among the nations, I will be exalted in the earth." (Psalm 46:10)

Come near to God and He will come near to you. Wash your hands, you sinners, and purify your hearts, you double-minded. (James 4:8)

Do your best to present yourself to God as one approved, a worker who does not need to be ashamed and who correctly handles the word of truth. (2 Timothy 2:15)

Be silent before Me, you islands! Let the nations renew their strength! Let them come forward and speak; let us meet together at the place of judgment. (Isaiah 41:1)

Your Word is a lamp to my feet and a light to my path. (Psalm 119:105)

All Scripture is breathed out by God and profitable for teaching, for reproof, for correction, and for training in righteousness. (2 Timothy 3:16)

Dear friends, God loves you and desires to spend time with you. He wants to hear your perspective about your problems, and He wants to share your joy and laughter! Our God is not distant, nor is He preoccupied. He is fully present, fully aware and understands anything you have going on before you say a word! He desires our attention and our focus. He encourages us to build a solid relationship with Him so that, in times of trial or uncertainty, we can stand on solid ground, knowing HE is in control everywhere and always and so that our faith will be refined and our relationship will be strengthened! God is NOT an incidental addition to our lives; our relationship with the commander of the angel armies is foundational to a life well lived!

So today, may we intentionally seek first His Kingdom and His righteousness. May we be still in His presence and present our very lives before His throne. Then, may we open our hearts to hear His wisdom and receive His reproof and correction so that we may grow in righteousness and relationship with God, our Father. Let us draw close to the source of His amazing light. Then, our reflections will light up the darkest of days, and our lives will encourage and bless the lives of those around us!

Have a great day! You are loved, may the favor of the Lord God rest upon us!

JULY 13

So, chosen by God for this new life of love, dress in the wardrobe God picked out for you: compassion, kindness, humility, quiet strength, discipline. Be even-tempered, content with second place, quick to forgive an offensive. Forgive as quickly and completely as the Master forgave you. And regardless of what else you put on, wear love. It's your basic all-purpose garment. Never be without it. (Colossians 3:12–13 MSG)

Love never gives up. Loves cares more for others than for self. Love doesn't want what it doesn't have. Love doesn't strut, doesn't have a swelled head, doesn't force itself on others, isn't always "me first," doesn't fly off the handle, doesn't keep score of the sins of others, doesn't revel when others grovel. Takes pleasure in the flowering of truth, puts up with anything, trusts God always. Always looks for the best, never looks back, keeps going to the end. Love never dies. (1 Corinthians 13:4–7 MSG)

Trust steadily in God, hope unswervingly, love extravagantly. And the best of the three is love. (1 Corinthians 13:13)

Almighty God, here we are again. We have been reading of Your power, Your provision, and Your grace, and today, we are thinking about love. But, Lord, the love of this world is so fickle. Here one day and gone the next! We love so that others will love us. We love ourselves more than we love You or anyone else. We are not quick to forgive an offense, nor is playing second fiddle something that comes naturally to us! Help! Teach us what real love looks like. Teach us how to love with compassion, kindness, and humility. Give us the quiet strength we will need to care more for others than for ourselves. Empower us to forgive offenses quickly and without keeping a mental list of wrongs. Show us what extravagant love looks like! And then help us to live it out day after day, offense after offense.

May love come to characterize us as Your daughters. May we begin to resemble You more and more every day! May the words of our mouths and the thoughts in our minds be pleasing to You, almighty God. Please continue to mold and make us into the women You created us to be. We love You, we seek Your guidance and Your will for our lives, and we surrender our stubbornness and our selfishness to You. Thank You for not giving up on us, for loving us with extravagance and forgiveness. We give our lives of love and service to You. Keep us on track, strengthen our resolve to follow You, and use us up for Your glory. In Jesus's holy name, we pray. So be it. Amen!

JULY 14

Each one should test their own actions. Then they can take pride in themselves alone, without comparing themselves to someone else. (Galatians 6:4)

Do nothing out of selfish ambition or vain conceit. Rather, in humility value others above yourselves. (Philippians 2:3)

Where there is strife, there is pride, but wisdom is found in those who take advice. (Proverbs 13:10)

The Fear-of-God means hating Evil, whose ways I hate with a passion - pride and arrogance and crooked talk. (Proverbs 8:13 MSG)

Good counsel and common sense are My characteristics; I am both Insight and Virtue to live it out. (Proverbs 8:14)

Do you see a person wise in their own eyes? There is more hope for a fool than for them. (Proverbs 26:12)

Therefore encourage one another and build each other up, just as in fact you are doing. (1 Thessalonians 5:11)

Carry each other's burdens, and in this way you will fulfill the law of Christ. (Galatians 6:2)

My command is this: Love each other as I have loved you. (John 15:12)

Pride, there are so many kinds of pride that bring us down to a level that only brings discouragement and disappointment. Today we will focus on spiritual pride, a vibe we may give off either intentionally or unintentionally. It gives the impression that we are *more* spiritual or superior spiritually than those around us. Watch out when this particular pride raises its ugly head because God detests spiritual pride! Actually, God hates all kinds of pride, but spiritual pride, I think, is particularly discouraging. My dear friends, each and every one of us is on a spiritual journey. God is intervening, teaching, reprimanding, and encouraging each and every one of us along the way. We are ALL a work in progress! It is not up to me, or to you, to evaluate and critique the progress along the way. If we constantly compare ourselves to others, we will constantly be disappointed! There will always be someone with more insight; wiser counsel; or deeper, more spiritual thoughts! So give it up! Give up comparing yourselves to others and be content with the beautiful, strong, kind woman God has created in You! You are enough! Our husbands, our friends, our kids are enough! The people in our lives may not be perfect, but they are being molded in the image of God, just as you and I are!

There are enough things and comments in this world that drag us down and discourage us. Let us instead live our lives in such a way that others will be encouraged and blessed. I love the saying, "I do not ask for mighty words to leave the crowd impressed, God grant my life may ring so true my neighbor will be blessed!" (Author Unknown).

Shine bright, sisters! Light the dark for those around you! The journey is long and encouragement goes a long way to lighten the load and invigorate the step! Have a great week, women of God! You are loved!

JULY 15

I have told you this so that My joy may be in you and that your joy may be complete. (John 15:11)

Now we see but a poor reflection as in a mirror; then we shall see face to face. Now I know in part, then I shall know fully, even as I am fully known. (1 Corinthians 13:12)

The LORD is slow to anger and abundant in lovingkindness, forgiving iniquity and transgression, but He will by no means clear the guilty, visiting the iniquity of the fathers on the children to the third and the fourth generations. (Numbers 14:18)

But You, O Lord are a God merciful and gracious, slow to anger and abundant in lovingkindness and truth. (Psalm 86:15)

The LORD is gracious and merciful; slow to anger and great in lovingkindness. (Psalm 145:8)

Ever feel like you have used up God's patience for you? Like you have doubted or not trusted one too many times? Like you have trampled on His grace and doubted His goodness to the point that He has thrown up His hands and said, "Enough! I'm finished with you!" If you have, you are not alone!

The great news is God has promised us He will NEVER leave or forsake us! God is indeed a God of unlimited abundance, unlimited grace and forgiveness! A God of sacrificial love and fierce loyalty to His children!

Instead of becoming frustrated with our imperfection, let us press on toward the finish line! When we fall, fail, or disappoint, ask for God's help to get up, dust off, and move on! As Mother Teresa has said, "We are not called to be perfect, just faithful."

You are greatly and eternally loved! You are daughters of the King!

JULY 16

You shall not make for yourself an idol in the form of anything in heaven above or on the earth beneath or in the waters below. You shall not bow down to them or worship them: for I, the Lord your God, am a jealous God, punishing the children for the sin of the fathers to the third and fourth generation of those who hate Me, but showing love to a thousand generations, of those who love Me and keep my commandments. (Exodus 20:4–5)

You are my lamp, O Lord; the Lord turns my darkness into light. (2 Samuel 22:29)

To whom will you liken Me and make Me equal and compare Me, that we may be alike? (Isaiah 46:5)

Put to death therefore what is earthly in you; sexual immorality, impurity, passion, evil desire, and covetousness, which is idolatry. (Colossians 3:5)

I used to think the scriptures about worshipping idols were outdated and didn't apply to the present time, but I was wrong. In fact, I think we are a nation deep in the throes of idol worship! We worship power, beauty, wealth, opinions, and personal satisfaction, just to name a few of our idols! We value our opinion over God's truth. We walk and talk the way we want to and then expect God to bless us! Wondering why we feel so "lost" and abandoned?

My dear sisters, God is a God of power! He is not weak or wimpy, waiting around in some corner hoping for us to choose Him or His way. Instead, He is, at this very moment, directing the course of history and, in fact, our very lives! He sees us—our hearts, our hurts—and questions and says, "Come to Me."

He sees the state of our world, the hatred and violence that permeate our culture and says, "Come. I Am the Way, the Truth and the Light!" (John 14:6). There is healing, life, redemption and joy in God's presence! And, wait for it, the closer we draw to Him and His brilliance, the brighter we shine!

Shine on, friends! The God of the universe loves you fiercely and is making a path for you to follow! I can think of no other place I would rather be!

JULY 17

Salvation is found in no one else, for there is no other name under heaven given to men by which we must be saved. (Acts 4:12)

By faith in the name of Jesus, this man whom you see and know was made strong. It is Jesus' name and that faith that comes through Him that has given this complete healing to him as you can all see. (Acts 3:16)

I tell you the truth, my Father will give you whatever you ask in My Name. Until now you have not asked for anything in My Name. Ask and you will receive and your joy will be complete. (John 16:23b–24)

Have you ever stopped to ponder how much power there is in just the name of Jesus? Demons flee when they hear us utter that name! Satan is defeated by that name! The Bible says that "every knee will bow and every tongue will confess that Jesus Christ is Lord." Just the name "Jesus" has power beyond our wildest imagining!

When we utter the name "Jesus," in faith, there is power! Over the course of my life, I have uttered that name at some of the lowest and weakest and most frightening moments of my life. I remember one night in particular, in 1992, when my heart and mind were reeling, unsettled, and afraid. I honestly felt "under attack" by something. I was up in the middle of the night, fearful and crying. I felt oppressed, but I couldn't understand why. I "felt" God whisper, "I'm here," and I spoke out loud the name, "Jesus." That's all, just "Jesus." Something amazing happened that I cannot explain or understand. The darkness I was feeling was instantly gone, and I mean AT THE

MOMEMT I uttered Jesus's name! I understood at that instant the POWER in His name! I can tell you, to this day, exactly where in my kitchen I was standing when I uttered His name that night. In fact, I have never thought about His name the same way since that night! There have been many other times when the name "Jesus" was all that I could muster as prayer. Upon the notifications of our daughter's hospitalizations, at my dad's death, at our daughter's death, just "Jesus" came out of my mouth and my heart. No eloquent prayer, no learned speech, just "Jesus HELP!" It was a plea for His power and His strength!

There is power and healing and strength in the name of Jesus! It is truly beyond our understanding!

I love you, sisters, but more importantly, Jesus loves you! Trust Him!

JULY 18

But He said to me, "My grace is sufficient for you, My power is made perfect in weakness." Therefore I will boast all the more gladly about my weaknesses, so that Christ's power may rest on me. (2 Corinthians 12:9)

Trust in Him at all times, O people; pour out your hearts to Him, for God is our refuge. (Psalm 62:8)

This righteousness is given through faith in Jesus Christ to all who believe. There is no difference between Jew and Gentile, for all have sinned and fall short of the glory of God, and all are justified freely by His grace through the redemption that came by Christ Jesus. (Romans 3:22–24)

But to each one of us grace has been given as Christ apportioned it. (Ephesians 4:7)

Do not be carried away by all kinds of strange teachings. It is good for our hearts to be strengthened by grace, not by eating ceremonial foods, which is of no benefit to those who do so. (Hebrews 13:9)

One thing that I think the Bible is very clear on is that grace is a daily need. God doesn't give us what we need for the months or years ahead; instead, He blesses us daily with His grace, His presence, and His wisdom. Our responsibility it to look toward Him, seek His face, and His presence every moment of every day. We would do well to come to the point where we realize fully that God's grace is sufficient for the day ahead. That His power will be exhibited in our weakness if we diligently seek Him. That God is indeed our refuge and strength. And, finally that without His gift of grace we all fall miserably short!

Sometimes we may not feel Him near, we may even question His provision or presence, but rest assured, my friends, God has PROMISED that He will NEVER leave or forsake us, and His promises are true! We need not bother looking anywhere else for fulfillment or peace. God alone is the source of those gifts. He can handle whatever we have on our hearts. His grace is sufficient! And His supply never runs dry!

JULY 19

In addition to all this, take up the shield of faith, with which you can extinguish all the flaming arrows of the evil one. (Ephesians 6:16)

This is the message we have heard from Him and declare to you: God is light; in Him there is no darkness at all. If we claim to have fellowship with Him yet walk in the darkness, we lie and do not live by the truth. But, if we walk in the light, as He is in the light, we have fellowship with one another, and the blood of Jesus, His Son, purifies us from all sin. (1 John 1:5–7)

If we claim that we experience a shared life with Him and continue to stumble around in the dark, we're obviously lying through our teeth - we're not living what we claim. But if we walk in the light, God Himself being the light, we also experience a shared life with one another, as the sacrificed blood of Jesus, God's Son, purges all our sin. (1 John 1:5–7 MSG)

Surely God is my salvation; I will trust and not be afraid. (Isaiah 12:2)

In Ephesians 6:16, we are reminded to "Take up our shield of faith." *In 1 John,* we are told, "God is light, in Him there is NO darkness." And, the Message translation reminds us that "if we claim a shared life (relationship) with Him and continue to stumble around in the dark...we're lying!" Friends, this faith, this relationship with the Living God that we are pursuing will challenge us and empower us like nothing else we have ever pursued! We need to daily pick up our shields of faith, and place our trust in Him. Regardless of how we may be "feeling" at any given moment!

I love it when I am reminded that my feelings have NOTHING to do with my faith! I may not *feel* God's presence within me, but that does not change the FACT that He is always with me! I may not feel loved, accepted, holy, but again, that does not affect the reality of who and what the Bible says I am! God tells us we are His beloved, His children, and His light-bearers. How we feel at any given moment doesn't actually change a thing. The devil would LOVE for us to believe otherwise! He would love for us to take our feelings as fact, to believe our fears are our reality, and to embrace the lies he tells each and every one of us daily! That, my dear sisters, is why it is *so* important to remember always what GOD says about us! To walk moment by moment in His light! To remind each other that we are saved by the blood of Jesus and that no matter what arrows the evil one shoots our way, we are the redeemed children of the King! Our faith is not a matter of feelings but of POWER and TRUST in the one who placed us here in this time and in this place for His purpose and His glory! Grab that shield and shine bright!

JULY 20

As the deer pants for streams of water, so my soul pants for You, O God. My soul thirsts for God, for the living God. When can I go and meet with God? (Psalm 42:1–2)

Those who look to Him are radiant; their faces are never covered with shame. (Psalm 34:5)

Do everything readily and cheerfully - no bickering, no second-guessing allowed! Go out in the world uncorrupted, a breath of fresh air in this squalid and polluted society. Provide people with a glimpse of good living and of the living God. Carry the light-giving message into the night so I'll have good cause to be proud of you on the day that Christ returns. (Philippians 2:14–15 MSG)

Let me think, please God, please others, or please myself? Oftentimes I find my thinking goes please myself, please others then, "Oh, I wonder what God thinks?"

As we grow closer and more intimate in our relationship with Jesus, there is a subtle and gradual shift that takes place in our thinking. We begin to think less of ourselves and desire to please Jesus more.

One of the phrases that I find myself muttering is "Less of me Lord, less of me. More of You!"

God has created us to have a deep, stubborn desire for Him. Even people who seem to have everything in life will admit they are seeking something that they don't have or understand. I was doing some research on suicide and was reading some accounts of people who had attempted it. Many spoke of an "emptiness" they simply could not fill. Others said they felt "hollow." I believe with all my heart that is the space that can only be filled by God. We were created for Him, by Him, and we will not become all He has created us to be without Him! We do indeed thirst for Him as a deer thirsts for water, whether we are aware of it or not.

He loves us, He calls us to live lives un-corrupted by the world around us. Lives that breath fresh air and give light to the communities around us. Lives that provide a glimpse of our living God and Savior! May our lives be radiant today, reflecting His great light!

JULY 21

My sheep listen to My voice; I know them, and they follow Me. (John 10:27)

And we know that in all things God works for the good of those who love Him, who have been called according to His purpose. (Romans 8:28)

Then you will call upon Me and come and pray to Me, and I will listen to You. You will seek Me and find Me when you seek Me with all your heart. (Jeremiah 29:12–13)

God promises that He is with us always. He will lead us and that He cares about us intimately! He knows what we are going to say even before we say it. He tells us that He loves us sacrificially. But are we listening? Do we expect to see divine intervention through-out out day? Do we look at the beauty surrounding us and see God, beauty's creator or do we plod through life, looking down, expecting Murphy's law to play itself out day after day after day? I think we oftentimes miss the surprises and blessings God has for us simply because we are not looking! Our hearts and our minds are so pre-occupied with our own agendas that we don't see God in the details of day-to-day life! My dear sisters, He is there! He is alongside you every single day. Not a moment goes by that He isn't thinking of you and calling out to you, "Seek Me." He has the answers we need, He will furnish the strength to finish this race of life, and He will shower a multitude of blessings upon us along the way! Personally, I don't want to go through life in a dogged religious plod, but rather in a spirited dance. Eagerly bouncing on toes of anticipation asking; "What's next, Papa?" God is FOR us and we will find Him when we seek Him with all our hearts!

JULY 22

I will instruct you and teach you in the way you should go; I will counsel you and watch over you. (Psalm 32:8)

Direct me in the path of Your commands, for there I find delight. (Psalm 119:35)

Let the morning bring me word of your unfailing love, for I have put my trust in you. Show me the way I should go, for to you I lift up my soul. (Psalm 143:8)

But in all these things we overwhelmingly conquer through Him who loved us. Romans 8:37

I can do all things through Him who strengthens me. (Philippians 4:13)

This morning while reading in Mark and Luke, I was reminded once again of the teachings of Jesus and of the awesome power of God! We are not victims in this world but, rather, conquerors! Our strength comes from the Lord. Our wisdom from God. Our hope is in Christ alone! The events of this world tend to beat the crap out of us! We worry, fret, stew, and imagine the worst! We dwell on the events in our lives that hurt us or discourage us instead of concentrating on the unimaginable power and love of Jesus Christ.

It is exceedingly hard to not feel discouraged or worried when we receive word of illness, struggle, or death. Unfortunately, we have all experienced or will experience these things in life. Thank goodness we serve a king who has the power to overcome! But, in the waiting, how do we trust God when things seem to be going horribly wrong?

How do we trust that God is in control when loved ones suffer and die? How do we pray? How do we cope and not lose heart?

My only response to that is to throw everything into God's hands! The fear, the uncertainty, and the anger, give it all to God! He is not offended by our anger or frustration at the events we are going through. He understands. He is big enough to handle anything we surrender to Him. Be honest with God then let Him use you and me to help. Extend God's grace by offering others encouragement, prayer, and a helping hand. With support and tears and an ironclad trust that God IS in control of ALL things ALL the time! whether we understand or agree. Then when you find that you do indeed have the strength you need and you feel the very hand of God holding you, you will KNOW that God's got this!

Friends, don't lose sight of our Lord, who knows us so intimately that He even knows how many hairs are on our heads. He loves us despite our doubts and questions and tells us, "I Am a God of power! Nothing is too hard for Me!"

JULY 23

O Lord, you have searched me and You know me. You know when I sit and when I rise; You perceive my thoughts from afar. You discern my going out and my lying down; You are familiar with all my ways. Before a word is on my tongue You know it completely, O Lord. Search me, O God, and know my heart; test me and know my anxious thoughts. See if there is any offensive way in me, and lead me in the way everlasting. (Psalm 139:1–4, 23–24)

There is no fear in love. But perfect love drives out fear, because fear has to do with punishment. The one who fears is not made perfect in love. (1 John 4:18)

God is love. When we take up permanent residence in a life of love, we live in God and God lives in us. This way, love has the run of the house, becomes at home and mature in us, so that we're free of worry on Judgement Day—our standing in the world is identical with Christ's. There is no room in love for fear. Well-formed love banishes fear. Since fear is crippling, a fearful life—fear of death, fear of judgment—is one not yet fully formed in love. (1 John 4:18 MSG)

Many years ago, I began telling God, "I want to hold nothing back from you, cleanse me from any wrong thinking or bring to mind unconfessed sin." I was amazed at how many things God brought to my mind over the years! Things that I didn't want Him messing in! Feelings of being wronged or wounded feelings from being hurt by others that I thought were long gone and buried. Over time and with continued prayer, I was reminded of things that I had forgotten. I was reminded of times I had spoken harshly to another, or been inattentive or uninterested when someone was taking to me. Oftentimes, these people were members of my own family! John Eldridge calls this wounding of ourselves or others "arrows." Friends, until our "arrow" wounds are placed in the light of God's presence, they stay as open sores. We can forget about them for a time, but when we remember the arrows, the pain is still there. Only God can fully heal us. I read somewhere that when we enter heaven, we will be covered in well-healed scars. For some reason, that analogy really spoke to me. The pain and the wounds are real, but God can and will heal the deepest wounds and cover it with a solid scar. The more scars we enter heaven with, the more vulnerable and willing to love we have been! A scarred soul gives witness to an open, loving heart!

God loves us so much, my friends, that He wants to heal us completely this side of heaven! He wants to heal our wounds so that we are free to move forward and risk reaching out to others to share His love and His healing with a hurting world! God is love, God is light, in Him there is no darkness at all!

JULY 24

We have this hope as an anchor for the soul, firm and secure. (Hebrews 6:19)

And now, dear children, continue in Him so that when He appears we may be confident and unashamed before Him at His coming. (1 John 2:28)

Jesus replied: "Love the Lord your God with all your heart and with all your soul and with all your mind." (Matthew 22:37)

Jesus said: "Love the Lord your God with all your passion and prayer and intelligence." (Matthew 22:37 MSG)

You will keep in perfect peace those whose minds are steadfast, because they trust in You. (Isaiah 26:3)

Guide me in Your truth and teach me, for You are God my Savior, and my hope is in You all day long. (Psalm 25:5)

We are all anchored to something. Sometimes it is the security we feel from having enough money or perhaps it's from our family or from our own self-esteem. God reveals to us that the only sure anchor is Him. When our lives fall apart and the things we cling to fall away, God's anchor holds firm. He is not effected by the events of this world or the problems in our lives. His anchor is unfailing and immovable! I know from personal experience that even though I have felt tossed around and battered by the storms of life, my anchor, my God has held me firm! I can say with bold confidence; "My Anchor Holds!"

JULY 25

Show me, Lord, my life's end and the number of my days; let me know how fleeting my life is. (Psalm 39:4)

Teach us to number our days, that we may gain a heart of wisdom. (Psalm 90:12)

For we are only of yesterday and know nothing, because our days on earth are a shadow. (Job 8:9)

Yet you do not know what your life will be like tomorrow. You are just a vapor that appears for a little while and then vanishes away. (James 4:14)

My days are like a lengthened shadow, and I wither away like grass. (Psalm 102:11)

The Dash

I read of a man who stood to speak at the funeral of a friend.
He referred to the dates on her tombstone;
from the beginning...to the end.

He noted that first came her date of birth and
spoke the following date with tears,
but he said what mattered most of all was
the dash between those years.

For that dash represents all the time that she
spent alive on earth and now only those

who loved her know what that little line is worth.
For it matters not, how much we own;
the cars, the house, the cash, what matters is how
we live and love and how we spend our dash.

So think about this long and hard…are there things
you'd like to change? For you never know how
much time is left, that can still be rearranged.

So when your eulogy's being read with your life's
actions to rehash…would you be proud of the things
they say about how you spend your dash?

—Linda Ellis

Lord, teach us to number our days. To remember how fleeting
are the moments of this life. And to live each day with our best
efforts to give generously and love extravagantly so that our "dash"
may have a lasting impact on those we love and leave behind.

JULY 26

B ut the Lord looks after those who fear Him, those who put their hope in His love. (Psalm: 33:18)

I asked the Lord for help, and he answered me. He saved me from all that I feared. The angel of the Lord camps around those who fear God and he saves them. (Psalm 34:4, 7)

Say to those with fearful hearts, "Be strong, do not fear; your God will come, He will come with vengeance; with divine retribution He will come to save you." (Isaiah 35:4)

Peace I leave with you; My peace I give you. I do not give to you as the world gives. Do not let your hearts be troubled and do not be afraid. (John 14:27)

We're frightened, and fear limits the joy we experience in our lives. So we live out our days trapped in an adventure-less existence. What exactly are we afraid of? Pain? Rejection? Are we afraid of making a mistake? Getting hurt? Being robbed or killed? Of getting a disease? Did you know that God is NEVER afraid, worried, or frenzied? Do you remember that His spirit lives in you?

Many years ago now, Lori and I took a group of ten girls to inner city Chicago on a mission trip. It never crossed my mind to be afraid. I felt secure in God's hand. I felt like he had led us there and that he would protect us, and you know what? he did!

After I got home, I was telling my mother and brother about our trip, and my brother came unglued! He told me how "stupid" I was and that "I didn't think it through!" At first, I was hurt, but then I realized that he was speaking out of fear for me. And I was amazed that that fear had not even entered My conscious thought. Yet years later, as my husband and I were preparing to leave on an international mission trip, I felt differently. When we went to the doctor to get our shots and malaria pills for travel, I began to feel a seed of fear creeping into my thinking, especially after the doctor explained all these illnesses we could get and the poor treatment available in other countries. I immediately went home and laid my fear at God's feet. I asked him to confirm that that was His will for us and that He would give me peace and remove all fear. I read these scriptures and was reminded that "God's got our back" and that He will be with us wherever we go.

I pray this peace for all of you as well as we deal with all sorts of things that upset our equilibrium, challenge our thinking and our faith. My dear sisters, God is good! All the time, God is good!

JULY 27

B ut the Lord said to Samuel, "Do not consider his appearance or his height, for I have rejected him. The Lord does not look at the things man looks at. Man looks at the outward appearance, but the Lord looks at the heart." (Samuel 16:7)

For I am convinced that neither death nor life, neither angels nor demons, neither the present nor the future nor any powers, neither height nor depth, not anything else in all creation, will be able to separate us from the love of God that is in Christ Jesus our Lord. (Romans 8:38–39 NIV)

And just to compare with The Message Bible translation: And who would dare tangle with God by messing with one of God's chosen? Who would dare even to point a finger? The One who died for us - who was raised to life for us! - is in the presence of God at this very moment sticking up for us. Do you think anyone is going to be able to drive a wedge between us and Christ's love for us? There is no way! Not trouble, not hard times, not hatred, not huger, not homelessness, not bullying threats, not backstabbing, not even the worst sins listed in Scripture; None of this fazes us because Jesus loves us. I'm absolutely convinced that nothing—nothing living or dead, angelic or demonic, today or tomorrow, high or low, thinkable or unthinkable—absolutely nothing can get between us and God's love because of the way that Jesus our Mater has embraced us. (Romans 38–39 MSG)

God sees you, my friends, He understands your concerns, questions, and doubts and loves you passionately! He is not scared off, offended, or angry at your questions. He wants you to bring them to Him, to seek His counsel, His advice, and more importantly, His presence. The enemy tries to get us to believe that we have to be wise; have it all together; never sin, cuss, doubt, or question (the list goes on and on) before God wants to be in our presence and answer us when we pray. Scripture, on the other hand, calls all of those preconditions a LIE! NOTHING can keep us from God's presence! Think about that. Nothing! I know enough about what God says to KNOW, that He is pleased with the fact that you are seeking Him, that you are questioning, learning, and wondering. God is a master of pursuit. He is pursuing you and me and will continue to do so. We tend to think it is us turning to God, but I think in reality we are not turning at all! God has us surrounded; we are just opening our eyes and hearts to His pursuit!

Today, hourly, if possible, take a second and remember just HOW much God loves you. Consider the things listed in the scripture—height, depth, angels, demons, events, troubles, concerns–NOTHING can separate us from God's love in Christ Jesus! Wow, are we EVER greatly and eternally loved!

JULY 28

My heart says of you, "Seek His face! Your face, Lord, I will seek." (Psalm 27:8)

Rather clothe yourselves with the Lord Jesus Christ, and do not think about how to gratify the desires of the sinful nature. (Romans 13:14)

Therefore, as God's chosen people, holy and dearly loved, clothe yourselves with compassion, kindness, humility, gentleness and patience. (Colossians 3:12)

Look to the LORD and His strength; seek His face always. (1 Chronicles 16:11)

God did this so that they would seek Him and perhaps reach out for Him and find Him, though He is not far from any one of us. (Acts 17:27)

Come near to God and He will come near to you. Wash your hands, you sinners, and purify your hearts, you double-minded. (James 4:8)

My mom used to say to my brothers and I when we were children, "Careful what you watch, read, or who you hang around with. Because if you put garbage in your mind and heart, you get a life of garbage out! Garbage in, garbage out!"

Conversely, if we fill our minds first thing in the morning with thoughts of Jesus, of what He has done for us, His great love for us and His tender mercy toward us, we will be more prone to extend those kindnesses to others. Friends, God desires us to earnestly seek Him, to desire to walk in His presence and seek His wisdom for our lives. And then He promises to transform us into people that look more and more like Him!

Dear Lord, today as we enjoy the beauty that surrounds us, the love of family and friends and the abundance we take for granted, may we be given such sweetness of spirit, such compassion, humility, and patience that we are, in turn, a blessing to those we come in contact with. Today, may we seek to exhibit Your character traits; Your kindness, gentleness, and self-control; Your love for others and for ourselves. May we, in turn, become more and more like you by the transformation of our minds. We acknowledge that the change we desire starts with bringing our hearts and minds to you on a daily basis. We love you, Lord! Walk closely with us today, and if we should wander off, bring us back into Your arms and Your will. Amen

JULY 29

Let me understand the teaching of your precepts; then I will meditate on Your wonders. (Psalm 119:27)

For the eyes of the Lord range throughout the earth to strengthen those whose hearts are fully committed to Him. (2 Chronicles 16:9)

Through Jesus therefore, let us continually offer to God a sacrifice of praise - the fruit of lips that confess His name. (Hebrews 13:15)

But seek first His kingdom and His righteousness, and all these things will be given you as well. (Matthew 6:33)

I love those who love Me, and those who seek Me find Me. (Proverbs 8:17)

Those who know Your name trust in you, for You, LORD, have never forsaken those who seek You. (Psalm 9:10)

Each one must give as he has decided in his heart, not reluctantly or under compulsion, for God loves a cheerful giver. (2 Corinthians 9:7)

One gives freely, yet grows all the richer; another withholds what she should give, and only suffers want. (Proverbs 11:24)

The scriptures today reminded me of something. God wants something from us! He desires that we spend time with Him in His word and in prayer. He desires that we respond to His kindness and goodness to us by giving Him our tithes and offerings. He expects us to offer up to Him our honest and heartfelt praise and worship. And you know, it is only fitting that our faith should be a two-way street. It isn't all about what we can GET from God, it is about how we respond to what God has done and is doing for us! I love the scripture in 2 Chronicles that says that God's eyes are looking for those who are fully committed to Him so that He can strengthen them!

I don't know about you, friends, but I need His strength! I need Him to instruct me and encourage me in the daily walk of life. I need His compassion, kindness, and wisdom to show me the way to go, the right response in difficult situations, and the discipline to seek His will. I need Him far more than He needs me! In fact, He doesn't NEED anything from me at all! He owns the cattle on a thousand hills (Psalm 50:10), the wealth in every mine, and everything I have is His. But He desires to have a relationship with me. He wants me to trust Him with everything I have and for everything I need, and in order to trust Him, I have to know Him and believe He loves and knows me.

I wish you could all visit the prison with me sometime when we volunteer there. These guys have screwed up big time. They are broken, broke, and hurting. But there is a group of guys that have come to believe in and trust God with their life inside, as well as with their future. They speak of a deep and reverent respect for God and His word. They are reading their Bibles, meeting in groups to pray for each other and to hold each other accountable. They are encouraging others to change their lives through the power of Jesus Christ! They cry about the regrets and shame they carry about their choices and encourage each other to stop blaming others, take responsibility for their own lives, and hand it over to God!

We serve a big, compassionate, forgiving God! He is afoot, my dear sisters! He loves us with a fierce passion and desires to strengthen us in our faith! Have a great week!

JULY 30

So do not fear, for I am with you; do not be dismayed, for I am your God. I will strengthen you and help you; I will uphold you with my righteous right hand. (Isaiah 41:10)

The Lord your God is with you, He is mighty to save. He will take great delight in you, He will quiet you with His love, He will rejoice over you with singing. (Zephaniah 3:17)

A righteous woman may have many troubles, but the Lord delivers her from them all. (Psalm 34:19)

I love all three of today's scriptures. But the scripture in Zephaniah that reminds us that God takes "great delight" in us, that He "rejoices over us with singing" just blows me away! How is it that the Lord of the universe, the hand that hung the moon and stars and stilled the storm, the mind that created everything we see and understand, as well as everything unseen and not understood by any mortal mind, takes delight in us? How is it possible that God rejoices over us with singing? Aren't we a misguided, stumbling, and struggling lot at times? Why then does the Lord of the angel armies rejoice and sing over us? Because, my dear sisters, we are His children! He loves us despite our flaws. He loves us with a cavernous, unrelenting, unrestrained love that we cannot begin to fathom this side of eternity! So today, just soak it in and rejoice in the untamed love of God! God is rejoicing over us, can you hear it?

JULY 31

Within Your temple, O God, we meditate on Your unfailing love. (Psalm 48:9)

Let the beloved of the Lord rest secure in Him, for He shields Him all day long, and the one the Lord loves rests between His shoulders. (Deuteronomy 33:13)

Delight in the Lord and He will give you the desires of your heart. (Psalm 37:4)

He says: "Be still, and know that I am God; I will be exalted among the nations, I will be exalted in the earth." (Psalm 46:10)

How can a young person stay on the path of purity? By living according to Your word. (Psalm 119:9)

Do your best to present yourself to God as one approved, a worker who does not need to be ashamed and who correctly handles the word of truth. (2 Timothy 2:15)

Whoever dwells in the shelter of the Most High will rest in the shadow of the Almighty. (Psalm 91:1)

I think today's scriptures are a good reminder for all or us. A reminder to fight for the precious time it takes to make our time spent with God in prayer and contemplation a priority. There are so many distractions that come in various forms, and quietness and prayer don't seem to fit in very well. I think of my morning God time like this: before the distractions come, I have prayed and asked God to help me be still. Before the business of life takes over, I have already asked God to come along with me throughout my day. Before the phone rings, the family wakes, or the dogs need out,

I have asked for forgiveness for my sins, failures, and shortcomings. The result is a lightness of heart, a sense of God's presence in my life, and a much-needed reminder of who is really in control. My time with God equips me with a surprising readiness to face whatever the day brings.

I remember well when our girls were just small and I decided that I wanted to be deliberate in setting a time every morning for time with God. At first, it was so difficult. My mind would wander to anything that flitted through it! My prayer then was "settle my mind." There were so many times I didn't get up early enough or wasn't motivated so that, when it was said and done, I had only spent about five minutes alone with God. But you know, five minutes a day is thirty-five minutes a week and hey! That was *way* better than what I was doing before that! It encouraged me to think that way. Eventually, five minutes led to ten then thirty then what is my usual now, about an hour. There have been many mornings that have varied from that routine, but you know, after a while, I really began to feel like I missed out when I skipped that time in the morning! On especially busy days, God has even awoken me as early as 4:30 a.m. or 5:00 a.m. and gently reminded me about our engagement.

I have never, ever regretted the time I have spent deliberately in His presence!

My dear sisters, there is power, hope, love, and blessing in His presence! You do not want to miss it!

Please, please remember, you are fiercely loved ALWAYS! Not just when you think you may be deserving but at every moment of every day!

AUGUST 1

B ut if any of you lacks wisdom, let her ask of God, who gives to all generously and without reproach, and it will be given to her. (James 1:5)

Teach me, and I will be silent; and show me how I have erred. (Job 6:24)

For You are my rock and my fortress. For Your Name's sake You will lead me and guide me. (Psalm 31:1)

Point out the road I must travel; I'm all ears, all eyes before You. Save me from my enemies, God—You're my only hope! (Psalm 143:8 MSG)

I'm sure now I'll see God's goodness in the exuberant earth. Stay with God! Take heart. Don't quit. I'll say it again; Stay with God! (Psalm 27:13–14 MSG)

Trust in the LORD with all your heart and do not lean on your own understanding. In all your ways acknowledge Him, and He will make your paths straight. (Proverbs 3:5–6)

Trust God from the bottom of your heart; don't try to figure out everything on your own. Listen for God's voice in everything you do, everywhere you go; He's the one who will keep you on track. Don't assume that you know it all. Run to God! Run from evil! (Proverbs 3:5–7)

You took nothing seriously, took nothing to heart, never gave tomorrow a thought. Well, start thinking, playgirl. You're acting like the center of the universe. (Isaiah 47:7 MSG)

Dear sisters, we are in a battle, not with flesh and blood but with the power of deception. Compliments of our greatest enemy. His lies whisper to us, and bombard us with thoughts like: "You don't need God. You've got this. You know what is best in this situation"; "You can figure this out. You are too busy to take time now to pray"; "He's not really got your best interests at heart. He's not listening, doesn't care, can't or won't help." Sound familiar? Our enemy wants to separate us from the only source of power and wisdom we will ever have in this life! His goal is to lead us to defeat, discouragement, and resentment and then blame God for it!

So our part is to plug in to the source of the wisdom, guidance, and power that God offers us each and every day. We don't have because we don't ask! God is in the giving business! He desires to fill us with His truth, His wisdom, and His strength; but sadly, too often, we are too busy or too proud to ask! The scripture in John 15:5 reminds us; "I am the vine; you are the branches. If you remain in Me and I in you, you will bear much fruit; apart from Me you can do nothing. This verse has stuck with me for a long time. Even when my heart is in the right place, wanting to do good, apart from God, my works and my will are nothing more than wind. If we want lives that matter, lives that have influence, bring encouragement and never give up. We need God! We need relationship with the commander of the angel armies! We need to be in the down on our knees, surrendered mode! Not our will but YOURS will be done, oh Lord! We must learn to look our enemy in the face and say, "Not today! I am a child of the King. And today, I am seeking His will and His purpose for my life!" Then we can simply put one foot in front of the other and watch Him work!

God is good! God is FOR us! He has called us, and He can and WILL equip us for whatever lies ahead! And, my dear friends, it's gonna be good! You are loved!

AUGUST 2

For all have sinned and fall short of the glory of God. (Romans 3:23)

It is obvious what kind of life develops out of trying to get your own way all the time; repetitive, loveless, cheap sex; a stinking accumulation of mental and emotional garbage; frenzied and joyless grabs for happiness, trinket gods, magic-show religion, paranoid loneliness, cutthroat competition; all-consuming-yet-never-satisfied wants; a brutal temper, an impotence to love or be loved; divided homes and divided lives; small-minded and lopsided pursuits; the vicious habit of depersonalizing everyone into a rival; uncontrolled and uncontrollable addictions; ugly parodies of community. I could go on. This isn't the first time I have warned you, you know. If you use your freedom this way, you will not inherit God's kingdom. (Galatians 5:19–21 MSG)

Put to death, therefore, whatever belongs to your earthly nature; sexual immorality, impurity, lust, evil desires and greed, which is idolatry. Because of these, the wrath of God is coming. (Colossians 3:5–6)

If anyone, then, knows the good they ought to do and doesn't do it, it is sin for them. (James 4:17–21)

Keep Your servant also from willful sins; may they not rule over me. Then I will be blameless, innocent of great transgression. May these words of my mouth and this meditation of my heart be pleasing in your sight, LORD, my Rock and my Redeemer. (Psalm 19:13–14)

We live in a culture that has redefined sin. We view it as normal, acceptable behavior, something to joke about and make light of, even joking that "the devil made me do it!" But our sin breaks the heart of God! We cause this heart break as a people and as a nation by our willful disobedience to His word and His authority. Somewhere along the way, we have grasped with both hands the concept of grace but have refused to address the issue of sin. We are quick to say, "God is for us, loves us, loves everyone," but are secretly hoping that God is blind and deaf! Blind to our willful disobedience and deaf to our careless and godless words.

My dear sisters, God is indeed FOR us, but He is also in the business of molding us and shaping us into versions of Himself. He wants to present us to the world as His children set apart for His purpose and His work. He desires for us to abandon anything that holds us back from this commission. Pride, envy, gluttony, lust, anger, greed, and sloth have to go! Instead, God wants to replace them with love, joy, peace, patience, kindness, goodness, faithfulness, gentleness, and self-control. We can't have it both ways. Either we are on God's side or on the side of the enemy. There is no middle ground! That being said, we can take a deep breath and praise God that He is the one who brings about change in us and convicts us of our sin so that we can bring it to Him and be forgiven. I believe we break the heart of God when we refuse to call sin, sin and thoughtlessly forget about the destruction and pain sin leaves in its wake! There is a reason God detests sinful behavior. It is because sin destroys relationships and lives, leaving in its wake despondent, depressed, addicted, half-dead people—people with no hope and no joy! God wants more for His daughters! There is much to be done, places to go, things to see, and hope to share! God is for us and wants the BEST for us! Let's not settle for less!

AUGUST 3

For if anyone thinks she is something when she is nothing, she deceives herself. (Galatians 6:3)

If you start thinking to yourselves, "I did all this. And all by myself. I'm rich. It's all mine!" well, think again. Remember that God, your God, gave you the strength to produce all this wealth so as to confirm the covenant that He promised to your ancestors as it is today. (Deuteronomy 8:17, 19 MSG)

"Proud" "Haughty," "Scoffer," are his names, Who acts with insolent pride. (Proverbs 21:24)

Through insolence comes nothing but strife. But wisdom is with those who receive counsel. (Proverbs 13:10)

Arrogant know-it-alls stir up discord, but wise men and women listen to each other's counsel. (Proverbs 13:10 MSG)

Who do you think it is you've insulted? Who do you think you've been bad-mouthing? Before Whom do you suppose you've been strutting? The Holy One of Israel, that's who! (2 Kings 19:22 MSG)

Everyone who is proud in heart is an abomination to the LORD, assuredly, she will not be unpunished. (Proverbs 16:5)

When pride comes, then comes dishonor. But with the humble is wisdom. (Proverbs 11:2)

Heavenly Father, may we be convicted this morning on the areas of pride in our lives, of attitudes of superiority that sometimes enter our thinking. Forgive us for wanting the desires of our hearts over whatever plans You may have for us. We confess that when we don't get our way, we whine and moan and question your authority over our lives. We quickly act just like the people in scripture, that when led out of Egypt and captivity, turned their attention to their own desires and other gods, thinking, "Well, if You won't do it my way, then You don't really care!" Forgive us, Father! Forgive our pride, our arrogance, our misguided sense of knowing what's best! Reveal to us the areas in our lives where pride rules! Help us to confess and release the pockets of pride that hold us back from an intimate relationship with You. We need You! We need friends and family who give us wise counsel, who keep us grounded in truth! Fill us with the wisdom that comes from Your hand. Give us patience to trust in Your timing and Your guidance. Lead us in the way that You know is best for us! We love You. We thank You for never giving up on us, and we willfully acknowledge Your authority over our lives. Pick us up when we stumble, reassure us when we doubt, and lead us on the path of Your choosing! We surrender our will to You! So be it. Amen.

AUGUST 4

Be prepared. You're up against more than you can handle on your own. Take all the help you can get, every weapon God has issued, so that when it's all over but the shouting you'll still be on your feet. Truth, righteousness, peace, faith, and salvation are more than words. Learn how to apply them. You'll need them throughout your life. God's Word is an indispensable weapon. In the same way, prayer is essential in this ongoing warfare. Pray hard and long. Pray for your brothers and sisters. Keep your eyes open. Keep each other's spirits up so that no one falls behind or drops out. (Ephesians 6:13–18 MSG)

The first thing I want you to do is pray. Pray every way you know how, for everyone you know. Pray especially for rulers and their governments to rule well so we can be quietly about our business of living simply, in humble contemplation. This is the way our Savior God wants us to live. (1 Timothy 2:1–3 MSG)

But I say to you, love your enemies and pray for those who persecute you. (Matthew 5:44)

But I have prayed for you, that your faith may not fail; and you, when once you have turned again, strengthen your sisters (brothers). (Luke 22:32)

Make this your common practice: Confess your sins to each other and pray for each other so that you can live together whole and healed. The prayer of a person living right with God is something powerful to be reckoned with. (James 5:16–17 MSG)

God sees hearts in a way we cannot. He sees the motives behind the actions and understands what we cannot see. God sees the brokenness, the abuse, the pain behind the actions of hurt people who hurt people. God sees a nation lost and wandering, confused and broken, refusing the grace and mercy that He is freely giving. No wonder His heart breaks! He offers us the weapons we will need to engage in the battle at hand, but we want no part of it! We have convinced ourselves that we don't need God, don't need to pray. We couldn't be more wrong!

Pray, dear sisters! Pray long and hard. Pray for mercy, forgiveness, peace, restoration, healing, and spiritual awakening! Bring all your prayers and petitions and lay them at the foot of the throne! God hears, God cares, and scripture reminds us that our prayers are a powerful weapon, something to be reckoned with!

May we grow in grace and with knowledge of the profound power of sincere prayer!

AUGUST 5

So teach us to number our days. That we may present to You a heart of wisdom. (Psalm 90:12)

Behold, the LORD's hand is not so short that it cannot save; nor is His ear so dull that it cannot hear. (Isaiah 59:1)

For "All flesh is like grass, and all its glory like the flower of the grass, the grass withers, and the flower falls off." (1 Peter 1:24)

Yet you do not know what your life will be like tomorrow. You are just a vapor that appears for a little while and then vanishes away. (James 4:14)

Take care of yourself, have a good time, and make the most of whatever job you have for as long as God gives you life. And that's about it. That's the human lot. Yes we should make the most of what God gives, both the bounty and the capacity to enjoy it, accepting what's given and delighting in the work. It's God's gift; God deal out joy in the present, the now. It's useless to brood over how long we might live. (Ecclesiastes 5:18–10 MSG)

Years ago, I heard someone say, "She's so heavenly minded, that she's of no earthly good!" It struck me as funny but got me to thinking. Seems to me there are three ways most people live their lives in regards to their death:

1.   Heavenly minded, dwelling on the time when they leave this earth. When they dwell here they miss the here and now, the blessings that God has for today!, the work we

have to do, and the effect we might be having on the world around us.

2. Fearful of death. Unwilling to give it a thought, pushing the idea off for another time because the idea is terrifying!

3. Realizing that "this is not our home" but living alive and well in the present place and in the present time. Knowing that when the number of our days is up, our God will bring us to Himself.

Working with hospice has been such a blessing for me. I cannot tell you how wonderful it is to enter the home or room of a person near death who is not afraid, not fighting but surrendering to, and even looking forward to, death. I think most people get to this point regardless of whether they are Christian or not, but for the Christian, there is a joy present that is unbelievable! Those without faith, in my limited experience, are resigned to the fact that death is near. Their reason for acceptance is simply because of the reality of the near future. Their only joy is the relief of pain. What a difference between the two! Yesterday, I was with a woman, weak, in pain, and very tired, who just kept mumbling to herself and to me how very "thankful" she was. Thankful for her life, her family, her friends, her faith! She is ready to "go home!"

We all know death is inevitable! But let's not waste a moment of living in the meantime! There are places to go, things to see and enjoy, and events to celebrate and work to be done! May we slide into death with a glass of champagne in one hand and the words, "Whew, what a ride," on our lips! (I heard that line at the funeral of a friend.)

As God's children, we get the best of both worlds! Joy in the present and peace at death!

Have a wonderful day. Shine bright!

AUGUST 6

Whan Jesus spoke again to the people, He said, "I Am the Light of the world. Whoever follows Me will never walk in darkness, but will have the light of life." (John 8:12)

The LORD is my light and my salvation—whom shall I fear? The LORD is the stronghold of my life - of whom shall I be afraid? (Psalm 27:1)

Every good and perfect gift is from above, coming down from the Father of the heavenly lights, Who does not change like shifting shadows. (James 1:17)

But the person who loves God is the one Whom God recognizes. (1 Corinthians 8:3)

You know me inside and out, you know every bone in my body; You know exactly how I was made, bit by bit, how I was sculpted from nothing into something. Like an open book, you watched me grow from conception to birth; all the stages of my life were spread out before You. The days of my life all prepared before I'd even lived one day. (Psalm 139:14–16 MSG)

My dear sisters, God knows us intimately and loves us anyway! There is absolutely nothing that we can tell Him that will shock or surprise Him. God sees us at our worst and chooses to redeem us anyway. He prepared the days of our life before we ever lived one of them! God created us, and He is in the details. We are safe bringing anything and everything to Him! Get to know Him, to trust Him, to bask in His presence. I promise you, you will never be the same!

Today, may we declare the praises of God, who called us out of darkness and into His wonderful light!

AUGUST 7

Rejoice always, pray continually, give thanks in all circumstances; for this is God's will for you in Christ Jesus. (1 Thessalonians 5:16–18)

Give thanks to the Lord, for He is good. His love endures forever. (Psalm 136:1)

Every good and perfect gift is from above, coming down from the Father of the heavenly lights, Who does not change like shifting shadows. (James 1:17)

And whatever you do, whether in word or deed, do it all in the name of the Lord Jesus, giving thanks to God the Father through Him. (Colossians 3:17)

The Lord is my strength and my shield; my heart trusts in Him, and He helps me. My heart leaps for joy, and with my song I praise Him. (Psalm 34:1)

Perhaps it takes a purer faith to praise God for unrealized blessings than for those we once enjoyed or those we enjoy now.

—A.W. Tozer

As we express our gratitude, we must never forget that the highest appreciation is not to utter words, but to live by them."

—John F. Kennedy.

I read a story a few years back. It was about a woman who battled depression and anxiety. A friend of hers advised her to keep a "thanksgiving journal" and to write down every day twenty things that she was thankful for. The story included some of her entries. The list was fun, funny, and challenging. One I remember to this day was, "The way the light catches the bubbles as I do dishes and makes them shine iridescent." It got me thinking about all the seemingly little things that make me smile or give me comfort.

So for the rest of the week, I challenge you to share with someone you love something that you are thankful for! I will start. I love birds, and over the years, I have felt that God communicates with me through their gentle presence. One evening, my husband and I were sitting on our deck talking about our day when a bird came and perched right on the arm of my chair. Another morning, early, while sitting at the table in the kitchen, I looked out my window and an owl was perched on the rail, looking right at me. He sat there for some time, even showing me how he could turn his head completely around. I am thankful for birds, their song, and their presence. Okay, your turn.

Dear sisters, God is good. God is for us. We have so much to be thankful for and so much to look forward to. Remember always you are loved!

AUGUST 8

I can do all this through Him who gives me strength. (Philippians 4:13)

Finally, be strong in the Lord and in His Mighty Power. (Ephesians 6:10)

My soul is weary with sorrow, strengthen me according to Your Word. (Psalm 119:28)

He gives strength to the weary and increases the power of the weak. (Isaiah 40:29)

But those who hope in the LORD will renew their strength. They will soar on wings like eagles; they will run and not grow weary, they will walk and not be faint. (Isaiah 40:31)

Love the Lord your God with ALL your heart and with ALL your soul and with ALL your mind and with ALL your strength. (Mark 12:30)

God is our refuge and strength, an ever-present help in trouble. (Psalm 46:1)

But You, LORD, do not be far from me. You are my strength; come quickly to help me. (Psalm 22:19)

And David was greatly distressed, for the people spoke of stoning him, because all the people were bitter in soul, each for his sons and daughters. But David strengthened himself in the LORD his God. (1 Samuel 30:6)

Reading today's scriptures reminded me of so many times in my life when I have been emotionally knocked to my knees: when I found out that a good friend of mine's daughter had aggressive leukemia, when we found out our daughter was pregnant at sixteen, when we heard a friend's diagnosis of ALS, when my father in law died, when my husband coded in an ER in Wyoming, the times our business was vandalized, the many times we have lost good friends and dearly loved family!

I remember the feelings so well, the sudden spike in blood pressure, a weakening in the knees and the feeling of lightheadedness. At those moments, I understood completely why some people pass out at bad news! All I could muster was "God, HELP!"

How I wish from the bottom of my heart that we could all avoid those times of difficulty and trial in our lives. Unfortunately, we live in a fallen world, and the Bible is very clear that times of trial and testing will come. But the scriptures are also very clear that the LORD is willing and able to be our source of strength! He promises to be "ever present" in times of trial. Not only that, He promises strength and increased power to those who turn to Him as their source of support. Honestly, sisters, I can say without hesitation, if I did not have the strength of the Lord to hold me up, I would be emotionally fragile and terribly depressed. The Lord, my God, has met me in every situation. He has strengthened me physically, emotionally, and spiritually to face whatever the situation entailed. He has held me up physically even as my knees buckled! He has given me words of encouragement when my heart was breaking, and He has carried me through more times than I can count. And I KNOW He will continue to carry me, and to carry you, until He calls us home.

God is good! God is FOR us! And God promises to be our strength when we have none. I pray that out of His glorious riches, HE may strengthen you with POWER through HIS SPIRIT in your inner being. (Ephesians 3:16).

Shine on, sisters! The world needs your light!

AUGUST 9

So do not fear, for I Am with you, do not be dismayed, for I Am your God. I will strengthen you and help you. I will uphold you with My Righteous Right Hand. (Isaiah 41:10)

But the Advocate, the Holy Spirit, whom the Father will send in My Name, will teach you all things and will remind you of everything I have said to you. Peace I leave with you; My Peace I give you. I do not give to you as the world gives. Do not let your hearts be troubled and do not be afraid. (John 14:26–27)

But He said to me, "My grace is sufficient for you, for My Power is made perfect in weakness." Therefore I will boast all the more gladly about my weaknesses, so that Christ's power may rest on me. That is why, for Christ's sake, I delight in my weaknesses, in insults, in hardships, in persecutions, in difficulties. For when I am weak, then I am strong. (2 Corinthians 12:9–10)

Therefore, since we are surrounded by such a great cloud of witnesses, let us throw off everything that hinders and the sin that so easily entangles. And let us run with perseverance the race marked out for us, fixing our eyes on Jesus, the pioneer and the perfecter of faith. For the joy set before Him He endured the cross, scorning its shame and sat down at the right hand of the throne of God. Consider Him Who endured such opposition from sinners, so that you will not grow weary and lose heart. (Hebrews 12:1–3)

ALL-mighty, ALL-powerful, ALL-knowing God, we're here before Your throne once again. We come in our weakness, our confusion, and our ineptitude to handle life on our own terms. We have bought in to the world's lie that we need to "figure things out for ourselves," "buck up," and be all things to all people. We confess to you now; we cannot! We need You, Lord! We need Your wisdom, Your power, and Your strength! We confess that we finally realize we cannot live well in victory and fearless without You. And oh, Father, we WANT to be fearless! How we desire to look at the events happening in our world and say without hesitation, "My God's got this!" Help us to surrender ALL that is dear to us into Your capable, loving hands. Help us to believe You when You tell us that You are directing our steps. Harden our hearts against the arrows of our enemy, who bombards us with negative, weak, fearful thoughts; and instead, direct our gaze to You. Remind us of the "great cloud of witnesses" cheering us on. Remind us of YOUR POWER, YOUR ABILITY, and YOUR PROVISION. Guide us in faithfulness and determination to daily gird ourselves with the "God weapons" and armor You have prepared for us. May we dress wearing the belt of truth, with feet ready for battle, fitted with the gospel of peace. Carrying the breastplate of righteousness, and the shield of faith, with which we can extinguish all the flaming arrows of the evil one. Wearing the helmet of salvation and carrying the sword of the Spirit. Dressed and ready for battle, no matter what, no matter where! GOD, remind us, remind us over and over and over that YOU ARE ABLE, YOU ARE STRONGER, YOU ARE IN CONTROL! Help us to let go and TRUST YOU! WE love YOU, use us for Your glory! So be it. Amen!

AUGUST 10

And those whom He predestined, He also called; and these whom He called, He also justified; and these whom He justified, He also glorified. (Romans 8:30)

God knew what He was doing from the very beginning. He decided from the outset to shape the lives of those who love Him along the same lines as the life of His Son... After He called them by name, He set them on a solid basis with Himself. And then, after getting them established, He stayed with them to the end, gloriously completing what He had begun. (Romans 8:29–30 MSG)

For the gifts and the calling of God are irrevocable. (Romans 11:29)

God's gifts and God's call are under full warranty—never canceled, never rescinded. (Romans 11:29 MSG)

Therefore I, (Paul) the prisoner of the Lord, implore you to walk in a manner worthy of the calling with which you have been called. (Ephesians 4:1)

I want you to get out there and walk - better yet, run! - on the road God called you to travel. (Ephesians 4:1 MSG)

I press on toward the goal for the prize of the upward call of God in Christ Jesus. (Philippians 3:14)

By no means do I count myself an expert in all of this, but I've got my eye on the goal, where God is beckoning us onward - to Jesus. I'm off and running, and I'm not turning back. (Philippians 3:14)

Fight the good fight of faith; take hold of the eternal life to which you were called, and you made the good confession in the presence of many witnesses. (1 Timothy 6:12)

But you, (Women of God); Run for your life from all this. Pursue a righteous life - a life of wonder, faith, love, steadiness, courtesy. Run hard and fast in the faith. Seize the eternal life, the life you were called to, the life you so fervently embraced in the presence of so many witnesses. (1 Timothy 6:11–12 MSG)

What God has planned for our life and how we envisioned our lives going may very likely be completely different. He gives us experiences and trials that we would have never signed up for. And to top it all off, He calls us to be faithful and obedient!

God calls us. God plans out our lives. God leads us. God pursues us, calls us each by name, prepares in advance good works for us to be about doing. Whether those works look like; raising children, cleaning house, making dinner, working outside the home, or volunteering in a soup kitchen, God calls us to live and work with integrity, with love, faith, and courtesy. God blesses us with families, homes, and jobs and encourages us to work as if working for Him! Sometimes, perhaps quite often, God calls us out of our comfort zone. He might call one to the ministry. Others He may call to teach, yet some to business. But whatever God has called you to, He has promised that He will stay with you until the end and bring to completion what He has begun in you! God promises us that His gifts are irrevocable, never canceled, and never rescinded. When God calls us He equips and leads us. May we learn to trust Him. You are greatly and eternally loved! Seize the life to which you were called! You are a child of the KING!

AUGUST 11

And my God will meet all your needs according to the riches of His glory in Christ Jesus. (Philippians 4:19)

Every good and perfect gift is from above, coming down from the Father of the heavenly lights, Who does not change like shifting shadows. (James 1:17)

And God is able to bless you abundantly, so that in all things at all times, having all that you need, you will abound in every good work. (2 Corinthians 9:8)

I will give thanks to You, Lord, with all my heart; I will tell of all your wonderful deeds. (Psalm 9:1)

And whatever you do, whether in word or deed, do it all in the name of the Lord Jesus, giving thanks to God the Father through Him. (Colossians 3:17)

Let them give thanks to the Lord for His unfailing love and His wonderful deeds for mankind, for He satisfies the thirsty and fills the hungry with good things. (Psalm 107:8–9)

Truly God, You alone are worthy of our gratitude! You created the beauty around us, the stars at night that take our breath away, and the sun by day that warms and delights us! You meet all our needs, both our physical needs and also our emotional and spiritual needs as well. You look at us, Your daughters, and You see us completely. You see our sins and our brokenness, but You also see our strength and beauty and potential. Give us eyes to see ourselves and others like You see them and us. Give us hearts of genuine gratitude. We are truly thankful for what You have done in our lives, even the little things, like producing gardens, bright flowers, and warm sunshine, that we take so much for granted. And as Americans, living in a blessed nation, much of what we take for granted, others are praying for! Give us eyes to see and hearts to appreciate the multitude of blessings that continually flow from YOUR HANDS! God, You ARE good! You are kind, compassionate, and forgiving! We are so quick to blame You when things don't go our way, to bemoan, "Oh, where is God? Why doesn't He show Himself," when in actuality, You are all around us. That breath we just took without effort—gift. That mind that works and that heart that beats without thought from us—gift. That healthy child, spouse, friend—gift. The material blessings, physical blessings, and spiritual blessings, all gifts that flow freely from Your generous hand. Forgive us for thinking that because things aren't going the specific way we had hoped for, that You are somehow absent or indifferent. Forgive us for taking so much for granted and praising and thanking You so little! Fill us up with gratitude! Open our eyes to see the magnitude of Your presence in our lives! We love you, Lord! We offer to You today our prayers and thanksgiving for our lives, for Your presence, protection, provision, and peace! Thank You that You aren't done with us yet. Fill us and use us we pray. Amen.

AUGUST 12

Have this attitude in yourselves which was also in Christ Jesus, who, although He existed in the form of God, did not regard equality with God a thing to be grasped, but emptied Himself, taking the form of a bond-servant, and being made in the likeness of men. humbled Himself by becoming obedient to the point of death, even death on the cross. (Philippians 2:5–8)

Let no one seek her own good, but that of her neighbor. (1 Corinthians 10:24)

But, the one who is the greatest among you must become like the youngest, and the leader like the servant. (Luke 22:27)

And whoever wants to be first among you must become your slave. For even the Son of Man came not to be served but to serve others and to give His life as a ransom for many. (Matthew 20:27–28)

Care for the flock that God has entrusted to you. Watch over it willingly, not grudgingly - not for what you will get out of it, but because you are eager to serve God. (1 Peter 5:2)

Never be lazy, but work hard and serve the Lord enthusiastically. (Romans 12:11)

"I am here to serve you today, Lord"—may this be our motto as we grow into the women of wisdom, strength and beauty that God created us to be. Keeping in mind that serving others will fulfill us in such a way that will delight us, challenge us and engage us far beyond anything we could imagine! A life lived with Christ is neither boring nor routine. May we live our lives enthusiastically, excited about what lies ahead but working diligently wherever God has placed us. Mother Teresa said, "God cannot use you where He has not placed you." So enter into this day believing that God has you where He wants you and embrace whatever He sets before you today. Live boldly with your whole heart and your whole attention, bouncing on eager toes of anticipation, asking, "What's next, Papa?" God's knows what He is doing friends, and He can be trusted!

AUGUST 13

Make every effort to live in peace with everyone and to be holy; without holiness no one will see the Lord. (Hebrews 12:14)

But just as He who called you is holy, so be holy in all you do; for it is written: "be holy, because I am holy." (1 Peter 1:15–16)

He has saved us and called us to a holy life—not because of anything we have done but because of His own Purpose and grace. This grace was given us in Christ Jesus before the beginning of time. (2 Timothy 1:9)

Do everything without grumbling or arguing, so that you may become blameless and pure, children of God without fault in a warped and crooked generation. Then you will shine among them like stars in the sky as you hold firmly to the Word of Life. (Philippians 2:14–16)

So roll up your sleeves, put your mind in gear, be totally ready to receive the gift that's coming when Jesus arrives. Don't lazily slip back into those old grooves of evil, doing just what you feel like doing. You didn't know any better then; you do now. As obedient children, let yourselves be pulled into a way of life shaped by God's life, a life energetic and blazing with holiness. God said, "I Am Holy; you be holy." You call out to God for help and He helps - He's a good Father that way. But don't forget, He's also a responsible Father, and won't let you get by with sloppy living. Your life is a journey you must travel with a deep consciousness of God. It cost God plenty to get you out of the dead-end, empty-headed life you grew up in. (1 Peter 1:13–20 MSG)

But you are the ones chosen by God, chosen for the high-calling of priestly work, chosen to be a holy people, God's instruments to do His work and speak out for Him, to tell others of the night-and-day difference He made for you - from nothing to something, from rejected to accepted. (2 Peter 2:9–10)

Whoa! Today's scriptures left me wanting to throw my hands up in the air and admit I am a failure at living a holy life! I fail repeatedly at acting right, saying the right words, and doing the right things! Sure, sometimes I get it right but all the time? I don't give everything away and I fail to guard my mind or my heart! I feel the need to put on some sackcloth and hang my head! I felt so overwhelmed because I fully realize that I am totally incapable of living a holy life on my own. So I did some reading. Holy in the original Greek means "set apart" or "separated onto God," set apart for use by God, for His purposes. Holiness is an attitude of the heart. It is more about relationship with the ONE who makes us holy than about anything we can do on our own. Being holy is to be dedicated to the Lord.

Speaking from personal experience, holiness is a process. I desire to live a life pleasing to God, but I stumble. I make mistakes. I get crabby, angry, greedy! I know what the scriptures say, and I fully believe that when we pick and choose what we want to believe in scripture, we stomp on the very truth of God. But isn't it more loving to exclude some of the scriptures that are hard to present in a loving manner? God surely doesn't mean EVERYTHING He says in scripture? Can I still be holy and discredit parts of scripture I don't agree with? Unfortunately, we, as a nation, have been doing just that for years! That being said, holiness is not something we can achieve by our own efforts. Holiness comes from an honest, open, repentant relationship with Jesus Christ. Holiness is not something WE do, it is something CHRIST does in and through us as we grow in relationship with Him.

My dear sisters, we ARE called to be holy, to be set apart from the world and the world's ways. But God does not call us out of this world. He asks us to fully dive in to the life He has placed us in to witness His strength and His transformative power in our lives and to tell others, "Follow me! My Father loves you!" We may not be perfect, but we are a holy work in progress!

AUGUST 14

The LORD your God is in your midst, a Mighty One Who will save; He will rejoice over you with gladness; He will quiet you by His love; He will exult over you with loud singing. (Zephaniah 3:17)

Who shows no partiality to princes, nor regards the rich more than the poor, for they are all the work of His hands. (Job 34:19)

But You, O Lord, are a God merciful and gracious, slow to anger and abounding in steadfast love and faithfulness. (Psalm 86:15)

I love those who love Me, and those who seek Me diligently find Me. (Proverbs 8:17)

Give thanks to the God of heaven, for His steadfast love endures forever. (Psalm 136:26)

Many of us have a hard time understanding the love of God.

I personally have struggled with understanding His great love for me. I used to live like His love was dependent on my performance on my walk of faith, which is idolatry. My mindset was, "I have to do something to make God love me more."

—Fritz Chery

God's unfailing love for us is an object fact affirmed over and over in the Scriptures. It is true whether we believe it or not. Our doubts do not destroy God's love, nor does our faith create it. It originates in the very nature of God, who is love, and it flows to us through union with His Beloved Son.

—Jerry Bridges

Friends, our enemy would love for us to believe that God's love for us is contingent on our performance or at least dependent on the level of our love for Him. But that is contrary to what scripture tells us. God loves us because of WHO He is. His love is steadfast and faithful. He rejoices over us; He calls us by name and He knows us intimately! To reflect on God's love for us is freeing and powerful! We can live lives of joyful anticipation for the future, lives of encouragement and trust. We can believe with our whole hearts that God loves us, protects and guides us. Knowing that He calls us His children and loves us immensely, shrug off that load of guilt and regret you are carrying and run into the arms of the Father who knows you by name and cherishes you! You are loved more than you can ever imagine!

AUGUST 15

I can do all this through Him Who gives me strength. (Philippians 4:13)

He gives strength to the weary and increases the power of the weak. (Isaiah 40:29)

My soul is weary with sorrow; strengthen me according to Your Word. (Psalm 119:28)

Finally, be strong in the Lord and in His mighty power. (Ephesians 6:10)

But You, Lord, do not be far from me. You are my strength; come quickly to help me. (Psalm 22:19)

Surely God is my salvation; I will trust and not be afraid. The Lord, the Lord Himself, is my strength and my defense; He has become my salvation. (Isaiah 12:2)

For the Lord your God is He who goes with you to fight for you against your enemies, to give you the victory. (Deuteronomy 20:4)

Our strength, my strength comes from God. When troubles come and threaten to overwhelm me, God holds me up. He has done so in the past, and I know I can count on Him in the future. God CAN and DOES heal, but it is at His discretion and not mine. How I wish it were not so. For so many years, I prayed for healing and restoration for our daughter only to be disappointed over and over and over again. I knew in my heart God HEARD me, but the answer was no. It was hard. It made me angry, but God continued to give me the strength I needed day after day, trial after trial, hospitalization after hospitalization. God never left my side. He sat with me through all the nights of tears and no sleep, through the bad news and the court appointments. He managed the details when we brought her kids into our home and away from their mom. He strengthened, sustained, held, and encouraged us to keep on when we wanted to throw our hands up, harden our hearts, and give in to depression and guilt. God carried us on many occasions when our own strength failed. He gave us words to encourage others when our hearts were shattered. God came through in a big way when He said "no" to our requests.

Frankly, ladies, God can do whatever He wants whenever He wants with no need for explanation to us. God is God, and we are not! But God does not operate out of a hard or cold heart. God sees the picture of our lives and the lives of those around us in its entirety. He sees our conception to death in one glance. He KNOWS what He is doing. He asks us to TRUST Him. He made us to take a small part in the grand scheme of His DESIGN. Sometimes our part is difficult, and we wander around like God has deserted us. But God promises us He will NEVER leave us or forget about us even for an instant. He IS working all things out for His purposes and for His glory. And He promises us that we will not be disappointed! God understands the "rippling effect" the lives of believers have on the lives of those around them. We, as believers, oftentimes don't see or understand that, even in our trials, our weariness, our depression and struggles, God is working. He is strengthening us, even holding us, through those difficult times so that, when He delivers us through the trial, we come forth stronger, braver, and shining brighter than ever before! God is FOR us! He FIGHTS for us! He has called, claimed, and equipped us for whatever lies ahead, AND He promises us He will walk with us every step of the way! He is able when we are not, strong when we are weak, and passionate to save! God is good all the time. God is good!

AUGUST 16

For the Word of God is living and active, sharper than any two-edged sword, piercing to the division of soul and of spirit, of joints and of marrow, and discerning the thoughts and intentions of the heart. (Hebrews 4:12)

God means what He says. What He says goes. His powerful Word is sharp as a surgeon's scalpel, cutting through everything, whether doubt or defense, laying us open to listen and obey. Nothing and no one is impervious to God's Word. We can't get away from it - no matter what. (Hebrews 4:12–13 MSG)

Call to Me and I will answer you, and will tell you great and hidden things that you have not known. (Jeremiah 33:3)

So shall My Word be that goes out from My mouth; it shall not return to Me empty, but it shall accomplish that which I purpose, and shall succeed in the thing for which I sent it. (Isaiah 55:11)

All Scripture is breathed out by God and profitable for teaching, for reproof, for correction, and for training in righteousness. (2 Timothy 3:16)

Every part of Scripture is God-breathed and useful one way or another—showing us truth, exposing our rebellion, correcting our mistakes, training us to live God's way. Through the Word we are put together and shaped up for the tasks God has for us. (2 Timothy 3:16 MSG)

My dear sisters, God STILL speaks! He speaks to us through circumstances, wise counsel, people, dreams and visions, thoughts, nature, supernaturally, through the Bible, and through the peace He places deep in our souls which defies the chaotic world in which we live. Our God is alive and well! He is intricately involved in the details of this world. The politics, the division, the power struggles, He sees it all! He knows how it will play out, and He is moving in ways we can neither see nor imagine. Our enemy is no match for God! Our God also is orchestrating the events and details in our lives and in the lives of all of His children.

There are two voices we are inundated with, the voice of God and the voice of the enemy. Now, it seems to me that we have gotten pretty good at listening to the voice of the enemy. That is the voice that tells us, "Don't bother trying. You'll never be good enough or never succeed." The voice that belittles, discourages, and destroys us. Yet God is whispering at the same time, "I love you. Trust Me, I have plans to empower you, to encourage you, to bring you hope and a bright future. Join with Me. I will help you. I will strengthen you and uphold you with My righteous right hand."

Friends, we have a choice daily to choose who we will tune out. My prayer is that we will all learn to turn off the voice of our enemy and embrace and believe God's promises for us. That we will become firm in our belief that God IS Who He says He is, that He CAN do what He says He can do, and that He loves us! Because when we learn to operate and live our lives out of love instead of fear and defeat, we become useful in the hands of our God! When we believe we are who HE says we are, He can use us for His purposes and for His glory, and then, dear sisters, we will laugh in the face of fear and our enemy will run from us in terror! God is BIGGER and STRONGER and more powerful than ANYTHING we are facing! God's GOT THIS and US!

AUGUST 17

Immediately his leprosy was cleansed. (Matthew 8:3)

And immediately Jesus stretched forth His hand, and caught him, and said unto him, O thou of little faith, wherefore didst thou doubt? (Matthew 14:31)

And immediately their eyes received sight. (Matthew 20:34)

And immediately the fever left her, and she ministered unto them. (Mark 1:31)

Immediately the leprosy departed from him, and he was cleansed. (Mark 1:42)

Immediately, from what I found this morning, the word is used fifty-five times in the King James Version (KJV). I glanced at the scriptures, and most of the time, it was used in regard to healing. It was also used in response to God: "immediately the disciples left that place," "immediately the cock crowed." God can move mountains, heal the sick, and respond to our prayers immediately! He has done it before and He can do it again! Sisters, God is STILL in the miracle business!

The scripture that spoke to me this morning was this one. From Matthew 5:13–16, The Message Bible:

> Let me tell you why you are here. You're here to be salt-seasoning that brings out the God-flavors of this earth. If you lose your saltiness, how will people taste godliness? You've lost your usefulness and will end up in the garbage. Here's another

way to put it: You're here to be light, bringing out the God-colors in the world. God is not a secret to be kept. We're going public with this, as public as a city on a hill. If I make you light-bearers, you don't think I'm going to hide you under a bucket do you? I'm putting you on a light stand. Now that I've put you there on a hilltop, on a light stand—shine! Keep open house, be generous with your lives. By opening up to others, you'll prompt people to open up with God, this generous Father in heaven.

I pray that we will respond immediately when God calls us to open up our lives to those around us!

Shine on, sisters!

AUGUST 18

Y ou are my hiding place; You will protect me from trouble and surround me with songs of deliverance. (Psalm 32:7)

God is our refuge and strength, an ever-present help in trouble. (Psalm 46:1)

So we say with confidence, "The Lord is my helper; I will not be afraid. What can mere mortals do to me?" (Hebrews 13:6)

You make Your saving help my shield, and Your right hand sustains me; Your help has made me great. You provide a broad path for my feet so that my ankles do not give way. (Psalm 18:35–36)

Keep me safe, my God, for in You I take refuge. (Psalm 16:1)

The Lord will fight for you; you need only to be still. (Exodus 14:14)

The Lord is with me; I will not be afraid. What can mere mortals do to me? (Psalm 118:6)

I keep my eyes always on the Lord. With Him at my right hand, I will not be shaken. (Psalm 16:8)

Even to your old age and gray hairs I AM He, I AM He Who will sustain you. I have made you and I will carry you; I will sustain you and I will rescue you. (Isaiah 46:4)

Face it, friends; we all run to something in times of trouble or hardship. Some run to alcohol, some to drugs, some to the arms of another man and some to God. In fact, there is a Christian song out with those lyrics, but I think it is true. God wants to be the source of comfort for us. He promises us He will rescue us and even carry us! But I think that somewhere, maybe pushed to the back of our minds, is this doubt that God is really for us, that He really has our best interests at heart. I think it is safe to say that, for most of us, when hardships come, we question God's presence. We question His motives and we question whether He loves us at all. Then we begin to internalize these feelings thinking, "He would love me if I was, wasn't, didn't, did. So right then, we have just declared God's promises null and void because of our performance! My dear sisters, God loves us! He protects us, He carries us, He sustains us, He rescues us! Let's LET Him! Let's let God be God and trust Him to mold and make us into the women He made us to be. Let's go to Him with our pleas and requests and troubles and mistakes and believe that He hears, that He cares, and that He is able to handle everything that comes our way. When we doubt God's love for us, His ability to answer prayer, and His provision, we are listening to the voice of our enemy who desperately wants us to believe that God cannot or will not! Sisters, OUR GOD CAN be trusted! HE is our fortress in times of trouble and adversity! He is able and He is willing! Not only is He the one to run to in trouble, but He delights in us! He is pleased when we are happy, when we are smiling and enjoying life. He wants to be part of that as well! God wants ALL of us, not just the leftovers! He wants to be our first thought in the morning and our last thought at night. He wants to hear our laughter as well as collect our tears. God is ever present, ever faithful, and ever watchful. So today, let's not be afraid to stand still in His presence and let Him fight for us. We are daughters of the KING! Let's believe it and claim it!"

AUGUST 19

But blessed is the one who trusts in the Lord, whose confidence is in Him. They will be like a tree planted by the water that sends out its roots by the stream. It does not fear when heat comes; its leaves are always green. It has no worries in a year of drought and never fails to bear fruit. (Jeremiah 17:7–8)

Trust in the Lord with all your heart and lean not on your own understanding; in all your ways submit to Him, and He will make your paths straight. (Proverbs 3:5–6)

When I am afraid, I put my trust in You. (Psalm 56:3)

When you pass through the waters, I will be with you; and when you pass through the rivers, they will not sweep over you. When you walk through the fire, you will not be burned; the flames will not set you ablaze. (Isaiah 43:2)

Let the morning bring me word of Your unfailing love, for I have put my trust in you. Show me the way I should go, for to you I entrust my life. (Psalm 143:8)

For we live by faith, not by sight. (2 Corinthians 5:7)

He will not let your foot slip - He Who watches over you will not slumber. (Psalm 121:3)

Trust—how many times in scripture have we read that word? How many devotional reading have discussed that word? How often have you thought about that word? "Do you trust Me?" "Do you trust that I AM who I say I am, that you are who I say you are?" Do we trust scripture as moral, ethical, and complete truth? Do we trust that God really has our best interests at heart? Do we trust Him?

I pulled out my journal from 2010. That year, I was earnestly seeking knowledge about trust. I wrote down many scriptures that spoke to me during that time, and one of them is from Isaiah 30:15–16 in The Message Bible translation: "Your salvation requires you to turn back to Me and stop your silly efforts to save yourself. Your strength will come from settling down in complete dependence on Me."

My dear sisters, we cannot save ourselves. We can never be good enough, moral enough, righteous enough, or holy enough to save ourselves! God does the saving! Now, honestly, I think that we are all at a point that we believe that, so here's my next thought. If God is able to save us from hell, is He not worthy of our trust? Should we not trust Him day in and day out, through the storms of life and the moments on the mountaintops? He intricately wove us together in our mothers' wombs, gave us our strengths, and our personality traits, as well as our physical traits. He ordained the exact moment when we would live on this earth from beginning to end. And He prepared good works for us to be doing in advance of our birth. So here're questions that beg to be asked, taken from the book, *Radical*:

> Have I become so preoccupied with and dismayed by circumstances that I doubt God's ability to handle things in His own way and in His own time? Then I too am a fool! Do I doubt God's sovereignty? Either He IS sovereign or He is NOT God! Do I have the foggiest idea of what sort of power I so blithely invoke? Do I believe He is Who He says He is? Lord heal my unbelief!"

Friends, God delights in using ordinary Christians, like you and me, who come to the end of themselves and choose to trust in Him!

So the question God asks us today is; "Do you find Me to be qualified to orchestrate your days?" Only as individuals can we honestly answer that. If we believe God is worthy of our trust, what is holding us back from complete surrender to Him? Lord, heal our unbelief!

Have a great week! You are loved by an all-consuming, all-powerful, wild, dangerous, unfettered, living God! Trust Him! You won't be disappointed?

AUGUST 20

This is the message we have heard from Him and declare to you; God is Light; in Him there is no darkness at all. If we claim to have fellowship with Him and yet walk in the darkness, we lie and do not live out the truth. But if we walk in the light, as He is in the light, we have fellowship with one another, and the blood of Jesus, His Son, purifies us from all sin, If we claim to be without sin, we deceive ourselves and the truth is not in us. If we confess our sins, He is faithful and just and will forgive us our sins and purify us from all unrighteousness. (1 John 1:5–9)

But you are a chosen people, a royal priesthood, a holy nation, God special possession, that you may declare the praises of Him Who called you out of darkness into His wonderful light. (1 Peter 2:9)

I saw that wisdom is better than folly, just as light is better than darkness. (Ecclesiastes 2:13)

The Light shines in the darkness, and the darkness has not overcome it. (John 1:5)

All mighty God, Your word tells us of Your attributes. It tells us that You are an all-consuming fire, that You are light, that You are all knowing and all powerful! We, as Your daughters, cannot draw near You without being bathed in Your light. Draw us nearer to Your presence. May we embrace this great love that beckons us and let it draw us nearer and nearer to You. As we grow in relationship with You and You reveal areas of sin in our lives, help us to willingly surrender those things to You. For You alone are able to purify us, heal us, and restore us. I think the world sees this great light that is Your presence but refuses to acknowledge it for fear of being found out, for fear of being exposed. But we, as Your children, walk willingly in Your presence. We desire to live lives that reflect Your great light, and we desire to light up the darkness that surrounds us. Help us! Forgive us when we fail and draw us back to Yourself. Without You, we stumble and flail around in the dark. Make us brave and bold to declare the hope we have found in Your presence. We love You, we thank You, and we boldly ask, as Your daughters, that You love us extravagantly, guide our steps, and order our lives so that, when we arrive home into Your presence, we may hear those words we so desperately want to hear: "Well done, good and faithful servant!" Amen.

AUGUST 21

For all have sinned, and fall short of the glory of God. (Romans 3:23)

Keep Your servant also from willful sins; may they not rule over me. Then I will be blameless, innocent of great transgression. May these words of my mouth and this mediation of my heart be pleasing in Your sight, LORD, my Rock and my Redeemer. (Psalm 19:13–14)

For your ways are in full view of the Lord, and He examines all your paths. The evil deeds of the wicked ensnare them; the cords of their sins hold them fast. (Proverbs 5:21–22)

Direct my footsteps according to Your Word; let no sin rule over me. (Psalm 119:133)

Above all, love each other deeply, because love covers over a multitude of sins. (1 Peter 4:8)

A good woman brings good things out of the good stored up in her heart, and an evil woman brings evil things out of the evil stored up in her heart. For the mouth speaks what the heart is full of. (Luke 6:45)

Sin. Unfortunately, in the world in which we live, sin is oftentimes ignored, justified, or even glorified. Our enemy has been having a wonderful time "redefining" sin and making sins against God and each other normal and accepted. But the Bible is very clear on the consequences of sin. Romans 6:23 says, "For the wages of sin is death, but the free gift of God is eternal life in Christ Jesus our Lord." Death! Eternal death! Eternal separation from God and banishment from heaven! That's some pretty serious consequences! Sin is deplor-able and unacceptable to God. The God we love and serve and run to is holy! Sin is an abomination to Him and, as such, needs to be dealt with.

Sometimes it is easier to see the sin in someone else's life. Sometimes, we see only the sin in our own. Either way, the only sin we can deal with immediately and completely is our own! When we were robbed and vandalized at the store, that was a sin against us. However, the anger and hatred and fear I felt were sins I had to own. In slowly forgiving the offenders and confessing my anger and bitterness, I was forgiven and healed. Speaking from experience, I can imagine that all of us are carrying around pockets of pain, rejection, and confusion caused by the sin of another, but by asking for forgiveness for our response to the pain, we are not justifying the sin against us, just admitting that we too have sinned and perhaps have lashed out in anger or judgment. Sin is a cancer that spreads and infects our thoughts as well as our actions. It has to go! Let's take ours to the very throne of God and leave it there, for our Father is gracious and forgiving. He loves us and directs our steps. Let us quickly throw out anything that stands in the way of His work in us!

You ARE LOVED!

AUGUST 22

Blessed are the gentle (meek) for they shall inherit the earth. (Matthew 5:5)

But let it be the hidden person of the heart, with the imperishable quality of a gentle and quiet spirit, which is precious in the sight of God. (1 Peter 3:4)

Cultivate inner beauty, the gentle, gracious kind that God delights in. (1 Peter 3:4 MSG)

But He gives a greater grace therefore it says, "God is opposed to the proud, but gives grace to the humble." (James 4:6)

But what happens when we live God's way? He brings gifts into our lives, much the same way that fruit appears in an orchard - things like affection for others, exuberance about life, serenity. We develop a willingness to stick with things, a sense of compassion in the heart, and a conviction that a basic holiness permeates things and people. We find ourselves involved in loyal commitments, not needing to force our way in life, able to marshal and direct our energies wisely. (Galatians 5:22–23)

The definition of meekness is "strength under control." Perhaps meekness could be defined as a determination to trust the hand that is holding us, not demanding our own way but believing that God can be trusted to handle the details and living with a willingness to be still in His presence and humble in our responses to the difficulties of life.

Personally, I think meekness and humility have been two of the virtues that our enemy has twisted and redefined. Our God cherishes a gentle and humble spirit, but the world calls that weak, even spineless. God says, "Look out for the needs of others." The world says, "Every man/woman for themselves. Me first!" God says, "Trust Me. I'm in control." The world says, "I'm in control!" Because of our enemy, life on this planet is a constant power struggle. MY way versus God's way. The funny thing is we mere mortals seem to think we know better than GOD!

I have made it a point to try to avoid people who leave destructive words, critical responses, and short-tempered reactions in their wake. They seem to go through life leaving a trail of emotional and relational debris in their path! My dear friends, may God's spirit so rule our lives and our words that the world cannot help but take notice. May the words and actions of our lives speak as a clear witness of the Holy Spirit that lives within us! God is FOR us! We don't need to bully our way through life. God's got THIS!

AUGUST 23

 T his resurrection life you received from God is not a timid, grave-tending life. It's adventurously expectant. God's Spirit beckons: There are things to do and places to go! (Romans 8:14–15 MSG)

You have not because you ask not. (Matthew 7:7)

But they who wait for the LORD shall renew their strength; they shall mount up with wings like eagles; they shall run and not be weary; they shall walk and not faint. (Isaiah 40:31)

Be strong and courageous. Do not fear or be in dread of them, for it is the LORD your God who goes with you. He will not leave you or forsake you. (Deuteronomy 31:6)

Little children, you are from God and have overcome them, for He who is in you is greater than he who is in the world. (1 John 4:4)

God's way is not a matter of mere talk, it's an empowered life! (1 Corinthians 4:18)

Oswald Chambers said, "God wants us to venture our all with total abandoned confidence in Him." Entrust yourself to God's hands. Throw yourself with abandon and total confidence unto God.

I absolutely LOVE the idea of praying BIG and asking BOLDLY! I fear that we have so marginalized God and tried to limit His influence in our lives (consciously or unconsciously) that we have forgotten WHO He is! My dear sisters, the God we are seeking, learning about, and pursuing is pursuing us! I realize I have said it a hundred times, but this God is ALL powerful, ALL knowing, ALL seeing, ALL understanding, ALL consuming, as well as ALL almighty! Absolutely nothing is too difficult for Him or beyond His understanding or His control. We have got to take Him out of the box we have limited Him to in our lives and let Him have control of all the details of our lives! God is FOR us!

I am so sick and tired of the notion that because we are Christians, we live our lives in this dogged, religious state—heads down, feet dragging, timid, and yes, grave tending! There is *so* much more to this life that God has given us. I am all in with the adventurously expectant life that God offers us. I am kneeling before His throne today and every day, asking BOLDLY for God to do mighty things in and through me! I am praying for wisdom, discernment, and a learned tongue to proclaim the truth that has set me free!

I want to be done with the "mere talk" mentality and grab with both hands the empowered life that He is offering! Will you join me? Because I am certain it's gonna be good! You are greatly and eternally loved! Let's live like it!

AUGUST 24

Throw wide the gates so good and true people can enter. People with their minds set on You, You keep completely whole, steady on their feet, because they keep at it and don't quit. Depend on God and keep at it because in the Lord God you have a sure thing. (Isaiah 26:3–4 MSG)

You will keep in perfect peace her whose mind is steadfast, because she trusts in You. Trust in the Lord forever, for the Lord, the Lord, is the Rock eternal. (Isaiah 26:3–4 NIV)

But the eyes of the Lord are on those who fear Him, on those whose hope is in His unfailing love. (Psalm 33:18)

They eyes of the Lord are on the righteous and His ears are attentive to their cry. (Psalm 34:15)

My soul finds rest in God alone; my salvation comes from Him. He alone is my rock and my salvation; He is my fortress, I will never be shaken. (Psalm 62:1–2)

However humble our circumstances or undramatic our talents, our true purpose has been revealed. We were meant to be this person at this time and place. Not only for ourselves, but for you and other people - we were meant to make a particular contribution to the world. And so we must do it well. Do it with faith and patience, with all our strength and passion.
—Marjorie Holmes

The middle of the night is oftentimes when I feel the need to work something out in my head. I never really get it worked out, just lose sleep! Perhaps that would be a good time to recite Psalm 62, "My soul finds rest in You Alone God, I will never be shaken!" The other verses I picked today are just to remind us that God's eyes are always on us. He is not just off somewhere, waiting for us to call on Him. He is always watching, always attentive to our cries. God isn't just with us in the difficult times, but He is right beside us on the good days. During the times we are laughing so hard that the tears are rolling down our faces, during the times we are so filled with love for our families and friends that we feel we could burst. I believe it brings Him so much joy when we include Him and consciously thank Him and think of Him in those times!

Early this morning, I was having a conversation with God, asking Him why I was working on this devotional every morning. I don't know if you have realized it or not, but I am fearful that I will wander off and do this for me, for my glory, and my personal reasons. I constantly ask God to use this devotional for His purpose and His glory. I frequently—okay, always—ask God, "What do you want me to say?" And today as once again I was having this conversation, I felt Him say, "Tell them how crazy I am about them! Tell them how proud of them I am for desiring to know Me better. Tell them I am for them! Tell them I chose them as my daughters, placed them exactly where I wanted them, and will be with them wherever they go—to the quilt retreats, basketball games, and in their homes—as well as with them on their adventures. Tell them I will be with their children and grandchildren as they move away and with them when they are ill. Tell them it is no accident they are seeking Me. Tell them I have been pursuing them."

I want you all so desperately to believe God's promises and believe that you are worth dying for because God thinks so!

You are loved so very, very much! Believe it!

AUGUST 25

The Spirit and the bride say, "Come!" Let the one who hears this say, "Come!" Let whoever is thirsty come, whoever wishes may have the water of life as a free gift. (Revelation 22:17)

The Father gives Me My people. Every one of them will come to Me, and I will always accept them. (John 6:37)

I ask the Father in His great glory to give you the power to be strong inwardly through His Spirit. I pray that Christ will live in your hearts by faith and that your life will be strong in love and be built on love. And I pray that you and all God's holy people will have the power to understand the greatness of Christ's love—how wide and how long and how high and how deep that love is. Christ's love is greater than anyone can ever know, but I pray that you will be able to know that love. Then you can be filled with the fullness of God. With God's power working in us, God can do much, much, more than anything we can ask or imagine. (Ephesians 3:16–20)

Good morning, lovely ladies!

Honestly, friends, I don't think we can imagine the great love of the Father for us, we are His children! I have a hard time getting around the fact that God loves me unconditionally. I certainly *feel* more *lovable* at some times over others, but I need to remember that God loves us always, no matter what, through thick and thin. He loves us through adversity and through celebration! We have a God who knows us intimately and loves us more than our little minds can grasp. I believe someday, when we step foot in heaven, we will be completely overwhelmed by the of the magnitude of God's love for us!

Today, let His love envelop you. Feel God's arms around you and hear Him whisper, "Come! Come with whatever is on your heart and mind." Hear Him remind you, "No one loves you more than I do." We are never, ever walking this journey alone, sisters! God is very near, extending the invitation to come to Him, lean on Him, and trust in Him. May we walk through this day remembering that "with God's power working in us, God can do much, much more than anything we can ask or imagine!"

Have a great day!

AUGUST 26

But the people who trust the Lord will become strong again. They will rise up as an eagle in the sky; they will run and not need rest; they will walk and not become tired. (Isaiah 40:31 NCV)

I only ask one thing from the Lord. This is what I want: Let me live in the Lord's house all my life. Let me see the Lord's beauty and look with my own eyes at His Temple. (Psalm 27:4)

Brothers and sisters, think about the things that are good and worthy of praise. Think about the things that are true and honorable and right and pure and beautiful and respected. (Philippians 4:8)

I remember hearing as a young girl, "You will only be as happy as you set your mind to be." I thought it a curious phrase then, but the older I get, the more wisdom I find in those words. Personally speaking, when I consistently remind myself of why my husband can be a pain in the you know what, or of how taken for granted I feel, or how I can never seem to catch up or make time for everyone I would like to, my happiness sinks to the depths and I feel frustrated and discouraged. However, when my thinking goes more like—Thank you Lord for a husband who loves me and for the blessings of family and friends. "Wow! Can you believe the beautiful place I get to live? I have certainly been blessed with family and wonderful friends. I am thankful for a house to clean, clothes to wash and food to pre-pare!"—when my thoughts go that way, my heart soars!

The Lord CAN make us strong again. He CAN grant us peace! I think the first step is for us to realize that our thoughts have power over us. God asks us to be thankful and to trust Him. If we take a minute and look back at our track record with God, we can see that HE has been faithful. Can God say the same about us? There have been times where I have felt that God was simply an angry, judgmental God who really couldn't care less about my happiness. But the truth of the matter is God loves us more than we can imagine. He desires us to be whole, healed, and joyful! After all, what kind of an impression do we leave when we walk through life feet dragging, head down, and a sour expression on our face? As for me, I am bouncing on eager toes of anticipation to see what God has in store for me and for you, my dear sisters in Christ! Have a great day!

AUGUST 27

So God raised Him to the highest place. God made His name greater than every other name so that every knee will bow to the name of Jesus - everyone in heaven, on earth, and under the earth. And everyone will confess that Jesus Christ is Lord and bring glory to God the Father. (Philippians 2:9–11)

Now this is what the Lord says. He created you, people of Jacob; He formed you, people of Israel. He says, "Don't be afraid, because I have saved you. I have called you by name, and you are Mine." (Isaiah 43:1)

I am the good shepherd. I know My own and My own know Me, just as the Father knows Me and I know the Father; and I lay down My life for the sheep. (John 10:14–15)

Before I formed you in the womb I knew you, and before you were born I consecrated you; I appointed you a prophet to the nations. (Jeremiah 1:5)

"Because she loves me," says the LORD, "I will rescue her; I will protect her, for she acknowledges my name." (Psalm 91:14, NIV)

I love this scripture in Isaiah because I love, love, love the idea that God has called each of us by name, not just a random "Hey, anyone that is interested, follow Me." No, God called us EACH by name: "Sherryl, follow Me"; "Marilyn, trust Me"; "Kim, give it to Me"; "Barb, I've got this." Not only does He call us by name, He knows us better than we know ourselves! He knows every word on our lips BEFORE we say it! He knit us together in our mothers' wombs and placed us each exactly where He wants us! The Lord of the universe can't get more personal than that! But did you catch it? At the end of Isaiah 43, verse 1? Not only does he KNOW us intimately, He says, "You are MINE"! wow! God doesn't disown us because we screw up or lose our temper or have questions and doubts. He claims us through it all! My dear sisters, once He calls us, He CLAIMS us! Let this sink in and drown out any remaining doubt. YOU ARE A CHILD OF GOD! He has called you, redeemed you, and will someday bring you home in to His glorious presence! It doesn't get any better than that!

AUGUST 28

Submit yourselves, then to God. Resist the devil and he will flee from you. Come near to God and He will come near to you. (James 4:7–8)

Therefore, there is no condemnation for those who are in Christ Jesus, because through Christ Jesus the law of the Spirit of life set me free from the law of sin and death. (Romans 8:1–2)

Surely God is my salvation; I will trust and not be afraid. (Isaiah 12:2)

The Lord will fight for you, and you have only to be silent. (Exodus 14:14)

You will not need to fight in this battle. Stand firm, hold your position, and see the salvation of the Lord on your behalf. (2 Chronicles 20:17a)

Submit yourselves therefore to God. Resist the devil, and he will flee from you. (James 4:7)

So many times we wonder why life is so difficult. As followers of Christ shouldn't our way be easy? Shouldn't it be smoothed out for us? I think we oftentimes forget the reality of the spiritual battle going on for our souls at any given moment. Satan HATES our allegiance to Christ and so the battle ensues. The good news is that although we do indeed live in a fallen world, the outcome of the battle is certain. GOD WINS! As children of God, we have no reason for fear! I think perhaps a call to endurance, trust, and faith in the one who holds us, protects us, and directs us is in order! God's got whatever you are going through. I wish you and I didn't have to walk through some of the hard stuff in our lives, but rest assured, if we endure through difficult times, joy will be just around the corner!

God is crazy about you! In fact, as His children, we are NEVER out of His sight or far from His intervention! So take a deep breath and step out with faith and remember always the hand that is holding yours and the power of the One fighting for you! Have a great week!

AUGUST 29

When they reached the place God had told him about, Abraham built an altar there and arranged the wood on it. He bound his son Isaac and laid him on the altar, on top of the wood. Then he reached his hand and took the knife to slay his son. But the angel of the Lord called out to him from heaven, "Abraham! Abraham!" "Here I am," he replied. "Do not do anything to him. Now I know that you fear God, because you have not withheld from Me your son, your only son." (Genesis 22:9–12)

Now to Him who is able to do immeasurably more than all we ask or imagine, according to His power that is at work within us. (Ephesians 3:20)

The Lord replied, "My Presence will go with you, and I will give you rest." (Exodus 33:14)

Honestly, I don't like the story about Abraham taking his son to sacrifice him, or that fact that God would ask him to do such a horrific thing! Yet when I think about it in the context of idol worship, I begin to understand what the Bible is saying through this story. The God of Abraham as well as the God of all of us is NOT content to play second fiddle! Nor is He content to occupy any place other than front and center in our lives. So many times we put our relationship with God on the back burner, thinking, "I will get to my spiritual life later. I have too many other things that are frankly more important to me right now." They may be good things, like family, friends, work, etc., but they are not the best thing. Only God deserves our worship!

It's kind of ironic. We try so desperately to smooth the way for our children and grandchildren, we worry about them, cry over them, and will defend them without a second thought. Yet God promises that HE will go with them, that HIS presence will be with them wherever they go. He tells us that we cannot begin to understand how "wide and long and high and deep" His love is! His presence in our loved ones' lives far surpasses ANYTHING we could ever do or even imagine for them. It's time to let go, sisters! Let go of the fear for the future, fear of harm, or fear of all the many dreaded things Satan wants us to dwell on. Instead, lets train our thinking to rest on God's power, His wisdom, and His strength. Let's pray for our family and friends in a spirit of surrender, surrendering them to God, lifting up their very souls to God for His purpose and His glory. Because we can trust it when scripture tells us that God is able to do immeasurably more than ALL we can ask or imagine! He loves us, my dear, dear friends! And He is worthy of center stage in our lives and deserving of our trust and worship!

AUGUST 30

O Lord, You have searched me and you know me. You know when I sit and when I rise; you perceive my thoughts from afar. You discern my going out and my lying down; you are familiar with all my ways. Before a word is on my tongue You know it completely, O Lord. (Psalm 139:1–4)

But now in Christ Jesus you who once were far away have been brought near through the blood of Christ. (Ephesians 2:13)

God made Him who had no sin to be sin for us, so that in Him we might become the righteousness of God. (2 Corinthians 5:21)

Become friends with God, He's already a friend with you. How? you ask. In Christ. God put the wrong on Him who never did anything wrong so we could be put right with God. (2 Corinthians 5:21 MSG)

Sit back a moment, sisters. Soak it in. Hear God whisper, "I am nearer than you dare believe, closer than the air you breathe. Before I formed you in your mother's womb, I knew you! I know your every thought…know your travel plans and your habits, nothing dear child, absolutely nothing can separate you from My Loving Presence."

And then to make it possible for us to have a relationship with an all-powerful, all-knowing, sin-hating God, He sent His Son to bear the weight of our sin on the cross so that we are without blemish as we approach the very throne of God!

Dear heavenly Father, it is with a joyful and grateful heart that we approach Your throne this morning. Thank you for loving us, for interceding for us, and for being our friend. May we learn to grasp the depth, width, and expansiveness of Your love for us so that we may in turn offer love and forgiveness to those in our lives. May YOUR glory be so bright in our lives that we do indeed bring light into the darkness of this world. May we leak Jesus on everyone we meet today in Jesus's precious name. So be it. Amen!

AUGUST 31

I hen God said to Moses, "I AM WHO I AM." When you go to the people of Israel, tell them, "I AM sent me to you." (Exodus 3:14)

Don't you know that you are God's temple and that God's Spirit lives in you? (1 Corinthians 3:16)

The Lord tell His secrets to those who respect Him; He tells them about His agreement. My eyes are always looking to the Lord for help. He will keep me from any traps. (Psalm 25:14–15)

Lord, tell me Your ways. Show me how to live. Guide me in Your truth, and teach me, my God, my Savior. I trust You all day long. (Psalm 25:4–5)

I don't know about you, sweet sisters, but, boy, oh boy, did I need the reminder this morning that God's spirit lives within me! I woke up early feeling overwhelmed, inadequate, and sad. Getting mom's house ready has proved challenging, as most things do. Things are going well, a little slower than planned, but hey, that's to be expected, right? Parent's night at school to kick off sports for the grandchildren living with us is a hard reminder for the kids that their mom will not be there. She will not be at a game ever again. Tears last night. Hey, I get that too! But it doesn't make it any easier. We have had a younger grandson since Monday and will till Sunday. He is a great, quirky kid. You can tell he is pretty much an only child; he is rather high maintenance. I am tired and feeling old! We are STILL working on our brick wall behind the house, and my husband has decided we need to finish it before our grandson goes back to school! I get that, but mom's house is still sitting with a to-do list! To top it off, I have been in long conversations with a friend whose son's funeral is this Saturday! My heart breaks for her, and I have been dreaming about that family and everything we have to do and not sleeping! THAT, my friends, is why I so desperately needed the reminder this morning that God's spirit lives in me. I not only need His spirit but His wisdom and His strength. I am painfully aware that I am ill-equipped and unprepared to handle this life on my own. I don't know WHY the Lord of the angel armies cares about carpet layers, plumbers, and carpet cleaners fitting into a tight schedule, or why He would want to be involved in the details of my life. But scripture reminds me that God is involved in all the moments of my life, and yours! So this morning, as I linger over my second cup of coffee, I am taking a deep breath, heading back to Menards (for the sixth time) and remembering who is holding, guiding, and loving me every minute of every day. He's got this! And He's got whatever you are experiencing in your life right now as well. You are loved more than you can ever, ever, EVER imagine! And someday, you will know without a shadow of a doubt that I am right on that count!

SEPTEMBER 1

Teach me to do Your will, for You are my God; Let Your good Spirit lead me on level ground. (Psalm 143:10)

Or do you think lightly of the riches of His kindness and tolerance and patience, not knowing that the kindness of God leads you to repentance? (Romans 2:4)

For everything created by God is good, and nothing is to be rejected if it is received with gratitude. (1 Timothy 4:4)

For You, Lord are good, and ready to forgive. And abundant in lovingkindness to all who call upon you. (Psalm 86:5)

O give thanks to the LORD for He is good; for His lovingkindness is everlasting. (1 Chronicles 16:34, Psalm 106:1)

Every good thing given and every perfect gift is from above, coming down from the Father of Lights, with Whom there is no variation or shifting shadow. (James 1:17)

O taste and see that the LORD is good; How blessed is the woman who takes refuge in Him! (Psalm 34:8)

God is good all the time. God is good!

Those of you that know my husband know that He is fond of saying, "God is good." In fact, it is the tagline on every text he sends. What you may not know is those words, "God is good" were also the "tag" line I used at our daughter's funeral in 2015. "God is good, all the time, God is good."

Sometimes we have to remind ourselves over and over about that truth. When our lives are hard, when there is pain and heartache, it is hard to remember and believe it. But the fact that we don't always believe it does not make it any less true, just like refusing to acknowledge night does not make it day! I think one of the reasons I personally doubt God's goodness at times is because I don't understand what God is doing. I, in my limited thinking, cannot imagine how He can possibly bring good out of some really difficult things. I can't figure it out, so I doubt God. I don't trust in His goodness, His wisdom, or His agenda, which, in all honesty, makes me a fool. How could I possibly understand what God is up to? How can I dare imagine I know better than God?

God warns us in His word that we will go through difficult times. Scripture says, "When you walk through the fire," not if. He is warning us, reminding us, preparing us for the difficulties of this life. My dear sisters, we live in a fallen world, a world at war with the ways of God. Our enemy is having his way destroying families, lives, and communities. Of course, we will be attacked. We are in a battle! But, and this is BIG, God is FOR us! He has our backs! He has tried to warn us, counsel us, and prepare us for whatever lies ahead! He is reminding us over and over again, "Stick with Me! I am good! I love you, care for you, and will protect you. I'VE GOT THIS!" Even though and even when we don't understand why God is allowing life to go the way it often times does, we can still believe and trust in God's goodness.

If we will just take a moment and reflect on all the way's that God has shown His true nature to us, we will be encouraged. God shows us His goodness in the provision and beauty that He supplies day in and day out. Nature speaks this loudly to some—the provision of food, health, and stability to others. God also shows His goodness by intervening in the lives of His children, sometimes through friends, pastors, or even strangers, providing encouragement or meeting our needs at just the right time. I am convinced that, when we die, we will be blown over by the sheer number of times God has intervened in our lives for our good! And then, finally, God outdid Himself in goodness when He sent Jesus to pay for our sin so that we could enter into relationship with Him.

My dear friends, God is good, ALL the time. God is good!

SEPTEMBER 2

Rejoice always, pray continually, give thanks in all circumstances; for this is God's will for you in Christ Jesus. (1 Thessalonians 5:16–18)

Do not be anxious about anything, but in every situation, by prayer and petition, with thanksgiving, present your requests to God. And the peace of God, which transcends all understanding, will guard your hearts and your minds in Christ Jesus. (Philippians 4:6–7)

Don't fret or worry. Instead of worrying, pray. Let petitions and praises shape your worries into prayers, letting God know your concerns. Before you know it, a sense of God's wholeness, everything coming together for good, will come and settle you down. It's wonderful what happens when Christ displaces worry at the center of your life. (Philippians 4:6–7 MSG)

Meanwhile, the moment we get tired in the waiting, God's Spirit is right alongside helping us along. If we don't know how or what to pray, it doesn't matter. He does our praying in and for us, making prayer out of our wordless sighs, our aching groans. He knows us far better than we know ourselves, knows our pregnant condition, and keeps us present before God. That's why we can be so sure that every detail in our lives of love for God is worked into something good. (Romans 8:26–27 MSG)

He has told you, woman, what is good; and what does the Lord require of you but to do justice, and love kindness, and to walk humbly with your God. (Micah 6:8)

We often times question, "What is God's will or plan for my life?" We pray for guidance, discernment, and wisdom to make God honoring decisions. Yet when we are living in relationship with God, God is already discerning our movements; guiding us in the direction He would have us go; closing doors when we turn the wrong way; and orchestrating the moments of our days, months, and years. I believe that God is so intricately woven into the daily fabric of our lives that, as His children, we would have to work hard to be separated from His will for us! Sure, we get distracted, take some wrong steps, and lose focus, but God does not! Two Timothy 2:19 says this, "Nevertheless, God's solid foundation stands firm, bearing this inscription: The Lord knows those who are His."

My dear sisters, we are KNOWN by God. He has called us, claimed us, and promised to be with us always. We are His! So I think that instead of worrying about God's will or plan for our lives, we should instead embrace where He has us in THIS moment, in THIS place, living out our days with an attitude of gratitude for what He has already done in our lives. Then look forward to the future with a heart of thankfulness for what He has in store because, you KNOW, it's gonna be good!

You are loved! You are called and you are claimed by the Creator Himself! You are a daughter of the KING!

SEPTEMBER 3

B ut they who wait for the LORD shall renew their strength; they shall mount up with wings like eagles; they shall run and not be weary; they shall walk and not faint. (Isaiah 40:31)

I believe that I shall look upon the goodness of the Lord in the land of the living! Wait for the Lord; be strong, and let your heart take courage; wait for the Lord! (Psalm 27:13–14)

The Lord is good to those who wait for him, to the soul who seeks Him. (Lamentations 3:25)

The Lord is not slow to fulfill His promises as some count slowness, but is patient toward you, not wishing that any should perish, but that all should reach repentance. (2 Peter 3:9)

Wait for the Lord; be strong, and let your heart take courage; wait for the Lord! (Psalm 27:14)

But as for me, I will look to the Lord; I will wait for the God of my salvation; my God will hear me. (Micah 7:7)

Waiting! There are not many things harder to do than to wait! But as God's children, we are asked to make our request known to God and then to wait on His timing. Sometimes God says no, but sometimes, when He says yes, He also says, "In My time." Now, personally, I oftentimes think I know better than God and rush ahead and try and fix or orchestrate things to happen in MY time. I am sure you all know how well that works out! Waiting is not something that comes naturally to us. We are used to getting what we want when we want it! The whole concept of "waiting on God" is foreign to us. We can only see or understand our immediate concerns about an issue.

But God, He sees the WHOLE picture, everyone involved and all the outcomes of any one decision or action. His response truly is worth the wait! So, my dear friends, let's ask God for help with whatever is weighing on us right now, and then, let us take courage, be strong, and wait for our Lord God to take action because He's got this!

SEPTEMBER 4

M ake every effort to live in peace with everyone and to be holy; without holiness no one will see the Lord. (Hebrews 12:14)

He has saved us and called us to a holy life - not because of anything we have done but because of His own purpose and grace. This grace was given us in Christ Jesus before the beginning of time. (2 Timothy 1:9)

In your relationships with one another, have the same mindset as Christ Jesus. (Philippians 2:5)

In all things show yourself to be an example of good deeds, with purity in doctrine, dignified, sound in speech which is beyond reproach, so that the opponent will be put to shame, having nothing bad to say about us. (Titus 2:7–8)

Therefore, since we have these promises, dear friends, let us purify ourselves from everything that contaminates body and spirit, perfecting holiness out of reverence for God. (2 Corinthians 7:1)

"Church ladies," they have a reputation that is a comedians fodder! *Saturday Night Live* has a great spoof about church ladies. I have personally known a few of the church ladies portrayed in numerous skits. Unfortunately, playing "holier than thou" or Miss Judgmental is probably NOT the image of Christ we would like to leave on the minds of those who may be watching us. Let me tell you about a few of the church ladies that have had a profound effect on my life.

My aunt Esther. Now she was a Christian woman, strong willed, wise, and not shy about pointing out errant behavior. In my case, it was a lack of appreciation for a gift I had been given by my parents for my birthday. I remember it well. My mom had given me a brush, comb, and mirror set for my eighth birthday. It was white with pink flowers. I was NOT impressed. Now, normally we didn't celebrate birthdays, so you would think that the fact that I got a gift at all would have thrilled me, but I was unappreciative. My aunt Esther took me aside and told me that she was disappointed in me for the way I acted. I knew she was right. I was ashamed and apologized to my mom. I can't remember Esther's exact words, but she expressed how much she loved me and knew I was capable of better behavior. I don't know why that had such a profound effect on me. Perhaps because I loved her so much, admired her, and enjoyed being with her. She was, in fact, the strongest woman I have ever met. She was like the glue that held my dad's family together. I have so many Esther stories that have inspired and encouraged me.

Another woman who was such a blessing for me was MaryAnn. She was one of the ladies in our church who helped out with anything going on. Funerals, potlucks, teas, Sunday school, Bible school, Easter breakfast. She was soft spoken, quick to laugh, and kinder than anyone I had ever encountered before. To this day, when I think of her, I thank God for allowing me to meet her as a young wife and mother. She had a profound effect on how I wanted to be in my interactions with others, especially those who would come after me. I wanted to leave the example that MaryAnn did!

My dear friends, I have said it before and I will say it again, our lives matter! They matter to God, our families, friends, and the world around us who is watching. May our lives so shine before men that they see our good works and glorify our Father in heaven!

The truth is that the manner in which we live our lives, day in and day out, is how the world perceives us. It is not the words we say, or the stories we tell. It is the way we live. When we consistently live our lives well and yet others speak badly about us, take heart, no one will believe it!

Shine bright, ladies! The world is watching! YOU ARE LOVED!

SEPTEMBER 5

This is eternal life, that they may know You, the only true God, and Jesus Christ whom You have sent. (John 17:3)

The very credentials these people are waving around as something special, I'm tearing up and throwing out with the trash—along with everything I used to take credit for. And why? Because of Christ. Yes, all the things I once thought were so important are gone from my life. Compared to the high privilege of knowing Christ Jesus as my Master, firsthand, everything I once thought I had going for me is insignificant—dog dung. I've dumped it all in the trash so that I could embrace Christ and be embraced by Him. I didn't want some petty, inferior brand of righteousness that comes from keeping a list of rules when I could get the robust kind that comes from trusting Christ—God's righteousness. (Philippians 3:7–9 MSG)

But grow in the grace and knowledge of our Lord and Savior Jesus Christ. To Him be the glory, both now and to the day of eternity. (2 Peter 3:18)

I am the Good Shepherd, and I know My own and My own know me. (John 10:14)

As I was reading this morning, I kept hearing the same thought running through my mind over and over. It was "Do you love Me?" "Yes, you may know some scripture and claim to understand some of its meaning, but, do you love Me?" "Is relationship with Me more important to you than anything else?" "Do you love Me?" "Do you trust Me?" "Do you consider me your friend, your confidant, your Savior?"

My dear sisters, Jesus doesn't want part of us, the cleaned-up, Sunday-best part. He wants ALL of us! He wants to be our first conscious thought of the morning and the last at night. He desires our total commitment and our total surrender. Faith isn't a Sunday morning pickup game; it is a lifestyle, a conscious thought day after day to trust Jesus Christ! It's an ALL or NOTHING kind of thing. Either we are all-in or we are not. Jesus isn't content with just a part of us. He desires an intimate relationship, flaws and all!

Remember, He knows us better than we know ourselves and loves us completely! Our enemy tells us over and over that Jesus will love us WHEN, when we get our act together, when we go to church more frequently, when we stop messing up. That old liar even goes so far as to tell us that we are not welcome to bring our messes to Christ, that we need to clean up first. Jesus says, "Come to Me now, in the middle of your mess. In the middle of your crisis, and in the middle of your questions. I AM all that you need."

So yes, study the Word, pray and repent, and repeat, but keep your eyes focused on Jesus. He is the author and perfecter of our faith, and HE will never let us down! You are loved! You are claimed! And you are a daughter of the KING!

SEPTEMBER 6

Those who know Your name trust in You, for You, LORD, have never forsaken those Who seek You. (Psalm 9:10)

But I trust in Your unfailing love; my heart rejoices in Your salvation. (Psalm 13:5)

Some trust in chariots and some in horses, but we trust in the name of the LORD our God. (Psalm 20:7)

But I trust in You, LORD; I say, "You are my God." (Psalm 31:14)

LORD Almighty, blessed is the one who trusts in You. (Psalm 84:12)

Trust in the LORD with all your heart and lean not on your own understanding; in all your ways submit to Him, and He will make your paths straight. (Proverbs 3:5–6)

Those who trust in themselves are fools, but those who walk in wisdom are kept safe. (Proverbs 28:26)

But now, this is what the LORD says - He who created you, Jacob, He who formed you, Israel, "Do not fear, for I have redeemed you; I have summoned you by name; you are Mine." (Isaiah 43:1)

May the God of hope fill you with all joy and peace as you trust in Him, so that you may overflow with hope by the power of the Holy Spirit. (Romans 15:13)

Trust—believing the word of God, believing that God knows better than we do; believing that His plan and His purpose trumps any plan of ours; trusting that even when the answer is no or not yet, God knows what He is doing; trusting that when what we may have planned for our lives is not exactly what God has planned, His way is superior; trusting that in the hurt, disappointment, and pain of life, God is still good. That He is still FOR us. That He is not finished with us yet. That the trial and frustrations and disappointments of life are nothing more than refining fire to strengthen us, to polish us, and to mold us into the image of God!

May we NEVER walk away from this LORD of love who desires the very best for us! May we never turn away and insist on our own way, even though our sight is limited. May we never demand that God listen to us, that He follow OUR lead. For my dear friends, along that path is destruction! Isaiah 55:8 reminds us that God's "thoughts are not our thoughts, neither are God's ways our ways." "My ways are FAR BEYOND anything you could imagine!"

I remember asking God, "How anything good could possibly come from this trial?" Honestly, I never got an answer, just the whispered thought, "Do you trust Me?" It was through those trials that I made the conscious decision to trust in God's sovereignty, wisdom, and righteousness. Don't get me wrong. I was still face down, tears streaming, begging for my way, but I surrendered (eventually) to the words and mind-set: "Your will be done." I kept begging but trusted God with the outcome!

Love you, friends! May we keep our eyes focused on God. He knows what He is doing everywhere and always! HE'S GOT THIS!

SEPTEMBER 7

Each one should test their own actions. Then they can take pride in themselves alone, without comparing themselves to someone else. (Galatians 6:4)

But He gives us more grace. That is why Scripture says; "God opposes the proud but shows favor to the humble." (James 4:6)

Humble yourselves before the Lord, and He will lift you up. (James 4:10)

This is what the LORD says: "Let not the wise boast of their wisdom or the strong boast of their strength or the rich boast of their riches but let her who boasts boast about this: that she understands and knows Me, that I am the Lord, Who exercises kindness, justice and righteousness on earth, for in these I delight," declares the Lord. (Jeremiah 9:23–24)

Do nothing out of selfish ambition or vain conceit. Rather, in humility value others above yourselves. (Philippians 2:3)

When pride comes, then comes disgrace, but with humility comes wisdom. (Proverbs 11:2)

Do you see a person wise in their own eyes? There is more hope for a fool than for them. (Proverbs 26:12)

Why is it that we think we deserve so much? Where did this attitude come from? Why are we such a group of people driven by what we think we are entitled to? "I want so I should get!" "She has this, so I should have it"; "I don't deserve to have problems, illnesses, or struggles"; "I want MY way!"; "I know best!" We have become a nation of foot-stomping toddlers just told no! Not only do we want our way, we will go to any extreme to get our way—theft, embezzlement, lying, cheating, backstabbing, exaggeration—all just part of the game! We walk around with a huge I emblazoned on our chest! "I deserve, I want, I expect!"—all of these are completely contrary to what God in His word asks of us. God asks us to "humble ourselves" and wait for Him to lift us up at the right time.

He even goes further to ask that the things we do in humility be kept quiet, not done in front of others. God sees. He understands motives and rewards obedience. What a shift from the direction of the culture we are living in!

It's time we test our own actions, stop comparing ourselves with others, and start questioning our own motives. Then we can begin to take pride in our surrendered obedience, allowing God to mold us into the women of faith He is calling us to be. May God look upon us and announce to heaven, "That one's mine!" Then, then, dear friends, we will shine even brighter because we will be reflecting more and more of the character of God.

Shine on, sisters!

SEPTEMBER 8

Jesus said to him, "I Am the Way, and the Truth and the Life. No one comes to the Father except through Me." (John 14:6)

I have come into the world as light, so that whoever believes in Me may not remain in darkness. (John 12:46)

Training us to renounce ungodliness and worldly passions, and to live self-controlled, upright, and Godly lives in the present age. (Titus 2:12)

For God gave us a spirit not of fear but of power and love and self-control. (2 Timothy 1:7)

But He's already made it plain how to live, what to do, what GOD is looking for in men and women. It's quite simple: Do what is fair and just to your neighbor, be compassionate and loyal in love, and don't take yourself too seriously—take God seriously. (Micah 6:8 MSG)

God's angel sets up a circle of protection around us while we pray… Worship God if you want the best; worship opens doors to all His goodness. (Psalm 34:7, 9 MSG)

Our Lord is great, with limitless strength; we'll never comprehend what He knows and does… He's not impressed with horsepower; the size our muscles means little to Him. Those who fear God get God's attention; they can depend on His Strength! (Psalm 147:5, 10–11 MSG)

Therefore, there is now no condemnation for those who are in Christ Jesus. (Romans 8:1)

When I read today's scriptures, my mind went to reasons to be thankful, and that is what these scriptures represent for me. Sometimes I think we get so caught up in our "asks" that we forget what God has already done for and in us. God has given us a spirit of courage, power, love, and self-control. He has promised to protect us, guide us, and deliver us. He has delivered us from the darkness and brought us into His glorious light. He promises us that He will be with us always, that He will protect us with His limitless strength, orchestrate our lives with His incomprehensible wisdom, and love us with more love and understanding than we can ever imagine. God is FOR us. That fact alone is worthy of our constant praise and thankfulness!

Scripture reminds us that we can depend on God. We can depend on HIS strength. The enemy wants us to forget that fact. He wants us to doubt God's goodness, God's ability, and God's love. But GOD's promises are firm. Our God is an unshakable fortress. Nothing and no one can undo or disrupt what God is doing in the lives of believers. May we grow in trust and gratitude as we reflect on God goodness to us.

We are loved! We are called out of darkness into HIS LIGHT! We are claimed by almighty GOD! WE ARE HIS! No power of hell can separate us from HIS LOVE!

Have a great day! Reflect brightly! Love extravagantly! Live boldly!

SEPTEMBER 9

On the other hand I am filled with power—with the Spirit of the LORD—and with justice and courage. (Micah 3:8)

I have filled him with the Spirit of God in wisdom, in understanding, in knowledge, and in all kinds of craftsmanship. (Exodus 31:3)

I know what it is to be in need, and I know what it is to have plenty. I have learned the secret of being content in any and every situation, whether well fed or hungry, whether living in plenty or in want. I can do all this through Him Who gives me strength. (Philippians 4:12–13)

Keep your lives free from the love of money and be content with what you have, because God has said, "Never will I leave your; never will I forsake you." (Hebrews 13:5)

But godliness with contentment is great gain. For we brought nothing into this world, and we can take nothing out of it. (1 Timothy 6:6–7)

Then he said to them, "Watch out! Be on your guard against all kinds of greed; life does not consist in an abundance of possessions." (Luke 12:15)

Better the poor whose walk is blameless than the rich whose ways are perverse. (Proverbs 28:6)

That each of them may eat and drink, and find satisfaction in all their toil - this is the gift of God. (Ecclesiastes 3:13)

Thinking about contentment and our constant desire for more, I have come to the simple conclusion that our desire for more is fear-based! We don't want to miss out. We feel empty in and of ourselves, so we feel a need to *fill* that space. We think the newest and fanciest gadget will surely do the trick or a new lover or new drink or new drug, ANYTHING to fill this void. Even Christians chase after such things. And again, I think it is out of fear. We doubt the goodness of God. We doubt His promise to care for us, to provide for us, and to stay with us. We doubt the core truths of scripture. We have God so boxed in this little box that we can understand that we simply cannot fathom the greatness of our God.

My dear friends, it is time to let our ideas about God out of this little confined space we have placed them in. It is time to fully embrace and believe that God IS who HE says He is. It's time to open our minds and hearts to the power, provision, strength, wisdom, and abundance of GOD. We are choosing to live small, frightened, timid, grave-tending lives when God is calling us to walk boldly and in freedom in HIM. He is telling us to quit looking down, quit dreaming small, and stop fretting our lives away.

He is reminding us that HE is the source of fulfillment, of plenty, and of abundance. HE alone is able to fill that void that keeps us always looking for the next best thing. HE IS ENOUGH! He is overflowing with kindness, mercy, forgiveness, and abundance! He wants to lavish us with good and perfect gifts from His storehouse of blessings! He wants to fill us so full with His spirit that we absolutely cannot help but leak Jesus on everyone we meet! GOD IS GOOD! GOD IS FOR US! ENOUGH SAID!

SEPTEMBER 10

Then Jesus said to His disciples, "If anyone wishes to come after Me he/she must deny herself and take up his cross and follow Me." For whoever wishes to save her life will lose it, but whoever loses her life for My sake will find it." (Matthew 16:24–25)

Anyone who intends to come with Me has to let Me lead. You're not in the driver's seat. I am. Don't run from suffering, embrace it. Follow me and I'll show you how. Self-help is no help at all. Self-sacrifice is the way, My way, to finding yourself, your true self. What kind of deal is it to get everything you want but lose yourself, your true self. What kind of deal is it to get everything you want but lose yourself? What could you ever trade your soul for? (Matthew 16:24–25 MSG)

I, God, generate all this. But doom to you who fight your Maker - you're a pot at odds with the potter! Does clay talk back to the potter? "What are you doing? What clumsy fingers!" Would a sperm say to a father "Who gave you permission to use me to make a baby?" Or a fetus to mother, Why have you cooped me up in this belly?" (Isaiah 45:9–10 MSG)

Are you satisfied with who you are? Are you content with the fact that God thought about you before He created you? Do you understand that He positioned you here in this time and in this place for His purposes? Do you accept that "the potter" knew you; crafted the details of your personality, your strengths and your weaknesses; and deliberately placed you here, right where you are? Do you believe that He loves you? That He is jealous for your love? That He desires all of you, not just your leftovers? Do you believe that He knows you completely and loves you anyway? He does! We are safe to surrender to His great love. We are safe to rest in the powerful arms that are holding us. We are safe to cry, mourn, question, and surrender to the loving arms of our Father. God's got this! I simply cannot say that enough. My dear sisters, let us pray, plead, and beg God for the concerns of our heart. Let us bow, kneel, and cry out to our Father for intervention, for healing, for peace. But may we never forget, God is FOR us. God loves us. God KNOWS what He is doing ALL the time! When we hurt, when we mourn, when we simply do not understand, may we rest in the knowledge that God KNOWS! May we be satisfied in the fact that God sees far more than we will ever see, He understands more than we will ever understand, and He loves us fiercely! May we rest and surrender to His plan and His purpose. And may we be satisfied in knowing that no matter what, God is in control. And God is good!

Have a great week! Fight to be all that God intended you to be and rest in the fact that you are greatly and eternally loved!

SEPTEMBER 11

God is our refuge and strength, a very present help in trouble. Therefore we will not fear though the earth should change and though the mountains slip into the heart of the sea, though its waters roar and foam, though the mountains quake at its swelling pride. (Psalm 46:1–3)

I will say to the LORD, "My refuge and my fortress, my God, in Whom I trust!" (Psalm 91:2)

The eternal God is a dwelling place, and underneath are the everlasting arms, and He drove out the enemy from before you, and said "Destroy!" (Deuteronomy 33:27)

And it will come about, while My Glory is passing by, that I will put you in the cleft of the rock and cover you with My Hand until I have passed by. (Exodus 33:22)

God is our refuge and strength, a very present help in trouble. (Psalm 46:1)

In the fear of the LORD there is a strong confidence, and His Children will have refuge. (Proverbs 14:26)

The name of the LORD is a strong tower, the righteous run to it and are safe. (Proverbs 18:10)

O LORD, my strength and my stronghold, and my refuge in the day of distress. To You the nations will come from the ends of the earth and say, "Our fathers have inherited nothing but falsehood, futility and things of no profit." (Jeremiah 16:19)

The LORD is my rock and my fortress and my deliver, my God, my Rock, in Whom I take refuge; My shield and the horn of my salvation, my stronghold. (Psalm 18:2)

God knows we are reading this. He knows the events of our world are frightening us. He knows this is the time to reassure us that He is in control! It is because of God's timing and God's love for us and all His children that He is reminding us today that, no matter what is happening, HE remains God, and He is God OVER ALL!

He remains in control of world events like hurricanes; like unstable leaders; like diseases, famines, and wars. We, as a nation and as a culture, have rejected Him and His ways, and He sees the mess we have made of things. He sees the selfishness and pride that has overtaken our world. Because of self-will, He has left us to decide the course we will take. The resulting disasters, I believe, are a result of these choices. God is indeed a loving Father, but He will not be mocked! He is God ALL MIGHTY; God ALL POWERFUL; God ever present, ever seeing; and God MOST HOLY! He IS our rock, our fortress, and our refuge! As His daughters, we can run to Him for protection and peace. We can expect Him to comfort us in His everlasting arms and cover us with His hand. His word tells us He will. And then, when the immediate storm has passed, it is time for us to climb out of our hiding place and reflect the light of His love so that others may see the goodness of God.

God's GOT THIS. He's got us. And no matter what, God is FOR us. We are loved, we are chosen, and we are claimed by the King of the universe. We have no reason to fear.

Have a great week! May we leak the joy of Jesus on everyone we meet!

SEPTEMBER 12

This in essence, is the message we heard from Christ and are passing on to you. God is light, pure light; there is not a trace of darkness in Him. If we claim that we experience a shared life with Him and continue to stumble around in the dark, we're obviously lying through our teeth—we're not living what we claim. But if we walk in the light, God Himself being the light, we also experience a shared life with one another, as the sacrificed blood of Jesus, God's Son, purges all our sin. If we claim that we're free of sin, we're only fooling ourselves. A claim like that is errant nonsense. On the other hand, if we admit our sins—make a clean breast of them—He won't let us down, He'll be true to Himself. He'll forgive our sins and purge us of all wrong-doing. If we claim that we've never sinned, we out—and—out contradict God—make a liar out of Him. A claim like that only shows off our ignorance of God. (1 John 5–10 MSG)

So here's what I want you to do, God helping you. Take your everyday, ordinary life – you're sleeping, eating, going-to-work and walking around life - and place it before God as an offering. Embracing what God does for you is the best thing you can do for Him. Don't become so well-adjusted to your culture that you fit into it without even thinking. Instead, fix your attention on God. You'll be changed from the inside out. Readily recognize what He wants from you, and quickly respond to it. Unlike the culture around you, always dragging you down to its level of immaturity. God brings the best out of you, develops well-formed maturity in you. (Romans 12:1–2 MSG)

Years ago, my husband and I heard Bob Goff (author of *Loves Does*) speak. Actually, we attended a two-day seminar, which was wild, fun, and inspiring! Anyway, I have lots of notes from the various speakers that were at that event. Bob Goff would consistently remind us to "get some skin in the game." Meaning get out there! Live your faith! Reach out with love and compassion to your fellowmen and leak Jesus on everyone you meet! "Leaking Jesus" was another one of his favorite sayings! Mother Teresa put it this way, "God does not ask that we do great things, but rather that we do ordinary things with great love."

Sometimes we think that we need to go to the mission field to serve God or abandon our families and our jobs. We may feel inadequate in our lives for Christ. We may feel like we are not doing enough, or WE are not enough! But we can only serve God where HE has chosen to place us. Where ever you are right now, that is your mission field.

That is precisely why I love The Message Bible translation from Romans 12, "Take your everyday, ordinary life, and place it before God as an offering." We can make a conscious choice to "be all in" for God wherever He has us. We can look for Him in the ordinary, everyday events of our lives and face the world and our families and friends with "great love." We can "shine the light of Christ" in the everyday, ordinary moments. And we can trust that God will bring out the best in us! Embrace the race, sisters! YOU ARE LOVED, CALLED and CLAIMED!

SEPTEMBER 13

For all have sinned and fall short of the glory of God. (Romans 3:23)

Put to death, therefore, whatever belongs to your earthly nature; sexual immorality, impurity, lust, evil desires and greed, which is idolatry. Because of these, the wrath of God is coming. (Colossians 3:5–6)

And that means killing off everything connected with that way of death; sexual promiscuity, impurity, lust, doing whatever you feel like whenever you feel like it, and grabbing whatever attracts your fancy. That's a life shaped by things and feelings instead of by God. It's because of this kind of thing that God is about to explode in anger. It wasn't long ago that you were doing all that stuff and not knowing any better. But you know better now, so make sure it's all gone for good; bad temper, irritability, meanness, profanity, dirty talk. (Colossians 3:5–8 MSG)

If anyone, then, knows the good they ought to do and doesn't do it, it is sin for them. (James 4:17–21)

Keep your servant also from willful sins; may they not rule over me. Then I will be blameless, innocent of great transgression. May these words of my mouth and this meditation of my heart be pleasing in Your sight, LORD, my Rock and my Redeemer. (Psalm 19:13–17)

Almighty God, Father of love and light, we come before Your throne, convicted of our need for forgiveness. Show us the ways we have sinned in thought, word, or deed. Convict us of our need to repent before You. Teach us, Your daughters, of the seriousness of sin! We don't want anything or anyone to come between us and our relationship with You. In our culture today, sin is scoffed at, joked about, and has become the status quo. Forgive us! For in accepting evil and sin as a part of everyday life, we have inadvertently made it acceptable. We are sorry; we are wrong! Help us to remember that sin is detestable to You regardless of what our culture tells us. Remind us of our unconfessed sin, cleanse us, renew us, and release us to better love You. And, Father, when we have confessed our sin to You and received Your forgiveness, help us to let it go to release that sin forever. We confess our enemy loves to continually wound us with our past sins and failures long after You have forgiven them. You promise us in Your word that, when we confess our sins with a sincere heart, You remember them no longer. May we move on believing Your promises.

Father, continue to mold us and make us into strong women of faith. We realize the culture we live in is watching, wondering what, if anything, makes us different from the world around us. Use us to reflect the light of Your glory, the light of Your forgiveness, and the light of Your strength! You ALONE are worthy of praise, of adoration, and of our worship! Remove the ties that bind us to our old way of life or anything that is offensive to You. Cleanse us, renew us, and forgive us in Jesus's holy name. So be it. Amen.

SEPTEMBER 14

But I am afraid that just as Eve was deceived by the serpent's cunning, your minds may somehow be led astray from your sincere and pure devotion to Christ. (2 Corinthians 11:3)

The thief comes only to steal and kill and destroy; I have come that they may have life, and have it to the full. (John 10:10)

Put on the full armor of God, so that you can take your stand against the devil's schemes. For our struggle is not against flesh and blood, but against the rulers, against the authorities, against the power of this dark world and against the spiritual forces of evil in the heavenly realms. Therefore put on the full armor of God, so that when the day of evil comes, you may be able to stand your ground, and after you have done everything, to stand. Stand firm then, with the belt of truth buckled around your waist, with the breastplate of righteousness in place, and with your feet fitted with the readiness that comes from the gospel of peace. In addition to all this, take up the shield of faith, with which you can extinguish all the flaming arrows of the evil one. (Ephesians 6:11–16)

Be alert and of sober mind. Your enemy the devil prowls around like a roaring lion looking for someone to devour. Resist him, standing firm in the faith, because you know that the family of believers throughout the world is undergoing the same kind of sufferings. (1 Peter 5:8–9)

I can't help but believe that Satan has really got the world bamboozled! I honestly think that many people look at God as some "cosmic cop," waiting and ready to imprison and punish us when we do wrong. Many reject God because they don't want to follow some list of rules or be held accountable for the way they have chosen to live. We have even gone so far as to glorify Satan and portray him as some funny, "anything goes" kind of guy who is always up for a party and a good time! When in truth, he is our greatest enemy and worst nightmare. His desire is to destroy us by poor choices, poor self-image, and hatred for almost everything. By blinding us to the horrendous nature of our enemy, we have been deluded into thinking we don't need God or anything He stands for. But, my friends, we are walking into our own destruction. God is FOR us. His word is not a list of laws as much as it is a list of directions for living a full and satisfying life. Our greatest enemy wants us to live lives of discouragement, fear, doubt, hatred, and sin. He wants us to be so destroyed by our own actions and reactions that there is no light left in us. He wants us as part of this great darkness around us.

My dear sisters, we cannot be neutral in this walk of life. Either we are on God's side, or we are on the enemy's side. There is no middle ground. God has come that we may have life and have it to the full. He has given us a way, through Jesus, to live lives of forgiveness and joyful anticipation of what lies ahead of us. We don't have to live in fear or dread. God is in control always. We may not understand the why, but we can rest assured of the *who*.

May we draw ever closer to our God of love and light. May we rise each morning fully equipped to face the arrows of our enemy (realizing that many times that attack takes place in our own minds), and may we reflect ever so brightly the light of our Lord and Savior who promises to walk with us always. May we be so near to our Lord that, upon our rising each morning, the forces of our enemy shout, "Damn, she's up!"

Shine bright, sisters! Your light is badly needed! YOU ARE LOVED!

SEPTEMBER 15

B̲ear with each other and forgive one another if any of you has a grievance against someone. Forgive as the Lord forgave you. (Colossians 3:13)

So, chosen by God for this new life of love, dress in the wardrobe God picked out for you: compassion, kindness, humility, quiet strength, discipline. Be even-tempered, content with second place, quick to forgive an offense. Forgive as quickly and completely as the Master forgave you. And regardless of what else you put on, wear love. It's your basic all-purpose garment. Never be without it. (Colossians 3:12–14 MSG)

Get rid of all bitterness, rage and anger, brawling and slander, along with every form of malice. Be kind and compassionate to one another, forgiving each other, just as in Christ God forgave you. (Ephesians 4:31–32)

The Lord our God is merciful and forgiving, even though we have rebelled against Him. (Daniel 9:9)

And when you stand praying, if you hold anything against anyone, forgive them, so that your Father in heaven may forgive you your sins. (Mark 11:25)

I've told you all this so that trusting Me, you will be unshakable and assured, deeply at peace. In this godless world you will continue to experience difficulties. But take heart! I've conquered the world! (John 6:33)

I believe forgiveness is crucial for us to pursue. When we are carrying a grudge or harboring unforgiveness in our hearts, it does damage to our soul. We become bitter, resentful, angry people. We wear our hurt and outrage for everyone to see. We hurt others without a second thought because we are hurt. Unforgiveness is a powerful tool of our enemy, and a tool that he uses with skill and frequency. So how then do we forgive someone who has wounded us deeply? How do we move past the hurt, betrayal, or grievance? Only by the power of God. Forgiveness is not a natural trait we are born with. In fact, quite the opposite. Forgiveness is a choice, a choice of our heart. God will honor our choice to forgive someone, and in fact, He will enable us to do it. Personally speaking, forgiveness is a process. It is a consistent surrender of an offense to God, surrendering the wound over and over until it no longer holds any pain, asking God to forgive the offender (sometimes through clenched teeth), and asking God to soften our hearts so that the offense no longer brings us pain. My dear sisters, when God asks us to do something, like forgive an offender, He is asking us to do so because He KNOWS what is best for us. He knows the fragile condition of our hearts, and He wants to free us from the bitterness of an unforgiving heart. No, it is NOT *okay* when someone betrays us or mistreats us. But by forgiving, we are NOT legitimizing what has been done, only releasing it from its power to harm us, to steal our joy and our peace. God is the perfect judge, and He can be trusted to set things right. We need to remember that, as others have harmed us, we have also wounded others, perhaps not intentionally or with malice, but we are also in need of forgiveness.

May we live in such a way that the attributes of God become second nature to us. May we purpose to live lives pleasing to God and available for His purpose and His glory. HE KNOWS what He is doing. He CAN be trusted.

Have a great day! Shine bright! Love deeply and extravagantly! Live bold, believing lives! God's got this!

SEPTEMBER 16

Know therefore that the LORD your God is God, the faithful God who keeps covenant and steadfast love with those who love Him and keep His commandments, to a thousand generations. (Deuteronomy 7:9)

But You, O Lord, are a God merciful and gracious, slow to anger and abounding in steadfast love and faithfulness. (Psalm 86:15)

Give thanks to the God of heaven, for His steadfast love endures forever. (Psalm 136:26)

The LORD your God is in your midst, a Mighty One Who will save; He will rejoice over you with gladness; He will quiet you by His love; He will exult over you with loud singing. (Zephaniah 3:17)

No, in all these things we are more than conquerors through Him Who loved us. For I am sure that neither death, nor life, nor angels nor rulers, nor things present nor things to come, nor powers, nor height nor depth, nor anything else in all creation, will be able to separate us from the love of God in Christ Jesus our Lord. (Romans 8:37–39)

None of this fazes us because Jesus loves us. I'm absolutely convinced that nothing—nothing living or dead, angelic or demonic, today or tomorrow, high or low, thinkable or unthinkable—absolutely nothing can get between us and God's love because of the way that Jesus our Master has embraced us. (Romans 8:37–39 MSG)

And who would dare tangle with God by messing with one of God's chosen? Who would dare even to point a finger? The One Who died for us—Who was raised to life for us!—Is in the presence of God at this very moment sticking up for us. Do you think anyone is going to be able to drive a wedge between us and Christ's love for us? (Romans 8:33 MSG)

I personally have a tough time getting my head around the FACT that I don't have to EARN God's favor. I somehow have it deep in my thinking process that, if I behave better, God will love me more. If I study His word, memorize it, quote it, teach or preach it, He will love me more and give me special treatment. The Bible teaches otherwise. We do not earn God's favor; it is a gift, sheer gift.

He loves us when we seek Him, and He loves us when we don't. He loves those who reject Him; He pursues those who aren't looking; and He lavishes us, ALL of us, with generous gifts and blessings we DO NOT deserve.

If God loves us no matter how we respond, why then do we bother to try and carve out some time in our day for time with God? That is a question we each have to answer for ourselves. Personally, there is a craving, or deep desire, in my soul to become more intimately in love with Jesus, to know Him better, to trust Him more, to begin to truly understand His deep and unconditional love for me. When I consistently remind all of you that "you are greatly loved," I mean it. I have experienced just momentary glimpses of that great love in my relationship with Jesus, and quite frankly, it was overwhelming. It literally took my breath away and brought tears to my eyes. You know that feeling when you are choking back tears and you have that huge lump in your throat that makes it unable to swallow? It felt like that. The magnitude of HIS love for us is mind-boggling. I cannot wait until, on the other side of this life, I can fully experience it.

God loves us, my dear sisters, more than my words can convey, more than we can grasp. He loves those who don't love Him. He pursues them, grieves over them, and mourns over them. And that, friends, is why we are here. If we can encourage, inspire, or love an unbeliever, we are revealing a little bit of God to that person. We are being the hands and feet of Christ, and we then move from being followers of Christ into being disciples of Christ.

Let your love shine, sisters! Love extravagantly, love boldly!

SEPTEMBER 17

But if from there you seek the Lord your God, you will find Him if you look for Him with all your heart and with all your soul. (Deuteronomy 4:29)

Let us hold unswervingly to the hope we profess, for He who promised is faithful. (Hebrews 10:23)

The Lord watches over all who love Him, but all the wicked He will destroy. (Psalm 145:20)

Look to the LORD and His strength; seek His face always. (1 Chronicles 16:11)

Now devote your heart and soul to seeking the LORD your God. (1 Chronicles 22:19)

And without faith it is impossible to please God, because anyone who comes to Him must believe that He exists and that He rewards those who earnestly seek Him. (Hebrews 11:6)

Today, I was struck by *our* part of this journey called faith. We are called to actively seek God, with ALL our heart and with ALL our soul. We are called to profess the hope we have in the Lord without being wishy-washy or lukewarm (unswervingly.) We are promised in return that God watches over us but also that He will DESTROY the wicked! Ouch! I sometimes prefer the "God loves everybody" or "God is so forgiving and kind that how we live doesn't matter" or "I don't have to live my faith, God knows I love Him" God!

I believe today's verses call us to action. To actively look for God; to seek His wisdom; His guidance and His instruction; to unswervingly cling to Him no matter what the world tells us; and to train our hearts, minds, and souls to love Him and trust His faithfulness. After all, my dear sisters, not one of us will get out alive. We will all be called to the judgment seat of Christ and be asked to give an account of how we lived our lives. I want our lives to matter, our hearts to be steadfast, and for us to be welcomed home with the words: "Well done, My good and faithful servants!"

Today may we earnestly seek the counsel and the wisdom of the Lord our God. May we strengthen our resolve to trust Him and cling tightly to the hand holding ours!

SEPTEMBER 18

The eternal God is your refuge, and underneath are the everlasting arms. He will drive out your enemy before you, saying, "Destroy Him!" (Deuteronomy 33:27)

I am confident of this: I will see the goodness of the Lord in the land of the living. Wait for the Lord; be strong and take heart and wait for the Lord. (Psalm 27:13–14)

With all humility and gentleness, with patience showing tolerance for one another in love. Therefore I, the prisoner of the Lord, implore you to walk in a manner worthy of the calling with which you have been called. (Ephesians 4:1–2)

Let your gentle spirit be known to all men. The Lord is near. (Philippians 4:5)

But the wisdom from above is first pure, then peaceable, gentle, reasonable, full of mercy and good fruits, unwavering, without hypocrisy. (James 3:17)

Go gently through this day, not pushing or elbowing for better position, not impatiently shifting from foot to foot, and not demanding your own way or "telling" God how you think He should do things or handle so and so. Gently! Oh, that we may become women known for our gentle strength, our gentle spirit, and our gentle hearts. Along with gentleness, may our hearts and minds be so attuned to God, so steadfast in our trust that NOTHING can upset us or disappoint us. Then add to gentleness, love, joy, peace, patience, kindness, goodness, faithfulness and self-control.

May we all be so filled with the "fruit of the spirit" that we leak Jesus on everyone we meet today.

SEPTEMBER 19

The Sovereign Lord has given me an instructed tongue, to know the word that sustains the weary. He wakens me morning by morning, wakens my ear to listen like one being taught. (Isaiah 50:4)

Why spend money on what is not bread, and your labor on what does not satisfy? Listen, listen to Me and eat what is good, and your soul will delight in the richest of fare. Give ear and come to Me; hear Me, that your soul may live. I will make an everlasting covenant with you, my faithful love promised to David. (Isaiah 55:2–3)

When He had received the drink, Jesus said, "It is finished." With that, He bowed His head and gave up His Spirit. (John 19:30)

And when Jesus had cried out again in a loud voice, He gave up His Spirit. At that moment the curtain of the temple was torn in two from top to bottom. The earth shook and the rocks split. The tombs broke open and the bodies of many holy people who had died were raised to life. (Matthew 27:50–52)

Can you even begin to imagine what it must have been like to be around at the time of Jesus's death? At the moment He died by giving up His Spirit, watching the massive curtain in the holy temple split in two? Then, and even stranger, many surrounding tombs broke open and dead bodies rose once again! The scriptures go on to say, "They (meaning the risen bodies) went into the holy city (where the curtain in the temple had been torn) and appeared to many people!" Sounds like something out of a horror movie!

I can't help but think that many of the people who had turned against Jesus and yelled for His death were right then shaking in their sandals! Thoughts like "What have we done!" or "The followers were right!" had to be running through their minds! Can you imagine the fear and regret that must have consumed them? My heart goes out to them! I cannot honestly say how I would have reacted if I were alive when Jesus walked the earth. Sure, I would love to think that I would have been a faithful follower, but, sincerely, I do not know how I would have reacted. Jesus said some pretty weird stuff while He walked among the people of His day, like "I am the Alpha (beginning) and the Omega (end) No one comes to the Father except through Me" and "This is my body (the communion bread) broken for you, this is My blood (the wine) shed for you, take and eat and drink." Whoa! I fear that I may have doubted His claim, may have thought, "He is a little too far out for my tastes." So, if I'm truthful, it is hard for me to condemn the doubters.

It is by grace alone that I can claim relationship with Jesus. God has given me the gift of faith in Him and ALL His claims. I can honestly say that I "believe the whole of scripture," even the parts I don't understand and cannot explain. I believe that God IS Who He says He is. I believe that God CAN do all the things He says He can do, and I am greatly and forever humbled that He walks with me (and you) as our constant companion!

Have a great week, my friends. The King of Kings is with you always!

SEPTEMBER 20

The Lord said to Elijah, "Go stand in front of Me on the mountain and I will pass by you." Then a very strong wind blew until it caused the mountains to fall apart and large rocks to break in front of the Lord. But the Lord was not in the wind. After the wind, there was an earthquake, but the Lord was not in the earthquake. After the earthquake, there was a fire, but the Lord was not in the fire. After the fire, there was a quiet, gentle sound. (1 Kings 19:11–12)

Lord, every morning You hear my voice. Every morning, I tell You what I need, and I wait for Your answer. (Psalm 5:3)

So faith comes from hearing, and hearing through the word of Christ. (Romans 10:17)

Call to me and I will answer you, and will tell you great and hidden things that you have not known. (Jeremiah 33:3)

I don't know about you friends, but personally, I wish God would speak to me through something LOUD and attention grabbing! Oftentimes, I have trouble calming my heart and mind to hear Him whisper. I know that this very subject has been a topic of conversation with many of you. How do we know when we are hearing God's voice? How do we know it is God and not our own thoughts? Honestly, I don't know for certain either. In my experience, when I feel a nudge to do or say something to someone, I ask, "Is this coming from you God or from me?" I usually don't hear anything very helpful, so if the nudge is still strong, I go forward. I then say something like "If this falls flat on its face and I look like an idiot, it's all on You, God." I have to admit I have said some things to perfect strangers that have left them looking at me like "What just happened?" and, in one instance, left a woman in tears. I don't know how our interaction ended up or what the end result (if any) was in most instances, but there have been a few times when I have been obedient to that nudge, and I have had the blessing of finding out that "my" (God's) timing was dead on! That the words I meekly and weakly wrote or said arrived at just the precise moment they needed to! Now, I would love to take credit for that and say it is all about me, but my whole heart KNOWS that it is indeed all about HIM!

One "tool" I use to determine if I will follow a nudge is considering, is it life affirming, encouraging, used for building someone up? I do not believe that God would EVER ask me to speak words of condemnation, judgment, or ridicule to another—heaven knows I'm a major work in progress myself!

Anyway, the point is God speaks and we struggle to hear. We either respond or not, but don't worry, God won't stop speaking to us. May we never stop listening!

I love you, dear friends! Have a great day and remember always how loved, valued, and unique you are to God!

SEPTEMBER 21

For whoever wants to save her life will lose it, but whoever loses her life for Me and for the gospel will save it. What good is it for a woman to gain the whole world, yet forfeit her soul? (Mark 8:35–36)

For You created my inmost being; You knit me together in my mother's womb. I praise You because I am fearfully made; Your works are wonderful, I know that full well. My frame was hidden from You when I was made in the secret place. When I was woven together in the depths of the earth, Your eyes saw my unformed body. ALL the days ordained for me were written in Your book before one of them came to be. (Psalm 139:13–16)

Now the Lord is the Spirit, and where the Spirit of the Lord is, there is freedom. And we, who with unveiled faces all reflect the Lord's glory, are being transformed into His likeness with ever-increasing glory, which comes from the Lord, who is the Spirit. (2 Corinthians 3:17–18)

Dear heavenly Father, we come before You today with praise and thanksgiving! Praise for Your great and undying love for us regardless of how we perform. We are thankful for the multitude of blessings you have poured into our lives, blessings for health, family, friends, homes, jobs, food and humor. We confess that we often take all the blessings for granted and focus on the problems and concerns of any given day. We are truly sorry, Lord. Help us to remember always that you knew us before we were even born, that you KNOW every day of every one of our lives, that NOTHING that we are facing or will ever face is going to take You by surprise. Please, Father, give us a glimpse of Your strength, of Your power, and of Your love for us. Please watch over those we love and care for as well as those we may not know that are going through things we cannot even imagine. You know them, Lord. You see them and we know that You care. Soften our hearts to care for others. Embolden us to bring big, bold prayers before Your throne. Transform us into Your likeness with ever-increasing glory. We love you Lord, and we surrender our lives to You. - Amen

SEPTEMBER 22

T hen the Lord God took dust from the ground and formed a man from it. He breathed the breath of life into the man's nose, and the man became a living person. (Genesis 2:7)

Happy are the people who know how to praise You. Lord, let them live in the light of Your presence. (Psalm 89:15)

So brothers and sisters, since God has shown us great mercy, I beg you to offer your lives as a living sacrifice to Him. Your offering must be only for God and pleasing to Him, which is the spiritual way for you to worship. Do not change yourselves to be like the people of this world, but be changed within by a new way of thinking. Then you will be able to decide what God wants for you; you will know what is good and pleasing to Him and what is perfect. (Romans 12:1–2)

So here's what I want you to do, God helping you. Take your everyday, ordinary life—your sleeping, eating, going-to-work, walking around life—and place it before God as an offering. Embracing what God does for you is the best thing you can do for Him. Don't become so well-adjusted to your culture that you fit into it without even thinking. Instead, fix your attention on God. You'll be changed from the inside out. (Romans 12:1–2 MSG)

Good morning, sisters! Quick question, what does the word worship mean to you? How do you worship God? For a long stretch of my faith life, I thought worship was something we did on Sunday mornings in church and with other believers. Honestly, that is a true statement. But I think there is another side of worship, a more personal type of worship. When we begin to believe that God is intimately involved in our lives, in our everyday, ordinary moments of life and when we cry out to God in our struggles, look to Him for strength and guidance, and laugh and thank Him when times are good, we begin to worship God with our very lives! The day-to-day, step-by-step ordinariness of our everyday lives turn into moments of awareness of His constant presence and goodness. We become acutely aware of His protection, guidance, and love for us, and we thank Him and praise Him without forethought. Thankfulness becomes a lifestyle and worship flows naturally! The definition of worship is the "feeling or expression of reverence and adoration for a deity (God)."

That "feeling of reverence" doesn't have to be limited to Sunday services; it can become an everyday act of the most routine part of our day.

Now, honestly, I know that my day-to-day life is not always filled with worship, nor am I thankful in all circumstances, but I do know and acknowledge the hand that is holding mine, and I do desire to become the woman He intended me to be. So it's a step in the right direction. Thankfully, God is along for the whole journey with me and with you, dear sisters.

May we willingly embrace what God is doing in and for us, may we fix our attention on God and let Him make us into the mighty women of faith He calls us to be!

SEPTEMBER 23

P eace I leave with you; My Peace I give you. I do not give to you as the world gives. Do not let your hearts be troubled and do not be afraid. (John 14:27)

In repentance and rest is your salvation, in quietness and trust is your strength. (Isaiah 30:15)

The weapons we fight with are not the weapons of the world. On the contrary, they have divine power to demolish strongholds. (2 Corinthians 10:4)

The world is unprincipled. It's dog-eat-dog out there! The world doesn't fight fair. But we don't live or fight our battles that way - never have and never will. The tools of our trade aren't for marketing or manipulation, but they are for demolishing that entire massively corrupt culture. We use our powerful God-tools for smashing warped philosophies, tearing down barriers erected against the truth of God, fitting every loose thought and emotion and impulse in the structure of life shaped by Christ. (2 Corinthians 10:3–5 MSG)

I remember years ago when I was in a Bible study about becoming "warriors for Christ." I don't remember what it was called. But it was a Beth Moore study. I remember the study, but what I still smile about is one of the women who was going to attend, but dropped out saying; "I don't want to fight or become a warrior." I didn't say it then, but think about it to this day, we ALL are warriors, my dear sisters, whether we want to be or not! It goes with becoming a follower of Christ! We are in a DAILY spiritual battle against the forces of evil in our world. But if we dwell on the evil and corrupt nature of our world, we may become fearful and troubled, so Jesus warns us in John, DO NOT LET your hearts be troubled and DO NOT be afraid. That's interesting. It almost sounds like an order? Perhaps an order from our Commander In Chief? Is He telling us, "Don't let your thoughts go down that road, pull them back, trust in Me. I've got this battle. I will supply your weapons and protect you." I do indeed think that is exactly what He is saying.

So how then do we prepare for this daily battle? It's really quite simple—prayer. Sarah Young says it this way, "You may appear to be doing nothing, but actually you are participating in battles going on within spiritual realms. You are waging war." I believe with ALL my heart, friends, that our prayers are more powerful and effective than we can ever imagine, not because of the way we are praying but because of WHO we are praying to! God, Commander of the Angel Armies, hears EVERY prayer we mutter no matter how simple or eloquent. He hears. He understands all parties involved. He sees the disease, the sickness, the brokenness. He understands their past and sees their future! He sends His army of angels to intervene and protect us and those we love and pray for. Our strength to continue in this battle comes in "quietness and trust!"

Have a great week, my fellow soldiers in Christ! Remember every moment how greatly and eternally loved you are no matter what battle you are currently fighting!

SEPTEMBER 24

The angel of the Lord found Hagar near a spring in the desert; it was the spring that is beside the road to Shur. And he said, "Hagar, servant of Sarai, where have you come from, and where are you going?" "I'm running away from my mistress Sarai," she answered. Then the angel of the Lord told her, "Go back to your mistress and submit to her." The angel added, "I will so increase your descendants that they will be too numerous to count." The angel of the Lord also said to her: "You are now with child and you will have a son. You shall name him Ishmael, for the Lord has heard of your misery. He will be a wild donkey of a man; and his hand will be against everyone and everyone's hand against him, and he will live in hostility toward all his brothers." She gave this name to the Lord who spoke to her, "You are the God who sees me," for she said, "I have now seen the One who sees me." (Genesis 16:7–14)

Where can I go from your Spirit? Where can I flee from Your presence? If I go up to the heavens, you are there; if I make my bed in the depths you are there. If I rise on the wings of the dawn, if I settle on the far side of the sea, even there your hand will guide me, Your right hand will hold me fast. (Psalm 139:7–10)

The Lord your God is with you, He is mighty to save. He will take great delight in you, He will quiet you with His love, He will rejoice over you with singing. (Zephaniah 3:17)

Good morning, sisters. Kind of some lengthy scriptures this morning, but both Psalm 139 and Zephaniah 3:17 are two of my personal favorites. When remembering the story of Hagar this morning, I was struck first of all by the words of the angel of the Lord when he spoke of the person the baby in her womb would become. It really hit me how intimately God knows us even before we are born He knows the kind of woman we will become. He says of one, "She will be a lover of people, outgoing, and fun-loving"; of another, "She will be a quiet, thoughtful woman"; and of still another, He may say, "She will be powerful and successful." Can you grasp the magnitude of the wisdom of God? Then in Psalm 139, the scripture explains in detail our inability to escape God. There is absolutely NO PLACE we can go to escape His presence. Not only does He know EXACTLY where we are but "even there His hand will guide us and hold us fast." Now, putting it all together, and then to top it off, not only does God know us before we are born, He goes with us everywhere and "He takes great delight in us. He rejoices over us with singing!"

That, my dear friends, is too wonderful for this little mind to comprehend! Have a great day embracing the love of the God who sees you, understands you, and rejoices over you with singing!

SEPTEMBER 25

T aste and see that the Lord is good, blessed is the woman who takes refuge in Him. (Psalm 34:8)

Make every effort to live in peace with everyone and to be holy; without holiness no one will see the Lord. (Hebrews 12:14)

They must turn from evil and do good; they must seek peace and pursue it. (1 Peter 3:11)

Peacemakers who sow in peace reap a harvest of righteousness. (James 3:18)

On the evening of that first day of the week, when the disciples were together, with the doors locked for fear of the Jews, Jesus came and stood among them and said, "Peace be with you!" (John 20:19)

Let the peace of Christ rule in your hearts, since as members of one body you were called to peace. And be thankful. (Colossians 3:15)

Peace, MY peace I give you, peace unlike the peace which is temporary that you find in the world. My peace is a calmness in your heart in the midst of turmoil, confusion, or trouble. My peace is not fleeting or superficial. The peace I give you fills up your whole being, body, mind, and soul. It is like water that seeps into the tiny cracks and fissures in your heart and mind, sealing the brokenness and restoring you. I love you more than you can imagine. I want all of you, not just your hurried prayers or monumental concerns but your laughter, your desires for yourselves and your families, and your wildest dreams and deepest darkest secrets! I want you to know Me and to think of Me as your closest friend. I have a fierce passion for you! I never let you out of my sight, and I hem you in from all sides as you walk through this life. I will NEVER leave you or even turn my back on you for a moment. You are mine! Take this peace I offer and go, be a light in the darkness! You are exactly where I want you right now in this time and this place! GO! I see You and I love you.

—Jesus

SEPTEMBER 26

God, investigate my life; get all the facts firsthand. I'm an open book to you; even from a distance, you know what I'm thinking. You know when I leave and when I get back; I'm never out of your sight. You know everything I'm going to say before I start the first sentence. I look behind me and you're there, then up ahead and you're there too—Your reassuring presence, coming and going. This is too much, too wonderful—I can't take it all in! (Psalm 139:1–6 MSG)

Now it is God who makes both us and you stand firm in Christ. He anointed us, set His seal of ownership on us, and put His Spirit in our hearts as a deposit, guaranteeing what is to come. (2 Corinthians 1:21–22)

No one will be able to stand up against you all the days of your life. As I was with Moses, so I will be with you; I will never leave you nor forsake you. (Joshua 1:5)

God knows us friends better than we know ourselves! He understands why we do what we do. He sees our hearts and loves us with a tender yet fierce passion! I sometimes question my own actions, "Why did I feel that way," "why did I respond this way," "why am I sad, discouraged, and disheartened?" God knows! He sees and understands the emotions that drive our reactions and actions. Sometimes, we nurse hurts for years, before we bring them to Him for healing. Sometimes, we don't even know what the wound is, let alone where it came from. But, God knows. As we pause, reflect, and bring our sincere hearts before Him, the light of His presence begins to heal and restore. And then, as we are healed from the fissures and cracks in our soul, He can fill us up to overflowing so that our believing lives are filled with His love and His compassion. Then, we can begin to overflow these gifts into the lives of the people He places around us!

As Bob Goff (*Love Does*) is fond of saying, "Go and leak Jesus on everyone you meet!"

SEPTEMBER 27

"I am with you and will watch over you wherever you go, and I will bring you back to this land. I will not leave you until I have done what I have promised you." (Genesis 28:15)

What, then, shall we say in response to this? If God is for us, who can be against us? (Romans 8:31)

Jesus Christ is the same yesterday and today and forever. (Hebrews 13:8)

Many are the plans in a person's heart, but it is the Lord's purpose that prevails." (Proverbs 19:21)

Therefore, my dear friends, as you have always obeyed—not only in My presence, but now much more in my absence—continue to work out your salvation with fear and trembling, for it is God who works in you to will and to act in order to fulfill His good purpose. (Philippians 2:12–13)

These scriptures really spoke to me today with the reminder that God is FOR us! He, along with unseen angels in the spiritual realm are "cheering us on" as we live out this walk of faith! I think sometimes we become overwhelmed because this life is difficult—disease, ALS, death of loved ones, depression, addiction, greed, the list goes on and on. Friends, we live in a fallen world! God is not the cause or the source of our problems. Satan is! God may allow us to walk through some dark and difficult places, but He promises us that He will NEVER leave us. He will never forget about us, Isaiah 49:16 tells us, "See, I have written your name of the palms of My hands." He has promised us that He will never forsake, forget, or abandon us! So take heart! If God is FOR us, and He promises us that He is, what can possibly come against us that can separate us from His love, comfort, and provision?

Have a wonderful week remembering that the Lord of the universe is only a whisper away! (Think how close He is to you always if a whisper is all it takes!) You are greatly and eternally loved!

SEPTEMBER 28

Let your speech always be gracious, seasoned with salt, so that you may know how you ought to answer each person. (Colossians 4:6)

Blessed are the merciful, for they shall receive mercy. (Matthew 5:7)

Let no corrupting talk come out of your mouths, but only such as is good for building up, as fits the occasion, that it may give grace to those who hear. (Ephesians 4:29)

For judgment is without mercy to one who has shown no mercy. Mercy triumphs over judgment. (James 2:13)

Put on then, as God's chosen ones, holy and beloved, compassionate hearts, kindness, humility, meekness, and patience. (Colossians 3:12)

Then Peter came to Jesus and asked, "Lord, how many times shall I forgive my brother when he sins against me? Up to seven times? Jesus answered, 'I tell you, not seven times, but seventy-seven times.'" (Matthew 18:21–22)

Then he adds, "Their sins and lawless acts I will remember no more." (Hebrews 10:17)

Forgiveness, we all want it when we mess up, God extends it, do we? Working with and getting to know some of the men from the minimum security prison where we volunteer, has impressed upon me the power of guilt. There are men walking around in there who have absolutely bought in to the lie of our enemy that tells us; "you are damaged goods". "Your offenses are unforgiveable." But the worst one and most damaging one in my opinion is this; "you have messed up too many times, there is no hope for you, you will only mess up again!" They come to church defeated, broken, in desperate need of forgiveness, yet expecting rejection and failure.

There are moments in the service, or in prayer afterward, or perhaps in their personal devotional time, when they feel His presence, but it doesn't last and their minds are immediately drawn back to all the times they have messed up. They don't feel worthy of forgiveness so they reject the idea that they really can be forgiven, renewed and loved. It is heartbreaking.

How do we, as children of God extend mercy and forgiveness to others? Do we forgive seventy times seven? Do we live compassionate lives, willing to extend mercy? Or, are we quick to judge, condemn and write off? Don't misinterpret my meaning here. As children of the King we are to acknowledge sin. Our sin as well as the sin of others. Pretending that nothing happened or that sin is no big deal, is a lie! But when sin breaks us and those we love, (which it always does), and when there is genuine regret and desire for forgiveness, do we extend it? How many times are we willing to do so? God has an amazing way of fixings broken things and broken people! Unfortunately personal brokenness is oftentimes the prerequisite of healing. We need to come to the point of complete and honest regret and sadness over our sins before a holy God. Then, and only then can true healing and restoration take place. My dear sisters, it isn't up to you and me to determine when someone is truly sorry. That is up to God. We are to repeatedly extend mercy, forgiveness, compassion and love to those in need of it. Which is all of us. The rest is up to God!

You are loved, called, claimed and forgiven! Extend the grace!

SEPTEMBER 29

And pray in the Spirit on all occasions with all kids of prayers and requests. With this in mind, be alert and always keep on praying for all the Lord's people. (Ephesians 6:18)

Then you will call on Me and come and pray to Me, and I will listen to you. (Jeremiah 29:12)

My prayer is not that you take them out of the world but that You protect them from the evil one. (John 17:15)

Is anyone among you in trouble? Let them pray. Is anyone happy? Let them sing songs of praise. (James 5:13)

But I tell you, love your enemies and pray for those who persecute you. (Matthew 5:44)

The LORD detests the sacrifice of the wicked, but the prayer of the upright pleases Him. (Proverbs 15:8)

May my prayer be set before You like incense; may the lifting up of my hands be like the evening sacrifice. (Psalm 141:12)

In the same way, the Spirit helps us in our weakness. We do not know what we ought to pray for, but the Spirit Himself intercedes for us through wordless groans. (Romans 8:26)

In my devotional time this morning, I was thinking how intertwined our lives are with others. I felt like God was reminding me that I see such an incredibly small piece of the whole picture. I live my life through such a tiny peephole. I can only see how things affect me. I pray for my concerns, my problems, my family, my church, my friends, my, my, my. I need to be reminded that God is concerned with the WHOLE of us! He loves us all! When we intercede in prayer for those in need, those in dire situations, those we do not know, I believe God is pleased! He knows them and HE loves them! When we pray globally, we begin to think globally! We are not on this planet alone to be waited on by a servant God. We are told in scripture to get out there, make a difference in the lives and circumstances God places before us! We ALWAYS have the ability to pray for others no matter where we may physically be.

I wonder sometimes if I forget about how powerful prayer is, not because of our words but because of the power, wisdom, and knowledge of the ONE hearing our words. God WANTS us to care. He wants us to mourn for others, to rejoice with others, and to have our hearts broken for the things that break His heart. He desires that we be transformed into HIS image. Prayer is one of the ways He does that transformation within us. So I challenge you. The next time you see or hear about a sad, difficult, or troubling situation that someone is in, PRAY! Pray long and hard for them and for God to intervene. I have heard it said that when we pray for others, we are standing in the gap for them. Many feel separated by a great chasm from God and the Holy Spirit. When we stand in that chasm for them, in that gap, we are making a way for them to draw closer to God! How powerful is that?

My dear sisters, may we intentionally become "gap dwellers" for those around us and even those continents away! If God is FOR them, and He most certainly is, then may we become advocates for them, using our prayers to "stand in the gap" and bring them home! We are all in this life together, and we ALL need God!

SEPTEMBER 30

I have fought the good fight, I have finished the race, I have kept the faith. (2 Timothy 4:7)

But you, woman of God, flee from all this, and pursue righteousness, godliness, faith, love, endurance, and gentleness. Fight the good fight of the faith. Take hold of the eternal life to which you were called and about which you made the good confession in the presence of many witnesses. (1 Timothy 6:11–12)

For we do not wrestle against flesh and blood, but against the cosmic powers over this present darkness, against the spiritual forces of evil in the heavenly places. (Ephesians 6:12)

This is no afternoon athletic contest that we'll walk away from and forget about in a couple of hours. This is for keeps, a life-or-death fight to the finish against the Devil and all his angels. Be prepared. You're up against far more than you can handle on your own. Take all the help you can get, every weapon God has issued, so that when it's all over but the shouting you'll still be on your feet. (Ephesians 6:12–13 MSG)

Blessed is the woman who remains steadfast under trial, for when she has stood the test she will receive the crown of life, which God has promised to those who love Him. (James 1:12)

My dear friends, the above scriptures are a call to action! A warning about the attack and strategy of our enemy. The Bible is clear about the fact that something is required of us! We are called to stand firm in our faith, to arm ourselves with the "God weapons" provided for us so that we will be equipped and ready to stand for what we believe. To stand firm on the word of God regardless of the jokes, insults, and persecution we may endure. Living in a free country, we have been spared some of the hardships others face on a daily basis, but we have also come under attack for what we believe, being called judgmental, unloving, close-minded, etc. Churches are full of teachings on what people "want to hear," abandoning truth and the word of God. We want to hear what we want to hear, and when told otherwise, we leave and look for a place that will make us feel good about ourselves. We look for a community of people who sit back and bask in grace and have absolutely no "skin in the game." Revelation 3:16 says, "So because you are lukewarm—neither hot not cold—I am about to spit you out of My mouth." That scripture has always bothered me. I worry. Am I lukewarm, afraid to take a stand for what I believe? Am I willing to speak up for what I believe, willing to intercede and advocate for others? Am I really so sure of my standing with Christ that I would lay down my life for what I believe? I pray, dear sisters, that none of us are ever placed in that position! But I also pray that it is a question that we wrestle with. How sure are you of the one with whom you place your trust? Are you willing to pursue His call on your life to the point of your own discomfort? This truly is "no afternoon athletic contest" that we are involved in. It is a fight to the finish with the greatest enemy of all time who would love nothing more than to devour us! Don't misunderstand me. God equips us after He calls us, but the fight is ours! We don't fight alone, but we must all fight the good fight of faith. It may be against our culture, or it may be a battle in our own mind, wondering, Am I convinced my faith is life defining, something that I desire more than anything else? For that is what God requires! He wants warriors, hands and feet that represent Him and are not afraid to follow where He leads! When it is all said and done and we breathe our last breath, I promise it will all be worth it. Ralph Erskine is quoted as saying, "Faith, without trouble or fighting is a suspicious faith, for true faith is a fighting, wrestling faith." Roll up your sleeves and armor up! It's gonna be good!

Have a great day. Remembering always that you are loved, called, and claimed by the commander of the angel armies and HE IS ABLE!

OCTOBER 1

And we all, who with unveiled faces contemplate the Lord's glory, are being transformed into His image with ever-increasing glory, which comes from the Lord, Who is the Spirit. (2 Corinthians 3:18)

Do not conform to the pattern of this world, but be transformed by the renewing of your mind. Then you will be able to test and approve what God's will is—His good, pleasing and perfect will. (Romans 12:2)

May the Lord direct your hearts into God's love and Christ's perseverance. (2 Thessalonians 3:5)

Create in me a clean heart, O God, and renew a steadfast spirit within me. (Psalm 51:10)

Therefore if anyone is in Christ, she is a new creature; the old things passed away; behold, new things have come. (2 Corinthians 5:17)

And I am sure of this, that He who began a good work in you will bring it to completion at the day of Jesus Christ. (Philippians 1:6)

Almighty Father, search us, examine our hearts, lay bare our thoughts and transform us into Your likeness. We admit that on our own we are powerless to make ourselves into Your image. You alone are the source of transformation! Fill us with Your Holy Spirit, convict us of sin, wrong thinking, selfishness, bitterness, pride, envy, lust, laziness, and indifference and, instead, fill us with the thoughts of Your spirit. Fill us with love, joy, peace, patience, kindness, goodness, faithfulness, and self-control! Continually pour Your goodness,

Your wisdom, and Your energy into us so that we may in turn reflect Your light. Lord, we surrender our lives to You. We trust You to will and to work in us for Your good purpose. We acknowledge that "talking the Christian talk" without true repentance and surrender is nothing more than a costume that we put on when it fits our purposes. Forgive us! Renew us! Transform us! Use us! Empower us! We surrender this world's hold on us and jump willingly into Your outstretched arms! We're depending on You!

Love us with all You've got! Amen!

OCTOBER 2

Therefore encourage one another and build each other up, just as in fact you are doing. (1 Thessalonians 5:11)

Have I not commanded you? Be strong and courageous. Do not be afraid. Do not be discouraged, for the LORD your God will be with you wherever you go. (Joshua 1:9)

The Lord Himself goes before you and will be with you; He will never leave you nor forsake you. Do not be afraid; do not be discouraged. (Deuteronomy 31:8)

Therefore, my dear brothers and sisters, stand firm. Let nothing move you. Always give yourselves fully to the work of the Lord, because you know that your labor in the Lord is not in vain. (1 Corinthians 15:58)

And let us consider how we may spur one another on toward love and good deeds, not giving up meeting together, as some are in the habit of doing, but encouraging one another - and all the more as you see the Day approaching. (Hebrews 10:24–25)

Be on your guard; stand firm in the faith; be courageous; be strong. (1 Corinthians 16:13)

Friends, how aware are you of the ability you have to speak life into the people around you? Do you ever leave words unspoken that would build up or encourage those God has placed in your path? Life-affirming words can accomplish more than we can ever imagine when spoken with sincerity and love.

Challenge for the week: Journal about a time that someone encouraged or challenged you that left an impact. Then, make a point of encouraging or challenging someone in your life this week.

I think it is fair to say that we all get complacent at times. We get lazy in our relationships, lazy in our self-discipline, and lazy in our time with the Lord. A little encouragement to keep at it or to aim higher can go a long way! I am sure you have all heard the old saying, "You will get out of it, what you put in to it." Sometimes our biggest struggles are with monotony and drudgery. We do the same things over and over with the same people week after week, and we lose sight of the fact that we have an opportunity to encourage and motivate and challenge those around us every day!

Shine bright, ladies! The world around you needs your light and your encouragement! Have a great week!

OCTOBER 3

But you are a Chosen race a royal priesthood, a Holy nation, a people for God's own possession, so that you may proclaim the excellences of Him Who has called you out of darkness into His marvelous light. (1 Peter 2:9)

For He chose us in Him before the creation of the world to be holy and blameless in His sight. In love He predestined us to be adopted as His daughters through Jesus Christ, in accordance with His pleasure and will. (Ephesians 1:4,5, NIV)

For we are His workmanship, created in Christ Jesus for good works, which God prepared beforehand so that we would walk in them. (Ephesians 2:10)

When He puts forth all His own, He goes ahead of them, and the sheep follow Him because they know His voice. (John 10:4)

But we should always give thanks to God for you, sisters beloved by the Lord, because God has chosen you from the beginning for salvation through sanctification by the Spirit and faith in the truth. (2 Thessalonians 2:13)

So, sisters, what does the word *holy* mean to you? By definition, it means set apart, sacred. But what does scripture mean when it says, "Be holy because I Am holy"? I encourage you to think about this even as I take a stab at the "holy purpose."

As children of God, heirs to the kingdom, and vessels for the potter's use, we are first called to be available to our Father so that we are ready and equipped to be used by God. I think sometimes we get this lofty picture in our minds about being holy, imagining angel status or life on a mission field! But we cannot be useful to God anywhere that HE has not already placed us. This is our mission field, so perhaps our holy purpose is being fulfilled every day in the ordinary, moment-by-moment events of our lives, in the way we respond to and love those that God has placed around us, in living out the relationship that we are experiencing with God, or in the desire for surrender and trust that is growing in our hearts. Perhaps being holy is being truthful, authentic, and gut-level honest with our Father, admitting our shortcomings and our frustrations with what we don't understand. Perhaps it is about desiring to become ALL that God has intended us to be, surrendering OUR will for HIS plan, trusting that we ARE who GOD says we are, and then living like we believe it.

Remember, friends, God has called you. He has chosen and equipped you. You are of great value to Him.

OCTOBER 4

Be imitators of me, just as I also am of Christ. (1 Corinthians 11:1)

But we all, with unveiled face, beholding as in a mirror the glory of the Lord, are being transformed into the same image from glory to glory, just as from the Lord, the Spirit. (2 Corinthians 3:18)

Our faces shining with the brightness of His face. And so we are transfigured much like the Messiah, our lives gradually becoming brighter and more beautiful, as God enters our lives and we become more like Him. (2 Corinthians 3:18 MSG)

A pupil is not above her teacher, but everyone, after she has been fully trained, will be like her teacher. (Luke 6:40)

Commit to the Lord whatever you do, and your plans will succeed. (Proverbs 16:3)

Above all else, guard your heart, for it is the wellspring of life. (Proverbs 4:23)

The person who lives in right relationship with God does it by embracing what God arranges for her. (Galatians 3:12 MSG)

Make a careful exploration of who you are and the work you have been given, and then sink yourself into that. Don't be impressed with yourself. Don't compare yourself with others. Each of you must take responsibility for doing the creative best you can with your own life. Don't be misled. No one makes a fool of God. What a person plants, she will harvest. The person who plants selfishness, ignoring the needs of others—ignoring God—harvests a crop of weeds. All she'll have for her life is weeds! But the one who plants in response to God, letting God's Spirit do the growth work in her, harvests a crop of real life, eternal life! (Galatians 6:4–8 MSG)

Right now, you and I are in the quarry. We're feeling the rumble of life's heavy machinery, the blunt edge of the shaping tools. The pounding blows are slowly separating us from our deep, rock-hard attachments to this world. But like living stones, we are being shaped and sized for placement in a faraway temple fit for the glory of God. This pain has a purpose. All this hammering and chiseling is taking us somewhere. Somewhere heavenly and eternal.

—Nancy Leigh DeMoss,
The Quiet Place.

I like the phrase, "We are in the quarry." And I like the idea that the frustrations and trials and temptations of this life are shaping us, molding, and fitting us into the likeness of Christ! Jesus's life on earth was anything but easy, so for us to expect anything else for ours is nothing short of unrealistic. Sure, this life is full of difficulties and disappointments, but the thing to remember is this is only a temporary situation. We can rise above the things that are weighing us down; we can stand tall and strong in our convictions because the "quarry" is not our home. What awaits us if far beyond anything we can imagine.

Let's let God's shaping hand do His work in our lives and look forward, bouncing on eager toes of anticipation to what lies ahead.

Because God is FOR us, He knows what He is doing, and He CAN be trusted.

You are greatly and eternally loved! Trust the hands that are shaping you!

OCTOBER 5

This is the confidence we have in approaching God; that if we ask anything according to His Will, He hears us. And if we know that He hears us - whatever we ask - we know that we have what we asked of Him. (John 5:14–15)

A person may think their own ways are right, but the LORD weighs the heart. (Proverbs 21:2)

The eyes of the Lord watch over those who do right, and His ears are open to their prayers. But the Lord turns His face against those who do evil. (1 Peter 3:12)

Humble yourselves, therefore, under God's Mighty Hand, that He may lift you up in due time. (1 Peter 5:6)

Let us not becomes weary in doing good, for at the proper time we will reap a harvest if we do not give up. (Galatians 6:9)

Now to Him Who is able to do immeasurably more than all we ask or imagine, according to His power that is at work within us. (Ephesians 3:20)

For My thoughts are not your thoughts, neither are your ways my ways, declares the LORD. (Isaiah 55:8)

Unanswered prayer—it's painful, challenging, and frustrating. When we KNOW that God can but God chooses not to. We are left wondering why. Was it because I am not good enough, worthy of an answer? Or we wonder, does God even hear at all? Our faith takes a hard hit, and we aren't sure anymore that God is good, or that He can be trusted with the deepest hurts and concerns of our hearts.

I have been there recently when I really don't want to pray, when I have the attitude, "What good does it do anyway?" or the thought, "You can't be trusted." It is times like these that I fight to bring my thoughts back to the God I have known since I was a small child. The God who is faithful, who can be trusted, who forgives and restores me. It helps me to remind myself that "my thoughts, are NOT God's thoughts." That God may be telling me no, and I am choosing to believe that He is not listening.

Sisters, God DOES hear our prayers. He understands the deepest longings of our heart, and He will never abandon us even when we turn our backs on Him. I believe that it is in these darkest moments of confusion and pain that God's spirit continually whispers to our hearts, "Trust Me in this"; "My timeline is different, and far superior to yours"; and "I have ALL the facts, see the whole picture and always know what is best." Our problem is that we are trying to figure out life's most difficult struggles with extremely limited vision. We see death as the end, failure! Yet perhaps it is a supreme deliverance, the most merciful answer possible.

We are trying to access the tough situations in life and fix them with clouded vision and without all the facts. One of the things I have learned to pray over the years is "Lord, bring all the facts to light. Show me just a fraction of what You know." We so often base our prayers on one-sided or limited truth about what we are praying for, really praying, without meaning to, for something that is contrary to God's best for ourselves or another!

When we are hurting, prayer is really the BEST option, and perhaps learning to say, (even through gritted teeth) "YOUR will be done," is the faith step we need to take to learn to trust HIM more! Because, friends, GOD IS FOR US!

OCTOBER 6

Then they despised the pleasant land. They did not believe in His Word, but grumbled in their tents. They did not listen to the voice of the LORD. (Psalm 106:24–26)

Then He said to them, "Beware, and be on your guard against every form of greed; for not even when one has an abundance does her life consist of her possessions." (Luke 12:15)

She who loves money will not be satisfied with money, nor she who has abundance with its income. This too is vanity. (Ecclesiastes 5:10)

Make sure that your character is free from the love of money, being content with what you have, for He Himself has said, "I will never desert you, nor will I ever forsake you." (Hebrews 13:5)

The verses above speak primarily about being discontented with possessions or with greed, but sometimes we are more discontented with God's behavior or response on our behalf. Somewhere along the way, we have come up with this notion that God is supposed to serve US, that He is in heaven, waiting for us to tell Him what we need, what to do, what we want. As absurd as this sounds when I write it, don't you agree that there is an element of truth in this statement? I have personally wondered, "Lord, but why? I am a Christian, why is this happening to me?" Perhaps the better response would be, "Lord, I don't understand what You are up to or why, but I am Your child, and I know that You can be trusted. I surrender my situation to You."

My dear sisters, God comes through for us all the time! He delivers us from evils we didn't even see coming. He directs our steps to keep us from disaster. He sends His mighty angels to protect us and reassure us. Yet because we averted those disasters and are even unaware of them, we grumble, "God doesn't care, doesn't see, isn't enough!"

May we jealously guard our hearts and minds against discontentment with God. Someday, when God's provision, protection, and guidance is revealed to us, we will be on our knees, on the ground, humbled and overwhelmed with the knowledge of God's sure and constant vigilance and intervention. Let's not wait! Begin thanking God today for working in the details of our lives regardless of whether we see what He is up to or not. May we learn to trust Him completely and let go of preconceived notions about how things are supposed to work in our lives. Let's let God BE God and rest in the assurance that He's got this!

Have a great week! Love you, ladies! Shine bright!

OCTOBER 7

For the Word of God is alive and active, sharper than any dou-ble-edged sword, it penetrates even to dividing soul and spirit, joints and marrow, it judges the thoughts and attitudes of the heart. (Hebrews 4:12)

All Scripture is God-breathed and is useful for teaching, rebuk-ing, correcting and training in righteousness, so that the servant of God may be thoroughly equipped for every good work. (2 Timothy 3:16–17)

Do not merely listen to the word, and so deceive yourselves. Do what is says. (James 1:22)

As for God, His way is perfect; the Lord's Word is flawless; He shields all who take refuge in Him. (Psalm 18:30)

Therefore everyone who hears these Words of Mine and puts them into practice is like a wise man who built His house on the rock. (Matthew 7:24)

Do everything without grumbling or arguing, so that you may become blameless and pure, children of God without fault in a warped and crooked generation. Then you will shine among them like stars in the sky as you hold firmly to the Word of life. (Philippians 2:14–16)

The unfolding of Your words gives light; it gives understanding to the simple. (Psalm 119:130)

In God, Whose word I praise—in God I trust and am not afraid. What can mere mortals do to me? (Psalm 56:4)

On a day-to-day basis, we are overrun with challenges that oftentimes leave us in a panic and lead to sleepless nights and mounting worry. At such times, we need to remember that God's word is our sanity. It teaches truth, and when we rely on Him, He protects our minds and our hearts by binding us to Him and reordering our perspective.

My dear sisters, GOD IS IN CONTROL! He has been since the beginning of time, and He will be until the end of time! Nothing happens without His complete knowledge. Nothing surprises Him, and nothing overwhelms Him. God is God, and even the most evil of the enemy run in terror at the mere mention of His name!

May we become so grounded in God's word that our foundation is firm! May we spend time studying scripture and committing it to memory so that when we feel threatened or worried or overwhelmed or downright afraid by what we see on the news and read in the papers, we remember God's words to us in scripture, "He shields all those who take refuge in Him."

"In God I trust and am not afraid." The world around us needs to know that, as daughters of the King, we are confident in the one who controls all things! We need to know and claim His promises: "So do not fear, for I am with you; do not be dismayed for I am your God, I will strengthen you and help you; I will uphold you with My Righteous Right Hand" and "For God has NOT given us a spirit of fear, but of power and of love and of a sound mind." Let's cling to and claim for ourselves these words of our Father so that we will not be shaken! May we shine among those in our world like stars as we hold firmly to God's word!

We are loved, protected, encouraged, equipped, and known by God. Let's live like it!

OCTOBER 8

Y ou adulteresses, do you not know that the friendship with the world is hostility toward God? Therefore whoever wishes to be a friend of the world makes herself an enemy of God. (James 4:4)

Do not love the world nor the things in the world. If anyone loves the world, the love of the father is not in them. For all that is in the world, the lust of the flesh and the lust of the eyes and the boastful pride of life, is not from the Father, but is from the world. (1 John 2:15–16)

Instructing us to deny ungodliness and world desires and to live sensibly, righteously and godly in the present age. (Titus 2:12)

Summing up; Be agreeable, be sympathetic, be loving, be compassionate, be humble. That goes for all of you, no exceptions. No retaliation. No Sharp-tongued sarcasm. Instead, bless—that's your job, to bless. You'll be a blessing and also get a blessing. (1 Peter 3:8 MSG)

As children of God, we must continually choose whom we will serve. We cannot have it both ways. We cannot be friends with the world and friends with God.

To be holy means to be set apart, set apart for God's purposes and God's use. Yet even as Christians, we don't want to be set apart or different. Very often, we are so much like the world around us that no one would even know that we consider ourselves to be God followers! We are quick to confess with our mouths, but our lives tell another story. We are as angry, bitter, crabby, greedy, self-centered, and as irritable as the next guy. We certainly can talk the talk, but when it comes down to walking the walk, we would rather not. We, as human beings, all seem to have an I problem: I deserve, I don't deserve, I want, I think, I, I, I, I, I.

What if instead of thinking, *I*, we thought You. "What do You, Father, want me to do, to possess, to work at?" "Where do You want me to spend my time, my money and my energies?" Or "How do You want me to respond in any given circumstance?" I think, by shifting the focus of our thinking away from ourselves we could begin to live lives of obedience and in doing so claim the promises at the end of that line of scripture that reads; "Be a blessing and also get a blessing."—It's a WIN-WIN!

Today, may we live lives of compassion and humility. Abandoning our friendships with the world and instead embracing this God who loves us fiercely, and desires for us to have an impact on the culture around us. Today, may we be a blessing to someone else.

You are loved, called, claimed, equipped, blessed! Live BIG, BOLD, BEAUTIFUL lives before the Master!

OCTOBER 9

Whoever brings blessing will be enriched, and one who waters, will herself be watered. The people curse her who holds back grain, but a blessing is on the head of her who sells it. 9 Proverbs 11:25–26)

But someone who does not know, and then does something wrong, will be punished only lightly. When someone has been given much, much will be required in return; and when someone has been entrusted with much, even more will be required. (Luke 12:48)

Remember this: The person who sows sparingly will also reap sparingly, and the person who sows generously will also reap generously. (2 Corinthians 9:6)

So encourage each other to build each other up, just as you are already doing. (1 Thessalonians 5:11)

Bear one another's burdens, and so fulfill the law of Christ. (Galatians 6:2)

And do not forget to do good and to share with others, for with such sacrifices God is pleased. (Hebrews 13:16)

So confess your sins to one another and pray for one another so that you may be healed. The prayer of a righteous person has great effectiveness. (James 5:16)

There are many ways to live out a life of gratitude. The scriptures above list a few of them. Through giving, encouragement, and through our prayers are all a good start. God has blessed us with, first and foremost, faith but also material blessings. He has given us physical blessings, such as health and medical care, and He has given us spiritual blessings as well. He has called us by name, placed us where He wants us and given us what we will need to do His will. He has claimed responsibility for us even for our past failures. He has offered forgiveness and reinstated us into His family. And finally, He has equipped us by giving us His spirit, living and breathing God within us, guiding us, encouraging us, directing our hands and feet as we walk out our faith.

Living a life of gratitude doesn't have to be difficult. It is rather an outpouring of, or response to, what God has already done for us. We are being filled to overflowing daily with the love, protection, and provision from God Himself. Our response in our lives of love is to simply leak on to others what is overflowing from us, His loved, protected, pampered daughters. Our Dad's got this! We don't need to hang on to our blessings with clenched fists. There is more love, grace, joy, peace, and blessing that we ourselves can contain! Let's go and spread the light of His love, and the gifts from His hands! Let's live boldly, joyfully, and gratefully in HIS presence and for His glory!

Have a great day! Shine bright! Live joyfully! Expect great things! We serve a God of excess!

OCTOBER 10

A wise woman will hear and increase in learning, and a woman of understanding will acquire wise counsel. (Proverbs 1:5)

Then the LORD came and stood and called as at other times, "Samuel, Samuel!" And Samuel said, "Speak, for Your servant is listening." (1 Samuel 3:10)

Listen to counsel and accept discipline, that you may be wise the rest of your days. (Proverbs 19:20)

This you know, my beloved sisters but everyone must be quick to hear, slow to speak and slow to anger. (James 1:19)

But prove yourselves doers of the word, and not merely hearers who delude themselves. For if anyone is a hearer of the word and not a doer, she is like a woman who looks at her natural face in a mirror; for once she has looked at herself and gone away, she has immediately forgotten what kind of person she was. (James 1:22–24)

Don't fool yourself into thinking that you are a listener when you are anything but, letting the Word go in one ear and out the other. Act on what you hear! Those who hear and don't act are like those who glance in the mirror, walk away, and two minutes later have no idea who they are, what they look like. (James 1:22–24 MSG)

Quiet time, devotional time, or prayer time, whatever you call it, it is crucial to a solid, honest relationship with our Father.

I think one of the reasons establishing a habit of time alone with God is so difficult is because our enemy is throwing everything he has at us in order that we would not make time alone with God a priority in our lives. Every time we turn our hearts and our minds toward God, he loses ground. Satan does NOT want us to discern God's voice, to grow in relationship with Him, and heaven forbid, ACT on what we are learning. We are not in a battle with flesh and blood on this issue. But the battle can be won. Make an effort every day. Whenever it comes to mind, set a few minutes aside for prayer, reading, or worship of God. Five minutes here, ten minutes there, five minutes again, it adds up. Don't listen to the voices that reprimand you, saying, "You messed up again." "Too late now." "Maybe tomorrow." When thoughts of God come in to your mind, pause, stop, and pray. Grab your Bible, grab a devotional, seek God's wisdom. God rewards obedience. He desires relationship. He WANTS to advise and counsel us. He just needs us to be focused on Him to hear Him.

Don't give up, sisters! I realize there are hundreds of things clamoring for our attention, but nothing, absolutely nothing, is more important than our hearts. God loves us. He desires to mold us into ALL that we can be. Our part is to give Him the time to do it. "Seek the Lord, Your God, with ALL your hearts, with ALL your mind, and with ALL your soul and all the rest will fall into place."

Let's commit to becoming women who hear and grow in learning and understanding. Let us earnestly seek God and listen to wise counsel and accept discipline. Then, when we glance at our reflection in the mirror we will be sure of who we are, Daughters of the King!

OCTOBER 11

Let your speech always be with grace, as though seasoned with salt, so that you will know how you should respond to each person. (Colossians 4:6)

But sanctify Christ as Lord in your hearts, always being ready to make a defense to everyone who asks you to give an account for the hope that is in you, yet with gentleness and reverence. (1 Peter 3:15)

Let your light shine before men in such a way that they may see your good works, and glorify your Father who is in heaven. (Matthew 5:16)

Therefore, we are ambassadors for Christ, as though God were making an appeal through us, we beg you on behalf of Christ, be reconciled to God. (2 Corinthians 5:20)

Witnessing—telling others what we believe and why. Are you comfortable with that, friends? Do you know what you believe and why? I think that, honestly, that is a difficult question. Sure, I know what I believe, but putting words to the why is difficult! In 1 Peter MSG, we are asked to "be ready to speak up and tell anyone who asks why you're living the way you are." As ambassadors for Christ, we need to realize that the way we live our lives, conduct ourselves in public and private, as well as the words we speak, or don't speak, are communicating to the world around us all the time! Thank God that He sent the Holy Spirit to live and breathe in us so that we will be equipped to better live lives pleasing to Him. On our own strength and merit, we will continually fail, but if we earnestly seek God and daily surrender our wills to His plan, God will work through us all the time.

Oswald Chambers says a couple of things that I think are quite relevant to today's devotion: "Look at God's incredible waste of His saints, (you and I, and all believers) according to the world's judgment. God seems to place His saints in the most useless places." And then we say, "God intends for me to be here because I am so useful to Him. Yet Jesus never measured His life by how or where He was of the greatest use. God places His saints where they will bring the most glory to Him, and we are totally incapable of judging where that may be." And again, Oswald says, "Once you have the right relationship with God through salvation and sanctification, remember that whatever your circumstances may be, you have been placed in them by God. The lives that have the greatest blessing to you are the lives of those people who themselves are unaware of having been a blessing."

My dear sisters, we are to be about living the lives of ambassadors of Christ today exactly wherever He has placed you, whatever your circumstances! This is not some future lofty goal but the everyday, "one foot in front of the other" daily life of His daughters!

I beg you, be ready to give an account to anyone who wants to know! Shine brightly, shine unabashedly (that's my new favorite word, it means without shame or apology, boldly, certain of one's position). Be fearless and wildly confident in the ONE in whom we place our trust!

There are places to go, things to experience, and joy unimaginable ahead as we claim our position as daughters of the KING!

OCTOBER 12

We demolish arguments and every pretension that sets itself up against the knowledge of God, and we take captive every thought to make it obedient to Christ. (2 Corinthians 10:5)

We use our powerful God -tools for smashing warped philosophies, tearing down barriers erected against the truth of God, fitting every loose thought and emotion and impulse into the structure of life shaped by Christ. (2 Corinthians 10:5 MSG)

This calls for patient endurance on the part of the people of God who keep His commands and remain faithful to Jesus. (Revelation 14:12)

Meanwhile, the saints stand passionately patient, keeping God's commands, staying faithful to Jesus. (Revelation 14:12 MSG)

Through Him we received grace and apostleship to call all the Gentiles to the obedience that comes from faith for His Name's sake. (Romans 1:5)

Through Him we received both the generous gift of His life, and the urgent task of passing it on to others who receive it by entering into obedient trust in Jesus. (Romans 1:5 MSG)

And this is love; that we walk in obedience to His commands As you have heard from the beginning His command is that you walk in love. (2 John 1:6)

That we love each other. Love means following His commandments, and His unifying commandment is that you conduct your lives in love. (2 John 1:6 MSG)

He replied, "Blessed rather are those who hear the Word of God and obey it!" (Luke 11:8)

But whoever looks intently into the perfect law that gives freedom, and continues in it - not forgetting what they have heard, but doing it - they will be blessed in what they do. (James 1:25)

Almighty, all-powerful, all-knowing God, we come before Your throne once again, thanking You for the blessings of abundance, health, family and relationships. For the beauty of creation, and the power of Your spirit! We ask that You would steady us, nudge us forward, and bring us back as we walk and wander on this path of obedience to You. Father, our hearts are willing to be obedient to Your teaching, but our minds wander and our flesh is weak. Help us to focus on Your command to "love one another," remembering that "love covers a multitude of sin!" Teach us to love not only those *like* us but those we don't understand as well. May our underlying motivation and emotion be, every day and always, love for others and a desire to see them turn to You. May we be bold and obedient in standing up for truth and right. May we speak up for those unable to do so themselves, and may we be obedient in looking after the needs of others. Enable us to take our thoughts captive, expose them to Your light, and discard any thought or emotion that is not pleasing to You. We confess, Lord, that, oftentimes, we give our emotions and feelings far more power in our lives than they should have! Help us to grasp and hold on to the fact that You ask us to obey what You teach regardless of how we may feel!

Father, banish fear and worry from our lives and replace it with total reliance and surrender to You! May we consistently do the hard work of relinquishment, letting go of anything and everything that stands in the way of our total and complete surrender to Your will and Your way. Because, Father, we know that we can't demand our way and expect Your will to be done. Mold us and make us into mighty women of faith, women who stand firm in the face of adversity, whose joy is untouchable, and whose faith is undeniable! Help us to remember that, everywhere and always, You are in control! Our part is to trust You.

We love You, Lord. Forgive us for doubting your sovereignty, Your wisdom, and Your ways! We confess that we are weary from trying to do life on our own. Forgive us, renew us, and empower us for Your glory! Amen!

OCTOBER 13

But in everything commending ourselves as servants of God, in much endurance in afflictions in hardships, in distresses. (2 Corinthians 6:4)

Well, now is the right time to listen, the day to be helped. Don't put it off, don't frustrate God's work by showing up late, throwing a question mark over everything we're doing. Our work as God's servants gets validated—or not—in the details. People are watching us as we stay at our post, alertly, unswervingly…in hard times, tough times, bad times, when we're beaten up, jailed, and mobbed, working hard, working late, working without eating, with pure heart, clear head, steady hand, in gentleness, holiness, and honest love, when we're telling the truth, and when God's showing His power, when we're doing our best setting things right, when we're praised and when we're blamed, slandered, and honored, true to our word, though distrusted, ignored by the world, but recognized by God, terrifically alive, though rumored to be dead, beaten within an inch of our lives, but refusing to die, immersed in tears, yet always filled with deep joy, living on handouts, yet enriching many, having nothing, having it all…I can't tell you how much I long for you to enter this wide-open, spacious life. We didn't fence you in. The smallness you feel comes from within you. Your lives aren't small, but you're living them in a small way. I'm speaking as plainly as I can and with great affection. Open up your lives. Live openly and expansively! (2 Corinthians 4–13 MSG)

Being a bond-servant is not a concept that we, in this day and age, are familiar with. In fact, the whole idea of servanthood is a foreign, unwelcome topic. Jesus, while living on earth as a man, said that He did not come to BE served but to serve. How different this world would look if we, in turn, lived that way. If daily we looked for a way and then followed through on serving those around us, not just our immediate families but the strangers around us. I think that, oftentimes, we enter in to relationships (Christianity included) for what we can get out of that relationship, not what we can give.

I don't want the hardship that these disciples endured, but I can truthfully say that I need to spend some time considering the cost of becoming a disciple of Jesus Christ. Would I withstand the persecution and not be quick to abandon my faith? What I do know is that my desire is to claim the open and expansive life that Jesus offers those who follow Him. I desire to open up my life and stop living a small ineffective life. Care to join me?

May God grant us the wisdom and strength to follow Him everywhere and always!

OCTOBER 14

The decisions of God are accurate down to the nth degree. (Psalm 19:9 MSG)

Clean the slate, God, so we can start the day fresh! Keep me from stupid sins, from thinking I can take over Your work. (Psalm 19:13)

God Himself bellows in thunder as He commands His forces. Look at the size of that army! And the strength of those who obey Him! God's Judgment Day—great and terrible. Who can possibly survive this? But there's also this, it's not too late—God's personal message!—"Come back to Me and really mean it! Come fasting and weeping, sorry for your sins!" Change your life, not just your clothes. Come back to God, your God! (Joel 2:10–13 MSG)

"These words I speak to you are not incidental additions to your life, homeowner improvements to your standard of living. They are foundational words, words to build a life on... But, if you just use my words in Bible studies and don't work them into your life, you are like a stupid carpenter who built his house on the sandy beach." (Matthew 7:24, 26 MSG)

The well-intentioned efforts we make to get it all together for God can very well get in the way of what God is doing for us. The main and central action is everywhere and always what GOD has done, is doing and will do for us. Our main and central task is to live in responsive obedience to God's action revealed in Jesus. Our part in the action is the act of faith

—from the introduction to Hebrews, MSG

When I looked for verses about "responding to God," I was taken to numerous verses on obedience. I searched verses on "bringing glory to God." I read verses on worship, praise, and the worthiness of God. So how DO we respond to God? The scripture says our response should be to worship God! But what does that really mean? How? By singing? By prayer? The conclusion I have come to is this, by our complete and total surrender to God and His will in our lives. Our response to God's gifts is trust and faith and surrender. Now, those are easy words to type but not so easy to master in our own lives. Oftentimes, my trust in God goes only as far as my understanding of God. Oswald Chambers says it this way,

> When we are afraid, the least we can do is pray to God. But our Lord has a right to expect that those who name His name have an underlying confidence in Him. God expects His children to be so confident in Him that in any crisis they are the ones who are reliable. Yet our trust is only in God up to a certain point, then we turn back to the elementary panic-stricken prayers of those people who do not even know God. We come to our wits' end, showing that we don't have even the slightest amount of confidence in Him or in His sovereign control of the world. To us He seems to be asleep, and we can see nothing but giant, breaking waves on the sea ahead of us. "O you of little faith!" What a stinging pain must have shot through the disciples as they surely thought to themselves, "We missed the mark again!" And what a sharp pain will go through us when we suddenly realize that we could have produced complete and utter joy in the heart of Jesus by remaining absolutely confident in Him, in spite of what we were facing!

Did you catch that last line? "We could have produced complete and utter joy in the heart of Jesus by remaining absolutely confident in Him." I am in total agreement that the things we do to "get it all together" for God, very often get in the way of what God is doing! God wants our heart of hearts. He wants us to come to Him in complete sincerity. Fasting and weeping, and truly sorry for our sins. Trusting that He is bigger, wiser, stronger, and greater than anything that is before us. God is in control, always and in every situation. Our response is to trust Him!

OCTOBER 15

You ask and do not receive, because you ask with wrong motives, so that you may spend it on your pleasures. (James 4:3)

If I regard wickedness in my heart, the Lord will not hear. (Psalm 66:18)

Because I called you and you refused, I stretched out My hand and no one paid attention; and you neglected all My counsel and did not want My reproof. (Proverbs 1:24–25)

There they cry out, but He does not answer because of the pride of evil men. Surely God will not listen to an empty cry, nor will the Almighty regard it. (Job 35:12–13)

Honestly, friends, I have very often felt that "my prayers fell on deaf ears." It took my forcing myself to believe the truths God tells us about Himself to believe that He did indeed hear and then realizing the answer I was getting or would get would not be in line with what I wanted. How did I know that God did indeed hear me? Because I trusted in the salvation and grace I received when I gave Jesus control of me. Now, I'm not saying that it wasn't and isn't a continual struggle for control, but my heart is willing. It is my flesh that is weak. I desire my way in my time and have the pride to believe I know best. For me, it is a daily surrender, repeating over and over, "I surrender my life to You. Your will be done."

Do not be mistaken. God HEARS the cries and prayers of His children. How and when He answers is completely up to Him. God understands our motives better than we do ourselves. He sees our stubbornness, our rebellion, our self-centeredness and addresses those things in our lives that are displeasing to Him. Oh, that we would fall to our knees in repentance and sorrow for the things that stand in the way of our right relationship with Him! We can't have it OUR way and claim to desire HIS way. Very often, the two are in conflict with each other.

May we learn to pray with complete surrender to the will of God! Because, you can be certain, His way is the best way! Every day, always and even when we simply do not comprehend what He is up to.

I believe that God has changed my heart for the prison ministry because of unanswered prayers for our daughter. God has given me a compassion and desire for these lost men of "lawlessness" to personally know Jesus Christ.

Sisters, I don't know what God is up to, but I do know that He can be trusted!

OCTOBER 16

Bear with each other and forgive one another if any of you has a grievance against someone. Forgive as the Lord forgave you. (Colossians 3:13)

Get rid of all bitterness, rage and anger, brawling and slander, along with every form of malice. Be kind and compassionate to one another, forgiving each other, just as in Christ God forgave you. (Ephesians 4:31–32)

And when you stand praying, if you hold anything against anyone, forgive them, so that your Father in heaven may forgive you your sins. (Mark 11:25)

Then Peter came to Jesus and asked, "Lord, how many times shall I forgive my brother when he sins against me? Up to seven times?" Jesus answered, "I tell you, not seven times, but seventy-seven times." (Matthew 18:21–22)

Love is patient, love is kind. It does not envy, it does not boast, it is not proud. It does not dishonor others, it is not self-seeking, it is not easily angered, it keeps no record of wrongs. Love does not delight in evil but rejoices with the truth. (1 Corinthians 13:4–6)

Let it go and let God have it. I was just thinking this morning that, oftentimes, something someone might say, just in passing, hurts something in us. And instead of just brushing it off and not giving it a second thought, we harbor the words, ponder them over and over, attach some meaning to them that is hurtful and malicious, and then turn that meaning inward, toward ourselves. So something said without forethought or intention now has the power to hurt us!

Our enemy loves it when we self-abuse! Just last night, someone said something that I continued to ponder, as I was getting ready for bed and again first thing this morning. I needed to simply let it go. It makes me wonder, how many times have I said something that was misconstrued or taken in a way not intended? Let's not get our knickers in a knot over something taken out of context or simply misunderstood! May we all learn to exercise forbearance. Life is short. Let's learn to not make it any harder than it already is.

God reminds us to forgive and let it go so that the little things don't zap our joy!

Have a fantastic day! God is in the details. Trust Him!

OCTOBER 17

Your thoughts - how rare, how beautiful! God, I'll never comprehend them! I couldn't even begin to count them - any more than I could count the sand of the sea. (Psalm 139:17–18)

Yet to all who did receive Him, to those who believed in His Name, He gave the right to become Children of God! (John 1:12)

Before I formed you in the womb I knew you, before you were born I set you apart; I appointed you as a prophet to the nations. (Jeremiah 1:5)

But you are the ones chosen by God for the high calling of priestly work, chosen to be a holy people, God's instruments to do His work and speak out for Him, to tell others of the night and day difference He made for you - from nothing to something, from rejected to accepted. (1 Peter 2:2–10 MSG)

Don't be afraid, I've redeemed you. I've called you by name. You're mine. When you're in over your head, I'll be there with you. When you're in rough waters, you will not go down. When you're between a rock and a hard place, it won't be a dead end—Because I AM GOD, your personal God, the Holy of Israel, your Savior. I paid a huge price for you; all of Egypt, with rich Cush and Seba thrown in! That's how much you mean to me! That's how much I love you! I'd sell off the whole world to get you back, trade the creation just for you... You're my handpicked servant. So that you'll come to know and trust Me, understand both that I am and Who I am. (Isaiah 43:2–6, 11 MSG)

With Your very own hands you formed me; now breathe Your wisdom over me so I can understand You. (Psalm 119:73 MSG)

We are a chosen people. Hand picked by God for the high calling of His work. We are called to be holy, to be His instruments and to tell others about Him. He's called us by name and paid a huge price for us.

He ordained where we would live, as well as what time in the world's history that we would live. And He has prepared works for us to be about doing. God is in the details. Even when we feel isolated or even abandoned, God has never left our side. He promises us that He works all things out for the good of those who love Him. Even the hard, confusing things. God's timing of events is far superior to our timing. His understanding we cannot even begin to comprehend. He asks that we trust Him, lean into Him, and ASK Him for what is near and dear to our hearts as well as what is troubling us. God is for us. He is deeply aware of the intimate details of our lives as well as the overall picture. He can be trusted. He promises to be with us always and everywhere.

So, today, take a deep breath and rejoice in Who is holding you. Trust that He is FOR you and live this day in joyful anticipation of what lies ahead for you. Because YOU, my friends, are children of the King, heirs to the throne and passionately loved by the very creator of the universe AND nothing is too hard for our Father or beyond His comprehension! HE's GOT THIS!

OCTOBER 18

But the wicked are like the tossing sea, for it cannot be quiet, and its waters toss up refuse and mud. "There is no peace," says my God, "for the wicked." (Isaiah 57:20–21)

Jesus answered them, "Truly, truly, I say to you, everyone who commits sin is the slave of sin." (John 8:34)

Her own iniquities will capture the wicked, and she will be held with the cords of her own sin. (Proverbs 5:22)

Righteousness exalts a nation, but sin is a disgrace to any people. (Proverbs 14:34)

Sound thinking makes for gracious living, but liars walk a rough road. A commonsense person lives good sense, fools litter the country with silliness. Irresponsible talk makes a real mess of things, but a reliable reporter is a healing presence. Refuse discipline and end up homeless; embrace correction and live an honored life. Souls who follow their hearts thrive; fools bent on evil despise matters of the soul. Become wise by walking with the wise; hang out with fools and watch your life fall to pieces. - Disaster entraps sinners, but God-loyal people get a good life. A good life gets passed on to the grandchildren, ill-gotten wealth ends up with good people. A refusal to correct is a refusal to love; love your children by disciplining them. (Proverbs 13:15–22 MSG)

I realize that I touched on this very topic not long ago, but our culture has so downplayed and even glorified the sin nature that we and our children and grandchildren are blind to the severe and certain consequences of "playing with sin." In the world we are living in, sin is "no big deal"—"everyone does it." When we call sin what it is—sin—we are called intolerant, unloving, and judgmental. So what is a Christian to do? I guess, first and foremost, address the sin issue in our own lives. Look at it for what it is, confess it, and move forward in faith, working at letting go of the sin that entangles us and holds us back. Then lovingly work with the people God has already placed before us, helping them to work through and untangle themselves from their sin. We can speak truth into the lives of our loved ones. We can represent walking the walk as well as talking the talk. We can hold ourselves accountable for the choices we make (or don't make) and then we can witness with our lives to those around us. Sin is serious! Our culture has made a mockery of sin, and its certain and ugly consequences. Sure, we can overlook the sin around us, thinking that we are being "loving" by doing so. But are we not loving them into hell? When I volunteer at the local prison, the prisoners often times will say things like "I wish I would have known the seriousness of my choices when I was younger" or "I didn't realize there was another way" or "I deserve what I get, my choices have brought me here." The men that seem to be willing to admit their mistakes, ask forgiveness and seek restoration with God are the ones that give us hope! Many of these men are now volunteering in their churches, speaking at Celebrate Recovery, and moving forward in forgiveness with their lives. But unfortunately, the consequences of their choices will follow them their whole lives. They are convicted felons, and as such, many options are no longer on the table for them. Restoration is possible, but first, the truth must be addressed head on. What sin is holding us back from closer relationship with Jesus Christ? It's a tough question to ask, but I promise you it is worth it.

Please, please don't misinterpret what I am saying here. I am not implying that I have it figured out, but God is gracious and revealing my sin to me little by little so as not to overwhelm me. He will be gracious with you as well!

YOU ARE LOVED!

OCTOBER 19

And do not be conformed to this world, but be transformed by the renewing of your mind, so that you may prove what the will of God is, that which is good and acceptable and perfect. (Romans 12:2)

As obedient children, do not be conformed to the former lusts which were yours in your ignorance. (1 Peter 1:14)

Thus you will know that I Am the LORD, for you have not walked in My statutes nor have you executed My ordinances, but have acted according to the ordinances of the nations around you. (Ezekiel 11:12)

So then let us not sleep as others do, but let us be alert and sober. (1 Thessalonians 5:6)

But friends, you're not in the dark, so how could you be taken off guard by any of this? Your sons of Light, daughters of Day. We live under wide open skies and know where we stand. So let's not sleepwalk through life like those others. Let's keep our eyes open and be smart. (1 Thessalonians 5:4–6)

Be imitators of me, just as I also am of Christ. (1 Corinthians 11:1)

Therefore be imitators of God, as beloved children, and walk in love just as Christ also loved you and gave Himself up for us, an offering and a sacrifice to God as a fragrant aroma. (Ephesians 5:1–2)

We are not called to merely survive in this world. As God's children, we are called to change this world to transform the darkness around us with the vibrant light of Christ!

As people living in this world, oftentimes, we find ourselves more worried about fitting in than in being obedient to what we know is truth. The world is constantly bombarding us with what is "acceptable" and "good," oftentimes telling us precisely what is contrary to scripture. It is good and acceptable to live together out of marriage. I remember when I was young, such a relationship was kept secret. Today, it is normal. It is good and acceptable to use whatever means necessary to get ahead today; it is even expected that people will lie and elaborate on their resumes. We are living in a time when the laws of moral truth are fading away.

That is why, as God's children, we are called to stand out from the rest of the world, to live lives that reflect our beliefs, to fight with passion conformity to this world, and to raise up the next generation to do the same! It will not be easy, but we need to remember that we are being "watched!" Others are observing how we live our lives, how we respond to trouble and heartache, how we react to things happening around us. We don't necessarily have to "speak" our beliefs, our lives speak for themselves.

By building up instead of tearing down, by loving in difficult circumstances, by forgiving, by walking away from gossip or rumor, by standing up for truth and being confident in the one who is in control, our lives shine, and the source of that light penetrates the darkness around us.

May we live this day in such a way that not a word is necessary! Shine bright, sisters!

OCTOBER 20

The Lord is my Shepherd, I shall not be in want. He makes me lie down in green pastures, He leads me beside quiet waters, He restores my soul. He guides me in paths of righteousness for His names sake. (Psalm 23:1–3)

By the seventh day God had finished the work He had been doing, so on the seventh day He rested from all the work. And God blessed the 7th day and made it holy, because on it He rested from all the work of creating that He had done. (Genesis 2:2–3)

(The charge of John the Baptist) To shine on those living in darkness and in the shadow of death, to guide our feet into the path of peace. (Luke 1:79)

Today reading, Psalm 23, I was struck by the words: "He guides me in paths of righteousness for HIS NAMES SAKE!" And it hit me! God is guiding our lives down paths that He has ordained. He is helping us to walk upright, He is refreshing us when we grow weary, He is restoring our souls to continue on whatever path He has placed us, and WHY? Because we identify with Him, because He calls us His children, because our lives reveal God's righteousness. It is for the sake of the reputation of His name. When we identify ourselves as believers, the world is watching, not God, but us! Am I living my life in front of others and my family in a way that consistently reveals God's righteousness? The answer to that is NO! But I am trying! I am learning to depend on Him more and more, even whispering in the midst of my day, "God help! May Your light so shine that others may see you in me!" My dear friends, as we identify more and more with Jesus Christ, He changes us. He softens our hearts, strengthens our resolve to follow Him, and leads us forward in our walk of faith. We will not change overnight, but we WILL change. God loves us too much to leave us where He found us. His love is transformative and powerful. When we willingly enter into relationship with Him, He changes us from the inside out. He draws us to Himself so that we do indeed "shine on those living in darkness and in the shadow of death." He promises us that HE WILL guide our feet into the path of peace. Our God can be trusted to bring to pass what He says He will. Let's let HIM to the leading today and keep our eyes open to what HE is up to.

Have a great day! You are greatly and eternally loved!

OCTOBER 21

Find rest, O my soul, in God alone; my hope comes from Him. He alone is my rock and my salvation; He is my fortress, I will not be shaken. My salvation and my honor depend on God; He is my mighty rock, my refuge. Trust in Him at all times, O people, pour out your hearts to Him, for God is our refuge. (Psalm 62:5–8)

"I Am the Alpha and the Omega," says the Lord God, who is, and who was, and who is to come, the Almighty. (Revelation 1:8)

But you are a chosen people, a royal priesthood, a holy nation, God's special possession, that you may declare the praises of Him who called you out of darkness into His wonderful light. (1 Peter 2:9)

Every good and perfect gift is from above, coming down from the Father of the heavenly lights, who does not change like shifting shadows. (James 1:17)

The scripture on Psalm 62 got me thinking this morning. Is God alone where I find my hope, my rest, and my strength? I would have to answer that "sometimes He is"; other times, my thinking is more like, "When all else fails, I'll turn to God." When my hope is floundering, my rest is unobtainable, and my strength is gone, then I cry out! I first try to fix things on my own. I work to patch up relationships, orchestrate events, and run the show that is my life. Then I hope for the best and keep my fingers crossed. Sound familiar? I've got it completely backward. I think the struggle is determining what is MY part in my relationship with God and what is GOD's part. Now I realize that I need to learn to trust God and His timing, but when?

After I have exhausted my own efforts? How often do I think I am moving forward in faith when I am actually running before God and getting in His way? Honestly, friends, I don't have the answer for that.

God is indeed our refuge. He is our source of strength, hope, and salvation. He was here at the very beginning of all things, and He will be here long after we are dead and gone.

He sees us, knows our struggles, and has chosen us. We are His beloved daughters. I think perhaps I just need to get out of His way.

Have a great week! You are greatly and eternally loved!

OCTOBER 22

T hough the fig tree does not bud and there are no grapes on the vines, though the olive crop fails and the fields produce no food, though there are no sheep in the pen and no cattle in the stalls, yet I will rejoice in the Lord, I will be joyful in God my Savior. (Habakkuk 3:17–19)

Splendor and majesty are before Him; strength and joy in His dwelling place. (1 Chronicles 16:27)

Consider it pure joy, my brothers and sisters, whenever you face trials of many kinds, because you know that the testing of your faith produces perseverance. (James 1:2–3)

Go, eat your food with gladness, and drink your wine with a joyful heart, for God has already approved what you do. (Ecclesiastes 9:7)

The prospect of the righteous is joy, but the hopes of the wicked come to nothing. (Proverbs 10:28)

Joy—what does that word mean to you? The scriptures speak of; "joy in the Lord," "joy in difficult circumstances," "joy in hardship, pain, uncertainty." How is it possible to be joyful when the world is spinning in confusion or chaos? How can those struggling with pain, illness, or addiction find joy in their present circumstances? Personally speaking, where was my joy when our daughter struggled with depression and addiction?

Joy is a word I think we often times confuse with happiness, and quite frankly, the two are NOTHING alike! I found my "joy" in difficult circumstances; in the unlikeliest of places; on my face, weeping before the Lord, desperate for His intervention, begging for His reassurance and for His healing. In the pain, I heard that still, small whisper, "I've got this. Put it in My hands," "I love her even more than you do," and "Trust Me even if you don't understand." The joy that resulted was a quiet resolve, a surrender of my wishes and even my very daughter, to the Lord. He asked me to surrender to His plan, His timing and ultimately His resolution. Strangely enough, there was a "joy" there. Not a "yippee, hooray" kind of joy, but a hard-fought war victory type of joy—exhausted, fearful, but at peace, knowing the Lord was taking it from my hands and into His. I think the key to my joy in the years of struggle was surrender! "Your will O Lord, not mine!"

I love you, ladies, but even better, the Lord of the universe, King of heaven, and leader of the angel armies loves you more! Together, there is nothing you can't handle, and come out leaking joy!

OCTOBER 23

I will ask the Father and He will give you another Helper to be with you forever - the Spirit of truth. The world cannot accept Him, because it does not see Him or know Him. But you know Him, because He lives with you and He will be in you. (John 14:16–17)

But I tell you the truth, it is better for you that I go away. When I go away, I will send the Helper to you. If I do not go away the Helper will not come. when the Helper comes, He will prove to the people of the world the truth about sin, about being right with God and about judgment. (John 16:7–8)

Then He told me, "This is the word of the Lord to Zerubbabel: You will not succeed by your own strength or power, but by My Spirit, says the Lord All-Powerful." (Zechariah 4:6)

I remember reading a little story years ago that spoke about someone dying, entering heaven and running to Paul, Peter, and the other disciples and asking, "Tell me, what was it like living with, and talking with Jesus?" And as the question was being asked the disciples were asking excitedly at the same time, "Tell us what was is like having God's spirit within you?"

Personally, I think I underestimate the power of God's spirit within me. I cannot grasp the concept with this little mind, so I doubt. We are God's children, endowed with His spirit, and encouraged to live lives of hope, joy and wisdom so that we may in turn reflect God's light for any who may be following. The scary thing is we ARE being followed! We may not know it, but within God's people is a *light*, a light that those seeking see. Maybe they don't understand what they are seeing, but they glimpse something that catches their eye and makes them consider the source. I remember when I was much younger and just getting involved with a church. There were women in that church whose lives "reflected" something! Something I couldn't quite put my finger on…but something I wanted for myself. I know now that I glimpsed God's light and God's spirit in their lives. And, I knew then, with certainty, it was something I wanted. My early life was directly affected by the light of my parents; Sunday school teachers; and my aunt Esther in particular, a woman in whom God's spirit lived so loudly that you couldn't help but take notice!

Glow bright, my dear sisters! Your life matters, and you are being observed! Reflect so brightly that others cannot help but take notice and seek our Father in heaven!

OCTOBER 24

Because he delights in me, he saved me. (Psalm 18:19)

As a man rejoices over his new wife, so your God will rejoice over you. (Isaiah 62:6)

Let the glory of the LORD endure forever; Let the Lord be glad in His works. (Psalm 104:31)

God saw all that He had made and behold, it was very good. And there was evening and there was morning the sixth day. (Genesis 1:31)

For the LORD takes pleasure in His people; He will beautify the afflicted ones with salvation. (Psalm 149:4)

The Lord thundered from heaven; the voice of the Most High resounded. (Psalm 18:13, NIV)

As a man rejoices over his new wife, so your God will rejoice over you. (Isaiah 62:5)

And you thought he saved you because of your decency. You thought he saved you because of your good works or good attitude or good looks. Sorry, if that were the case your salvation would be lost when your voice went south or your works got weak. There are many reasons God saves you: to bring glory to himself, to appease his justice, to demonstrate his sovereignty. But one of the sweetest reasons God saved you is because he is fond of you. He likes having you around. He thinks you are the best thing to come down the pike in quite a while.

If God had a refrigerator, your picture would be on it. If he had a wallet, your photo would be in it. He sends you flowers every spring and a sunrise every morning. Whenever you want to talk, he'll listen. He can live anywhere in the universe, and he chose your heart… Face it friend. He's crazy about you! (Max Lucado, *A Gentle Thunder*)

I was reading through Psalm 18 this morning and was reminded of God's power, "The Lord thundered from heaven; the Most High raised his voice, and there was hail and lightning" (Psalm 18:13) and then I was humbled by verse 19b, "Because he delights in me, he saved me."

It is a hard thing to get our head around, this love of God! We don't earn it; we certainly don't deserve it and Thank GOD He doesn't remove it when we mess up. Some words that have hit home with me were again spoken at the prison ministry on Sunday. God doesn't just love us after we confess our sin and failures, He loves us THROUGH them. At our daughter's funeral, the pastor said, "She didn't die alone. God was right there with her," and I believe that. He is with us every moment of every day, good, bad, boring, productive. Why, I can't fathom! Certainly, He has better things to do.

Rejoice, my friends, in the knowledge that YOU ARE DEEPLY, PASSIONATELY LOVED!

OCTOBER 25

Lᴏʀᴅ, make me to know my end and what is the extent of my days. Let me know how transient I am. (Psalm 39:4)

For we are only of yesterday and know nothing, because our days on earth are as a shadow. (Job 8:9)

Yet you do not know what your life will be like tomorrow. You are just a vapor that appears for a little while and then vanishes away. (James 4:14)

My days are like a lengthened shadow, and I wither away like grass. (Psalm 102:11)

Thus He remembered that they were but flesh, A wind that passes and does not return. (Psalm 78:39)

Like a flower he comes forth and withers He also flees like a shadow and does not remain. (Job 14:2)

Good morning, friends! My husband and I were rocked by the news of a dear friend's sudden death. I haven't been able to get him off my mind. I have been thinking about the tether that holds us here to this life and to all that we know or understand.

It is asking a lot of us, Father, to believe in what we cannot see or even begin to comprehend! Did our friend know You? Is he somewhere near you now? Does he see our daughter? Did his mom meet him at his death?

Without Your intervention, Lord, we are all lost. Without the gift of faith, we will be lost eternally. Pour down Your spirit upon us, Lord. The lost are wandering around, not even knowing they are lost! We may be made in Your image, but we are slow of mind, thinking we can figure things out on our own terms and following what we WANT to believe. But You are ultimate truth; us not wanting to believe doesn't change that fact. The cord holding us here is thin and easily broken. Open our hearts to receive you fully. Move so mightily among your people that the lost can't help but take notice and turn to You.

You, O Lord, are our only hope! Claim us for Your own and deliver us home when our short time here is done.

Satan is subtle, sneaky at best. He convinces us that there is always next week to catch up with friends, next summer to go camping, a better time to speak of God with our children and grandchildren. So consequently, friendships will wither, prayers will be unspoken, and memories not made. All because the mundane, ordinary days deaden our hearts to the gifts of the moment! He (Satan) tells us we have many moments. God tells us otherwise. God tells us to live wisely, fully, that our time here is short (but a breath). He (God) reminds us to love extravagantly and forgive offenses. He reminds us to enjoy the life we have been given and to use it for His glory.

Just some thoughts I wanted to share. You, my friends are deeply, eternally loved! Live today like you believe it!

OCTOBER 26

And the peace of God, which transcends all understanding, will guard your hearts and your minds in Christ Jesus. (Philippians 4:7)

But when he (Peter) saw the wind, he was afraid and, beginning to sink, cried out, "Lord save me!" (Matthew 14:30)

Let us fix our eyes on Jesus, the author and perfecter of our faith, who for the joy set before Him endured the cross, scorning its shame, and sat down at the right hand of the throne of God. (Hebrews 12:2)

And who would dare tangle with God by messing with one of God's chosen? Who would dare even to point a finger? The One who died for us—who was raised to life for us—is in the presence of God, at this very moment, sticking up for us. Do you think anyone is going to be able to drive a wedge between us and Christ's love for us? (Romans 8:33–35, MSG).

Opposition comes where do we look? Our husbands, coworkers, employees, children drive us nuts, where do we look? Our own thoughts depress and discourage us; where do we look? Fix your eyes (hearts and thoughts) on Jesus the perfecter of our faith.

I certainly don't know what the definition of "perfect" faith is, but my guess would be that our FIRST impulse, our first thought would be to bring everything before the throne of God. Lay it at the feet of Jesus and then walk forward in our life. Unburdened by the very things we just discarded there. The scripture in Romans from the Message Translation says: "Who would dare to tangle with one of God's chosen"; that's you and me, beloved sisters! Nothing we are up against in our lives can or will separate us from the love of God, so why not let Him have it in the first place and move forward in faith. My dear friends, we carry so much around on our shoulders day after day that we have little or no control over. It is time to surrender it all to the one who can affect outcomes. He is able! And He is willing. Are you?

OCTOBER 27

Then He said to him (Peter) follow Me. (John 21:19)

For our light and momentary troubles are achieving for us an eternal glory that far outweighs them all. So we fix our eyes not on what is seen, but on what is unseen. For what is seen is temporary, but what is unseen is eternal. (2 Corinthians 4:17–18)

The Sovereign Lord is my strength; he makes my feet like the feet of a deer, he enables me to go on the heights. (Habakkuk 3:19)

For I, the Lord your God, hold your right hand; it is I who say to you, "Fear not, I am the one who helps you." (Isaiah 41:13)

Do not be anxious about anything, but in everything by prayer and supplication with thanksgiving let your requests be made known to God. (Philippians 4:6)

The LORD is my rock and my fortress and my deliverer, my God, my Rock, in Whom I take refuge, my shield, and the horn of my salvation, my stronghold. (Psalm 18:2)

Good morning! As we begin a new day of seeking God's presence, may we be reminded to take "deep breaths" of his word, His wisdom, and His perfect will for our lives. And when the road ahead gets bumpy, confusing, or frustrating, may we remember to grasp His hand tightly and hold on! We are in for quite a ride.

I don't know about you, but I know that when my trust is in the one who calmed the seas and raised the dead; my fear for the future goes away. Like a child when they see their mom or dad come into the room, I relax when I remember that God holds all results, events, and each one of us in His all-knowing, all-seeing, all-understanding hand. We are indeed in "good hands," so sit back and enjoy the ride. Hang on tight to the hand of the Lord of the universe as He leads you. He has things in store for you today. There are places to go; things to do; and people to meet, love, and encourage. Keep your eyes open and your hearts thankful, and I will try and do the same.

You are greatly and eternally loved!

OCTOBER 28

My heart says of you, "Seek His face!" Your face, Lord, I will seek. (Psalm 27:8)

Don't fret or worry. Instead of worrying, pray. Let petitions and praises shape your worries into prayers, letting God know your concerns. Before you know it, a sense of God's wholeness, everything coming together for good, will come and settle you down. It's wonderful what happens when Christ displaces worry at the center of your life. (Philippians 4:6–7 MSG)

You will seek Me and find Me when you seek Me with all your heart. (Jeremiah 29:13)

Look to the LORD and His strength; seek His face always. (1 Chronicles 16:11)

And without faith it is impossible to please God, because anyone who comes to Him must believe that He exists and that He rewards those who earnestly seek Him. (Hebrews 11:6)

Come near to God and He will come near to you. Wash your hands, you sinners and purify your hearts, you double-minded. (James 4:8)

We are not alone, sisters. No situation we will ever face, will be faced without the Lord our God right beside us. I am convicted for *our* part however. We are saved by grace through faith, a done deal. But is there more? I read something some time ago that made sense to me about our part and the scripture in Jeremiah feeds into it: "You will find me when you seek me with all your heart." It basically said that our part is to seek God with all our hearts. There is no neutral ground. Whether we understand it or not, as Christians, we belong to God. We are marked with His seal. Otherwise, we would be marked with the seal of the world and our enemy, Satan. We simply cannot have it both ways. So what does it mean to seek God with our whole heart? To me it means that it is a priority in my life. It means putting my relationship with Christ at the TOP of my to-do list. It means taking time out of a busy day to spend time alone with Him in prayer and conversation. It means pursing Him with my WHOLE heart and not just my leftover time and energy. It entails the sacrifice of my time and attention. But unless I am willing to honestly seek Him, I will never come to know Him as the friend, confidant, and lover of my soul that He is. My, and your, sacrifice of time will be richly rewarded. He is worth the effort. I am certain of that. Have a great day.

OCTOBER 29

For each will have to bear her own load. (Galatians 5:5)

For we all must appear before the judgement seat of Christ so that each one may receive what is due for what she has done in the body, whether good or evil. (2 Corinthians 5:10)

Therefore sisters, be all the more diligent to make your calling election sure, for if you practice these qualities you will never fall. Message—So friends, confirm God's invitation to you, His choice of you. Don't put it off, do it now. Do this, and you'll have your life on a firm footing, the streets paved, and the way wide open into the eternal kingdom of our Master and Savior, Jesus Christ. (2 Peter 1:10)

Whatever you do, work heartily, as for the Lord and not for men. (Colossians 3:23)

So whoever knows the right thing to do and fails to do it, for her it is sin. (James 4:17)

The point is this; whoever sows sparingly will also reap sparingly, and whoever sows bountifully will also reap bountifully. (2 Corinthians 9:6)

We are not responsible for what other people do or say, but we are always responsible for how we respond. I know we have all heard that, but admittedly, it is difficult to not lash out when insulted or mistreated. If you have lived any length of time at all, you have probably been at the receiving end of a verbal assault that left you wondering, *What was that about?* Let me give you an example.

Years ago now, I was checking at the grocery store. On one particularly hot day, a woman came through the check-out lane where I was working. She threw a big of ice on the counter and began ranting at me about the heat! She yelled and screamed at me about "how miserably hot it was," and I was left dumbfounded and wondering, *What was that about?* I knew it wasn't my fault it was hot. But I was overwhelmed and angered by the tongue lashing! I had to walk away and compose myself so I wouldn't take it out on the next person in line. I was responsible for how I responded to her. I was responsible for how I treated the next customer. In the same breath, I must admit that there have been times when I have taken my hurt and anger out on someone totally undeserving. Unfortunately, it is usually those closest to me.

Scripture repeatedly reminds us that God is concerned with ALL the details of our lives. He knows and cares when we are hurt or sad, but He is also concerned about how we react in any given situation. He asks us to reflect Him at ALL the moments in our lives. Not just in our best Sunday moments, but in the trenches of life when we encounter difficult people and frustrating circumstances. When we are frustrated, bored, sad or happy, how do we respond? Just some food for thought.

Have a good day. You are fiercely loved by God. He is calling us to come to Him; He has much to teach us for the journey ahead. Pack a lunch, there's a lot to learn!

OCTOBER 30

How priceless is Your unfailing love! Both high and low among men find refuge in the shadow of Your wings! Your righteousness is like the mighty mountains, Your justice like the great deep! (Psalm 36:7–9)

I will bless her with abundant provisions; her poor will I satisfy with food. (Psalm 132:15)

When they had all had enough to eat, He said to His disciples, "Gather the pieces that are left over. Let nothing be wasted." So they gathered them and filled 12 baskets with the pieces of the 5 barley loaves left over by those who had eaten. (John 6:12–13)

Every good gift and ever perfect gift is from above, coming down from the Father of lights with Whom there is no variation or shadow due to change. (James 1:17)

But the LORD is the true God; He is the living God and the everlasting King. At His wrath the earth quakes, and the nations cannot endure His indignation. (Jeremiah 10:10)

Great is the Lord, and greatly to be praised, and His greatness is unsearchable. (Psalm 145:3)

Good morning! I was struck by the words in today scriptures because they humbled me in my tracks. The reminders of God's great power and abundance made me realize that I constantly UNDERESTIMATE God! I remind myself on occasion to ask bold, believing prayers, big prayers, prayers that to me seem impossible! Sisters, the God we serve is ALMIGHTY, ALL POWERFUL, ALL KNOWING! There is absolutely NOTHING that is difficult for Him! There is no detail too small or too large for Him. He can feed the multitudes, still the storm and silence the wind! He is ALWAYS able. But here's the thing. We don't get what we ask because sometimes we ask with the wrong motives. God has a plan for your life that is uniquely you. The plan for my life or Barb's life or Sherryl's life may be hugely different, but I can promise you, that if you continue to seek Him, ask for direction and wisdom, HE WILL bring His plan for your life to fruition. So go ahead, friends, ask BIG, WILD prayers of God, seek Him always and hang on. He is able and you can bet it's gonna be good.

You are greatly and eternally loved!

OCTOBER 31

Surely God is my salvation; I will trust and not be afraid. The Lord, the Lord, is my strength and my song; He has become my salvation. (Isaiah 12:2)

Surely you have granted her eternal blessings and made her glad with the joy of your presence. (Psalm 21:6)

Where can I go from your Spirit? Or where can I flee from Your presence? If I ascend to heaven, You are there; If I make my bed in Sheol, behold You are there. If I take the wings of the dawn, if I dwell in the remotest part of the sea, even there your hand will lead me, And your right hand will lay hold of me. If I say, "Surely the darkness will overwhelm me, and the light around me will be night," Even the darkness is not dark to You, and the night is as bright as the day. Darkness and light are alike to You. (Psalm 139:7–12)

Surely, God is our salvation. He is our strength and our song. He has granted us joy and blessings, and watches over us no matter where we wander. Our lives are an open book to Him. He knows us intimately. He is grieved by the envy we feel in our hearts and by the insecurities we claim as part of who we are. He sees it all! I wonder sometimes if He doesn't look at us and think: "Why is she trying so hard to impress Me or those around her?" "Why does she not see that she is beautiful just the way I created her," "Why is she trying to hide from Me, and push Me away?" "Doesn't she realize how much I love her?" This ever present, all-knowing God loves us, my friends! He died on our behalf so that all the stupid stuff we do and say could be washed clean by His sacrifice on our behalf! So as for me,

I am embracing the joy He gives and singing a new song, a song of joy, restoration, and anxious anticipation of what lies ahead! God is FOR us! He LOVES us! We can trust that it's indeed going to be worth singing about!

NOVEMBER 1

Do not be anxious about anything, but in every situation, by prayer and petition, with thanksgiving, present your requests to God. And the peace of God, which transcends all understanding, will guard your hearts and your minds in Christ Jesus. (Philippians 4:6–7)

Let the peace of Christ rule in your hearts, since as members of one body you were called to peace. And be thankful. And whatever you do, whether in word or deed, do it all in the name of the Lord Jesus, giving thanks to God the Father through Him. (Colossians 3:15, 17)

I will give thanks to You, Lord, with all my heart; I will tell of all Your wonderful deeds. (Psalm 9:1)

Let your roots grow down into Him, and let your lives be built on Him. Then your faith will grow strong in the truth you were taught, and you will overflow with thankfulness. (Colossians 2:7)

Every good gift and every perfect gift is from above, coming down from the Father of Lights with Whom there is no variation or shadow due to change. (James 1:17)

God is good. God is WORTHY of our gratitude. He is worthy even when we don't feel like it, even when we feel that He is distant or uninterested, and even when things aren't going our way or frustration threatens to overwhelm us. God calls us to be thankful even in the midst of the trials and difficulties of this life. And why? Because our enemy cannot stand to be around hearts that give thanks and honor to God. Because when we turn our hearts to thankfulness, it leaves no room for complaining. Because thankfulness invites God's presence in our lives and enables Him to refresh us and pour out His blessings upon us. It reminds us that God is the giver of all good gifts. Thankfulness reminds us that we have so much to be thankful for. And finally, thankfulness reminds us that we are not in control but that we serve a mighty God who is! It takes our focus off of ourselves and places it back squarely where it belongs—on God! Today and every day, may we choose an attitude of gratitude!

You are loved! You are called! You are claimed, equipped, and protected! Get out there! Be ready to give account of God's power in your life! You are where you are supposed to be. Trust God to use you for His glory!

NOVEMBER 2

With all humility and gentleness, with patience, showing tolerance for one another in love. (Ephesians 4:2)

He has told you, O man, what is good, and what does the Lord require of you but to do justice, to love kindness, and to walk humbly with your God. (Micah 6:8)

So, as those who have been chosen of God, holy and beloved, put on a heart of compassion, kindness, humility, gentleness and patience. (Colossians 3:12)

And My people who are called by My name humble themselves and pray and seek My face and turn from their wicked ways, then I will hear from heaven, will forgive their sin and will heal their land. (2 Chronicles 7:14)

The fear of the Lord is the instruction for wisdom, and before honor comes humility. (Proverbs 15:33)

Humility—a modest or low view of one's own importance. Pride, in one form or another, is almost always at the root of our most difficult issues. Many of our insecurities and fears are rooted in pride. We as a people and nation are so obsessed with our own self-interests that we pridefully ignore the needs of others. Proverbs 16:18 says, "Pride goes before destruction, a haughty (prideful) spirit before a fall." The Bible warns over and over in both the old and new testaments about the danger of pride. God detests a prideful heart. Pride is the driving force that powers a "me first" generation. Pride sees itself as the most important in any and all relationships. Pride drives us to greed and brokenness. God calls on us to humble ourselves before Him; to consider the needs of others before our own; and to live a life of compassion, kindness, humility, gentleness, and patience. All virtues that our current culture portrays as weak and ineffective.

Pride has many faces and not all pride is wrong. Pride in our performance, doing our best in all we do is a healthy pride. But when pride becomes our motivation or excuse and our way of life, look out! When we think that we know better than God, when we think one race or people group is superior to another, when we look down on those that are different than us or demand our own way, destruction will follow. Before we can fully surrender to God's will for our lives, we need to let go of the areas of pride that are hindering our walk. Ask God to reveal to you the areas of pride in your own life. From experience, I can attest that He will! Then come before Him with humility and honesty, so He can work within and through you in ways you could never imagine! God desires to bless and exult you in His time and for His purpose, but humility is that most important first step!

Humbleness is not a sign of weakness but of a sincere warrior's heart!

NOVEMBER 3

Oh come, let us worship and bow down; let us kneel before the Lord, our Maker! (Psalm 95:6)

Submit yourselves therefore to God. Resist the devil, and he will flee from you. (James 4:7)

So whether you eat or drink or whatever you do, do it all for the glory of God. (1 Corinthians 10:31)

Love the Lord your God with all your heart and with all your soul and with all your mind and with all your strength. (Mark 12:30)

Everything is from Him and by Him and for Him. Glory belongs to Him forever! Amen! (Romans 11:36)

For in Him all things were created; things in heaven and on earth, visible and invisible, whether thrones or powers or rulers or authorities, all things have been created through Him and for Him. (Colossians 1:16)

In everything you do, put God first, and He will direct you and crown your efforts with success. (Proverbs 3:6)

Set you minds on things above, not on earthly things. (Colossians 3:2)

You can't put God first without being saved. When you trust in Christ you become a light. That is what you are now. You start to imitate Christ Who put His Father first in all He did. Your life will start to reflect the life of Christ. You will seek to submit to the will of your Father, spend time with your Father in prayer, serve others, etc. When you put God first you think of yourself less. Not my will, but your will Lord. Not my glory, but for Your glory Lord.

—Fritz Cherry

Almighty Lord, may thoughts of You be our first thoughts of the day, our anchor at midday, and our last conscious thought at night. May we determine our actions by focusing on You; looking to You over and over and over again throughout our day; and seeking Your wisdom, truth, and guidance in the everyday, ordinary things of this life. Teach us to live lives that are pleasing to You, lives that reflect Your great light and light up the darkness around us! Help us to loosen the grip we have on the trappings of our worldly life. They are things that don't last, things that fight for our attention. Fill us with Your spirit, with Your power, discernment, and energy so that when we have fulfilled our purpose here on this earth, we may be welcomed home with the words we so long to hear, "Well done, good and faithful servant!" We love you, Lord! We thank You for Your patience with us and goodness toward us. Mold us and make us more and more like You. So be it. Amen.

NOVEMBER 4

The one who offers thanksgiving as her sacrifice glorifies Me; to one who orders her way rightly I will show the salvation of God! (Psalm 50:23)

Make a joyful noise to the Lord, all the earth! Serve the Lord with gladness! Come into His Presence with singing! Know that the Lord, He is God! It is He Who made us; and we are His; we are His people, and the sheep of His pasture. Enter His gates with thanksgiving, and His courts with praise! Give thanks to Him; bless His Name! For the Lord is good; His steadfast love endures forever, and His faithfulness to all generations. (Psalm 100:1–5)

You are my God; I will extol You. This is the day that the Lord has made; let us rejoice and be glad in it. (Psalm 118:28–29)

The steadfast love of the Lord never ceases; His mercies never come to an end; they are new every morning; great is your faithfulness. The Lord is my portion, says my soul, therefore I will hope in Him. (Lamentations 3:22–24)

If we were able to go back in time and ask Paul what God expected of us, I think he would say, "Don't repay evil for evil… Seek to do good to everyone… Always rejoice… Pray without ceasing… Give thanks in all circumstances."

May our almighty God fill our hearts to overflowing today and throughout this week with His love. May He fill us with thankfulness for His provision and a desire for spiritual renewal. May we earnestly seek His discipline and His protection, mindful that God always knows what He is doing, even when our lives are difficult and circumstances are hard to understand. May we go through our day with a strong assurance and confidence in the one who is in control. May we trust the hand of the one who is holding ours, and may we in turn light the way for those that are following us. Sisters, be strong in your faith. Overflow with thankfulness. Shine bright. Remember ALWAYS that you are greatly and eternally loved.

NOVEMBER 5

But this is what I commanded them, saying, "Obey My voice, and I will be your God, and you will be My people; and you will walk in the way which I have commanded you, that it may be well with you." (Jeremiah 7:23)

We are destroying speculations and every lofty thing raised up against the knowledge of God, and we are taking every thought captive to the obedience of Christ. (2 Corinthians 10:5)

The world is unprincipled. It's dog-eat-dog out there! The world doesn't fight fair. But we don't live or fight our battles that way—never have and never will. The tools of our trade aren't for marketing or manipulation, but they are for demolishing that entire massively corrupt culture. We use our powerful God tools for smashing warped philosophies, tearing down barriers erected against the truth of God, fitting every loose thought and emotion and impulse into the structure of life shaped by Christ. Our tools are ready and at hand for clearing the ground of every obstruction and building lives of obedience into maturity. (2 Corinthians 10:3–6 MSG)

Do you think all God wants are sacrifices—empty rituals just for show? He wants you to listen to Him! Plain listening is the thing, not staging a lavish religious production. Not doing what God tells you is far worse than fooling around with the occult. Getting self-important around God is far worse than making deals with your dead ancestors. (1 Samuel 15:22–23 MSG)

After reading today's scriptures, my mind went immediately to "If you're going to talk the talk, you need to walk the walk." It is far easier to give lip service to what we believe than it is to live it out day after day, decision after decision, thought after thought! It is far easier to shout, "Love your neighbor!" than it is to forgive our spouse for the fiftieth time for the same irritating thing, or to say, "God's got this!" than it is to believe it when there seems to be no evidence to that fact. It is far easier to "go to church" on Sunday and call it good. than it is to live it out every day, moment by moment!

Friends, God wants relationship with us! Not just our Sunday best or our temporary enthusiasm for Christianity. He loves us at our worst moments, And He is near in our moments of crisis. He has already equipped us with the tools we will need to fight for our beliefs and to live lives of obedience. HE desires to transform our lives so that, at every turn, we resemble Him more and more. If we will simply stay near in thought and conversation, we will be transformed by His Light and His teachings and His wisdom. HE does the transformation, our part is to trust Him and surrender to His authority. "He Who began a good work, will bring it to completion in our lives." It's a promise!

NOVEMBER 6

What marvelous love the Father has extended to us! Just look at us—we're called children of God! That's who we really are. But that's also why the world doesn't recognize us or take us seriously; because it has no idea who He is or what He's up to. Dear friends, that's exactly who we are; children of God! And that's only the beginning. Who knows how we'll end up! What we know is that when Christ is openly revealed, we'll see Him (1 John 3:1–3 MSG)

But you are a chosen people, a royal priesthood, a holy nation, God's special possession, that you may declare the praises of Him who called you out of darkness into His wonderful light. (1 Peter 2:9)

Put on then, as God's chosen ones, holy and beloved, compassionate hearts, kindness, humility, meekness, and patience. (Colossians 3:12)

For you are all children of light, children of the day. We are not of the night or the darkness. (1 Thessalonians 5:5)

Therefore, we are ambassadors for Christ, God making His appeal through us. We implore you on behalf of Christ, be reconciled to God. (2 Corinthians 5:20)

You are the light of the world. (Matthew 5:13)

For we are God's fellow workers. You are God's field, God's building. (1 Corinthians 3:8)

Friends, how we feel about God or ourselves at any given moment has oftentimes very little to do with the truth. We may feel that God has abandoned us. God says; "I will never leave you or forsake you." I may feel insignificant or unimportant. God says, "I am

God's workmanship, created in Christ to do good works." I may feel discouraged or defeated, but God says, "I can do all things through Christ Jesus." I may feel under attack by thoughts or circumstances, but God says, "I can quench all the fiery darts of the wicked one with my shield of faith." I may feel overcome by the darkness of the world around me, but God says, "I am light." I may feel like I can never be enough, but God says, "I am forgiven of all my sins and washed in His blood," that "I am greatly loved by God," that "I am strengthened with all might according to His glorious power," and that "The devil flees from me!" God calls us His "chosen ones," "holy and beloved," "children of Light," and names us as His ambassadors for Christ!

Don't you see? We are to take every thought captive and bring it into God's glorious light. He loves us far more than we can even begin to imagine. Don't let the enemy waste a moment of your time with his discouraging lies. You are a daughter of the KING, and as His heirs, we are loved, protected, claimed, equipped, and empowered to handle anything life throws our way.

You've GOT THIS! Because, my dear sisters GOD'S GOT YOU!

NOVEMBER 7

- 1 Thessalonians 5:17—"Pray continually."
- 1 John 5:14–15—"This is the confidence we have in approaching God; that if we ask anything according to His will, He hears us. And if we know that He hears us—whatever we ask—we know that we have what we asked of Him."
- 1 Chronicles 16:11—"Look to the Lord and His strength; seek His face always."
- Ephesians 6:18—"And pray in the Spirit on all occasions with all kinds of prayers and requests. With this in mind, be alert and always keep on praying for all the Lord's people."
- Jeremiah 29:12 —"Then you will call on me and come and pray to Me, and I will listen to you."
- Matthew 5:44—"But I tell you, love your enemies and pray for those who persecute you."
- Romans 12:12—"Be joyful in hope, patient in affliction, faithful in prayer."
- James 5:16—The prayer of a righteous person is powerful and effective."

Even though I have been a believer since I was a little girl, I am still amazed and quickly forget about the important discipline of PRAYER! There are so many scriptures on prayer that I can't begin to add them all. Think about it for a second. When we pray, the Commander of the Angel Armies hears our prayer! The God who called down fire on a soaking wet altar, the God who parted the sea, the God who raised the dead and created the world hears us. Not only that, He responds. Now I know that sometimes we feel like our prayer falls on deaf ears, but the answer to prayer is up to God. That part is not our responsibility. Being faithful in prayer is what is asked of us. Sisters, God hears us. He delights in our prayers; they rise to Him as sweet smelling incense.

I believe with all my heart that, someday, when we see Jesus face to face, we will see the impact of the prayers that we have said. Those said in fear, in doubt, in anger, in exasperation, and in faith, God hears them all! We will also be able to see the impact of the prayers said on our behalf, prayers that perhaps changed the course of our lives or someone else's! Prayer is powerful because our God is powerful!

Have a great week, friends! You are greatly and eternally loved! Prayers continue for many concerns as well as all of you.

NOVEMBER 8

But to you who are listening I say: Love your enemies, do good to those who hate you, bless those who curse you, pray for those who mistreat you. If someone slaps you on one cheek, turn to them the other also. If someone takes your coat, do not withhold your shirt from them. Give to everyone who asks you, and if anyone takes what belongs to you, do not demand it back. (Luke 6:27–30)

Though I walk in the midst of trouble, You preserve my life. You stretch out Your hand against the anger of my foes; with Your Right Hand you save me. (Psalm 138:7)

Do not repay evil with evil or insult with insult. On the contrary, repay evil with blessing, because to this you were called so that you may inherit a blessing. (1 Peter 3:9)

Let all bitterness and wrath and anger and clamor and slander be put away from you, along with all malice. Be kind to one another, tender-hearted, forgiving each other, just as God in Christ also has forgiven you. (Ephesians 4:31–32)

See to it that no one comes short of the grace of God; that no root of bitterness springing up causes trouble, and by it may be defiled. (Hebrews 12:15)

Then Jesus said to His disciples, "if anyone wishes to come after Me, she must deny herself, and take up her cross and follow Me. For whoever wishes to save her life will lose it, but whoever loses her life for My sake will find it." (Matthew 16:24–25)

But now O Lord, You are our Father, we are the clay, and You our potter, and all of us are the work of Your Hand. (Isaiah 64:8)

In the above Scriptures, we are challenged to "Love our enemies, bless those who curse us, and pray for those mistreating us." We are asked to "Let all bitterness and wrath and anger, clamor and slander come to an end in our lives. Instead, we are encouraged to be kind, tenderhearted, and forgiving.

There is so much life advice in just these few scriptures. If we refuse to forgive those who hurt us, we grow bitter and resentful. We carry that bitterness with us whether we realize it or not. We carry it into every conversation, every interaction, and every thought we have. We become obsessed with being a victim and forget about our birthright as daughters of the King. We forget that God empowers us to overcome and rise above adversity. It is only through the complete surrender to the will of our Father that we will remember WHOSE we are. And not only remember whose we are, but WHO we are in Christ. Through our surrender of OUR will to GOD's will, we will be strengthened, encouraged, and be a delight to our Father in heaven. Indeed, we can do ALL things through Christ, who gives us the strength and courage.

So, my dear friends, whatever lies before you this day, or this week, take a minute this morning and remember who is in control and whose you are. We don't walk this life alone. In fact, we are being cheered on and encouraged by a "great cloud of witnesses." God is FOR us. We are His beloved. May we believe it and claim it.

NOVEMBER 9

But the Lord is faithful, and He will strengthen you and protect you from the evil one. (2 Thessalonians 3:3)

Be strong and courageous. Do not be afraid or terrified because of them, for the LORD your God goes with you, He will never leave you or forsake you. (Deuteronomy 31:6)

So do not fear, for I AM with you, do not be dismayed, for I AM your God. I will strengthen you and help you; I will uphold you with My Righteous Right Hand! (Isaiah 41:10)

The righteous person may have many troubles, but the LORD delivers her from them all. (Psalm 34:18)

God is our refuge and strength, an ever-present help in trouble. (Psalm 46:1)

Have mercy on me, my God, have mercy on me, for in You I take refuge. I will take refuge in the shadow of Your Wings until the disaster has passed. (Psalm 57:1)

Though I walk in the midst of trouble, You preserve my life. You stretch out Your Hand against the anger of my foes; with Your Right Hand you save me. (Psalm 138:7)

I give them eternal life, and they shall never perish; no one will snatch them out of My Hand. My Father, Who has given them to Me, is greater than all; no one can snatch them out of My Father's Hand. I and the Father are One. (John 10:28–30)

Enemies: in our lives on this earth we will meet different kinds. There are external enemies as well as internal enemies that wage war against our spirits, our hearts, and our minds. Personally, the enemy that gives me the most difficulty is the internal kind. He bombards me with thoughts of insufficiency, inadequacy, ineptitude, and unworthiness all dangled in my mind by the enemy—all embraced and invited in by Me! I believe the enemy of our souls throws all sorts of attacks at us and watches for our reaction, to see where to intensify his efforts. With one, he dangles pride, another power, and yet another; he takes advantage of areas of insecurity. Once we believe his lies, he works to use them for our downfall. We need to remember that.

God loves us. He protects us from harm by external forces, but He is perfectly capable of protecting us from the internal attack as well. I think the problem is that we embrace the lies of the enemy, believe them, and never surrender them to God. We tell ourselves, "I'll work on that" or "I'll clean up first" and THEN, "I will come to the Lord with surrender." My dear sisters, God wants you right now. He will take you as is. He is not embarrassed, disgusted, or ashamed of you or me. He cares deeply for us and wants to free us from the lies the enemy has fed us, lies that we have believed and hated ourselves for. Remember that old saying, "God loves you right where you are, but He loves you too much to leave you there." I think that rings true. It is God Himself who will work in us to will and to act for His good purpose. He will do the housecleaning in our hearts, the debriding and bandaging of old and long-embraced wounds, the restoration of joy and peace that can only happen through the powerful healing hands of our Lord and Father.

So starting this minute, scramble into the outstretched hands of the Father. Let Him protect, heal, and restore our hearts to their intended state. We are safe in His hands and in the shelter of His wings. God's got this!

NOVEMBER 10

Examine yourselves to see whether you are in the faith; test yourselves. Do you not realize that Christ Jesus is in you—unless, of course, you fail the test? (2 Corinthians 13:5)

Do not merely listen to the Word, and so deceive yourselves. Do what it says. Anyone who listens to the Word but does not do what it says is like someone who looks at her face in a mirror and, after looking at herself, goes away and immediately forgets what she looks like. (James 1:22–24)

Do not conform to the pattern of this world, but be transformed by the renewing of your mind. Then you will be able to test and approve what God's will is—His good, pleasing and perfect will. (Romans 12:2)

Let us examine our ways and test them, and let us return to the Lord. (Lamentations 3:40)

I have considered my ways and have turned my steps to Your statues. I will hasten and not delay to obey Your commands. (Psalm 119:59–60)

Don't pick on people, jump on their failures, criticize their faults—unless, of course, you want the same treatment. The critical spirit has a way of boomeranging. It's easy to see a smudge on your neighbor's face and be oblivious to the ugly sneer on your own. Do you have the nerve to say, "Let me wash your face for you,' when your own face is distorted by contempt? It's this whole traveling road-show mentality all over again, playing a holier-than-thou part instead of just living your part. Wipe that ugly sneer off your own face, and you might be fit to offer a washcloth to your neighbor. Don't be flip with the sacred. Banter and silliness give no honor to God. Don't reduce holy mysteries to slogans. In trying to be relevant, you're only being cute and inviting sacrilege. (Matthew 7:1–6 MSG)

Self-examination—what is it that drives me to respond the way I do or do the things I do? I like The Message Bible translation of the "speck in your brother's eye versus the log in your own" topic. It is oftentimes easy for us to see and remember and dwell on thoughts of how someone has hurt us, allowing bitterness, judgment, and a heart hardness to slowly suck the love out of us. It is then that self-righteousness comes in, slowly at first, but soon filling every corner and crevice in our heart. We didn't mean for it to happen, but left unexamined and exposed to His light, it continues to fester and ooze until it contaminates all the other relationships in our life as well.

Personally, I struggle with unforgiveness and a spirit of bitterness in a relationship that is often difficult for me. That is why self-examination and confession is good for me. God WILL reveal (when we ask) areas of thinking, motivation, and hurt in our lives that are causing a reflex reaction in us, a reaction that is contrary to God's will for us, a critical reaction that results in a sneer or an holier-than-thou attitude that is ugly and offensive both to God and to others.

Why would we want to do the hard work of self-examination? Because, my dear friends, living a life of contempt, or unforgiveness, eats away at our joy, at our peace and at our sense of well-being. God desires us to be filled with joy, peace, patience, kindness, faithfulness, goodness, gentleness, and self-control. When left unchecked, bitterness, unforgiveness, anger, and self-righteousness take up the space in hearts where the fruit of the spirit belongs. It takes the skip out of our step and replaces it with a heavy, dragging, head-down, shoulders stooped step and demeanor that cries out anything but the forgiven, free, loved daughter of the KING!

We are loved, forgiven, called, and claimed! May we do the hard work of getting rid of any attitudes that stand in the way!

NOVEMBER 11

I will give thanks to you Lord, with all my heart; I will tell of all your wonderful deeds. (Psalm 9:1)

And cultivate thankfulness. Let the Word of Christ, the Message, have the run of the house. Give it plenty of room in your lives. Instruct and direct one another using good common sense. And sing, sing your hearts out to God! Let every detail in your lives—words, actions, whatever—be done in the name of the Master Jesus, thanking God the Father every step of the way. (Colossians 3:16–17 MSG)

Give thanks to the Lord, for He is good, His love endures forever. (1 Chronicles 16:34)

The LORD is my strength and my shield; my heart trusts in Him, and He helps me. My heart leaps for joy, and with my song I praise Him. (Psalm 28:7)

Every good and perfect gift is from above, coming down from the Father of the heavenly lights, Who does not change like shifting shadows. (James 1:17)

Do you see what we've got? An unshakable kingdom! And do you see how thankful we must be? Not only thankful, but brimming with worship, deeply reverent before God. For God is not an indifferent bystander, He's actively cleaning house, torching all that needs to burn, and He won't quit until it's all cleansed. God Himself is Fire! (Hebrews 12:28–29)

I have heard it said that silent gratitude isn't much good to anyone.

Almighty God, we come into Your presence this morning with thanksgiving and praise. Praise for who You are, for what You have already accomplished in our lives, and for what You have in store for us. We thank You for health, families, friends, homes, the abundance of food and abundance of stuff. We thank You for the beauty and diversity of Your creation. We are thankful for those who teach us and encourage us in our faith, for the friends and family that grow us and support us and make us laugh. We thank you for the trials and problems that have drawn us closer and closer to You. We thank you for the clean air we breathe, the pets that share our lives, and the jobs that pay our bills. We thank you for those in authority over us, for the police, the firemen, the health care workers, and the facilities that are there to help us in times of need. We thank you for the beauty of the sunrises and the ferocity and power of Your thunderstorms. We thank You for those around us who make this world a better place, those who love You and love others. We thank you for the "light" that emanates from You and brings hope and healing to this world. We thank you for the rain; for the sunshine; and for the beautiful, glistening white snowfalls of winter. Just looking at the beauty on earth makes us desire a glimpse of the incredible beauty of heaven. We love you, Father. We know we don't tell You enough just how thankful we are. Remind us that you have cared for us since birth, heck, conception, and You won't stop until You deliver us home. Remind us who You are. Remind us of Your great love for us. We sometimes forget that we have such a great, powerful, unstoppable redeemer; and when we remember, we bounce on eager toes of anticipation, asking, "What's next, Papa?" We love You. Thank You for loving us. Amen.

Remind someone today why you are thankful for them. I am thankful to all of you for taking this journey of faith alongside me. May our good and gracious God grow us into everything He intends for us!

NOVEMBER 12

Let your heart therefore be wholly devoted to the LORD our God, to walk in His statutes and to keep His commandments as at this day. (1 Kings 8:61)

And you, your lives must be totally obedient to God, our personal God, following the life path He has cleared, alert and attentive to everything He has made plain this day. (1 Kings 8:61 MSG)

Teach me Your Way, O LORD I will walk in Your truth; unite my heart to fear Your name. (Psalm 86:11)

I have set the LORD continually before me; because He is at my right hand, I will not be shaken. (Psalm 16:8)

For the eyes of the LORD move to and fro throughout the earth that He may strongly support those whose heart is completely His. (2 Chronicles 16:9)

So that you will walk in a manner worthy of the Lord, to please Him in all respects, bearing fruit in every good work and increasing in the knowledge of God. (Colossians 1:10)

For you have been bought with a price; therefore glorify God in your body. (1 Corinthians 6:20)

For if we live, we live for the Lord, or if we die, we die for the Lord; therefore whether we live or die, we are the Lord's. (Romans 14:8)

Are you giving God your extras or your everything?

I have said it before, and I will repeat it here, God wants ALL of us, not just our leftovers—our leftover time, our leftover thoughts, our leftover energy. God wants us first. Before we try and fix the problem, God wants us to come to Him; before we start our busy schedule, He wants our time; and before we head out the door, God wants our hearts and our focus on Him. God wants us here and now, precisely where He has placed us. I think sometimes that when we think about serving God, we envision some distant land or future setting. But we cannot be of use to God where God has not placed us. I don't know why God has us where He has us, but I do know that HE KNOWS. Serving God with the whole of our lives is not some lofty, unobtainable future goal. We can begin today, here and now. The words from Romans 12 MSG lays it out for us:

> So here's what I want you to do, God helping you. Take your everyday, ordinary life —your sleeping, eating, going to work and walking around life—and place it before God as an offering. Embracing what God does for you is the best thing you can do for Him. Don't become so well adjusted to your culture that you fit into it without even thinking. Instead, fix your attention on God. You'll be changed from the inside out. Readily recognize what He wants from you, and quickly respond to it…love from the center of who you are don't fake it. Run for dear life from evil, hold on for dear life to good. Be good friends who love deeply, practice playing second fiddle. Don't burn out; keep yourselves fueled and aflame. Be alert servants of the Master, cheerfully expectant. Don't quit in hard times, pray all the harder. Help needy Christians; be inventive in hospitality.

And there you have it, sisters. That is how we can love God with the whole of our lives.

Shine bright. Leak Jesus. Your heart of love and compassion is desperately needed in our homes, communities, and world. You are loved! Be bold, be convicted!

NOVEMBER 13

At that time I will search Jerusalem with lamps, and I will punish the people who are complacent, those who say in their hearts, "The Lord will not do good, nor will He do ill." (Zephaniah 1:12)

For what will it profit a woman if she gains the whole world and forfeits her soul? Or what shall a woman give in return for her soul? (Matthew 16:26)

Therefore, confess your sins to one another and pray for one another, that you may be healed. The prayer of a righteous person has great power as it is working. (James 5:16)

Thus says the Lord: "Let not the wise woman boast in her wisdom, let not the mighty man boast in his might, let not the rich boast in their riches, but let her who boasts boast in this, that she understands and knows Me, that I Am the Lord who practices steadfast love, justice, and righteousness in the earth. For in these things I delight, declares the Lord." (Jeremiah 9:23–24)

If we confess our sins, He is faithful and just and will forgive us our sins and purify us from all unrighteousness. (1 John 1:9)

Whoever conceals their sins does not prosper, but the one who confesses and renounces them finds mercy. (Proverbs 28:13)

Repent, then, and turn to God, so that your sins may be wiped out, that times of refreshing may come from the Lord. (Acts 3:19)

Having been raised in the church, I have heard many of the themes of scripture repeated over and over. I have oftentimes sat through a service with hardly a thought about what was being said, my mind distracted, my thoughts all over the place. I struggled then, and struggle now, with complacency—"Oh, I'm okay. I'm for-given,"—unaware and unconcerned that there is still a raging battle going on for my soul and yours!

I think that is precisely why we need to remember the price that was paid for our redemption and for our forgiveness. Sin is deplor-able to God. ALL sin is ugly and unacceptable to God, not just the BIG sins we see others involved in but our own. Bitterness, selfish-ness, unforgiveness, hatred, envy, greed, discrimination, all of these things are sins. How I wish that, once we entered into relationship with Jesus Christ, all of these sins would no longer be part of our experience. But unfortunately, we all know too well that they are. Our enemy will continue to blast us with lies of complacency as long as we walk this earth, wanting us to believe that we are superior to those around us in one way or another, wanting us to believe that we don't need to ask for forgiveness because we are good enough, and hoping that we will believe his lies that he (the enemy) tells us about ourselves and our God! The reason that we need to continually exam-ine our hearts and our lives is because God does not want us to fall into a mind-set of complacency, of lukewarm Christianity. Our God is a "consuming fire!" He is NOT an unconcerned, absent Father. Rather, He wants us to live this life He has given us with a passion for truth and righteousness. He wants to use us to be His hands and His feet, His voice for His glory! But first, we need to be aware of the sin in our own lives. The scripture says, "Why do you look at the speck of sawdust in your brother's eye and pay no attention to the plank in your own eye?" First, let us examine ourselves, ask God to reveal and forgive areas of sin in our own lives, and then we will be available to be of use to our Father.

My dear sisters, there are places to go and things to do while we still have life and breath. Our time here is of great value to God. He wants to use us, to strengthen us, and to empower us for His glory. Let's not let the sin of complacency get in our way. Let's get out there, reflecting brightly the light of the one who calls us His daughters. Let us bounce on eager toes of anticipation, asking, "What's next Papa?" and expect our Father to come through for us at every twist and turn of this crazy life! Hang on friends, It's going to be good!

NOVEMBER 14

Let the Word of Christ richly dwell within you, with all wisdom teaching and admonishing one another with psalms and hymns and spiritual songs, singing with thankfulness in your hearts to God. (Colossians 3:16)

So Jesus was saying to those Jews who had believed Him, "If you continue in My Word, then you are truly disciples of Mine." (John 8:31)

If you abide in Me, and My Words abide in you, ask whatever you wish, and it will be done for you. (John 15:7)

Be diligent to present yourself approved to God as a workman who does not need to be ashamed, accurately handling the Word of truth. (2 Timothy 2:15)

Holding fast to the Word of life, so that in the day of Christ I will have reason to glory because I did not run in vain nor toil in vain. (Philippians 2:16)

But He answered and said, "It is written, man shall not live on bread alone, but on every Word that proceeds out of the mouth of God." (Matthew 4:4)

All Scripture is breathed out by God and profitable for teaching, for reproof, for correction and for training in righteousness, that the woman of God may be competent, equipped for every good work. (2 Timothy 3:16–17)

For the Word of God is living and active, sharper than any two-edged sword, piercing to the division of soul and spirit, of joints and of marrow, and discerning the thoughts and intentions of the heart. (Hebrews 4:12)

How can we claim to be followers of Jesus Christ if we don't know what He teaches? How can we cry out, "Lord, Lord" when we haven't the foggiest Who HE is? Many years ago, I heard the phrase, "Sitting in church Sunday after Sunday no more makes you a Christian that sitting in a chicken coop makes you a chicken." This faith we are pursuing, this God we are seeking is alive and well. In fact, scripture reminds us that God's word is "living and active, discerning the thoughts and intentions of the heart." Our God, Lord, Savior, Father, Provider, Healer desires that we live in relationship with Him. He wants us to know Him intimately, to trust Him completely, and to seek Him earnestly. Jeremiah 9:24 says, "'But let the one who boasts boast about this; that they have the understanding to know Me, that I Am the LORD, Who exercises kindness, justice and righteousness on earth, for in these I delight,' declares the Lord."

Thank God, that we have easy access to His word. I pray that we will not become so absorbed and exhausted in taking care of all our day-by-day obligations that we lose track of the time and doze off, oblivious to God. When we take the time to get to know God better, He fills us with energy, wisdom, and insight to live lives that are not only pleasing to Him, but lives that bring love and light to others. How can we continue to do all the things we do as women, mothers, daughters, wives, sisters, and friends if we are not filled by God? We cannot "leak Jesus" if we are not being continually filled by Jesus. We will run dry and end up exhausted, depressed, and discouraged.

My dear friends, God is the source of our energy. He is the source of our joy. He ALONE can fill us up with love, joy, peace, wisdom, encouragement so that we can, in turn, encourage, love, and give to those around us. GO be the light. Reflect the radiance of our Father. His gifts never run dry. Have a great day. You are greatly and eternally loved.

NOVEMBER 15

Y ou are worthy, our Lord and God, to receive glory and honor and power, for You created all things, and by Your will they were created and have their being. (Revelation 4:11)

The Lord says, "These people come near to Me with their mouth and honor Me with their lips, but their hearts are far from Me. Their worship of Me is based on merely human rules they have been taught." (Isaiah 29:13)

Therefore, since we are receiving a kingdom that cannot be shaken, let us be thankful, and so worship God acceptably with reverence and awe, for our God is a consuming fire. (Hebrews 12:28–29)

You alone are the LORD, You made the heavens, even the highest heavens, and all their starry host, the earth and all that is on it, the seas and all that is in them. You give life to everything, and the multitudes of heaven worship You. (Nehemiah 9:6)

All the nations You have made will come and worship before You, Lord; they will bring glory to Your name. For You are great and do marvelous deeds, You alone are God. (Psalm 86:9–10)

Shout for joy to the Lord, all the earth. Worship the Lord with gladness; come before Him with joyful songs. Know that the Lord is God. It is He who made us, and we are His; we are His people, the sheep of His pasture. Enter His gates with thanksgiving and His courts with praise; give thanks to Him and praise His name. For the Lord is good and His love endures forever; His faithfulness continues through all generations. (Psalm 100)

Friends, how do you worship God? What does the word *worship* mean to you?

Personally, I have always wondered how to worship God in a manner that is pleasing to Him. I have consistently been more concerned about asking for my needs and desires to be met than I have about worshiping God. When I think about worship pictures of sackcloth, ashes, and fasting come to mind. I have never been able to fast, at least with food. But I read an article about fasting that included many different types of fasting. Actually, the act of taking time each morning, or evening, for a devotional time with the Lord is a type of fasting. Anything that takes time away from our normal routine and sets it aside for time with the Lord is a form of fasting. The whole premise behind fasting, I believe, is to prepare our hearts for worship. God wants us to worship Him "in spirit and in truth." He desires for our hearts (our innermost, intimate, vulnerable selves) to come before Him in worship. He is not at all concerned with outward appearances. He is focused on our hearts! Are we humble before Him? Do we realize (and confess) the extent of our sin? Do we believe that He is worthy of our worship?

My dear sisters, in this side of eternity where we now reside, we cannot begin to fathom everything God has done and does for us every day. All the times He has intervened on our behalf, either to protect us or challenge us in order to grow us into the daughters we are becoming. All the people He has put in our path to encourage and help; and all the prayers He has answered, some before we have even asked. I honestly believe that, when we meet the Lord face to face, we will be completely overwhelmed and finally understand the depth of God's love for us. God is worthy of our worship now. Let us come before Him with humble and willing hearts with hands raised, knees bent, and songs on our lips. For great is our God, and worthy of honor and glory and praise. There is absolutely NOTHING that fazes, frightens, or intimidates HIM. May we, through worship, begin to discern the magnitude of His wisdom, power, and authority. NOTHING and NO ONE can stand before HIM unless He allows it. He is far bigger than our little minds can grasp. And He's holding us, helping us, and loves us. That alone is reason for worship.

NOVEMBER 16

Who will bring any charge against those whom God has chosen? it is God who justifies. Who is he that condemns? Christ Jesus, who died—more than that, who was raised to life—is at the right hand of God and is also interceding for us. (Romans 8:33–34)

And who would dare tangle with God by messing with one of God's chosen? Who would dare even point a finger? The One who died for us—who was raised to life for us!—is in the presence of God at this very moment sticking up for us. Do you think anyone is going to be able to drive a wedge between us and Christ's love for us? There is no way! (Romans 8:33–34 MSG)

Therefore, since we have a great High Priest who has gone through the heavens, Jesus the Son of God, let us hold firmly to the faith we profess. (Hebrews 4:14–16)

For we do not have a high priest who is unable to sympathize with our weaknesses, but we have one who has been tempted in every way, just as we are—yet was without sin. Let us approach the throne of grace with confidence, so that we may receive mercy and find grace to help us in our time of need. (Hebrews 4:15–16)

Now that we know what we have—Jesus, this great High Priest with ready access to God—let's not let it slip through our fingers. We don't have a priest who is out of touch with our reality. He's been through weakness and testing, experienced it all—all but the sin. So let's walk right up to Him and get what He is so ready to give. Take the mercy, accept the help. (Hebrews 4:15–16 MSG)

Well, my dear sisters in Christ, it has been a while since we have started this devotional together, I hope you are being blessed, spending time with God's word and in His presence. I wish we could meet and discuss what has surprised us and what God is doing in our lives. God has indeed noticed the progress you have made since you first resolved to live in His presence.

I love The Message Bible translation in both of these scriptures today: "Who would dare tangle with God by messing with one of God's chosen," and that "one" is each of us my friends! We are indeed God's chosen, His children, and His beloved! Take a minute and let that sink in! Who would DARE tangle with God by "driving a wedge between us and Christ's love for us?" Satan will try, but he has already lost the battle. We are marked and sealed by Christ as His children.

And then the Hebrews passage: "So let's walk right up to Him and get what He is so ready to give. Take the mercy, accept the help." God is ready and fully equipped to handle whatever we bring to Him whenever we hand it over! What's holding us back? May your faith be strengthened and your hearts soar as you dwell in the presence of the almighty God! You are so very greatly loved! Never, ever let people or circumstances tell you otherwise!

NOVEMBER 17

T herefore, since we are surrounded by such a huge crowd of witnesses to the life of faith, let us strip off every weight that slows us down, especially the sin that so easily trips us up. And let us run with endurance the race that God has set before us. (Hebrews 12:1)

Put on the full armor of God, so that you will be able to stand firm against the schemes of the devil. Therefore, take up the full armor of God, so that you will be able to resist in the evil day, and having done everything, to stand firm. (Ephesians 6:11, 13)

But resist him, firm in your faith, knowing that the same experiences of suffering are being accomplished by your brethren who are in the world. (1 Peter 5:9)

Be on the alert, stand firm in the faith, act like men, be strong. (1 Corinthians 16:13)

Let us hold fast the confession of our hope without wavering, for He who promised is faithful. (Hebrews 10:23)

Good morning, friends! As we begin another week in our walk of faith, I just wanted to encourage you to remember the "crowd of witnesses" surrounding us and tune our ears to hear them "cheering us on!" This race we are in is not for the faint of heart, nor is it a sprint! It is a marathon with twists, turns, hills, and valleys! But take heart! The prize at the end of the race will be well worth any frustrations, pain, or exhaustion along the way! You are loved mightily, dear sisters, and the God of the universe, the one in control of ALL things at ALL times has called you by name and placed you exactly where He wants you! So lace up your sneakers, pull on your spandex, and quiet your mind to hear the encouragement of heaven that is calling you on! People are watching you! You may not realize it, but your life matters greatly to God. Let Him use you to be His hands and feet to those He has already placed in your path!

NOVEMBER 18

If my people who are called by My name humble themselves, and pray and seek My face and turn from their wicked ways, then I will hear from heaven and will forgive their sin and heal their land. (Proverbs 11:14)

I urge, then, first of all, that petitions, prayers, intercession and thanksgiving be made for all people—for kings and all those in authority, that we may life peaceful and quiet lives in all godliness and holiness. (1 Timothy 2:1–2)

Also, seek the peace and prosperity of the city to which I have carried you into exile. Pray to the LORD for it, because if it prospers, you too will prosper. (Jeremiah 29:7)

For lack of guidance a nation falls, but victory is won through many advisers. (Proverbs 11:14)

That same power that broke prison chains, raised Lazarus from the dead, and parted the Red Sea is the same power that healed the blind man and delivered the delirious from demons, and that same power is at work still today.

He is the same yesterday, today, and forever!

May we stand together and pray for God to heal our land and strengthen His people. May we pray for all those in authority over us. May we pray for God's miraculous intervention, for blind eyes to be opened, for many to see the power of our Lord as they have never experienced before!

And for times when it's difficult to know even what to pray, we can trust these words as a place to begin: "The Spirit helps us in our weakness. For we do not know what to pray for as we ought, but the Spirit Himself intercedes for us, with groanings too deep for words" (Romans 8:26).

"We are never left to fend for ourselves, wrestling in worry, consumed with fear, or driven toward hate. He reminds us He is with us, He will help us, and He hasn't lost control, but has a plan. And His purposes will prevail. He hears our prayers. He knows our needs. There's great power in uniting together, turning our hearts toward God and praying on behalf of America, our nation." - Bishop Ron McRae.

"Blessed is the nation whose God is the Lord, the people He chooses for His inheritance" (Psalm 33:12).

May we be diligent and faithful in praying for our communities, schools, workplaces, and country! God hears us when we pray. He delights in answering prayer and always knows what is best! As warriors, we need to remember the power of the One with whom we place our trust!

NOVEMBER 19

Y ou are the light of the world. A city set on a hill cannot be hidden. Nor do people light a lamp and put it under a basket, but on a stand, and it gives light to all in the house. In the same way, let your light shine before others, so that they may see your good works and give glory to your Father who is in heaven. (Matthew 5:14–16)

Whoever does not bear her own cross and come after Me cannot be My disciple. (Luke 14:27)

So Jesus said to the Jews who had believed in Him, "if you abide in My word, you are truly My disciples, and you will know the truth, and the truth will set you free." (John 8:31–32)

A new commandment I give to you, that you love one another: just as I have loved you, you also are to love one another. By this all people will know that you are My disciples, if you have love for one another. (John 13:34–35)

Back in 2013, I was reading the Oswald Chambers devotional, *My Utmost for His Highest*, and these thoughts are in relation to that time.

Oswald makes a differentiation between being "saved" and "being a disciple." Anything (father, mother, wife, children, etc.) can compete with our relationship with God. "I may prefer to belong to my mother etc. then, Jesus said, you cannot be my disciple... this does not mean that I will not be saved, but it does mean that I cannot be entirely His... Our Lord makes his disciples His very own possession, becoming responsible for them." See (Matthew 28:19) – Oswald Chambers

This confuses me. I guess I thought salvation and discipleship were the same thing? Didn't God save us to send us? Does salvation make us disciples? I believe the point Oswald Chambers is making is that, as disciples, God demands our total surrender to Him. He demands that He be first and foremost in our lives. That means that we listen and obey when God directs our steps. We can so easily get tripped up by thinking that we KNOW what God's will for us is, and we wonder if we can possibly already be doing what He wants with our surrendered lives. Isn't my life too mundane, to uneventful, too ordinary? I am not on a mission field or preaching the gospel. Actually, we are all on a mission field every day with everyone we encounter even if it is the same people day after day. We preach with our lives as example. We trust God by not falling apart when trials come. By praising and worshiping THROUGH the storms of life. We witness when we least expect to. God's Holy Spirit pours through the lives of believers and drips on everyone in close proximity. I think one of Satan's great lies is "You are not doing enough, good enough or Christian enough!" We listen, become discouraged, and feel unworthy. I believe God is saying, "Just live in close communion with Me. I (I being important here) will work through you. I will touch, encourage, and reach out to those I place in your path through you, not because of you." We are all referred to as "vessels" for God's use. First, we need to be filled with Jesus then let Him use our hands and feet wherever we find ourselves.

So today, simply show up. Let the Holy Trinity do the rest.

NOVEMBER 20

God's way is not a matter of mere talk - it is an empowered life. (1 Corinthians 13:13)

Praise the Lord O my soul, and forget not His benefits - who forgives all your sins and heals all your diseases. (Psalm 103:2–3)

We humans keep brainstorming options and plans, but God's purpose prevails. (Proverbs 19:21 MSG)

Don't panic, I'm with you. There's no need to fear for I Am your God. I'll give you strength. I'll help you. I'll hold you steady, keep a firm grip on you. (Isaiah 41:9–10 MSG)

Keep your heart with all vigilance, for from it flow the springs of life. (Proverbs 4:23)

Create in me a clean heart, O God, and renew a right spirit within me. (Psalm 51:10)

Do not be conformed to this world, but be transformed by the renewal of your mind, that by testing you may discern what is the will of God, what is good and acceptable and perfect. (Romans 12:2)

God all mighty; God all powerful; God all knowing; God, commander of the angel armies, calls you and I His children! So then, why on earth do we worry and stew and fret about the difficulties of this life? Think of your own children. Do you listen when they tell you their problems? Wouldn't you move heaven and earth to help them? Don't you delight in giving them gifts? Now imagine our Father in heaven! His word tells us "He delights in us," "He knit us together in our mother's womb," "He ordained every day of our lives before one of them came to be." Does that sound like a God who is uninterested or uncaring? God loves to hear from us, my friends! He hears every whimper, catches every tear, and never misses a word of any conversation. His purposes will prevail. He forgives, heals, and delights in us. All we need to live an empowered life is to believe that God IS who He says He is. To talk to Him through prayer and to continually turn our minds and thoughts to Him. Believe God's in charge, and He delights in giving good gifts to His children. Believe that NO MATTER WHAT is going on, God's got it. He is aware of all the ins and outs of any situation, of all the souls involved, and He can be trusted to do what brings Him glory. He is bigger, stronger, and wiser than we can even begin to imagine. And, drum roll please, HE IS CRAZY ABOUT US.

NOVEMBER 21

Above all else, guard your heart, for it is the wellspring of life. (Proverbs 4:23)

May the words of my mouth, and the meditation of my heart be pleasing in your sight, O Lord, my Rock and my Redeemer. (Psalm 19:14)

Dear friend, take my advice, it will add years to your life. I'm writing out clear directions to Wisdom Way, I'm drawing a map to Righteous Road. I don't want you ending up in blind alleys or wasting time making wrong turns. Hold tight to good advice, don't relax your grip. Guard it well—your life is at stake! Don't take Wicked Bypass; don't so much as set foot on that road. Stay clear of it; give it a wide berth. Make a detour and be on your way. (Proverbs 4:10–15 MSG)

So often the words of the enemy that we hear in our thoughts sound so much like ourselves that we discount the source. How many times have you heard, "You will never get it right"; "God isn't interested in you until you get your act together"; "You are a disappointment, failure, looser, etc." As for myself, the answer would be, "Too many times to count." Satan loves to get into our thoughts, and our heads as well as our hearts and tell us that God is not who He says He is, or that God is somehow incapable or worse yet unwilling to intervene in our lives! All of the above are lies, deceptions of the serpent! God's language to us goes something like this, "I love you, my child," "I willingly gave my life for you so that your sin will not count against you!" "I will NEVER leave or abandon you," "You can trust Me."

The great deceiver on the other hand, has to twist his words to make them sound appealing to us. He would never speak truth to let us know that, by ignoring God or choosing our own way, we are, in fact, choosing his. Can't you hear him whisper, "You don't need God," "He is such a kill-joy," "My way is fun, freedom" while all the while the serpent is hoping to kill and destroy, as well as bring worry, misery and confusion.

That's why, my dear sisters., we must get in the habit of guarding our hearts! Guard them against the lies of our enemy. Hang on to God and His will for our lives for dear life so that we may experience the freedom and joy in the life that God has in store for us.

Love you, friends! Have a great day holding tightly the hand that is holding yours!

NOVEMBER 22

The world (Satan) is unprincipled. It's dog-eat-dog out there! The world (Satan) doesn't fight fair. But we don't live or fight our battles that way - never have and never will. The tools of our trade aren't for marketing or manipulation, but they are for demolishing that entire massively corrupt culture. We use our powerful God-tools for smashing warped philosophies, tearing down barriers erected against the truth of God, fitting every loose thought and emotion and impulse into the structure of life shaped by Christ. Our tools are ready at hand for clearing the ground of every obstruction and building lives of obedience into maturity. (2 Corinthians 10:3–6 MSG)

Finally, brothers and sisters, whatever is true, whatever is noble, whatever is right, whatever is pure, whatever is lovely, whatever is admirable – if anything is excellent or praise worthy – think about such things. (Philippians 4:8)

I would imagine that every one of us can relate in some way to today's first scripture. It's those little, nagging frustrations in our marriages, workplaces, and homes that Satan uses to begin to drive his massive wedge of dissatisfaction. "He doesn't treat me with the respect, kindness, consideration I deserve"; "Why is everything around here my responsibility?" "I work harder, longer, better than everyone else"—these thoughts when given center stage in our thinking begin to take over the entire place! These "little" thoughts begin to build and consequently consume our thinking. That is exactly what our enemy is hoping for, our complete and total dissatisfaction with our spouses, workplace, and lives. My dear sisters, our enemy

WANTS us to be miserable. That is his primary purpose. But take heart. God's word is clear; there is another way. We are warned to "take every thought CAPTIVE" and consider the source. Is it from God or the enemy? How do we know? The enemy wants to tear us down, destroy and break us. God, on the other hand, wants to build us up, encourage, strengthen, and use us.

There are things we can do to take control of our thought life. We can, first and foremost, accept responsibility for what we are thinking. We can intentionally focus our minds on the right things. We can choose to think about the good and the beautiful. We can think through our problems rather than just react with the first emotion that comes to our minds. We can learn to discipline our minds to focus on the right things.

So today, dear sisters, don't give Satan that opening he needs to get into our thoughts. Slam that door shut. Let's turn our thoughts to whatever is good, pure, and beautiful and let us all be transformed minute by minute by the renewing of our minds. God is far more powerful than ANYTHING our enemy can throw at us.

You are greatly and eternally loved!

NOVEMBER 23

Finally, be strong in the Lord and in His mighty power. Put on the full armor of God so that you can take your stand against the devil's schemes. For our struggle is not against flesh and blood but against the rulers, against the authorities, against the powers of this dark world and against the spiritual forces of evil in the heavenly realms. (Ephesians 6:10–12)

And that about wraps it up. God is strong and He wants you strong, So take everything the Master has set out for you, well-made weapons of the best materials. And put them to use so you will be able to stand up to everything the devil throws your way. This is no afternoon athletic contest that we'll walk away from and forget about in a couple of hours. This is for keeps, a life-or-death fight to the finish against the devil and all his angels. Be prepared. You're up against far more than you can handle on your own. Take all the help you can get, every weapon God has issued, so that when it's all over but the shouting you'll still be on your feet. (Ephesians 6:10–13 MSG)

Almighty God, we come before Your throne, asking you to equip us with the weapons that we will need for the battle before us. We have heard and sadly believed the lics that our enemy has whispered to us in the trials, storms, and dark nights of our lives, and we fear we have let him in. We believe that we are what he tells us we are and question that You love us. We question Your call on our lives, and we wonder why you would ever claim us. Help us now to deliberately, intentionally, and consistently guard our hearts and our minds against Satan's attacks! Gird us in Your truth, wisdom, and strength! Turn our hearts to praise and thanksgiving and our minds to the truth of who You say we are! We are children of the King! We are Your beloved! Remind us always that You are stronger, wiser, and always prepared for anything the world throws at us! Teach us to examine our thoughts and guard our hearts with a determined diligence! May we take every thought captive and expose it to Your powerful light! And may we begin to fully embrace the FACT that You love us with an incredible, fierce passion!

We love you, Lord. We desire to become more and more like you and we banish the enemy in Your holy, all-powerful name! So be it. Amen!

NOVEMBER 24

Don't fret or worry. Instead of worrying, pray. Let petitions and praises shape your worries into prayers, letting God know your concerns. Before you know it, a sense of God's wholeness, everything coming together for good, will come and settle you down. It's wonderful what happens when Christ displaces worry at the center of your life. (Philippians 4:6–7 MSG)

Whoever believes in me, as the Scripture has said, streams of living water will flow from within him/her. (John 7:38 NIV)

Do not get drunk on wine, which leads to debauchery (cheapening your life). Instead, be filled with the Spirit, Speak to one another with psalms, hymns and spiritual songs. Sing and make music in your heart to the Lord. Always giving thanks to God the Father for everything, in the name of the Lord Jesus Christ. (Ephesians 5:18-20)

Make every effort to live in peace with everyone and to be holy; without holiness no one will see the Lord. (Hebrews 12:14)

When you are around other people, do you try to impress them, or do you wear yourself out trying to gain acceptance? Our efforts to win other people's approval is emotionally and physically exhausting! When we focus on our need to only please one, that being God, a lot of the pressure to please others, to meet real or imagined expectations fades. I think that, perhaps, our desire to be the center of attention, or witty or whatever it is that motivates us, is actually insulting to God. Do we not think that we are enough just the way we are? Do we question our creator and doubt how he created us? Granted, we are all gifted in different and diverse ways. I believe we were created to embrace the gifts we've been given and then "run with them" for God's glory. Now the Bible is clear that we are to make every effort to get along with others. But getting along with or being accepted by others should never be our primary focus. Central to our thinking should be the thought, "What does God think of me?" "Is God pleased with the woman I am becoming?" and "Am I focused on living a life that is pleasing to Him?" My dear sisters, we cannot embrace the culture around us and fit in without even thinking about it. Just as we need to take our thoughts captive, we are reminded to keep Christ at the center of our lives and live out of that relationship. When we focus on what people around us are thinking of us, we are taking our eyes off God and exhausting ourselves in the process! God loves us, and we are enough!

NOVEMBER 25

For it is by grace you have been saved, through faith - and this is not from yourselves, it is the gift of God - not by works, so that no one can boast. For we are God's workmanship, created in Christ Jesus to do good works, which God prepared in advance for us to do. (Ephesians 2:8–9 NIV)

Saving is all His idea, and all His work. All we do is trust Him enough to let Him do it. It's God's gift from start to finish! We don't play the major role. If we did, we'd probably go around bragging that we'd done the whole thing! No, we neither make nor save ourselves, God does both the making and saving. He creates each of us by Christ Jesus to join Him in the work he does; the good work he has gotten ready for us to do, work we had better be doing. (Ephesians 2:8–9 MSG)

And I ask Him that with both feet planted firmly on love, you'll be able to take in with all followers of Jesus the "extravagant dimensions of Christ's love. Reach out and experience the breadth! Test its length! Plumb the depths! Rise to the heights! Live full lives, full in the fullness of God." (Ephesians 3:16–19 MSG)

I pray that out of His glorious riches He may strengthen you with power through His spirit in your inner being so that Christ may dwell in your hearts through faith. And I pray that you, being rooted and established in love, may have power, together with all the saints to grasp how wide and long and high and deep is the love of Christ, and to know this love that surpasses knowledge—that you may be filled to the measure of all the fullness of God. (Ephesians 3:16–19 NIV)

Trust in Him at all times, O people; pour out your hearts to Him, for God is our refuge. (Psalm 62:8 NIV)

So trust Him absolutely, people; lay your lives on the line for Him. God is a safe place to be. (Psalm 62:8 MSG)

Good morning, friends! What spoke to me today was actually from the scripture in Ephesians, "Live full lives, full in the fullness of God"!

Since I was a little girl, I have always prayed that "my life would matter," that there was a grander purpose for my being here. I have always wanted to live a full life, one of excitement and adventure without fear or restraint. But then life happens, and next thing I know, I was caught in a routine: work, kids, housework, then grandkids, housework, etc., nothing very glorious or exciting! I am reminded today that, no matter how I feel or even perform, God is still loving me, watching over me, and calling me to a full life, a life lived on purpose with a wild expectation of what God is up to and with a spirit that anxiously anticipates what's next. I am determined to give the best that is in me to the people and experiences He has ordained for me! I believe that I am exactly where God wants me in this time and in this place, and you are too! We are here for His purpose. I may not see it this side of eternity, but it's enough. I will rest and thrive in the fullness of His love for me.

And you know, He is crazy about each one of you! I believe He looks at you with joy and overflowing love, saying, "This one's mine!" Have a great day, friends! You are greatly and eternally loved!

NOVEMBER 26

No one has ever seen God; but if we love one another, God lives in us and His love is made complete in us. (1 John 4:12)

But the fruit of the Spirit is love, joy, peace, patience, kindness, goodness, faithfulness, gentleness and self-control. Against such things there is no law. (Galatians 5:22)

When Jesus spoke again to the people He said, "I am the light of the world. Whoever follows Me will never walk in darkness, but will have the light of life." (John 8:12)

The people living in darkness have seen a great light; on those living in the land of the shadow of death a light has dawned. (Matthew 4:6)

The light shines in the darkness, and the darkness has not overcome it. (John 1:5)

Billy Graham in his book, *Where I Am*, says this, "I have traveled to every continent in the world and have been a witness to the difference God's light makes in the people who possess Him. We are His light in a dark world."

As a little girl, I remember singing, "This little light of mine, I'm gonna let it shine." My dear sisters, we are called to be "light bearers," to shine brightly in a world mired in sin, deceit, hatred, arrogance, and pride. The thing is, this light isn't generated by us. It is the light of the knowledge of Jesus Christ and all we are doing is simply reflecting His great light. The closer we are to the source, the brighter we shine.

Shine bright, friends. Remembering always how Jesus has tenderly, gently called you to Himself. He loves you, and He will equip you for whatever He has called you to!

NOVEMBER 27

O Lord Almighty; blessed is the woman who trusts in you. (Psalm 84:12)

Those who know Your name will trust in you, for You Lord, have never forsaken those who seek You. (Psalm 10:10)

But I trust in you, O Lord: I say, "You are My God" - My times are in your hands. (Psalm 31:14–15)

To you, O Lord, I lift up my soul; in You I trust, O My God. (Psalm 25:1–2)

Trust in Him at all times, O people; pour out your hearts to Him, for God is our refuge. (Psalm 62:8)

Let the morning bring me word of Your unfailing love, for I have put my trust in You. Show me the way I should go, for to You I lift up my soul. (Psalm 143:8)

Therefore do not worry about tomorrow, for tomorrow will worry about itself. Each day has enough trouble of its own. (Matthew 6:34)

A little while back, when things with our daughter were in turmoil, I earnestly sought out verses of scripture with the word *trust* in them. I found *so* many verses that remind us, encourage us, and direct us to trust in God. One of my favorites is the one above, Psalm 143. I prayed that verse many, many times. I am constantly reminded that my ways are NOT God's ways, and my thoughts are not God's thoughts. I cannot fix other people. I cannot fix overwhelming poverty, disease, disaster, political messes, broken hearts, or addictions. But I can lift all of these things to God! I can seek wisdom and insight to see where I could help with what He is doing and trust that He's got the rest! We live in a broken world. Thankfully, we know the one who has the solution and the power to make things right! So, take a deep breath, step out in faith and help with the immediate needs and concerns right in front of you. Then, place your worries in the hands of the one who created you, and trust in Him to make things beautiful in His time. Remember always that He calls you His children and His beloved! Have a great week!

NOVEMBER 28

Though the fig tree does not bud and there are no grapes on the vines, though the olive crop fails and the fields produce no food, though there are no sheep in the pen and no cattle in the stalls, yet I will rejoice in the Lord, I will be joyful in God my Savior. (Habakkuk 3:17–18)

God is our refuge and strength, an ever-present help in times of trouble. (Psalm 46:1)

In everything give thanks, for this is the will of God in Christ Jesus concerning you. (1 Thessalonians 5:18)

Give thanks to the God of heaven, for His lovingkindness (graciousness, mercy, compassion) endures forever. (Psalm 136:26 AMP)

The Lord is my strength and my shield; in Him my heart trusts, and I am helped; my heart exults, and with my song I give thanks to Him. (Psalm 28:7)

Thankfulness—it is the love language of the heart! When people express gratitude, happiness seems to follow at its heel! I have so very many things to be thankful for today. Sure, I could dwell on the loss and pain of the past, but even when I think about it, I find so very many reasons to be thankful!

I want to briefly share our experience at the minimum security prison where my husband and I volunteer on Sundays. The prisoners wanted to do a service where they took the lead. They invited some of the men who don't usually come to church or had never come on Sunday morning. One of the inmates did the announcements and introductions and three of the men gave their personal testimony of what God has done and is doing in their lives. I so wish you all could have heard it! It was AMAZING! I was so overwhelmed by God's saving love for us, the lost, forgotten, and misguided, this ragtag bunch of misfits that God calls His sons and daughters! Talk about brokenness! These guys are drug dealers, thugs, pornography addicts, and drug and alcohol lost souls. They spoke of how they tried to kill themselves, how they almost succeeded multiple times, and how much hurt and pain they have inflicted on their families and friends. It was unbelievable, the level of honesty with which they spoke! When they spoke of God's love and help in their lives, it wasn't a "high in the sky" thought, it was an "in the trenches, grabbed by the scuff of your neck" kind of intervention! Boy, do we underestimate the saving love of Jesus Christ! That alone is cause for not just thanksgiving but a CELEBRATION! Oh, sisters, this God who loves us loves us with a passion so fierce that we are not able to stand against it! He is FOR us! He pursues us, and He is NEVER far from us! For that I am eternally grateful!

NOVEMBER 29

Y ou will keep in perfect peace her whose mind is steadfast, because she trusts in you. (Isaiah 26:3)

For it is God who works in you to will and to act according to His good purpose. (Philippians 2:13)

"I tell you the truth, anyone who will not receive the kingdom of God like a child will never enter it." (Mark 10:16)

But to all who did receive Him, who believed in His name, He gave the right to become children of God. (John 1:12)

The Spirit Himself bear witness with our spirit that we are children of God. (Romans 8:16)

By this it is evident who are the children of God, and who are the children of the devil; whoever does not practice righteousness is not of God, nor is the one who does not love her brother. (1 John 3:10)

See what kind of love the Father has given to us, that we should be called children of God; and so we are. The reason why the world does not know us is that it did not know Him. (1 John 3:1)

What speaks to me today is the scripture in Mark, receiving the kingdom of God like a child. For me it invokes images of God holding our hands. The visual that keeps coming to my mind is of a child holding her mother's hand then pulling away. I remember this happening often with our three daughters. Sometimes, I would let go and stand nearby and watch to see where they were going. Other times, I would grab their wrists because it was easier to hang on to, and I would pull them after me. I think that represents God and myself sometimes! At times, I grasp His hand tightly, willingly, and gladly. Other times, I pull away and wander off. I think He watches like an attentive parent, concerned but willing to let me have my own way. And at different times, my hands are *so* full of the stuff of this life, stuff like problems, desires, frustrations, fear, and anger that He has to grab me by the wrist and lead me in the direction He wants. I don't want to be like a willful child that continually tugs away from His grip or tries to run the other direction because He WILL let me wander off for a time because He has given me free will. Thankfully, He will never leave me or lose sight of me. Instead, I want to come to Him as a loving child, fully trusting that God has whatever is up ahead, helping me walk away from what is behind, knowing that the hand I am holding is fully capable to guide me through anything and then guide me home!

NOVEMBER 30

Blessed are the peacemakers, for they shall be called daughters of God. (Matthew 5:9)

Deceit is in the heart of those who devise evil, but counselors of peace have joy. (Proverbs 12:20)

So then we pursue the things which make for peace and the building up of one another. (Romans 14:19)

If possible, so far as it depends on you, be at peace with all men. (Romans 12:18)

Pursue peace with all men, and the sanctification without which no one will see the Lord. (Hebrews 12:14)

But the wisdom from above is first pure, then peaceable, gentle, reasonable, full of mercy and good fruits, unwavering, without hypocrisy. (James 3:17)

"If possible, so far as it depends on you, be at peace with all men (people)." (Romans 12:18) Peacemakers are the ones who put their own emotions, frustrations, and feelings aside and deescalate a situation. As mothers, we are pretty skilled at that if we have more than one child. The petty squabbles of childhood are a frequent call for peacemaking. Unfortunately, many adults take the childhood mindset of demanding their own way far into adulthood, so the need for intervention and maintaining the peace is a skill used in the workplace, as well as in committees, boardrooms, and bedrooms across our nation! When emotions and anger have freedom to dominate a conversation, little is accomplished and feelings are hurt. So then, how do we become skilled at peacemaking? It is by pursuing the best "peacemaker" the world has ever known. It is through our relationship with the Prince of Peace!

In face the word *peace* is used in the Bible 429 times! I think that would give us a pretty good indication that as daughters of the King we are called to be peacemakers. The verse in James 3 gives us the tools we need to maintain peace. First, a gentle and peaceful spirit. Then we are to be reasonable, full of mercy, and skilled at good deeds. Finally, we are to be unwavering in our faith and without hypocrisy. It's a tall order, but remember, friends, we are equipped by a BIG God! He will give us what we need when we need it if we will pursue relationship with Him. May our lives be so intertwined with the Prince of Peace that His thoughts become OUR thoughts and His ways become our ways!

Have a great day! You are loved, called, and equipped for whatever comes your way this week! Peace to you and yours!

DECEMBER 1

For even the Son of Man did not come to be served, but to serve, and to give His life a ransom for many. (Mark 10:45)

Let no one seek her own good, but that of her neighbor. (1 Corinthians 10:24)

Let a man regard us in this manner, as servants of Christ and stewards of the mysteries of God. (1 Corinthians 4:1)

We are servants of Christ, not His masters. We are guides into God's most sublime secrets, not security guards posted to protect them. (1 Corinthians 4:1 MSG)

Don't push your way to the front, don't sweet-talk each other, be deep-spirited friends. Put yourself aside, and help others get ahead. Don't be obsessed with getting your own advantage. Forget yourselves long enough to help others get ahead. (Philippians 2:3–4 MSG)

Therefore, my beloved sisters, be steadfast, immovable, always abounding in the work of the Lord, knowing that in the Lord your labor is not in vain. (1 Corinthians 15:58)

It is absolutely clear that God has called you to a free life. Just make sure that you don't use this freedom as an excuse to do whatever you want to do and destroy your freedom. Rather, use your freedom to serve one another in love; that's how freedom grows. For everything we know about God's Word is summed up in a single sentence: Love others as you love yourself... But what happens when we live God's way? He brings gifts into our lives, much the same way that fruit appears in an orchard—things like affection for others, exuberance about life, serenity. We develop a willingness to stick with things, a sense of compassion in the heart, and a conviction that a basic holiness permeates things and people. We find ourselves involved in loyal commitments, not needing to force our way in life, able to marshal and direct our energies wisely. (Galatians 5:13–14, 22–23 MSG)

What are people most likely to remember about you? That you helped them out, remembered them in difficult times, or that you were quick to respond and generous?

We each have an opportunity and a responsibility to leave a legacy. Five to ten years after you are gone from this earth, how will you be remembered? Personally, there are a couple of things I want. First and foremost I want to hear the words: "Well done, good and faithful servant," from my Lord when I meet Him face-to-face. And second, I want to be remembered as a woman who had exuberance for life, a friend and family member who loved deeply and extravagantly! I want to be remembered as generous, faithful, committed, and kind! (so, friends, after I'm gone, forget all those times I was anything less!). I want my character to be remembered. It is unimportant what I accomplished, what I stored up, or what I acquired. What I want to be remembered for is my heart!

How about you? What do you want to be remembered for? What kind of legacy are you hoping to leave? What will other's say at your funeral? Now I know that we are oftentimes less than we want to be, but at your best, what is your legacy?

You are loved, called, and claimed! Shine bright! Leave a legacy to be remembered!

DECEMBER 2

T ruly, truly, I say to you, whoever believes in Me will also do the works that I do; and greater works than these will she do, because I am going to the Father. (John 14:12)

You are the light of the world. A city set on a hill cannot be hidden. Nor do people light a lamp and put it under a basket but on a stand, and it gives light to all in the house. In the same way, let your light shine before others, so that they may see your good works and give glory to your Father Who is in heaven. (Matthew 5:14–16)

Therefore, my beloved, as you have always obeyed, so now, not only as in My presence but much more in My absence, work out your own salvation with fear and trembling, for it is God Who works in you, both to will and to work for His good pleasure. (Philippians 2:12–13)

For we are His workmanship, created in Christ Jesus for good works, which God prepared beforehand, that we should walk in them. (Ephesians 2:10)

Nevertheless, the firm foundation of God stands, having this seal, "The Lord knows those who are His," and everyone who names the name of the Lord is to abstain from wickedness." (2 Timothy 2:19)

The introduction to Hebrews in The Message Bible translation puts our responsibility this way, "It seems odd to have to say so, but too much religion is a bad thing. We can't get too much of God, can't get too much faith and obedience, can't get too much love and worship." But religion, the well-intentioned efforts we make to "get it all together" for God, can very well get in the way of what God is doing for us. The main and central action is everywhere and always what God has done, is doing, and will do for us. Jesus is the revelation of that action. Our main and central task is to live in responsive obedience to God's action revealed in Jesus. Our part in the action is the act of faith.

Are we known by God? Absolutely! Are we the light of the world? Scripture tells us we are; furthermore, scripture reminds us that we are to let that light shine, not hide it or dim it. Are we of use to God? "We are His workmanship, created for good works."

My dear friends, God created us. He placed us here in this time and in this place for His purposes and for His glory. He knew what He was doing. He knitted us together in our mother's wombs for His well-designed plan. We need to remember that God can use anyone regardless of how the world perceives them. We are not insignificant people; we are God's workmanship! We are the work of His HANDS, and we are the "light of the world." It's a pretty intimidating example of WHO scripture says we are, that is why the intro to Hebrews is vital lest we become overwhelmed and become legalistic! "Our part in the action is the act of faith," trusting who GOD says we are and then trusting GOD to work in and through us for His glory and believing that we are being held in the very hand of GOD and daily commissioned for His use.

Get out there, sisters! Shine bright! You are loved and you are His!

DECEMBER 3

Search me, O God and know my heart. Try me and know my anxious thoughts. See if there be any hurtful way in me and lead me in the everlasting way. (Psalm 139:23–24)

How many are my iniquities and sins? Make known to me my rebellion and my sin. (Job 13:23)

Examine me, O Lord, and try me. Test my mind and my heart. (Psalm 26:2)

And thou shalt love the Lord thy God with all thy heart, and with all thy soul, and with all they mind, and with all thy strength; this is the first commandment. (Mark 12:30)

Love the Lord God with all your passion and prayer and intelligence and energy. And here is the second: Love others as well as you love yourself! There is no other commandment that ranks with these. (Mark 12:30–31 MSG)

By this shall all know that ye are my disciples, if ye have love for one another. (John 13:35)

Love one another. In the same way I loved you, you love one another. This is how everyone will recognize that you are my disciples—when they see the love you have for each other. (John 13:35 MSG)

Sometimes the best and most necessary thing we can do is to stop and consider our hearts and our souls, stopping whatever we are doing, sitting still and doing some self-examination. Asking God to show us areas in our lives where we are slowly but surely stepping back from Him. Ask Him to reveal thoughts or motivations that we might have that we really don't want God to know about. Ask Him to shed light on attitudes that are anything but loving, and thoughts that will destroy us. Our enemy is watching us, waiting to undermine our love and devotion to God. The devil loves it when we harbor self-hatred or insecurity, and he uses that to pull us away from God. Friends, we need to learn to trust and believe what God says about us. We may harbor the fear of losing financial security or become obsessed with a passion for money! Thus, wealth becomes our idol. We may harbor hurt, pain, or resentment toward another that we don't want to let go of, so we refuse to expose it to God's light. Thus, rejecting God's healing and restoration.

God is FOR us; He desires to heal and direct and empower us. But first, we must be willing to bring our authentic selves before Him. To surrender our wills and our desires at His feet so that He can work His will in us. The scripture says, "Love the Lord, your God, with all your heart, with all your mind, and with all your soul and love your neighbor as yourself." Don't you see that, until we can learn to love ourselves, faults, weaknesses and all, we can never love another! I am not talking about a self-serving, self-centered love. But rather, an acceptance of who we are as God's daughters. I believe God is telling us, "Hey kids, love ME with all your heart, trust that you are made worthy of My great love for you, and GET OUT THERE and love those I place around you!"

May we, as God's children, live lives that are pleasing to Him. May we allow Him to transform us into the mighty women of faith He intended us to be! You are greatly loved! Pass it on!

DECEMBER 4

So do not fear, for I am with you; do not be dismayed, for I am your God. I will strengthen you and help you; I will uphold you with My righteous right hand. (Isaiah 41:10)

When I am afraid, I put my trust in You. (Psalm 56:3)

Do not be anxious about anything, but in every situation, by prayer and petition, with thanksgiving, present your requests to God. And the peace of God, which transcends all understanding, will guard your hearts and your minds in Christ Jesus. (Philippians 4:6–7)

Peace is what I leave with you; it is not my own peace that I give you. I do not give it as the world does. Do not be worried and upset; do not be afraid. (John 14:27)

For God has not given us a spirit of fear, but of power and of love and of a sound mind. (2 Timothy 1:7)

But now, this is what the LORD says… Fear not, for I have redeemed you; I have summoned you by name; YOU ARE MINE. (Isaiah 43:1)

Have I not commanded you? Be strong and courageous. Do not be terrified; do not be discouraged, for the Lord, your God will be with you wherever you go. (Joshua 1:9)

Humble yourselves, then, under God's Mighty Hand so that He will lift you up in His own good time. Leave all your worries with Him, because He cares for you. (1 Peter 5:6–7)

We can trust that our very life and everything in it is safely resting in God's hands!

Oswald Chambers in his devotional, *My Utmost for His Highest*, has much to say about worry: "Believe God is always the God you know Him to be when you are nearest to Him. Then think how unnecessary and disrespectful worry is" and "If we are obsessed by God, nothing else can get into our lives—not concerns, nor tribulation, nor worries. And now we understand why our Lord so emphasized the sin of worrying. How can we dare to be so absolutely unbelieving when God totally surrounds us? To be obsessed by God is to have an effective barricade against all the assaults of the enemy."

There are so many scriptures on worry in the Bible that I cannot begin to list them all. And why do you think that is? Because God knew that worry and fear would be one of the tools of our enemy. The great deceiver wants us to live our lives in a state of fear, always expecting the worst, doubting God's ability to handle things, and anxious and frightened at all times. Yet God intends for us to trust Him and be the rock and source of strength to those around us quaking in their boots. My friends, we are called to be strong, to be courageous, and to not be discouraged. All of these seem to be unreasonable demands in this difficult and, yes, frightening time in which we live, but the SOURCE of our strength is the factor that makes all the difference. As His children, we draw our strength, courage, and determination from HIM. And He is able and willing to take on whatever lies ahead. We can count on Him. God's got us, friends. He will never leave us. He will never turn His back on us. He is willing and able to be our strength and our courage. We just need to turn to Him.

Have a great week, warriors! YOU ARE LOVED and YOU ARE HIS!

DECEMBER 5

But someone will say, "You have faith and I have works." Show me your faith apart from your works, and I will show you my faith by my works. You believe that God is one; you do well. Even demons believe—and shudder! (James 2:18–20)

Let love be genuine. Abhor what is evil; hold fast to what is good. (Romans 12:9)

And we also thank God constantly for this, that when you received the Word of God, which you heard from us, you accepted it not as the word of men but as what it really is, the Word of God, which is at work in you believers. (1 Thessalonians 2:13)

And it is my prayer that your love may abound more and more, with knowledge and all discernment, so that you may approve what is excellent, and so be pure and blameless for the day of Christ, filled with the fruit of righteousness that comes through Jesus Christ, to the glory and praise of God. (Philippians 1:9–11)

For our boast is this, the testimony of our conscience, that we behaved in the world with simplicity and godly sincerity, not by earthly wisdom but by the grace of God, and supremely so toward you. (2 Corinthians 1:12)

Lives that are not the same in private as they are by reputation.
Are artificial lives. Jesus's words to the church in Sardis expressed
this very concern. Many of those first-century church members
were apparently like an alarming number of people who line
the seat cushions of our churches today - people who are nice

enough, who look and sound Christian, but have never truly
bowed the knee and surrendered their lives to the Savior.

—Nancy Leigh DeMoss,
The Quiet Place

If you're going to talk the talk, you'd better walk the walk! You know, sisters, I think we make following Christ too difficult. What God wants from us is our hearts! He wants a relationship with us. A few moments of our time every day to talk to Him, to thank Him for His gifts, to tell Him about our hurts and concerns, to surrender our wills to His plan, and to trust that He hears and that He cares. Really, I think it IS that simple! Scripture reminds us that "it is God who works in you to will and to act in order to fulfill His good purpose" (Philippians 2:13, NIV). Or as the Message translation puts it, "Be energetic in your life of salvation, reverent, and sensitive before God. That energy is God's energy, an energy deep within you; God himself willing and working at what will give him the most pleasure. My dear friends, we just need to show up, to bring our honest, authentic selves and place them before God. Hiding nothing, pretending nothing, and expecting, in return, the great and lavish love of the Father who is crazy about us. He will do the work within us. God desires His best for us, and asks us not to settle for anything less! God is FOR us! He is all powerful and all mighty! And He promises us that when we surrender our lives to Him, He will take care of the rest! So simply put, if we want to live authentic, sincere, loving lives, we need to spend time with the one we call Lord! He's always available to talk!

You are greatly and eternally loved!

DECEMBER 6

O Lord, You have examined my heart and know everything about me. You know when I sit down or stand up. You know my thoughts even when I'm far away. You see me when I travel and when I rest at home. You know everything I do. You know what I am going to say even before I say it, Lord. I can never escape from Your Spirit! I can never get away from Your Presence! If I go up to heaven, You are there; if I go down to the grave, You are there. You made all the delicate, inner parts of my body and knit me together in my mother' womb… You watched me as I was being formed in utter seclusion, as I was woven together in the dark of the womb. You saw me before I was born. Every day of my life was recorded in Your book. Every moment was laid out before a single day had passed. How precious are Your thoughts about me, O God. They cannot be numbered! I can't even count them; they outnumber the grains of sand! And when I wake up, You are still with me! (Psalm 139:1–4, 7–8, and 15–18)

Our true identity is found not in what we do for Christ, how hard we pursue Him, or how others view us. Rather it is found in our belonging to Jesus Christ, Whom God says we are (a beloved daughter of His), and how God sees us now in Christ. Our identity stems from an authentic relationship with God that He initiated in love.

"God has revealed this astounding truth to me—that God is and has been pursing me with His radical love all my life! Our pursuit of Him is important, but most important is our response to His loving us.

"It is easy to believe that the Christian life is all up to us. Yet even godly men and women get tired of chasing after God. God's pursuit of us has absolutely nothing to do with our level of obedience, our righteousness, or dedication to spiritual disciplines. It has never been about our faithfulness to God; It's about HIS faithfulness. Spiritual disciplines do not activate God's love for us or cause Him to come closer to us. God is the heavyweight in the Christian life. It is about His strength, His ability, His love, His longing, His resolve to stay in relationship with us. God longs for an intimate relationship even more than we do. Capturing our heart with His love is one of God's all-consuming passions that is constantly in His thoughts.

—Jim Feiker

My dear sisters, the creator of the universe is pursuing us. He longs for us to love Him back in response to HIS great love for us. He will NEVER leave our presence. He will never walk away or give up, but it helps me to remember that God is also pursuing those I love and care most deeply about. He loves them and pursues them as He does me. It humbles me to remember that God FIRST loved me. My love for Him is simply in response to what He has already done in my life. My love is fickle, dependent on my circumstances, my feelings or my gut. God's love is never-ending, all-consuming and fierce. Oh, that we might learn to love HIM as He loves us.

DECEMBER 7

Make me know Your ways, O Lord; Teach me Your paths. Lead me in Your truth and teach me, for You are the God of my salvation; for You I wait all the day. (Psalm 25:4–5)

But if any of you lacks wisdom, let her ask of God, who gives to all generously and without reproach, and it will be given to her. (James 1:5)

For You are my rock and my fortress; for Your name's sake You will lead me and guide me. (Psalm 31:3)

Teach me Your way, O Lord; I will walk in Your truth; unite my heart to fear Your name. (Psalm 86:11)

Let me hear Your lovingkindness in the morning; for I trust in You; teach me the way in which I should walk; for to You I lift up my soul. (Psalm 143:8)

I will bless the Lord Who has counseled me; indeed, my mind instructs me in the night. I have set the Lord continually before me; because He is at my right hand, I will not be shaken. (Psalm 16:7–8)

Nevertheless I am continually with You; You have taken hold of my right hand. With Your counsel You will guide me, and afterward receive me to glory. (Psalm 73:23–24)

Trust in the Lord with all your heart and do not lean on your own understanding. In all your ways acknowledge Him, and He will make your paths straight. (Proverbs 3:5–6)

What door is God opening for you? How do you know if it is indeed God opening the door? Both are good questions. Both left me thinking. So I did some investigation. What I came up with was three ways to recognize if the door that is opening is indeed being opened by God. First, does it align with God's word? God will never ask us to do something that is contrary to scripture. The door we want to go through may look exciting or inviting, but if by taking that job or entering that relationship we are going to be asked to do things that compromise what we know to be true, then it is safe to say that is not a door we should enter. Second, when we walk through a door God opens for us, we can expect confirmation from His word or others that know and love Him. And finally, if the door that is open before us seems to be more than we can manage on our own; it is probably worth investigating! God loves to push us and prod us and stretch us and grow us! He loves to lead us into new adventures that we simply understand we could never handle by our own power or ability.

My dear friends, until we take our last breath, God will continue to challenge us, push us and nudge us out of complacency! There are places to go, things to see, and new adventures to be experienced. We simply need to show up, seek His guidance and surrender to His plan because YOU KNOW it's gonna be good!

DECEMBER 8

T rust God from the bottom of your heart; don't try to figure out everything on your own. Listen for God's voice in everything you do; everywhere you go; He's the one who will keep you on track. (Proverbs 3:5–7 MSG)

Hold tight to good advice; don't relax your grip. Guard it well—your life is at stake! (Proverbs 4:13 MSG)

But He's already made it plain how to live; what to do, what God is looking for in men and women. It's quite simple; do what is fair and just to your neighbor, be compassionate and loyal in your love, And don't take yourself too seriously—take God seriously. (Micah 6:8 MSG)

My dear brothers and sisters, take note of this: Everyone should be quick to listen, slow to speak and slow to become angry. (James 1:19)

He replied, "Blessed rather are those who hear the word of God and obey it." (Luke 11:28)

Call to me and I will answer you and tell you great and unsearchable things you do not know. (Jeremiah 33:3)

Trusting God in the storms of life is an ongoing challenge for every one of us. We want to hear His voice, want to be able to readily discern it, but we question, "Is that You, Lord?" We get so focused on wondering if it is from God that we lose sight of the obvious! Does what we are hearing align with scripture? Is it life affirming? Would our Christian friends support and encourage us in this? If the answer is yes, then step forward with faith. God is able to pull us back if we have misunderstood. He is able to direct our steps and lead us in the way He has chosen for us! We don't need to let ourselves be hindered with doubts and negative or destructive thoughts on our walk of faith. Yes, the devil is a dangerous adversary, but our God has him quaking in his boots and looking to flee! We are children of the King: "And who would dare tangle with God by messing with one of God's chosen? Who would dare even to point a finger? The One who died for us—Who was raised to life for us! - is in the presence of God at this very moment sticking up for us. Do you think anyone is going to be able to drive a wedge between us and Christ's love for us?" (Romans 8 33–38 MSG).

So, my dear sisters, instead of worrying about the lies of the enemy, focus instead on the one who will defeat him for us! Banish anxiety about not being strong enough, smart enough, or holy enough on our own. We aren't and never will be, but the one we put our faith in, HE IS strong enough! Run to Him. Don't relax your grip on Him. He's got this!

DECEMBER 9

I will instruct you and teach you in the way you should go; I will counsel you and watch over you. (Psalm 32:8 NIV)

"Martha, Martha", the Lord answered, "you are worried and upset about many things, but only one thing is needed. Mary has chosen what is better, and it will not be taken away from her." (Luke 10:41–42)

But our citizenship is in heaven. And we eagerly await a Savior from there, the Lord Jesus Christ, who by the power that enables him to bring everything under his control, will transform our lowly bodies so that they will be like his glorious body. (Philippines 3:20–21)

This is good, and pleases God our Savior, who wants all people to be saved and to come to a knowledge of the truth. (1 Timothy 2:3–4)

Then He said to them all: "Whoever wants to be my disciple must deny themselves and take up their cross daily and follow Me." (Luke 9:23)

Oh, taste and see that the Lord is good! Blessed is the woman who takes refuge in Him. (Psalm 34:8)

Or do you presume on the riches of His kindness and forbearance and patience, not knowing that God's kindness is meant to lead you to repentance? (Romans 2:4)

I think many, if not all, of us have asked the same question: If God is REALLY good, then why so much heartache, pain, and confusion? As believers, shouldn't we then have a pass on all the bad stuff life has to offer?

I have been reading a book by Rick Warren that addresses this better than I can, so I will quote him:

> God wants his children to bear his image and likeness…let me be clear; you will never become God, or even a god.
>
> The desire to be a god shows up every time we try to control our circumstances, our future, and people around us. But as creatures, we will never be the Creator. God doesn't want you to become a god; he wants you to become godly, taking on his values, attitudes, and character… God's ultimate goal for your life on earth is not comfort, but character development. He wants you to grow up spiritually and become like Christ… Many Christians misinterpret Jesus' promise of the "abundant life" to mean perfect health, a comfortable lifestyle, constant happiness, full realization of your dreams and instant relief from problems through faith and prayer. In a word, they expect the Christian life to be easy. They expect heaven on earth. This self-absorbed perspective treats God as a genie who simply exists to serve you in your selfish pursuit of personal fulfillment. But God is NOT your servant, and if you fall for the idea that life is supposed to be easy, either you will become severely disillusioned or you will live in denial of reality. Never forget that life is not about you! You exist for God's purposes, not vice versa… God gives us our time on earth to build and strengthen our character for heaven.
>
> Not exactly what I want to hear as a Christian. I do honestly prefer the idea that, through faith and prayer, God will take away every problem,

concern, and pain, but unfortunately, the Bible says otherwise.

This life will be hard, but we will NEVER walk it alone. And all along our journey, there will be a multitude encouraging us along, cheering for us to keep trusting and finish strong.

How I wish I had words of comfort for all the hard things in life. I would share them with you my friends, and also with my own weary heart, but alas, I don't. One thing I do know, how we live matters! It matters to God, and He has PROMISED to never leave us.

DECEMBER 10

W hat a stack of blessing you have piled up for those who worship you, Ready and waiting for all who run to you to escape an unkind world. You hide them safely away from the opposition. As you slam the door on those oily, mocking faces, you silence the poisonous gossip Blessed God! (Psalm 31:19–20 MSG)

Jacob left Beersheba and set out for Haran. When he reached a certain place, he stopped for the night because the sun had set. Taking one of the stones there, he put it under his head and lay down to sleep. He had a dream in which he saw a stairway resting on the earth, with its top reaching to heaven and the angels of God were ascending and descending on it. There above it stood the Lord, and he said; "I am the Lord the God of your father Abraham and the God of Isaac. I will give you and your descendants the land on which you are lying. Your descendants will be like the dust of the earth, and you will spread out to the west and to the east, to the north and to the south. All peoples on earth will be blessed through you and your offspring. I am with you and will watch over you wherever you go, and I will bring you back to this land. I will not leave you until I have done what I have promised you." When Jacob awoke from his sleep, he thought, "Surely the Lord is in this place, and I was not aware of it." (Genesis 28:11–16)

I love the imagery of angels coming back and forth between heaven and earth. Do you realize that, most of the time, the Bible mentions angels, they are doing battle, fighting against evil and fighting for God's people? They are not the gentile, harmless, white, winged, singing do-gooders we envision them to be. I don't know, but there is something that gives me great peace when I think about God's power and the might of His angel armies. My dear friends, there is so much more going on around us that we are totally unaware of. There is a fierce spiritual battle going on for our souls. The enemy can see clearly those who belong to the LORD, and he doesn't like it. The LORD protects us in ways we will never see or understand this side of heaven. Scripture tells us in Psalm 139:5 NLT, "You go before me and follow me. You place Your hand of blessing on my head." We cannot see Him going before or behind or hemming us in on either side, but we can rest assured that He DOES. Although our lives and beliefs may be under attack by nonbelievers and the devil himself, God and His armies are MORE powerful than the enemy and all his attacks. Surely, the Lord IS with you wherever you go today, and whatever you come up against He is willing and able to fight for you. Pause for a second. Close your eyes. Can't you feel His presence surrounding you, keeping you safe and loving you. You and I are wrapped in His powerful arms of protection and guarded by the angel Armies of God! Believe it!

DECEMBER 11

But, me He caught—reached all the way from sky to sea, He pulled me out of that ocean of hate, that enemy chaos, the void in which I was drowning. They hit me when I was down, but God stuck by me. He stood me up on a wide-open field, I stood there saved—surprised to be loved! (Psalm 18:16, 19)

I wonder why you care, God—why do you bother with us at all? All we are is a puff of air, we're like shadows in a campfire. (Psalm 144:3–4 MSG)

He's not impressed with horsepower, the size of our muscles means little to Him. Those who fear God get God's attention, they can depend on His strength. (Psalm 147:10–11 MSG)

There is far more to your life than the food you put in your stomach, more to your outer appearance than the clothes you hang on your body. Look at the birds, free and unfettered, not tied down to a job description, careless in the care of God. And you count far more to Him than birds. (Matthew 6:25–26 MSG)

Therefore I tell you, do not worry about your life, what you will eat or drink; or about your body, what you will wear. Is not life more important than food, and the body more important than clothes? Look at the birds of the air; they do not sow or reap or store away in barns, and yet your Heavenly Father feeds them. Are you not much more valuable than they? (Matthew 6:25–26 NIV)

Value. My dear sisters, why do so many of us doubt our value? Why do we measure ourselves against others and not embrace the unique person that God designed each one of us to be? God doesn't make mistakes, cheap seconds, or flawed people! As God's chosen, God's masterpieces, and God's vessels, we sometimes get caught up in the mess, the darkness, and the sin of this world and begin to believe the enemy's lies. Friends, we are God's. He tells us how much He loves us over and over again in His word. He sent His beloved Son, Jesus, to die for us. He continually pulls us out of the "chaos, the void" in which we find ourselves and sticks by us. It's time to give Satan the boot and send him packing. Kick some enemy butt.

WE BELONG TO GOD. NOTHING can separate us from His love. We are His. Next time you doubt your value, remind the enemy of whose we are, and he'll go running!

DECEMBER 12

Make a careful exploration of who you are and the work you have been given, and then sink yourself into that. Don't be impressed with yourself. Don't compare yourselves with others. Each of you must take responsibility for doing the creative best you can with your own life. Don't be misled; No one makes a fool of God. What a person plants, he will harvest. The person who plants selfishness, ignoring the needs of others–ignoring God!—harvests a crop of weeds. All she'll have to show for her life is weeds! But the one who plants in response to God, letting God's Spirit do the growth in her, harvests a crop of real life, eternal life. (Galatians 6:4–5, 7–8 MSG)

Psalm 119:88, And let me live whole and holy, soul and body, so I can always walk with my head held high. (Psalm 119:88 MSG)

Have you ever noticed how refreshing it is when someone takes responsibility for something that has happened? I have noticed it in basketball when someone throws a bad pass then pats their chest and mouths, "Me." I have heard it in meetings when someone speaks up and says, "That was rude of me. I'm sorry." I have heard it in my home when someone says, "My bad." The world doesn't stop. I don't think less of that person, in fact, just the opposite. Blaming others gets us nowhere. In the same breath, it does us no good to continue to berate and blame ourselves for our mistakes. I think God's message to us in times of mistake and failure is to "keep moving," "admit your mistake and move forward." Perhaps you didn't have the best upbringing or the most understanding spouse. Perhaps your parents weren't loving, interested or capable. It's okay to acknowledge that and to admit the impact it has had on you. But then, GET MOVING. Quit blaming and start embracing what God has in store for you. Because, you know, He's in the restoration business and His plans are always good.

Have a wonderful day. May you walk through this day with your head held high and your hand firmly grasping the hand that is holding yours.

DECEMBER 13

As water reflects a face, so a woman's heart reflects the woman. (Proverbs: 27:19)

Summing it all up, friends, I'd say you'll do best by filling your minds and meditating on things true, noble, reputable, authentic, compelling, gracious - the best, not the worst, the beautiful, not the ugly, things to praise, not things to curse. Put into practice what you have learned. (Philippians 4:8)

The good woman out of the good treasure of her heart brings forth what is good; and the evil woman out of the evil treasure brings forth what is evil; for her mouth speaks from that which fills her heart. (Luke 6:45)

We are destroying speculations and every lofty thing raised up against the knowledge of God. And we are taking every thought captive to the obedience of Christ. (2 Corinthians 10:5)

Almighty God, I fear that far too often we let our minds take us to places of fear, to what-ifs and "worst that could happen" thoughts. Sometimes we camp there, filling our hearts and our minds with all-consuming fear. Forgive us. Help us in times like these to "take every thought captive." Let us bring them to Your light instead of harboring them in darkness. Remind us to focus our thoughts on You, Father. Continually bring to mind the many times you have interceded in our lives and the multitude of times you have answered prayers and straightened our paths. Remind us of Your strength that you make available to us. Remind us of Your wisdom that understands all circumstances and sees all parties involved. Remind us of

Your faithfulness and Your promise to never leave or forsake us. And then, wrap Your loving arms around us and give us peace. Today, Father, and every day following, we surrender our thought life to You. We will promise to be intentional in our praise and thanksgiving and leave the negative thoughts that are screaming for our time out in the cold. We love You, Lord; we desire to be more and more like You. We desire hearts that trust You and a willingness to surrender our fears to You. We thank you, Father, for who you are and for what You are doing in our lives. And we love You! Amen

DECEMBER 14

For the kingdom of God is not a matter of talk but of power. - Message - God's Way is not a matter of mere talk; it's an empowered life. (1 Corinthians 4:20)

I pray also that the eyes of your heart may be enlightened in order that you may know the hope to which He has called you, the riches of His glorious inheritance in the saints, and His incomparably Great Power for us who believe! (Ephesians 1:18–19)

But I do more than ask—ask the God of our Master Jesus Christ, the God of glory—to make you intelligent and discerning in knowing Him personally, your eyes focused and clear, so that you can see exactly what it is he is calling you to do, grasp the immensity of this glorious way of life He has for His followers, oh, the utter extravagance of His work in us who trust Him—endless energy, boundless strength! All this energy issues from Christ. (Ephesians 1:18–20 MSG)

He determines the number of stars; He give to all of them their names. Great is our Lord, and abundant in power; His understanding is beyond measure. (Psalm 147:4–5)

Jesus replied, "Your mistake is that you don't know the Scriptures, and you don't know the power of God." (Matthew 22:29)

Don't you just love the scriptures that speak of God's great power? In one of my journals, I have a list of references to God's power. I think I enjoy dwelling on His strength because so often I have none of my own.

Our victory in faith begins with right thinking. We have to be convinced that God cares about us, that He desires to act on our behalf and that He hears us when we cry out to Him. We need to believe that His Power is sufficient in all circumstances and that it is available to us when we ask. God is pleased when we ask Him to help us, to guide and strengthen us. He sees our hearts and knows when we struggle with desiring His will for our lives. He can help with that too. Just be honest, tell Him how you feel, that you fear surrendering your will to Him. He knows it anyway. Surrender is a scary thing, - letting go of our will and TRUSTING God with our lives is frightening stuff. But, it is the first step to complete and utter dependence on God.

My dear friends, God is crazy about you. He understands completely what you are going through. He knows what you are worried about as well as what brings you joy. And He CARES. He cares enough to forgive over and over again and waits for us to ask Him to intervene in our lives so that by His Spirit working in our lives, we will be filled to overflowing with "endless energy and boundless strength."

Have a great week. Remember that God desires to bless you with an empowered life, a life abounding with energy and strength. God is strong. He wants to make us strong. May we begin to see the utter extravagance of His work in us.

DECEMBER 15

All verses today are from The Message Bible translation.

Point out the road I must travel; I'm all ears, all eyes before you. Save me from my enemies, God—You're my only hope! Teach me how to live to please you. (Psalm 143:9–10)

Everything God does is right—the trademark on all His works is love. God's there, listening for all who pray, for all who pray and mean it. (Psalm 145:17–18)

God's in charge—always! (Psalm 146:10)

Our Lord is great, with limitless strength; we'll never comprehend what He knows and does. He's not impressed with horsepower; the size of our muscles means little to Him. Those who fear God get God's attention; they can depend on His strength. (Psalm 147:5, 11)

Trust God from the bottom of your heart; don't try to figure out everything on your own. Listen for God's voice in everything you do, everywhere you go; He's the One who will keep you on track. (Proverbs 3:5–6)

Our Lord is great with limitless strength. We'll never comprehend what He knows and does and that's okay. In fact, His wisdom and power is beyond our comprehension. His intervention, detail and timing are inclusive of All of His children. And the lives touched by God have a far-reaching ripple effect that we, with human eyes, cannot even imagine! May we live with such trust and faith in our God almighty that wherever and whenever He chooses to use us, our lives might be of great value to Him regardless of whether we comprehend it or not. May the wisp that is our lives be used by God for His purposes and His glory.

All-knowing God, we come before Your throne, not as immature angels or angels in training, but as women of God, imperfect, but placed in this world now, in this place, for Your specific purpose. May we live our lives well! May we trust You to use us where You have placed us and turn our doubt and insecurity over to You! You ARE sufficient. You ARE capable and more than enough in all situations in which we find ourselves. Heavenly Father, may Your light shine through us, and may our lives glorify You! We are all in and ready to "put some skin in the game." So be it! Amen.

DECEMBER 16

Y ou shall not worship them or serve them for I, the LORD your God, am a jealous God, visiting the iniquity of the fathers on the children, on the third and the fourth generations of those who hate Me. (Exodus 20:5)

For you shall not worship any other god, for the LORD, Whose name is Jealous, is a jealous God. (Exodus 34:14)

For the LORD your God is a consuming fire, a jealous God. (Deuteronomy 4:24)

How long, O Lord? Will You be angry forever? Will Your jealousy burn like fire? (Psalm 79:5)

For you have been bought with a price; therefore glorify God in your body. (1 Corinthians 6:20)

The gospel says that we, who are God's beloved, created a cosmic crisis. It says we, too, were stolen from our True Love and that He launched the greatest campaign in the history of the world to get us back. God created us for intimacy with Him. When we turned our back on Him He promised to come for us. He sent personal messengers; He used beauty and affliction to recapture our hearts. After all else failed, He conceived the most daring of plans. Under the cover of night He stole into the enemy's camp incognito, the Ancient of Days disguised as a newborn. The Incarnation, as Phil Yancey reminds us, was a daring raid into enemy territory. The whole world lay under the power of the evil one and we were held in the dungeons of darkness. God risked it all to rescue us. Why? What is it that He sees in us that causes Him to act the jealous lover, to lay siege both on the kingdom of darkness and on our own idolatries as if on Troy - not to annihilate, but to win us once again for Himself? This fierce intention, this reckless ambition that shoves all conventions aside, willing literally to move heaven and earth—what does He want from us?

We've been offered many explanations. From one religious camp we're told that what God wants is obedience, or sacrifice, or adherence to the right doctrines, or morality. Those are the answers offered by conservative churches. The more therapeutic churches suggest that no, God is after our contentment, or happiness, or self-actualization, or something else along those lines. He is concerned about all these things, of course, but they are not His primary concern. What He is after is US—our laughter, our tears, our dreams, our fears, our heart of hearts."

—Curtis and John Eldredge,
The Sacred Romance

My dear sisters, where would we be if God had not sent His Son to redeem and rescue us from the dungeon of darkness that our enemy longs to hold us captive in? What if God didn't care about recapturing our hearts or laying siege on the kingdom of our enemy. Where would we be if we were left to our own devices and to fend for ourselves? The thought is overwhelming! How is it possible that this fierce and holy God cares enough about us to sacrifice His pure, sinless Son on our behalf?

This Christmas, along with the warm, fuzzy thoughts, may we remember the daring rescue, the fierce love and pursuit of a holy and just Father! May our thoughts linger on the daring raid into enemy territory that was launched on our behalf! May we remember the price that God, through Jesus Christ, was willing to pay for our hearts! May we remember that God is a "jealous lover," not willing to share our hearts with the world. God wants all of us! May we learn to crave all of HIM!

DECEMBER 17

Each one should test their own actions. Then they can take pride in themselves alone, without comparing themselves to someone else. (Galatians 6:4)

The LORD Almighty has a day in store for all the proud and lofty, for all that is exalted (and they will be humbled.) (Isaiah 2:12)

But He gives us more grace. That is why Scripture says: "God opposes the proud but shows favor to the humble." (Jams 4:6)

Humble yourselves before the Lord, and He will lift you up. (James 4:10)

Do nothing out of selfish ambition or vain conceit. Rather, in humility value others above yourselves. (Philippians 2:3)

When pride comes, then comes disgrace, but with humility comes wisdom. (Proverbs 11:2)

My dear friends, we have been saved because God saw fit to send His Son and lower Himself to our level so that we might be set right with Him. How dare then do we exalt ourselves, demand our rights, or fight Him for control of our lives? Do we take His sacrifice for granted? Do we entertain the notion, for even a second, that He didn't NEED to die for us?

Holy Lord, I am moved today by how unthinkably prideful I am. How I have somehow decided that YOU should act in response to what I see as best. Forgive me. Forgive me for directing YOU on how to order my steps! Forgive my frustration with You when I don't think You are listening or that You care. Forgive my pride in believing that I know best, that I can handle the details of my life without

You. Father, make me mindful of Your great kindness to me. Remind me of my place in Your kingdom. Remind me that I am the clay, not the potter! Remind me that You ALWAYS and without exception know what is best for me and for those I love. Remind me that You don't need my approval, my permission, or my insight to work Your will for my life. I KNOW that my best option is surrender, total and complete surrender to whatever You have in store for me. Please, Father, help me to surrender the reigns of my life to You. You alone are worthy, You alone are holy, and You alone are God! And one more thing, Lord, when things don't go the way I expected or wanted, remind me that You are still in control, that You are still God, and that You are still in the details. Your will be done. I surrender. Amen.

DECEMBER 18

At that time the sign of the Son of Man will appear in the sky, and all the nations of the earth will mourn. They will see the Son of Man coming on the clouds of the sky, with power and great glory. And He will send His angels with a loud trumpet call, and they will gather His elect from the four winds, from one end of the heavens to the other. (Matthew 24:30–31)

For the Son of Man is going to come in His Father's glory with His angels, and then He will reward each person according to what He/She has done. (Matthew 16:27)

Do not let your hearts be troubled. Trust in God; trust also in Me. In My Father's house are many rooms; if it were not so, I would have told you. I am going there to prepare a place for you. And if I go and prepare a place for you, I will come back and take you to be with Me that you may also be where I am. (John 14:1–3)

So Christ, having been offered once to bear the sins of many, will appear a second time, not to deal with sin but to save those who are eagerly waiting for Him. (Hebrews 9:28)

I give them eternal life, and they will never perish, and NO ONE will snatch them out of My Hand. My Father, Who has given them to me, is greater than all, and no one is able to snatch them out of the Father's Hand. I and the Father are one. (John 10:28–30)

"I am the Alpha and the Omega," says the Lord God, "Who is and Who was and Who is to come, the Almighty." (Revelation 1:8)

And then they will see the Son of Man coming in clouds with great power and glory. (Matthew 24:31)

I love reflecting on the return of Jesus. On HOW He will return in great glory and unimaginable power. I am reminded of the scripture, in Romans 14, where it is written, "Every knee will bow, and every tongue confess, that Jesus Christ is Lord."

My dear sisters, do you realize how blessed we are in that we will not be taken by surprise? We will not be saying, "I wish I had sought Him" and "I wish I had acknowledged and known Him." We are being held in the very hand of God. His Word promises us that NO ONE can "snatch us from His hand." Our LORD and SAVIOR knows us. He calls us His daughters and calls each one of us by name. We are HIS and we will be with Him some day in paradise.

Our Savior is coming again in power and glory! HALLELUJAH!

DECEMBER 19

Look to the LORD and His strength; seek His face always. (1 Chronicles 16:11)

If My people, who are called by My name, will humble themselves and pray and seek My face and turn from their wicked ways, then I will hear from heaven, and I will forgive their sin and will heal their land. (2 Chronicles 7:14)

I pray that the eyes of your heart may be enlightened in order that you may know the hope to which He has called you, the riches of His glorious inheritance in His holy people. (Ephesians 1:18)

Then you will call on Me and come and pray to Me, and I will listen to you. (Jeremiah 29:12)

Is anyone among you in trouble? Let them pray. Is anyone happy? Let them sing song of praise. (James 5:13)

But I tell you, love your enemies and pray for those who persecute you. (Matthew 5:44)

Watch and pray so that you will not fall into temptation. The spirit is willing, but the flesh is weak. (Matthew 26:41)

The LORD detests the sacrifice of the wicked, but the prayer of the upright pleases Him. (Proverbs 15:8)

May my prayer be set before You like incense; may the lifting up of my hands be like the evening sacrifice. (Psalm 141:2)

Be joyful in hope, patient in affliction, faithful in prayer. (Romans 12:12)

The LORD is near to all who call on Him, to all who call on Him in truth. (Psalm 145:18)

The LORD is far from the wicked, but He hears the prayer of the righteous. (Proverbs 15:29)

Then Jesus told His disciples a parable to show them that they should always pray and not give up. (Luke 18:1)

God has promised to be with us in all the seasons of our life. He has promised to order our steps in accordance with His plan for our lives. He has promised to be with us always. But if we genuinely want to grow in relationship with our Lord, we need to spend time in prayer with Him, telling Him the deepest desires of our hearts and honestly laying our fears, complaints, and questions at His feet. Ask God boldly for wisdom in dealing with whatever is at the forefront of your thinking. Ask for patience, for protection, for peace in the most difficult of situations you find yourself. Ask God to give you the words to speak when necessary or the knowledge to be silent! Ask God to give you a heart like His, a gentle, yet strong spirit that can rise above circumstances. Seek His joy that is overflowing along with a trust that is steadfast. Ask God BOLDLY; bring your BIG dreams and aspirations to Him. I think so very often we pray weak, fearful prayers, not remembering that at the throne we are approaching sits a powerful, wise, Herculean, unstoppable, fierce, and mighty GOD!

So today, as you pray to our Father in heaven, take a moment and remember the unbelievable strength and wisdom of the ONE we are approaching. Stop praying little and believe that the ONE who hears is capable of more than we can ever dream or imagine.

Approach His throne boldly, climbing on to the lap of the ONE who knows us completely and loves us extravagantly.

My dear sisters, God desires to spend time with you. He calls you, and me, into relationship with Him so that everywhere and always we will know and believe who has our back. Who is protecting, guiding and pushing us forward in faith. We serve a GREAT and HOLY God. Let's not waste a minute in getting to know Him better!

DECEMBER 20

For He says, "In the time of My favor I heard you, and in the day of salvation I helped you." I tell you, now is the time of God's favor, now is the day of salvation. (2 Corinthians 6:2)

The world and its desires pass away, but whoever does the will of God lives forever. (1 John 2:17)

He has made everything beautiful in its time. He has also set eternity in the human heart, yet no one can fathom what God has done from beginning to end. (Ecclesiastes 3:11)

In their hearts humans plan their course, but the LORD establishes their steps. (Proverbs 16:9)

Teach us to number our days, that we may gain a heart of wisdom. (Psalm 90:12)

Be very careful, then, how you live—not as unwise but as wise, making the most of every opportunity, because the days are evil. Therefore do not be foolish, but understand what the Lord's will is. (Ephesians 9:15–17)

Oh, that we would have the wisdom to manage our time well! In the introduction to Proverbs in The Message Bible translation, it is written this way:

> Wisdom has to do with becoming skillful in honoring our parents and raising our children, handling our money and conducting our sexual lives, going to work, and exercising leadership, using words well and treating friends kindly, eating and

drinking healthily, cultivating emotions within ourselves and attitudes toward others that make for peace. Threaded through all these items is the insistence that the way we think of and respond to God is the most practical thing we do. In matters of everyday practicality, nothing, absolutely nothing, takes precedence over God.

I think God cares about how we manage our time because He knows how much time we have. He knows the plans and purposes He has for each one of us, and He knows our tendency to procrastinate. Time management matters because every day that we are given matters. There are truly places to go and things to do every day of our lives that God gives us breath. There are hugs to be given, encouragement and thankfulness to be expressed, prayers to be said, and songs of thanksgiving to be sung. There are memories to be made, laughter to be shared, and light to be reflected. There are dragons (yes, dragons,) to be slayed and loved ones to be kissed. There is time for forgiveness and self-reflection and tippy-toe excitement and expectation. After all, our GOD is BIG, BOLD, and LIMITLESS in ability and knowledge, and HE doesn't want us to waste a moment of this glorious life HE has given us. So sisters, send that note of encouragement or thanks. Call your mom and dad. Hug those babies and grandbabies. Love the people God has placed in your life with extravagance. After all, HE loves you extravagantly. He calls us to live big, bold, beautiful lives. He has given us so many blessing to enjoy. Let's not waste a minute more.

DECEMBER 21

(Elizabeth's Song) In a loud voice she exclaimed: "Blessed are you among women, and blessed is the child you will bear! But why am I so favored, that the mother of my Lord should come to me? As soon as the sound of your greeting reached my ears, the baby in my womb leaped for joy. Blessed is she who has believed that what the Lord has said to her will be accomplished." (Luke 1:42–45)

(Mary's Song) And Mary said: "My soul glorifies the Lord and my spirit rejoices in God my Savior, for He has been mindful of the humble state of His servant. From now on all generations will call me blessed, for the Mighty One has done great things for me—Holy is His name. His mercy extends to those who fear Him, from generation to generation. He has performed mighty deeds with His arm; He has scattered those who are proud in their inmost thoughts. He has brought down rulers from their thrones but has lifted up the humble. He has filled the hungry with good things but has sent the rich away empty. He has helped His servant Israel, remembering to be merciful to Abraham and his descendants forever, even as He said to our fathers." (Luke 1:46–55)

(Zechariah's Song) Praise be to the Lord, the God of Israel, because He has come and has redeemed His people. He has raised up a horn of salvation for us in the house of His servant David (as He said through His holy prophets of long ago), salvation from our enemies and from the hand of all who hate us - to show mercy to our fathers and to remember His holy covenant, the oath He swore to our father Abraham: to rescue us from the hand of our enemies, and to enable us to serve Him without fear in holiness and righteousness before Him all our days. And you, my child, will be called a prophet of the Most High; for you will go on before the Lord to prepare the way for Him, to give His people the knowledge of salvation through the forgiveness of their sins, because of the tender mercy of our God, by which the rising sun will come to us from heaven to shine on those living in darkness and in the shadow of death, to guide our feet into the path of peace. (Luke 1:68–79)

But the angel said to them, "Do not be afraid. I bring you good news of great joy that will be for all the people. Today in the town of David a Savior has been born to you; He is Christ the Lord. This will be a sign to you: You will find a baby wrapped in cloths and lying in a manger." (Luke 2:10–12)

Glory to God in the highest, and on earth peace to me on whom His favor rests. (Luke 2:14)

(Simeon's Song) Sovereign Lord, as You have promised, You now dismiss Your servant in peace. For my eyes have seen Your salvation, which You have prepared in the sight of all people, a Light for revelation to the Gentiles and for glory to Your people Israel. (Luke 29–32)

Whew! That was a lot of typing! Many of these verses are quite familiar and many have been used in various Christmas songs over the years. I love how God's people have worshiped Him with singing all throughout the Bible. I personally love the singing part of each and every service at church. But the inmate service at the prison has proven to be a powerful place of worship for both my husband and me. To hear those men singing loudly, many with hands raised, often brushing away tears, sometimes off-key and oblivious and unbothered by it. Watching men raising their voices to God in pure worship is emotionally touching. I cannot help but think that their beautiful, honest song is rejoiced over in heaven. I often wish that I could worship and sing and raise my hands without any thought of self-consciousness all the time. That my heart would always be so engrossed in worshiping my God that everything else would fade into the background. For we know HE IS WORTHY of ALL our praise and ALL our worship. This Christmas, let go of your fear and anxiety about the quality of your voice. Raise it wholeheartedly to Him in worship. Sing long and loud those Christmas songs you love. Teach them to your children and grandchildren. Worship God with your whole heart. He loves you, and He longs for relationship with you. Rejoice in His presence.

DECEMBER 22

The weapons we fight with are not the weapons of the world. On the contrary, they have divine power to demolish strongholds. We demolish arguments and every pretension that sets itself up against the knowledge of God, and we take captive every thought to make it obedient to Christ. (2 Corinthians 10:4–5 NIV)

The world is unprincipled. It's dog-eat-dog out there! The world doesn't fight fair. But we don't live or fight our battles that way - never have and never will. The tools of our trade aren't for marketing or manipulation, but they are for demolishing that entire massively corrupt culture. We use our powerful God-tools for smashing warped philosophies, tearing down barriers erected against the truth of God, fitting every loose thought and emotion and impulse into the structure of life shaped by Christ. Our tools are ready at hand for clearing the ground of every obstruction and building lives of obedience into maturity. (2 Corinthians 10:3–6 MSG)

Almighty God, commander of the angel armies, we come before your throne this morning, admitting that we let our feelings determine how we live our days. There are days, Father, when we don't feel loved, forgiven, or acceptable in your sight, and so we live like You are not with us. We go through our day without so much as a thought about You. We feel abandoned by You, like You don't care, and consequently, we live like we believe it! We are sorry. Please forgive us for letting our feelings overrule what we know is true. That You are with us always and that You love us, forgive us, and strengthen us. That You are for us! We are asking, Father, that beginning again today, we would believe in Your love and power. That we would come to You in sincerity and trust. Please remove any barriers separating us, including preoccupation with the things of this life and the excessive busyness we all are consumed by. We pray that we might listen intently for "that still small voice" and obey it when we hear it. That we might live in Your presence, realizing that You are always with us. Lord, steadily grow us into the women of faith, trust, and quiet strength that You have created us to be. We love you, Lord! We determine to "take every thought captive" and, if it is not from You, to dismiss it immediately! Please guide our steps, soften our hearts, and quiet our thoughts. We trust You, praise You, and thank You for what You have done and for what You are going to do in and through us. In Jesus's all-powerful name. Amen!

DECEMBER 23

But if you just use My Words in Bible studies and don't work them into your life, you are like a stupid carpenter who build his house on the sandy beach. When a storm rolled in and the waves came up, it collapsed like a house of cards. (Matthew 7: 24–25 MSG)

If you grow a healthy tree, you'll pick healthy fruit. If you grow a diseased tree, you'll pick worm-eaten fruit. The fruit tells you about the tree. "You have minds like a snake pit! How do you suppose what you say is worth anything when you are so foul-minded? It's your heart, not the dictionary, that gives meaning to your words. A good person produces good deeds and words season after season. An evil person is a blight on the orchard. Let me tell you something; every one of these careless words is going to come back to haunt you. There will be a time of Reckoning. Words are powerful, take them seriously. Words can be your salvation. Words can also be your damnation." (Matthew 12:33–37 MSG)

My mom used to remind us over and over again, "If you can't say something nice, don't say anything at all." I have found myself using that phrase with my grandchildren. There is enough negativity, accusation, and excuses spoken in one of our everyday lives to last a lifetime. So instead, let us focus our thoughts on what is good, kind, beautiful, inspiring, loving and nourishing to our souls. Building habits that with practice and time will produce "healthy fruit," the kind of fruit the Bible talks about in Galatians 5:22–23: "But the fruit of the Spirit is love, joy, peace, forbearance, kindness, goodness, faithfulness, gentleness and self-control." May we continually speak encouraging, kind, and loving words, words that are sincere and honest and can be used for building others up, spoken from a heart overflowing with the goodness of God! May we remember that our words have the power to hurt or to encourage. And may we use all that we are learning about the goodness and love of God, and incorporate it into the way we interact with those around us!

God loves us, friends, and He loves those around us as well; may we learn to become a voice of encouragement, and a light in the darkness! You are loved, you are called, and you are claimed! Rejoice!

DECEMBER 24

But seek first the kingdom of God and His righteousness, and all these things will be added to you. (Matthew 6:33)

Commit your work to the Lord, and your plans will be established. (Proverbs 16:3)

Do not lay up for yourselves treasurers on earth, where moth and rust destroy and where thieves break in and steal, but lay up for yourselves treasurers in heaven, where neither moth nor rust destroys and where thieves do not break in and steal. For where your treasure is, there your heart will be also. (Matthew 6:19–21)

He must increase, but I must decrease. (John 3:30)

For those who live according to the flesh set their minds on the things of the flesh, but those who live according to the Spirit set their minds on the things of the Spirit. (Romans 8:5)

Yes, sisters, it's Christmas Eve! I imagine that you have all run yourselves to the point of exhaustion, trying to get the house ready, groceries purchased, meals prepared, gifts wrapped, and house decorated. I commend you! I know how much work it all is, but I also know that all the extra effort makes for some wonderful memories and traditions. My prayer for all of us is that we have not been so consumed by all the trappings of Christmas that we have lost sight of the most important thing, that being the humble birth of our Lord and Savior! I understand the busyness of Christmas, but I would be amiss if I didn't remind us all of God's desire to be FIRST in our lives, to seek first His kingdom and HIS righteousness, to first commit our work to Him, to first nourish our souls and spirits at His feet!

Almighty God, it's us again, your exhausted, distracted daughters. We humbly come before You now with thankful hearts and repentant spirits. We confess that we have been so caught up in the glitz and busyness of Christmas that we have lost sight of you! We have focused our attention on the worldly things and missed You! We are sorry. We ask that you would soften our hearts to the true beauty of the gift you gave us at Christmas; the gift of Your only Son; the pure, holy sacrifice offered on our behalf! Shift our focus and our thinking back to what is important, the true reason for celebration the gift of Jesus! We love you, Lord. We thank you and we ask that You would be so close to us tomorrow, on Christmas Day, that we would not lose sight of You for even a second! We are grasping Your hand now, and we are hanging on with joy and expectation for what lies ahead! We praise you for what You have done for us and for the good and perfect gift of Christmas, the baby in the manger, the savior of our souls! Amen.

DECEMBER 25

For unto you is born this day in the city of David a savior, which is Christ the Lord. And this shall be a sign unto you; Ye shall find the babe wrapped in swaddling clothes, lying in a manger. And suddenly there was with the angel a multitude of the heavenly host praising God, and saying, Glory to God in the highest, and on earth peace, good will toward men. (Luke 2:11–14)

HALLELUJAH! Jesus is born! Can you even begin to imagine the sound of a "multitude of the heavenly host" praising God? It must have been completely overwhelming! And to think that the angels appeared FIRST to the lowliest of people, the shepherds! That tells us a lot about this God we worship. With God, we are ALL worthy of redemption and are all in need of a savior! There is no class system, no one superior to another; we are all God's beloved children!

Have a wonderful Christmas. Ponder the gift of Jesus and rejoice in knowing that God had you and I in mind when He sent His Son!

DECEMBER 26

"If you can?" said Jesus. "Everything is possible for she who believes." (Mark 9:23)

Jesus said, "If? There are no if's among believers. Anything can happen." (Mark 9:23 MSG)

By faith we understand that the universe was formed at God's command, so that what is seen was not made out of what was visible. (Hebrews 11:3)

I know what I'm doing. I have it all planned out—plans to take care of you, not abandon you, plans to give you the future you hope for. When you call on Me, when you come and pray to Me, I'll listen. "Yes, when you get serious about finding Me and want it more than anything else, I'll make sure you won't be disappointed." (Jeremiah 29:11–12 MSG)

Have you ever stopped to wonder just what "God's vision for you" is? Ever wonder why He placed you here and now in the exact circumstances of your life? Ever question how your life could be best used for His glory? Honestly, I do almost every day: "Why am I here?" "What is the purpose for my life in this season?" and "There's got to be more?"

Those are just some of the questions I wrestle with. Dear friends, we can rest assured and take great delight in the fact that God sees where we are, knows where we are going and is going to empower us to get there in His timing! Furthermore, He has it all planned out, and He will take care of us along the way! I can promise you we won't be disappointed! Scripture reminds us that "our lives are not our own," that "we belong to God." And we know that everything God created is good, including us!

So, Soul Sisters, we can throw off what hinders us. We can forgive ourselves for our mistakes and shortcomings (God has) and move forward in joyous anticipation of what God has in store for us because, as you well know, it's gonna be good!

Have a great day trusting in the God who knows you, loves you, and has a purpose for your life!

DECEMBER 27

For this reason I remind you to fan into flame the gift of God, which is in you through the laying on of my hands, for God gave us a spirit not of fear but of power and love and self-control. (2 Timothy 1:6–7)

Each one should use whatever gift she has received to serve others, faithfully administering God's grace in its various forms. If anyone speaks, she should do it as one speaking the very words of God. If anyone serves, she should do it with the strength God provides, so that in all things God may be praised through Jesus Christ. To Him be the glory and the power for ever and ever. Amen. (1 Peter 4:10–11)

Everything in the world is about to be wrapped up, so take nothing for granted. Stay wide-awake in prayer. Most of all, love each other as if your life depended on it. Love makes up for practically anything. Be quick to give a meal to the hungry, a bed to the homeless—cheerfully. Be generous with the different things God gave you, passing them around so all get in on it; if words, let it be God's words; if help, let it be God's hearty help. That way, God's bright presence will be evident in everything through Jesus, and He'll get all the credit as the One mighty in everything - encores to the end of time, Oh, yes! (1 Peter 4:7–11 MSG)

God's various gifts are handed out everywhere, but they all originate in God's Spirit. God's various ministries are carried out everywhere, but they all originate in God's Spirit. God's various expressions of power are in action everywhere, but God Himself is behind it all. Each person is given something to do that shows who God is. (1 Corinthians 12:4–6 MSG)

Good morning, friends! It is a beautiful new day with a brand-new opportunity to start again! If you are breathing, and I would sincerely hope you all are, it simply means that God has work for you to do. That He is not finished with you yet. There are places to go, things to do, words to say, encouragement to give, and kindnesses to extend. We serve a mighty God and an involved, motivated King, who is empowering His warriors to go and fight the good fight. Give a meal to the hungry, and a bed to the homeless. Speak the truth in love and love others extravagantly! We are ALL gifted in one way or another with God's good gifts, for His glory. Just thinking of all of you, I can imagine some of your gifts. Some are creative, some organized, some of you are word wise, some serve with kindness and compassion, some of you are gentle and good listeners, and some are generals leading the charge! Regardless of the gift, God has indeed equipped all of us with what He sees fit for His purpose and His glory. May we be about using these gifts. Today as you think about your giftings, please don't take them for granted or think them insignificant. God KNEW what He was doing when He created you, and you are exactly right! You are uniquely equipped to be this person, in this time and in this place that God wants for His purposes. Believe it! Rise to the occasion of the challenges of this day. God is in the details, and you are equipped for whatever He calls on you to do!

You've got this, sisters! You are greatly and eternally loved! Believe it and claim it! Have a great week!

DECEMBER 28

I do not cease to give thanks for you, remembering you in my prayers. (Ephesians 1:16)

I thank my God in all my remembrance of you. (Philippians 1:3)

We always thank God, the Father of our Lord Jesus Christ, when we pray for you. (Colossians 1:3)

May the Lord reward you for your kindness. (Ruth 1:8)

May the Lord, the God of Israel, under whose wings you have come to take refuge, reward you fully for what you have done. (Ruth 2:12)

I thank God for you—the God I serve with a clear conscience, just as my ancestors did. Night and day I constantly remember you in my prayers. (2 Timothy 1:3)

The Lord bless you and keep you; the Lord make His face shine upon you, and be gracious to you; the Lord lift up His countenance upon you, and give you peace. (Numbers 6:24–26)

Thanking others by sending notes is one of the topics near and dear to my heart. There is nothing as wonderful as receiving a thank you note out of the blue. Realizing that someone has taken the time to give thanks for words that were spoken, a kindness that was extended to them or the act of a kind deed. Along the journey of our lives, there will have been many people who have touched us, encouraged us, challenged us, and pushed us. All are worthy of our thanks. I encourage you to think today of the people who have influenced your life, from the time you were young until today. Perhaps it was a teacher or a parent of a friend, maybe it was stranger or a grandparent. Think long and hard then take a minute and write them a note. Let them know the influence they have had on you and thank them for taking the time to make the difference.

I promise you, the receiver will be blessed, and so will you.

DECEMBER 29

"For I know the plans I have for you," declares the Lord, "plans to prosper you and not to harm you, plans to give you hope and a future. Then you will call upon Me and come and pray to Me, and I will listen to you. You will seek Me and find Me when you seek Me with all your heart." (Jeremiah 29:11–12)

Be very careful then, how you live—not as unwise but as wise, making the most of every opportunity, because the days are evil. (Ephesians 5:15–17)

The Lord is not slow in keeping His promise, as some understand slowness. Instead He is patient with you, not wanting anyone to perish, but everyone to come to repentance. (2 Peter 3:9)

He has shown you, O mortal what is good. And what does the Lord require of you? To act justly and to love mercy and to walk humbly with your God. (Micah 6:8)

I think it is fair to say that we have all heard it said, and in fact, I have said it myself, "God has a plan for your life." He does indeed, my sisters! He has a plan and purpose for every life that He has created, which includes all of us! No matter where you live, who your family is, or what you personally think about it, God has a plan!

He has a plan to prosper us. Now, sometimes we read that verse and think God promises to make us rich. He may. I don't know His plans. But I do know that God will prosper us in our faith if we stick with Him! And when we grow in faith and in trust, we grow in hope! And we all know the power of hope! People who are hopeless, who have forgotten that God has a plan for them, become sad, depressed, unable to find any joy in this life and, perhaps, even suicidal. Hope is powerful! Hope is found in faith and trust in the Lord Jesus Christ! Hoping in Someone far greater than ourselves. Trusting in this God who created us, placed us where He wants and Who guides our steps. Our part is to simply seek Him, minute by minute, step by step until He brings us home, into His presence. Because you know what? It's going to all be worth it! The best is yet to come!

Have a great week! You are loved, protected, and guided by the creator of the universe, and He doesn't make mistakes!

DECEMBER 30

There's more to come: We continue to shout out praise even when we're hemmed in with troubles, because we know how troubles can develop passionate patience in us, and how that patience in turn forges the tempered steel of virtue, keeping us alert for whatever God will do next. In alert expectancy such as this, we're never left feeling shortchanged. Quite the contrary—we can't round up enough containers to hold everything God generously pours into our lives through the Holy Spirit! (Romans 5:3–5 MSG)

Isn't everything you have and everything you are sheer gifts from God? (1 Corinthians 4:7b MSG)

"Not my will, but Yours"—these are some very difficult words to say to God when we are struggling with something we really want or think we deserve. I remember so clearly one of the first times in my life I uttered those very words, through clenched teeth, I might add! It was back in 1982. There was a three-story house just down the road from where we were living that was for sale. It had a screened in porch on the front, was three stories tall and had a lot of character! I really wanted that house. I talked my husband into letting us go and look at it. That was a mistake! I then wanted it even more! We talked it over and basically came to the conclusion that we can't afford it. It needed too much work, new plumbing and electrical (it was built in 1920). I was crushed! I begged God to "make it work!" I knew in my heart that our decision was right, but oh, I wanted that house.

Finally, after much begging and crying, I prayed sincerely, albeit it through clenched teeth, "Your will be done God...not mine!"

Finally, I was a peace. It was one of the hardest prayers I had ever prayed! It is not an easy thing to do to surrender our will to God's. But after I did, the powerful desire that had consumed me was gone! Now (and it doesn't always work this way) here's the kicker! A couple of years later, that very house again came on the market. This was after a young (electrician) couple moved in and completely rewired and re-plumbed the house! Their dad had bought the house for them, and he knew we were interested, so he did everything he could to put us in that house, even offering to finance it until we could sell ours! God, You are *so* good!

Many years later, going through so many difficult struggles with our daughter and after begging God for years to "fix her," I finally cried out, again through clenched teeth, "Not my will, but Yours be done." Once again, that powerful peace surrounded me, and I knew God had it. This surrender didn't have the happy ending the first one did, but the peace I received from God in both was undeniable. God is good! God is faithful! God knows what's best and loves us too much to give us everything we want or think we deserve!

You are greatly and eternally loved, sisters! Trust God with whatever is frustrating you today then sit back and bask in the peace He gives!

DECEMBER 31

T herefore do not be anxious about tomorrow, for tomorrow will be anxious for itself. Sufficient for the day is its own trouble. (Matthew 6:34)

Delight yourself in the Lord and He will give you the desires of your heart. (Psalm 37:4)

I can do all things through Him who strengthens me. (Philippians 4:13)

So teach us to number our days that we may get a heart of wisdom. (Psalm 90:12)

Oh Lord, we confess that, as Your daughters, we have found many ways to deal with our own sense of being not enough. Some of us criticize, some of us just want to blend in and not cause a fuss, and some of us simply want to hide in the corner. None of these reactions are how You created us to be. Father, I want so desperately for all of us as Your beloved daughters to learn to live wild, free, authentic lives before You. Help us to remember that You have given us great authority through Christ. We are called into action, and scripture tells us that You are making Your appeal through us.

"We are not called to sit on our hands in silence. We are called by our great God to run wild into our culture, calling out an incredible message of life. God loves you, World. God loves you and made a way for you. Come with us. You don't have to live lost and alone. Our Dad has a place for you. He sees you as His ultimate treasure." (Jess Connolly and Hayley Morgan, *Wild and Free*).

Friends, I get it! We try to desperately to protect ourselves so the world can't hurt us that we wall ourselves up to God! Help us to take to heart that that the opposite of faith isn't doubt: it's control. Personally, Father, You opened my eyes when I finally understood the meaning of "meekness," which we find in Your word. The Greek word used for meekness in scripture actually means "exercising God's strength under His control." We are delighted that You have called us into lives of worth, value, and strength under Your control. We love You; we thank You. Please, almighty Lord, help us to become the women you made us to be. Amen.

My dear sisters, I don't know that I have succeeded, but through this devotional, I have tried to convey to you that I believe in you, that God loves you profoundly, and that there is a world around each one of you that needs your love, your light, and the grace that only you can give. I have hoped that you are growing personally in your faith through the reading and application of God's word, but that you are also changing the relationships and world around you by the evidence of your faith.

My earnest prayer for all of you is stated well by Johnnie Moore in his book, *Dirty God*:

> That your presence makes your church, or your town or your workplace, a better place, and that your contribution to the world will be filled with the love and grace of Jesus. I hope that you'll be the salt that seasons the earth and light that illuminates it's dark places. I hope you'll be a source of hope for the hopeless, and that you'll spend time with those who need Jesus more than anything else in the world. I hope you'll give your money and time, your heart and your energy, and that you'll take personally your part in Jesus' mission to heal a broken world. - I hope you will follow Him not just into the palaces we've built and that we call sanctuaries, but into the slums and orphanages as well - that you'll bear the burdens of widows and care for the elderly and make sure that the present suffering of many alive today

will not also be a prophecy of their future. I hope that you'll work with me to free this world of the chains of spiritual darkness, suffering, and poverty - of child labor and sexual slavery, of abuse and evil, of hatred, pain and loneliness... Each of us has the power to spread within our world an extra layer of the grace of God. We must not take this opportunity for granted. We should grab this chance so tightly our knuckles turn white!

Some wish to live within the sound
Of church or chapel bell
I want to run a rescue shop
Within a yard of Hell.

—C. T. Studd

ABOUT THE AUTHOR

Kim Krull was born and raised in a small town in South Dakota. She and her husband Dennis have raised three daughters, losing one to addiction, and gaining sons (in laws) and grandchildren along the way. She is a devout journal keeper, a passionate Christian, and a first-time author. She enjoys blogging and encouraging others to trust God and to grow in their faith. She and her husband have experienced success in their careers as small business owners, and her faith has endured numerous tragedies that have sent her reeling and doubting the goodness of God. The first blow was the death of the child of a dear friend. The second, a friend's diagnosis and subsequent death from ALS. And the third was the addiction struggles and untimely death of her own daughter. Kim was a volunteer EMT for many years and was present at some of the most difficult and frightening times in people's lives. She currently volunteers with the hospice organization and embraces the privilege of spending time with those facing their fears at the end of their lives. She also volunteers in prison ministry and has witnessed firsthand the regret, shame, and consequences of our decisions. Her experiences have taught her about the fragility, brevity, and beauty of life. Her heart is for women to become all that God intended them to be. To encourage them to grow in strength, in faith, and in relationship with Jesus Christ. Kim's writing style is passionate and authentic. She is honest about the difficulty of life and the struggle of faith. She is also confident and sincere about the power and ability of God. Kim has lived her life with a passion for others and, as a result, has been scarred and battered. She believes that everyone matters, that life is for embracing, and that scars are a sign of strength. She is adamant that we underestimate God, and she wants this book to remind you that this life is for embracing and that the very God who called you to Himself will equip you for whatever He has placed in your path.

CPSIA information can be obtained
at www.ICGtesting.com
Printed in the USA
JSHW030241171220
10319JS00001B/1